# The Emergence
# of Victorian
# Consciousness

# THE
# EMERGENCE
# OF
# *Victorian*
# *Consciousness*

## THE SPIRIT OF THE AGE

*EDITED BY GEORGE LEVINE*

THE FREE PRESS, NEW YORK

COLLIER-MACMILLAN LIMITED, LONDON

Copyright © 1967 by The Free Press

A DIVISION OF THE MACMILLAN COMPANY

*Printed in the United States of America*

Collier-Macmillan Canada, Ltd., Toronto, Ontario

Library of Congress Catalog Card Number: 67–24458

FIRST PRINTING

For
Marge,
David,
and Rachel

# Contents

# Introduction

TWENTIETH-CENTURY CULTURE HAS PROVIDED us with a language to describe our peculiar personal and social difficulties. In popular use this language is a hodge-podge of psychological, sociological, scientific, political, and philosophical (particularly existential) terminology: so we speak of our *angst*, of repression, of ego, id or libido, of class conflict, of the masses and conformity and the quest for identity, of the revolution of rising expectations, of the collapse of tradition, and so on. Any moderately literate man might add a dozen more. The language is symptomatic not only of the way in which special disciplines become popularized (and, perhaps, corrupted through popularization) but also, far more important, of a pervasive modern self-consciousness that seems to grow from the fundamental uncertainties that govern much of our lives. It reveals a general awareness that despite (or because of) the revolutionary developments in the possibilities of life provided by technology, society has thus far been unequal to its own growth and alteration.

Few of the problems created by the growth of technology and democracy are, however, unique to the twentieth century. If we penetrate the facade of Victorian complacency and hypocrisy, we can see quite clearly in those years, almost as in a mirror, the reversed image of our very selves. The revulsion from Victorianism that characterized the first several decades of this century was a revulsion from an aspect of ourselves that was never, in fact, destroyed. Although turning with contempt from what we have simple-mindedly identified as Victorian prudery, Victorian complacency, Victorian ornateness and bad taste, what we most dislike about Victorianism is something we, perhaps unhistorically, think of as naivete. We have rejected the Victorian responses to the new industrial society because, although we live, sometimes proudly, among the consequences of those responses, they seem in all their multifariousness to be symptomatic of a need and therefore a willingness, however tenuous and complex, to believe in the possibility of satisfactory resolution. The pride of the twentieth century is in its toughness and disillusion. We face up, because we must, to realities, and the central reality is that there is no certainty— except in man's capacity for brutality and destruction.

Nevertheless, we have not allowed ourselves to accept the incompatibility of our realism with our quests for resolution. We share, though more guardedly, the Victorians' optimism, if only because the alternative is an enervating despair, and we have learned from them that optimism need not be facile and unqualified. Even at their worst, the Victorians have much to teach us. Where earlier we needed to emphasize that they had failed in many ways and that their greatest writers, like Tennyson, Dickens, and George Eliot, wrote literature that at its best was profoundly flawed, we are coming to see that their failure results frequently from an admirable if naive ambition to do things on a large scale, with reckless disregard for small scale perfection. We can, moreover, see that their triumphs are genuine and all the more remarkable for being achieved amidst the first full onslaught of the technological and democratic revolutions that were to transform Western civilization. We can turn to the Victorians now with something other than nostalgia for the good old days when things were simple. For them life was perhaps even more difficult and complicated than it is now, if only because the traditions available to them had little relevance to their world. The Victorians were not unaware of this. G. Kitson Clark has remarked that "in the first quarter of the nineteenth century it was becoming increasingly clear that what was politically, socially, intellectually, and spiritually a new society was growing up in England for which neither the institutions, nor the ideas, that had been inherited from the eighteenth century would suffice."[1] We, at least, have a tradition of over one hundred years of

1. G. Kitson Clark, *The Making of Victorian England* (1962), p. 39.

industrial civilization, a tradition created by the Victorians themselves. And if we could understand how that tradition developed, we
would be in a much better position to understand ourselves.

The dawn of the Victorian period has, therefore, a peculiar
importance to the twentieth century, and it is from that dawn that
the essays collected in this volume are drawn. They illustrate something of the enormous expansion of self-consciousness that was leading
to the first serious and sustained analyses of industrial society and its
malaises. The early and pre-Victorian writers, occupied largely in the
journalism of their day, managed to create a body of writing—for the
reviews and weekly newspapers, in tracts and speeches—that in many
cases has great intrinsic merit and achieves the quality of art. The
quality of writing in the great reviews was, even at its most partisan
and vicious, remarkably high. Writers had leisure to expand and
develop ideas so that many ostensible reviews—in fact, independent
essays—are the length of modern books. And within the liberty of
space, despite their apparent service to a particular party or editorial
commitment, these men created profound and moving critiques of
their culture. Of course, only a fraction of what is included in this
volume has claim to the permanence of art; but even the most
evanescent journalism has its fascination. By examining some of this
writing, it becomes possible to make important inferences about what
went wrong.

I have arbitrarily limited the period from which the essays are
drawn to the years from 1824, when Byron died and the last of the
great quarterly reviews, the *Westminster*, was founded, to 1837, when
Victoria came to the throne. Between those years England clearly
changed directions and began to find ways to accommodate the new
society, ways that would be developed through the reign of Victoria
until the people who proposed the changes would have been shocked
at where they had led.

After Napoleon's defeat at Waterloo in 1815, England postponed
for a few years consideration of the problems created by the new
society. The general reaction against democratic principles that ran
throughout Europe after 1815 manifested itself in England in many
repressive acts. In 1817, for example, the Habeas Corpus Act was
suspended, and in 1819 strong restrictions were imposed on public
meetings and on the sale of "blasphemous and seditious" literature.
The Tories, whose views were largely those of the landed aristocracy,
were in power at the time of Waterloo and remained in power under
Lord Liverpool until, as a result of his death in 1827, of the passage
of Catholic Emancipation, and of agitation for reform, they were
finally ousted in 1830. The threat of the French Revolution—a threat

that, in one way or other, hung over the Victorians until quite late—was extremely influential in the formation of policy. Tories saw the political crises of the post-Napoleonic years, as Asa Briggs has remarked, "in terms not of high food prices, unemployment and misery but of a 'deluded people,' driven astray by malicious and treacherous agitators; an inflammatory press, seizing on every grievance; underground conspiracies, bound together by secret oaths, intimidation and crime; and woolly-minded supporters in high places, bewitched by the March of Mind and the advance of 'liberal principles'."[2]

But even under the Tories between 1820 and 1825, this view tended to bend a bit, and Peel and Canning, as members of Liverpool's cabinet, were instrumental in easing some of the restrictive pressures on what was generally coming to be known as "the spirit of the age." Thus, the early years from which the essays in this volume are drawn can be seen as the opening years of the reform that would come to characterize the whole Victorian period. Briggs argues that between 1825 and 1830 the Tory view largely broke down. After repeal of the Test Acts in 1828 and the passing of Catholic Emancipation in 1829, the adoption of the Reform Bill in 1832 formally initiated a new world.

It is the growth of this new world, with all its inherent promise of further change, that makes the central subject of this book. The profligacy of Regency days, when George IV could sport in the comically oriental and lavish Royal Pavilion at Brighton, was somberly, chastely exorcised; the repressive post-Napoleonic acts were slowly ameliorated; a whole class of articulate artisans and workmen grew up whose demands for the working classes terrified their rulers, but whose demands have, through the years, been met.

Nevertheless, the changes that took place in Victorian administration, in the relations of the classes, and in the distribution of the franchise seem, for the most part, to have come only in spite of the resistance of the classes in power. The Whigs had as profound a sense of the tradition of the landed aristocracy as the Tories, and when Melbourne became Prime Minister first in 1834 and more permanently in 1835, large scale reform was far from the center of his thoughts. "He believed," says Sir Llewellyn Woodward, "in letting things alone at a time when there was every reason for not letting them alone."[3] Despite the intense sensitivity to the difficulties of the time on the part of many writers represented in this volume, there were very few

2. Asa Briggs, *The Age of Improvement* (1959), p. 214.
3. Llewellyn Woodward, *The Age of Reform* (rev. ed., 1962), p. 99.

among them and among the traditional ruling classes who were ready to yield up without qualification essentially medieval traditions and privilege. But the changes created by industrialization, and particularly by the resultant urbanization, forced the best legislators, if only reluctantly, to yield, and produced the legislation that was to turn England into the only major industrial nation to achieve industrialization without a major revolution.

In what seems now a representatively complex way, post-Napoleonic society refused to divide itself up into the bad guys and the good guys. On the one hand, the Whigs were responsible for many of the movements toward democratization, but they were largely from great traditional families themselves. Even Macaulay, one of the few great Whigs who did not come from such a family, though immensely pleased with the 1832 Reform Bill (since it enfranchised only the safely middle class and wealthy), was altogether opposed to any extension of the franchise beyond the limits set by the Bill. On the other hand, the Tories, apparently more conservative than the Whigs, produced some of the most able, humane, and progressive politicians—for example, Sir Robert Peel (whose leadership was crucial in Catholic Emancipation and in repeal of the Corn Laws in 1846), and the Seventh Earl of Shaftesbury (who was enormously active in the amelioration of the sufferings of the poor, in social reform, and in philanthropic work). Moreover, the philosophical radicals, under the intellectual leadership of Jeremy Bentham, whose formulation of utilitarianism centered on the principle of "the greatest happiness of the greatest number," in many cases supported legislation that seemed brutally indifferent to ordinary human needs (for example, the Poor Law Act of 1834). Their support for the economic principle of *laissez faire* was, indeed, liberal for its time; but its effect in many cases was to prevent government interference where it was badly needed. John Stuart Mill, perhaps the greatest of the utilitarians, so far modified his earlier positions that by the end of his career he was espousing a modified socialism. Even the great moral reformers, the "Clapham Sect" of Evangelicals, although they did all they could to improve the manners and morals of society, were for the most part on the side of what William Hazlitt called, with biting contempt, "legitimacy"—inherited power and rank.

But given the enormous handicaps against which the spirit of reform struggled, it was, after all, the spirit of the age; and the ultimate achievements of the Victorians in improving the conditions of the lower classes and their steps toward a genuinely democratic society were, I think, more than admirable. At the very end of the period with which this book deals, the Chartist Movement officially began. This movement introduced into the minds of a large proportion of Victorians what was to be the last great threat of revolution. It sputtered out a failure in 1848, but its aims—formulated as early as 1836 in the pamphlet, *The Rotten House of Commons*, included here,— have by now long since been achieved. Moreover, England and, accordingly, America, have learned to look to the details of ordinary urban and industrial living: to provide street lamps, proper sewage, controls over smoke and pollution, child-labor laws, limits on working hours, universal education, and so on. Most of the aspects of modern urban life that we take for granted now were unheard of at the start of the nineteenth century. By stumbling and groping, with a great expense of human misery, the English had to create a world in keeping with the enormously complex and shifting society of a modern industrial nation. That even now more needs to be done than has yet been accomplished is less a reflection of Victorian failure than of the overwhelming difficulty of the problems.

Unfortunately, the achievements made in the material conditions of society were not matched or even approached by the achievements affecting the inner quality of ordinary human lives. Concern for this problem frequently got in the way of progressive legislation and led many to believe that a democratic society was incompatible with firmly held values. It is too easy to dismiss this attitude as merely reactionary. The ugliness of Victorian and modern cities is a reflection of the ugliness of many human lives. The "cash nexus" that Carlyle described and lamented in *Past and Present* (1842) seems at times to be the sole nexus and ordinary human relations appear to be at base exclusively utilitarian and mercantile. Not only are men inadequately related to other men, but one part of each man's life seems inadequately connected to another. Contemporary *angst* and *malaise*, or whatever it happens to be called at the moment, is reflected both in the intensity of work and play and in the division between work and play. The utopian schemes of Robert Owen and of the Victorian Positivists (some of whose ideas are reflected, via St. Simon and Auguste Comte, in the essays of Carlyle and Mill included in this volume), and the views of art and architecture espoused by Pugin (taken up more extensively by Ruskin and Morris afterward) represent an attempt to restore to human life the sense of oneness, of integrity, of identity, which these writers believed had been lost in the modern world. Pugin's assumption is that the physically beautiful can only be created by the spiritually beautiful and, therefore, that a more authentic expression of Christian spirit is found in the medieval Catholic Church than in modern Protestantism. The Victorian notion that only good men could be good artists might be seen to grow in part out of this idea.[4]

But it is not simply Catholic bias that associates Protestantism with ugliness. Clearly, not only utilitarianism but also evangelical Christianity contributed to much of the ugliness that we recognize as Victorian. In keeping with a long Puritan tradition, the Evangelicals distrusted any commitment to the beautiful because this commitment seemed to them to be opposed to the good. Thus, the utilitarians (like Mr. Gradgrind in Dickens' *Hard Times*) might turn away from the beautiful because it was not useful (although, of course, this was not by any means a necessary consequence of the utilitarian position), but the Evangelicals objected with equal vigor because beauty tended to encourage immorality. Matthew Arnold, in his *Culture and Anarchy* (1867), described this distinction between the moral and the useful on the one side and the beautiful on the other as the distinction between Hebraism and Hellenism. Thus, the position taken up by Arthur Henry Hallam in his essay on Tennyson became a distinct minority view in the years that followed, and the career of Tennyson himself suggests a rejection of it. The moral burden of the Victorian writer was, in many cases, too much for him to carry. Like Tennyson's Lady of Shalott, who grew tired of the shadows of art and attempted to engage herself in ordinary life, he was cursed, at least in the twentieth century view, to die as an artist.

Science, of course, made its inroads on Religion, and the Victorian age (indeed, for many of the major Victorians, the pre-Victorian age as well) was the great age of anguished rejection of faith. There are few things more painful than the loss of religion by people who want desperately not to lose it. In Germany, David Friedrich Strauss had already written his *Das Leben Jesu*, which attempted to reconstruct the life of the historical Jesus by scientific analysis of the language of the Bible, and to show him, though respectfully, not as God but as man. In England, independently, Charles Hennell produced a similar work, *An Inquiry Concerning the Origin of Christianity*. His attempt to sustain some sort of faith in the face of the evidence he had discovered in the Bible itself is both deeply moving and thoroughly characteristic of the period which followed.

But for many people, Christianity remained a vital and life-giving force. One alternative to Hennell's discoveries was Newman's Catholicism, which entailed an almost total avoidance of the issues as they were being formulated by more skeptical and worldly men. But Newman's slow and elaborate progress towards Catholicism entailed a

4. See Kenneth Clark, *The Gothic Revival* (1928), esp. p. 188.

brilliant analysis of the relation of reason to faith, an analysis that establishes a firm bulwark against scientism. He settled finally in a view which he regarded as impregnable: that there is no halfway house between Catholicism and atheism. The Oxford Movement, of which Newman was the real leader until his conversion to Catholicism in 1845, seemed a curious anachronism, nevertheless. While some were engaged in strenuous efforts to make Christianity relevant once more to the needs of ordinary men, Newman and his fellow Tractarians devoted themselves to defending Anglicanism from the inroads of the state, and to proving that the apostolic succession was authentically the possession of the Anglicans, who composed, therefore, the true Catholic Church.

On the other hand, Thomas Arnold and Samuel Taylor Coleridge were turning from any arguments which might seem sectarian and were suggesting a reconstruction of the Church of England in a way that would incorporate all schism and restore harmony. By 1834 Coleridge had died, but he left many disciples, among them the great F. D. Maurice, who extended the broad church view and argued for a Christian socialism, which would engage itself in the great social problems of the day. And Arnold, of course, left his mark on English education and on a whole generation of Englishmen who had been educated at Rugby when he was headmaster, and who carried with them his powerful moral bias. The crucial point, however, is that for Newman, Arnold, and Coleridge, Christianity was both essential and real. Whatever they may have thought, their systems were what they were because the pressures of the times were making Christianity as it had existed more and more irrelevant to citizens of the new society.

What followed among the great writers who found Catholicism, Anglicanism, and Dissent inadequate was a series of attempts to construct a substitute for the apparently dying religion. Matthew Arnold gives us "culture," Thomas Carlyle the "hero," George Eliot "duty," and Walter Pater "experience." At the same time strenuous and partly successful attempts to return to the old religion continued. One should not forget that among the lower classes dissenting religion exercised a powerful influence. Indeed, Elie Halevy suggests that England managed to avoid revolution largely because the dissident impulses of the inarticulate were channeled off in religious expression.[5]

But everywhere amid the confusion of the age it is possible to

5. Elie Halevy, *History of the English People in the Nineteenth Century*, (trans. 1949–1950), "Preface" to Vol. II. It should be noted that many historians now believe that for a large—though not very articulate—part of the Victorian population, religion had become essentially irrelevant.

discern a gnawing self-consciousness such as Carlyle described in his *Characteristics*. It was, for example, during this period that classes, even as the divisions between them began in some ways to break down, first came to be strictly defined and identified. Education, as Raymond Williams remarks, became organized "on a more rigid class basis," and the whole structure of society was concluding a shift from "a system of social orders, based on localities, to a national system of social classes."[6] The workingman, however, was finding spokesmen and some means of education. Against conservative resistance, which really preferred purely moral education, and under the leadership of George Birkbeck and Lord Brougham, Mechanics' Institutes were being established in which laborers with the time and energy might study scientific and technical subjects. Demagogues and humanitarians were delivering lectures and speeches to them. And in the days of economic depression (as, for example, in 1824–25 and 1836–37), strong attempts were made to give unity to a working class that consisted of an impossibly heterogeneous variety of subclasses.

Every class had its periodicals to define and defend its aims and to view the spirit of the age from its own special angle. The *Edinburgh Review*, founded in 1802, was the spokesman for the great Whig families; the *Quarterly Review*, founded in 1809 to do battle with the *Edinburgh*, represented the Tories and landed aristocracy; *The Westminster Review*, founded to do battle with both, became the spokesman for the middle-class philosophical radicals, like Bentham and James Mill. The weekly *Examiner*, originally under the editorship of Leigh Hunt, was a strong anti-establishment paper, advocating radical reform. And the extraordinary burst of journalistic activity was providing outlets for the "lower orders," although, except for some provincial working-class newspapers, most of them were rather patronizingly produced by the wealthy, or by get-rich-quick journalistic speculators. *Gentleman's Magazine* in 1825 listed about thirty-five weeklies published in London, sold for no more than three or four pence, and obviously directed to the poor. But whatever the quality or the purpose of the publications, the increased dissemination of knowledge, especially among the lower classes, widely known as the March of Mind, was making the country extremely articulate about its own condition.

Carlyle was probably right in arguing that self-consciousness was a sign of disease, at least in the sense that the self-consciousness he observed grew out of a radical and painful reconstitution of the social

6. Raymond Williams, *The Long Revolution* (1961), p. 156.

order. But this self-consciousness was, as Carlyle also recognized, probably the only possible cure, even if the cure was to be achieved only in spontaneity and unselfconsciousness.

If self-consciousness itself had been sufficient for the cure, however, the cure would have come soon. Periodicals were full of essays about the spirit of the age or the signs of the times, commenting on social problems, proposing solutions. And these essays often evoked rebuttals in other periodicals and pamphlets. It was, moreover, during the period of Melbourne's administration after 1835 that the tradition of appointing Royal Commissions to provide information concerning legislation was firmly established. Statistical societies were founded, and England busily surveyed itself.

Perhaps most striking, two art forms were achieving great popularity—the autobiography and the novel. Popular taste was inclining to realism, toward a literature that dwelt in detail on the facts of contemporary life. Few major writers neglected to write autobiographies or, at least, to leave provision for full scale biographies after their deaths. In many cases, an autobiography was a writer's chief work; certainly *Sartor Resartus*, published serially in *Fraser's Magazine* in 1833 and 1834, was Carlyle's masterpiece. After his friend Hallam's death in 1833, Tennyson turned to the writing of the spiritual autobiography that, published in 1850, was to make him the most important Victorian poet—*In Memoriam*. Newman had a deep autobiographical impulse that found public expression in 1864 with his *Apologia pro vita sua*. Coleridge, of course, produced his *Biographia literaria* in 1817, and Wordsworth's great work, *The Prelude*, was to have been only a prelude to a great autobiographical epic. In 1829, Whittaker, Treacher, and Company were advertising a series of books called *Autobiography*, of which by then twenty-eight volumes had been published at three shillings and six pence, a price designed to gain a relatively popular audience. Finally, the kinship between autobiography and novel was made clear during the Victorian age proper in such famous semiautobiographical novels as Dickens' *David Copperfield*, Thackeray's *Pendennis*, and George Eliot's *Mill on the Floss*.

Under the pressure of this impulse to study the here and now, and as the reading public expanded and power spread downwards through society, the old ideal literature of heroism (which in fact had long been fading) died out. The characteristic Victorian novel is one in which the hero is rather an ordinary man, at least in his circumstances, and as an individual relatively powerless to shape his own fate. Although Victorian didactic literature constantly insists on the necessity of self-help, one of the dominant themes of a major tradition within Victorian fiction is the powerlessness of the individual. (*Vanity Fair*, it will be remembered, is subtitled *A Novel Without a Hero*.) In his own way, John Stuart Mill recognized the validity of this theme in his essay, *Civilization*. "By the natural growth of civilization," says Mill, "power passes from individuals to masses, and the weight and importance of an individual, as compared with the mass, sinks into greater and greater insignificance."

It was the curious paradox of the time, as writers like Carlyle saw it, that as democracy grows and the ordinary man seems to gain importance, he in fact diminishes in significance and loses his sense of identity and purpose. Clearly, this view partially accounts for Carlyle's prolonged and fruitless quest for a hero who would lead his times out of darkness. And such a view promotes a resurgence of interest in the past, and particularly in the Middle Ages. There Carlyle and many others found a harmonious and integrated society, hierarchically structured, where great and good men might lead. Among the people who, as individuals, counted most in society, democracy was greeted with a serious ambivalence; even John Stuart Mill, that outspoken champion of liberty, felt that before democracy came it was essential that the society be prepared, that the lower classes be educated, and that the tyranny of the majority be prevented.

It is not strange, therefore, that self-consciousness manifested itself most intensely in a conflict between past and present. Even the Benthamites, who ignored history and attempted to reconstitute society on purely rational and unhistorical principles, could not accept the idea of a complete shift in power from the traditional possessors (that is, the wealthy) to the laboring classes. When Mill began edging away from strict rationalistic utilitarianism, he recognized that Bentham's major flaw was precisely his refusal or inability to attend to history and thus to the facts of human nature. To fill the gap created by Bentham's fallibility, he turned to Coleridge and learned from him the importance of history and of the principle of conserving what is best in institutions inherited from the past, even though obsolete. Coleridge (with, to be sure, Scott's historical novels) was the great propagandist for historicism, and significantly, history became the third of the major Victorian genres, along with autobiography and the novel. Many of the most famous Victorian writers were primarily historians, as, for example, Carlyle, Macaulay, and J. A. Froude. If these historians were not terribly "scientific" or "objective," and if they took liberties with dialogue and dramatized excessively, they nevertheless were extremely important to the furtherance of historical

inquiry. The novelistic qualities of their histories, moreover, suggest
that historical writing, as well as autobiography and fiction, grew out
of the age's interest in the real and, paradoxically, in the present.
Those qualities helped too, incidentally, in making their histories
among the most readable (or at least most interesting) ever written.
Of course, the same concern for the relation between past and present
is apparent in Victorian fiction. Only Dickens, among the major
novelists, looked back with contempt on the past. One need think
only of George Eliot and Thomas Hardy to recall how often and how
effectively Victorian novels focus dramatically on the tensions between
past and present. Finally, of course, in prose directly concerned with
the spirit of the age, past and present frequently provide the way into
the subject: in Mill's essays on Bentham and Coleridge, in Carlyle's
*Past and Present*, in Pugin's *Contrasts*, in Southey's *Colloquies*, even
in Macaulay's review of that book.

That the past was to lose out was, given the *Zeitgeist*, inevitable,
but it was not for lack of trying—or of shouting. The pure conservative opinion may be seen in David Robinson's crotchety and vociferous
essay of 1830, in which the spirit of the age is explicitly recognized
(and done battle with) as the spirit of democracy:

> . . . the wholesome control and guidance of the master, landlord
> and other superiors, must exist, or amidst the mass of the people
> morals cannot; if the lower classes be not kept in order by morals,
> and the influence of the master, etc. nothing can keep them so
> but despotism in the ruler. The body of them, from the want
> of knowledge and understanding, must always be incapable of
> exercising the elective franchise in a proper manner without
> counsel; and in consequence, if they be not led by their superiors,
> they will by demagogues and traitors; they must follow the for-
> mer, duly divided into balanced parties for public good, or they
> will follow the latter in an irresistible whole for public evil.[7]

But this argument, directed immediately against the Reform Bill, was
very close to the argument Macaulay used for the Reform Bill. The
threat of what might happen if the past did not yield to the present
was a powerful political argument among the ruling class for making
concessions to the present. But the concessions, like the Reform Bill
of 1832, were small and grudging, thrown to the populace with the
hope of placating them a while longer. We can, at any rate, see in
Robinson's statement why the age was so much concerned with edu-

7. [David Robinson] "Letter to Christopher North, Esquire, on the
Spirit of the Age, By One of the Democracy," *Blackwood's Edinburgh Magazine*, XXVIII (Dec. 1830), 900–920.

cating the lower classes to the values of the higher; why Evangelical tracts preached submission, humility, self-denial; why, even when the sanctions of religion were gone, the same ideals were preached by secular moralists; and why resistance to the spirit of the age was so intense that the great reforms seemed to come despite rather than because of the attitudes of the leaders.

The great hope was that the present would take shape under the control of the past, with its traditions of order, grace, hierarchy, and culture. It is easy enough to look back now and see that the liberals were not really liberal after all, and to see in the duality of their behavior not the overwhelming difficulty of the problems they faced, but mere hypocrisy. Writers like Carlyle, who became increasingly disillusioned about the possibilities of order, must appear in their rage and intolerance as despicable protofascists. But the truth seems to be that we have found no alternative ideal. Representative modern artists and critics tend to be as intolerant of genuinely democratic society as were the Victorians. They preach against vulgarity and "kitsch" (that hybrid pseudo-culture named by Dwight MacDonald) and against the decay of the language. Where they are deeply engaged in social issues they tend, like many of the disciples of that great Victorianesque critic, F. R. Leavis, to look toward an uncorrupted popular culture, or to cleave to the ancient traditions of humane letters and culture—the very traditions in which the great Victorians grew up; and at the same time to raise the lower culture of the "masses" to the level of that tradition. It is not easy now, upon consideration, to reject that tradition, embodying as it does the finest aspects of the intellectual and spiritual history of the West, although it may appear to have led us to a dead end. It is the same tradition toward which most of the essays in this volume are directed. For those liberal writers who recognized the need to move toward increased democracy and increased concern for the lower orders, we can feel a strong sympathy; we can regard them as superior to their times because it was they who helped move us to whatever amelioration of the material conditions of ordinary people we have achieved. But we cannot forget that many of them were torn by a problem which is ours, and that every step they took toward democratization seemed to them and to their contemporaries to be a step away from "the best that has been thought and said" in the Western world.

Of necessity, the arrangement and selection of the essays in this volume have been somewhat arbitrary. I have tried to include many essays having an intrinsic and permanent merit as art, but to select only such essays would have been to misrepresent the age badly. My central concern has been to give a cross section of the intellectual, spiritual, and social currents of the time, and this entailed my selecting much that is mere journalism or worse. However, these lesser pieces provide an important background to the major ones and serve to increase our appreciation of the intelligence and skill required to move beyond the ordinary vision of the time. Other considerations also entailed selectivity. I have not, for example, selected from one of the finest relevant books—William Hazlitt's *Spirit of the Age* (1825)—in some ways the most fitting opening for this volume. That book, however, makes no generalized statements sufficient to give a sense of what Hazlitt is up to. Only by viewing the whole work and Hazlitt's judgments of all the important figures he chooses to treat can one infer his total conception of his times. Obviously, the limits of space imposed by this volume make that impossible. Space, too, has led me to omit letters and private journals from this volume. These, of course, are in some ways even more revealing than published material; but since a choice had to be made, I thought it more economical to stay with published material that had a wide public and was therefore certain to represent wide segments of opinion.

Even while attempting to give a full view of the various movements of the time, it has been necessary to be extremely selective. I have not, therefore, given adequate representation to the Evangelical Movement. That movement, which grew up in the late eighteenth century, had already diffused its influence very widely by 1825. So powerful had it become that in the morally unexceptionable novels of Dickens, who shared many of the Evangelical attitudes, rigidly Evangelical figures are frequently inhuman, at times, villainous. Both William Wilberforce, the leader of the movement, and Hannah More, its most prolific propagandist, were in their declining days in the period covered in this book; both died in 1833, the former at 74, the latter at 87. Nevertheless, the work of their movement forms one of the major components of the age: it leads to moral reform, major legislation, extensive philanthropic activity, prudishness among the respectable, glorification of the family (to become the center of concern in Victorian society), and to the stern moral emphasis of so many of the greatest Victorian writers, many of whom, like Macaulay, Newman, and George Eliot, grew up directly under its influence.

I have also found it necessary to bring together under section headings many not very homogenous activities. In the first section I have gathered some of the most famous and representative statements of the large problem of the spirit of the age. These, by their very nature, cover so much ground that they are not easily set under any less generalized heading. In the second section are collected essays to demonstrate some of the variety of attitudes toward the increased diffusion of knowledge beyond its traditional, that is, upper class, recipients. This March of Mind, as it was both seriously and comically named, is perhaps the single most important fact about the times. For many of the writers, this movement seemed to be the inevitable fore-runner of full democracy and could be traced back to the invention of the printing press. In the third section, again rather arbitrarily, I have brought together essays that, in one way or other, throw light on some special problems of social growth, particularly the problems of reform, material progress, crime, and the labor movement (in some of its various manifestations). The final two sections deal with religion and the arts. In the latter I have, for the sake of simplicity and be-cause of its greater importance in Victorian England, confined myself largely to literature.

This volume should help to suggest, sometimes in great detail, most of the main currents of the time, to bring forward some of the great writers in lesser-known works, and to anticipate the major developments that we recognize clearly among the Victorians and, indeed, among ourselves. For anyone interested in pursuing the sub-ject of this book, I recommend as a start extensive browsing through the immensely readable and fascinating journals of the time, begin-ning perhaps with the great reviews. Such reading makes for an educa-tion in itself, and suggests how much we have lost by forsaking that sometimes heinous practice of anonymous reviewing and by depriving ourselves of the leisure time required for the writing and reading of extended essays. This deprivation might be seen as another sign of the decline in the humane tradition the Victorian writers were defending.

I want to thank several people who have been helpful at various stages of the book, and in particular, Michael Wolff of Indiana Uni-versity, with whom I first discussed the volume. G. Robert Stange of the University of Minnesota had some very helpful suggestions. Walter Houghton of Wellesley College helped identify certain anony-mous essays. Peter Maxwell of The Free Press was particularly and intelligently encouraging. And, inevitably though none the less gen-uinely, I want to thank my wife for helping me through the whole arduous business.

GEORGE LEVINE

[All numbered footnotes throughout the text are the editor's, unless otherwise indicated.]

# I

# THE SPIRIT OF THE AGE:

# SOME MAJOR STATEMENTS

Lord Byron . . . panders to the spirit of the
age, goes to the very edge of extreme and
licentious speculation, and breaks his neck
over it.

WILLIAM HAZLITT
*The Spirit of the Age*

THOMAS CARLYLE

# Signs of the Times*

THOMAS CARLYLE (1795–1881), ESSAYIST AND
historian, exercised over the first generation of Victorians the
influence of a spiritual leader and prophet. His idiosyncratic
and outspoken criticism of the "game-keeping" aristocracy
and the dilatory and windy Parliament, his profound sense
of the injustice of the social system, and, particularly, his attempt
to build a new faith out of the ashes of the old, made him a sage to
whom almost all the great of his time paid deference. But his deeply
humanitarian motives were perverted by deep frustrations concerning the development of the country, and in the twentieth century he has been widely condemned as a ranting protofascist. His
passionate need for justice, order, unity, and spiritual certainty
drove him to positions in his later years that can only be regarded
as vicious (see, for example, his violent pamphlet of 1849, *The
Nigger Question*).

* From *Edinburgh Review*, XLIX (June, 1829), 439–59.

For the first forty years of his life he lived on the brink of poverty and supported himself by writing essays on literature, particularly German literature. From the German Romantics he learned how he might come to terms with the materialism and rationalism of the new age (described in the essays included here). His first great success, however, came only with the publication of his *French Revolution* (1837).

In the two essays included here, Carlyle can be seen breaking out of his long apprenticeship and assuming the role of prophet. These essays, his first ventures into independent thought and social analysis, foreshadow clearly his later development. But it should be noted that both essays display something of Carlyle's occasionally redeeming humor and retain a genuine, if grim, optimism.

It is no very good symptom either of nations or individuals, that they deal much in vaticination. Happy men are full of the present, for its bounty suffices them; and wise men also, for its duties engage them. Our grand business undoubtedly is, not to *see* what lies dimly at a distance, but to *do* what lies clearly at hand.

> Know'st thou *Yesterday*, its aim and reason?
> Work'st thou well *To-day*, for worthy things?
> Then calmly wait the *Morrow's* hidden season,
> And fear not thou, what hap soe'er it brings!

But man's 'large discourse of reason' will look 'before and after' and, impatient of 'the ignorant present time,' will indulge in anticipation far more than profits him. Seldom can the unhappy be persuaded that the evil of the day is sufficient for it; and the ambitious will not be content with present splendour—but paints yet more glorious triumphs, on the cloud-curtain of the future.

The case, however, is still worse with nations. For here the prophets are not one, but many; and each incites and confirms the other—so that the fatidical fury spreads wider and wider, till at last even a Saul must join in it. For there is still a real magic in the action and re-action of minds on one another. The casual deliration of a few becomes, by this mysterious reverberation, the frenzy of many; men lose the use, not only of their understandings, but of their bodily senses; while the most obdurate, unbelieving hearts melt, like the rest, in the furnace where all are cast, as victims and as fuel. It is grievous to think that this noble omnipotence of Sympathy has been so rarely the Aaron's-rod of Truth and Virtue, and so often the Enchanter's-rod of Wickedness and Folly! No solitary miscreant, scarcely any solitary maniac, would venture on such actions and imaginations, as large communities of sane men have, in such circumstances, entertained as sound wisdom. Witness long scenes of the French Revolution! a whole people drunk with blood and arrogance—and then with terror and cruelty—and with desperation, and blood again! Levity is no protection against such visitations, nor the utmost earnestness of character. The New England Puritan burns witches, wrestles for months with the horrors of Satan's invisible world, and all ghastly phantasms, the daily and hourly precursors of the Last Day; then suddenly bethinks him that he is frantic, weeps bitterly, prays contritely—and the history of that gloomy season lies behind him like a frightful dream.

And Old England has had her share of such frenzies and panics; though happily, like other old maladies, they have grown milder of late: and since the days of Titus Oates,[1] have mostly passed without loss of men's lives, or indeed without much other loss than that of reason, for the time, in the sufferers. In this mitigated form, however, the distemper is of pretty regular recurrence—and may be reckoned on at intervals, like other natural visitations; so that reasonable men deal with it, as the Londoners do with their fog—go cautiously out into the groping crowd, and patiently carry lanterns at noon; knowing, by a well-grounded faith, that the sun is still in existence, and will one day reappear. How often have we heard, for the last fifty years, that the country was wrecked, and fast sinking; whereas, up to this date, the country is entire and afloat! The 'State in Danger' is a condition of things, which we have witnessed a hundred times; and as for the church, it has seldom been out of 'danger' since we can remember it.

All men are aware, that the present is a crisis of this sort; and why it has become so. The repeal of the Test Acts, and then of the Catholic disabilities,[2] has struck many of their admirers with an indescribable astonishment. Those things seemed fixed and immovable—

1. Titus Oates brought to London in 1678 the story of a Popish plot. After the death of the judge before whom Oates swore the truth of his story, London went wild with fear and rage.
2. The repeal of the Test Acts (1828) and the passage of Catholic Emancipation (1829) were two of the most important legislative acts ushering in the age of reform. Through them, Dissenters and Roman Catholics were given equal rights with Anglicans in many aspects of legal and business life.

deep as the foundations of the world; and, lo! in a moment they have
vanished, and their place knows them no more! Our worthy friends
mistook the slumbering Leviathan for an island—often as they had
been assured, that Intolerance was, and could be, nothing but a Monster; and so, mooring under the lee, they had anchored comfortably in
his scaly rind, thinking to take good cheer—as for some space they
did. But now their Leviathan has suddenly dived under; and they can
no longer be fastened in the stream of time; but must drift forward
on it, even like the rest of the world—no very appalling fate, we think,
could they but understand it; which, however, they will not yet, for
a season. Their little island is gone, and sunk deep amid confused
eddies; and what is left worth caring for in the universe? What is it
to them, that the great continents of the earth are still standing; and
the polestar and all our loadstars, in the heavens, still shining and
eternal? Their cherished little haven is gone, and they will not be
comforted! And therefore, day after day, in all manner of periodical or
perennial publications, the most lugubrious predictions are sent forth.
The king has virtually abdicated; the church is a widow, without join-
ture; public principle is gone; private honesty is going; society, in short,
is fast falling in pieces; and a time of unmixed evil is come on us. At
such a period, it was to be expected that the rage of prophecy should
be more than usually excited. Accordingly, the Millenarians[3] have
come forth on the right hand, and the Millites[4] on the left. The Fifth-
monarchy[5] men prophesy from the Bible, and the Utilitarians from
Bentham. The one announce that the last of the seals is to be opened,
positively, in the year 1860; and the other assure us, that 'the greatest
happiness principle' is to make a heaven of earth, in a still shorter
time. We know these symptoms too well, to think it necessary or safe
to interfere with them. Time and the hours will bring relief to all
parties. The grand encourager of Delphic or other noises is—the Echo.
Left to themselves, they will soon dissipate, and die away in space.

Meanwhile, we too admit that the present is an important time—

3. Millenarians believe that Christ's reign of one thousand years on
earth is rapidly approaching.
4. Millites, in Carlyle's language, are probably the followers of James
Mill, the leading disseminator of Jeremy Bentham's utilitarian views. In this
essay and in *Characteristics*, Carlyle mounts a strong attack against the utilitarians, whom he called "profit and loss" philosophers. Their insistence that
all human action is determined by the pursuit of pleasure and the avoidance
of pain led him to speak contemptuously of them as men who thought it possible to "grind out virtue from the husks of pleasure."
5. Fifth Monarchy Men were extreme Puritans who, like the Millenarians, believed that Christ's reign ("the fifth monarchy") was at hand.

as all present time necessarily is. The poorest day that passes over us is the conflux of two Eternities! and is made up of currents that issue from the remotest Past, and flow onwards into the remotest Future. We were wise indeed, could we discern truly the signs of our own time; and, by knowledge of its wants and advantages, wisely adjust our own position in it. Let us then, instead of gazing idly into the obscure distance, look calmly around us, for a little, on the perplexed scene where we stand. Perhaps, on a more serious inspection, something of its perplexity will disappear, some of its distinctive characters, and deeper tendencies, more clearly reveal themselves; whereby our own relations to it, our own true aims and endeavours in it, may also become clearer.

Were we required to characterise this age of ours by any single epithet, we should be tempted to call it, not an Heroical, Devotional, Philosophical, or Moral Age, but, above all others, the Mechanical Age. It is the Age of Machinery, in every outward and inward sense of that word; the age which, with its whole undivided might, forwards, teaches, and practises the great art of adapting means to ends. Nothing is now done directly, or by hand; all is by rule and calculated contrivance. For the simplest operation, some helps and accompaniments, some cunning, abbreviating process is in readiness. Our old modes of exertion are all discredited, and thrown aside. On every hand, the living artisan is driven from his workshop, to make room for a speedier, inanimate one. The shuttle drops from the fingers of the weaver, and falls into iron fingers that ply it faster. The sailor furls his sail, and lays down his oar, and bids a strong, unwearied servant, on vaporous wings, bear him through the waters. Men have crossed oceans by steam; the Birmingham Fireking has visited the fabulous East; and the genius of the Cape, were there any Camoens now to sing it, has again been alarmed, and with far stranger thunders than Gama's. There is no end to machinery. Even the horse is stripped of his harness, and finds a fleet fire-horse yoked in his stead. Nay, we have an artist that hatches chickens by steam—the very brood-hen is to be superseded! For all earthly, and for some unearthly purposes, we have machines and mechanic furtherances; for mincing our cabbages; for casting us into magnetic sleep. We remove mountains, and make seas our smooth highway; nothing can resist us. We war with rude nature; and, by our resistless engines, come off always victorious, and loaded with spoils.

What wonderful accessions have thus been made, and are still making, to the physical power of mankind; how much better fed, clothed, lodged, and, in all outward respects, accommodated, men now are, or might be, by a given quantity of labour, is a grateful reflection which forces itself on every one. What changes, too, this addition of power is introducing into the social system; how wealth has more and more increased, and at the same time gathered itself more and more into masses, strangely altering the old relations, and increasing the distance between the rich and the poor, will be a question for Political Economists—and a much more complex and important one than any they have yet engaged with. But leaving these matters for the present, let us observe how the mechanical genius of our time has diffused itself into quite other provinces. Not the external and physical alone is now managed by machinery, but the internal and spiritual also. Here, too, nothing follows its spontaneous course, nothing is left to be accomplished by old, natural methods. Every thing has its cunningly devised implements, its pre-established apparatus; it is not done by hand, but by machinery. . . . Instruction, that mysterious communing of Wisdom with Ignorance, is no longer an indefinable tentative process, requiring a study of individual aptitudes, and a perpetual variation of means and methods, to attain the same end; but a secure, universal, straightforward business, to be conducted in the gross, by proper mechanism, with such intellect as comes to hand. Then, we have Religious machines, of all imaginable varieties—the Bible Society, professing a far higher and heavenly structure, is found, on enquiry, to be altogether an earthly contrivance, supported by collection of monies, by fomenting of vanities, by puffing, intrigue, and chicane—and yet, in effect, a very excellent machine for converting the heathen. . . . Then every machine must have its moving power, in some of the great currents of society: Every little sect among us, Unitarians, Utilitarians, Anabaptists, Phrenologists,[6] must each have its periodical, its monthly or quarterly magazine—hanging out, like its windmill, into the *popularis aura*, to grind meal for the society.

   With individuals, in like manner, natural strength avails little. No individual now hopes to accomplish the poorest enterprise single-handed, and without mechanical aids; he must make interest with some existing corporation, and till his field with their oxen. In these days, more emphatically than ever, 'to live, signifies to unite with a party, or to make one.' Philosophy, Science, Art, Literature, all depend on machinery. No Newton, by silent meditation, now discovers the

   6. Phrenologists believe that there is an intimate connection between the physiological, the moral, and the spiritual. The cult had an enormous prestige for a while, even among quite serious and intelligent people, who thought it possible to read character by determining the contours of the head.

system of the world from the falling of an apple; but some quite other than Newton stands in his Museum, his Scientific Institution, and behind whole batteries of retorts, digesters, and galvanic piles, imperatively 'interrogates Nature,'—who, however, shows no haste to answer. In defect of Raphaels, and Angelos, and Mozarts, we have Royal Academies of Painting, Sculpture, Music; whereby the languishing spirit of Art may be strengthened by the more generous diet of a Public Kitchen. Literature, too, has its Paternoster-row mechanism, its Trade dinners, its Editorial conclaves, and huge subterranean, puffing bellows;[7] so that books are not only printed, but, in a great measure, written and sold, by machinery. National culture, spiritual benefit of all sorts, is under the same management. No Queen Christina, in these times, needs to send for her Descartes: no King Frederick for his Voltaire, and painfully nourish him with pensions and flattery: But any sovereign of taste, who wishes to enlighten his people, has only to impose a new tax, and with the proceeds establish Philosophic Institutes. Hence the Royal and Imperial Societies, the Bibliothèques, Glypcothèques, Sechnothèques,[8] which front us in all capital cities, like so many well-finished hives, to which it is expected the stray agencies of Wisdom will swarm of their own accord, and hive and make honey. In like manner, among ourselves, when it is thought that religion is declining, we have only to vote half a million's worth of bricks and mortar, and build new churches. . . .

These things, which we state lightly enough here, are yet of deep import, and indicate a mighty change in our whole manner of existence. For the same habit regulates, not our modes of action alone, but our modes of thought and feeling. Men are grown mechanical in head and in heart, as well as in hand. They have lost faith in individual endeavour, and in natural force, of any kind. Not for internal perfection, but for external combinations and arrangements, for institutions, constitutions—for Mechanism of one sort or other, do they hope and struggle. Their whole efforts, attachments, opinions, turn on mechanism, and are of a mechanical character.

We may trace this tendency, we think, very distinctly, in all the great manifestations of our time; in its intellectual aspect, the studies it most favours, and its manner of conducting them; in its practical

7. Puffing was the word for what we now call advertising. Serious writers were sorely annoyed by the way publishers exaggerated the virtues of their books. Advertising, puffing one's own importance, seemed to Carlyle (as it, at least sometimes, should seem to us) degrading and immoral.

8. Libraries, museums for sculpture and for technology. The *Edinburgh Review* misprinted the last word, which should read *Technotèques*.

aspects, its politics, arts, religion, morals; in the whole sources, and throughout the whole currents, of its spiritual, no less than its material activity.

Consider, for example, the state of Science generally, in Europe, at this period. It is admitted, on all sides, that the Metaphysical and Moral Sciences are falling into decay, while the Physical are engrossing, every day, more respect and attention. In most of the European nations, there is now no such thing as a Science of Mind; only more or less advancement in the general science, or the special sciences, of matter. The French were the first to desert this school of Metaphysics; and though they have lately affected to revive it, it has yet no signs of vitality. The land of Malebranche, Pascal, Descartes, and Fenelon, has now only its Cousins and Villemains,[9] while, in the department of Physics, it reckons far other names. Among ourselves, the Philosophy of Mind, after a rickety infancy, which never reached the vigour of manhood, fell suddenly into decay, languished, and finally died out, with its last amiable cultivator, Professor Stewart.[10] In no nation but Germany has any decisive effort been made in psychological science; not to speak of any decisive result. The science of the age, in short, is physical, chemical, physiological, and, in all shapes, mechanical. Our favourite Mathematics, the highly prized exponent of all these other sciences, has also become more and more mechanical. Excellence, in what is called its higher departments, depends less on natural genius, than on acquired expertness in wielding its machinery. Without undervaluing the wonderful results which a Lagrange, or Laplace,[11] educes by means of it, we may remark, that its calculus, differential and

9. Victor Cousin (1792–1867) was a French philosopher who equated consciousness with sensation, reason, and the personal element of will. Abel-François Villemains (1790–1870) was a French critic and historian of literature who argued strongly for the liberty of the press.

10. Dugald Stewart (1753–1828), professor of Moral Philosophy at Edinburgh University, was a disciple of Thomas Reid (1710–96). Reid attempted to refute David Hume's sceptical empiricism and became the exponent of "common sense" philosophy. He thought that Hume's philosophy merely caused confusion because it questioned what all knew to be true; the function of philosophy, he argued, was to understand better the meaning of the propositions we accept. The senses, he thought, provide adequate evidence of the reality of the outside world we believe in.

11. Joseph Louis, Comte Lagrange (1736–1813), was a great mathematician who developed the calculus of variations. His most famous book was the *Méchanique analytique* (1788). Pierre Simon, Marquis de Laplace, was regarded as the greatest theoretical astronomer since Newton. Disturbances in the planetary system, he argued, in fact led to the stabilizing of it. His *Méchanique céleste* appeared in five volumes between 1799 and 1825. Carlyle, it should be remembered, began his academic career as a mathematician.

integral, is little else than a more cunningly-constructed arithmetical mill, where the factors being put in, are, as it were, ground into the true product, under cover, and without other effort on our part, than steady turning of the handle. We have more Mathematics certainly than ever; but less Mathesis. Archimedes and Plato could not have read the *Méchanique Céleste*; but neither would the whole French Institute see aught in that saying, 'God geometrises!' but a sentimental rodomontade.

From Locke's time downwards, our whole Metaphysics have been physical; not a spiritual Philosophy, but a material one. The singular estimation in which his Essay was so long held as a scientific work (for the character of the man entitled all he said to veneration), will one day be thought a curious indication of the spirit of these times. His whole doctrine is mechanical, in its aim and origin, in its method and its results. It is a mere discussion concerning the origin of our consciousness, or ideas, or whatever else they are called; a genetic history of what we see in the mind. But the grand secrets of Necessity and Freewill, of the mind's vital or non-vital dependence on matter, of our mysterious relations to Time and Space, to God, to the universe, are not, in the faintest degree, touched on in their enquiries; and seem not to have the smallest connexion with them.

The last class of our Scotch Metaphysicians had a dim notion that much of this was wrong; but they knew not how to right it. The school of Reid had also from the first taken a mechanical course, not seeing any other. The singular conclusions at which Hume, setting out from their admitted premises, was arriving, brought this school into being; they let loose Instinct, as an undiscriminating bandog, to guard them against these conclusions—they tugged lustily at the logical chain by which Hume was so coldly towing them and the world into bottomless abysses of Atheism and Fatalism. But the chain somehow snapped between them; and the issue has been that nobody now cares about either—any more than about Hartley's, Darwin's, or Priestley's[12] contemporaneous doings in England. Hartley's vibrations and vibrati-

12. David Hartley (1705–57), philosopher, doctor, member of the Royal Society, built his philosophy on the principle of the association of ideas. He was a materialist, who believed he was not a materialist, and argued that all mental phenomena grow out of "vibratiuncles," or little vibrations of the nerves. Erasmus Darwin (1731–1802), the grandfather of Charles Darwin, was himself a famous scientist. He wrote, among other things, scientific poems ("The Loves of the Plants," for example) which mark him as a confused forerunner of his grandson's fully developed evolutionary theory. Evolution was "in the air" long before Charles Darwin wrote. Joseph Priestley, the discoverer of oxygen, was a liberal philosopher and Unitarian. He helped turn Unitarianism from a biblical religion to one which relied heavily on a natural religion.

uncles one would think were material and mechanical enough; but our continental neighbours have gone still farther. One of their philosophers has lately discovered, that 'as the liver secretes bile, so does the brain secrete thought'; which astonishing discovery Dr Cahanis, more lately still, in his *Rapports du Physique et du Morale de l'Homme*, has pushed into its minutest developements. The metaphysical philosophy of this last enquirer is certainly no shadowy or unsubstantial one. He fairly lays open our moral structure with his dissecting-knives and real metal probes; and exhibits it to the inspection of mankind, by Leuwenhoeck microscopes and inflation with the anatomical blow-pipe. Thought, he is inclined to hold, is still secreted by the brain; but then Poetry and Religion (and it is really worth knowing) are 'a product of the smaller intestines.'

This condition of the two great departments of knowledge; the outward, cultivated exclusively on mechanical principles—the inward finally abandoned, because, cultivated on such principles, it is found to yield no result—sufficiently indicates the intellectual bias of our time, its all-pervading disposition towards that line of enquiry. In fact, an inward persuasion has long been diffusing itself, and now and then even comes to utterance, that except the external, there are no true sciences; that to the inward world (if there be any) our only conceivable road is through the outward; that, in short, what cannot be investigated and understood mechanically, cannot be investigated and understood at all. We advert the more particularly to these intellectual propensities, as to prominent symptoms of our age; because Opinion is at all times doubly related to Action, first as cause, then as effect; and the speculative tendency of any age, will therefore give us, on the whole, the best indications of its practical tendency.

Nowhere, for example, is the deep, almost exclusive faith, we have in Mechanism, more visible than in the Politics of this time. Civil government does, by its nature, include much that is mechanical, and must be treated accordingly. We term it, indeed, in ordinary language, the Machine of Society, and talk of it as the grand working wheel from which all private machines must derive, or to which they must adapt, their movements. Considered merely as a metaphor, all this is well enough; but here, as in so many other cases, the 'foam hardens itself into a shell,' and the shadow we have wantonly evoked stands terrible before us, and will not depart at our bidding. Government includes much also that is not mechanical, and cannot be treated mechanically; of which latter truth, as appears to us, the political speculations and exertions of our time are taking less and less cognisance.

Nay, in the very outset, we might note the mighty interest taken in *mere political arrangements*, as itself the sign of a mechanical age. The whole discontent of Europe takes this direction. The deep, strong cry of all civilized nations—a cry which, every one now sees, must and will be answered, is, Give us a reform of Government! A good structure of legislation—a proper check upon the executive—a wise arrangement of the judiciary, is *all* that is wanting for human happiness. The Philosopher of this age is not a Socrates, a Plato, a Hooker, or Taylor, who inculcates on men the necessity and infinite worth of moral goodness, the great truth that our happiness depends on the mind which is within us, and not on the circumstances which are without us; but a Smith, a De Lolme,[13] a Bentham, who chiefly inculcates the reverse of this—that our happiness depends entirely on external circumstances; nay that the strength and dignity of the mind within us is itself the creature and consequence of these. Were the laws, the government, in good order, all were well with us; the rest would care for itself! Dissentients from this opinion, expressed or implied, are now rarely to be met with; widely and angrily as men differ in its application, the principle is admitted by all.

Equally mechanical, and of equal simplicity, are the methods proposed by both parties for completing or securing this all-sufficient perfection of arrangement. It is no longer the moral, religious, spiritual condition of the people that is our concern, but their physical, practical, economical condition, as regulated by public laws. Thus is the Body-politic more than ever worshipped and tended: But the Soul-politic less than ever. Love of country, in any high or generous sense, in any other than an almost animal sense, or mere habit, has little importance attached to it in such reforms, or in the opposition shown them. Men are to be guided only by their self-interests. Good government is a good balancing of these; and, except a keen eye and appetite for self-interest, requires no virtue in any quarter. To both parties it is emphatically a machine: to the discontented, a taxing-machine; to the contented, a 'machine for securing property.' Its duties and its faults are not those of a father, but of an active parish constable. . . .

To us who live in the midst of all this, and see continually the faith, hope, and practice of every one founded on Mechanism of one kind or other, it is apt to seem quite natural, and as if it could never

13. Adam Smith (1723–1827) was the famous founder of what became the science of political economy and authority for the doctrine of *laissez faire,* free trade. His *Wealth of Nations* (1776) became an internationally important book very quickly. Jean Louis de Lolme (1740–1806) was a Swiss journalist who wrote a study of English political institutions.

have been otherwise. Nevertheless, if we recollect or reflect a little, we shall find both that it has been, and might again be, otherwise. The domain of Mechanism—meaning thereby political, ecclesiastical, or other outward establishments—was once considered as embracing, and we are persuaded can at any time embrace, but a limited portion of man's interests, and by no means the highest portion.

To speak a little pedantically, there is a science of *Dynamics* in man's fortunes and nature, as well as of *Mechanics*. There is a science which treats of, and practically addresses, the primary, unmodified forces and energies of man, the mysterious springs of Love, and Fear, and Wonder, of Enthusiasm, Poetry, Religion, all which have a truly vital and *infinite* character; as well as a science which practically addresses the finite, modified developements of these, when they take the shape of immediate 'motives,' as hope of reward, or as fear of punishment.

Now it is certain, that in former times the wise men, the enlightened lovers of their kind, who appeared generally as Moralists, Poets, or Priests, did, without neglecting the Mechanical province, deal chiefly with the Dynamical; applying themselves chiefly to regulate, increase, and purify the inward primary powers of man; and fancying that herein lay the main difficulty, and the best service they could undertake. But a wide difference is manifest in our age. For the wise men, who now appear as Political Philosophers, deal exclusively with the Mechanical province; and occupying themselves in counting up and estimating men's motives, strive by curious checking and balancing, and other adjustments of Profit and Loss, to guide them to their true advantage: while, unfortunately, those same 'motives' are so innumerable, and so variable in every individual, that no really useful conclusion can ever be drawn from their enumeration. But though Mechanism, wisely contrived, has done much for man, in a social and moral point of view, we cannot be persuaded that it has ever been the chief source of his worth or happiness. . . .

Or, to take an infinitely higher instance, that of the Christian Religion, which, under every theory of it, in the believing or the unbelieving mind, must ever be regarded as the crowning glory, or rather the life and soul, of our whole modern culture: How did Christianity arise and spread abroad among men? Was it by institutions and establishments, and well-arranged systems of mechanism? Not so; on the contrary, in all past and existing institutions for these ends, its divine spirit has invariably been found to languish and decay. It arose in the mystic deeps of man's soul; and was spread abroad by the 'preaching of the word,' by simple, altogether natural and individual efforts; and flew, like hallowed fire, from heart to heart, till all were purified and illuminated by it; and its heavenly light shone, as it still shines, and as sun or star will ever shine, through the whole dark destinies of man. Here again was no Mechanism; man's highest attainment was accomplished, Dynamically, not Mechanically. Nay, we will venture to say that no high attainment, not even any far-extending movement among men, was ever accomplished otherwise. Strange as it may seem, if we read History with any degree of thoughtfulness, we shall find, that the checks and balances of Profit and Loss have never been the grand agents with men; that they have never been roused into deep, thorough, all-pervading efforts by any computable prospect of Profit and Loss, for any visible, finite object; but always for some invisible and infinite one. The Crusades took their rise in Religion; their visible object was, commercially speaking, worth nothing. It was the boundless, Invisible world that was laid bare in the imaginations of those men; and in its burning light, the visible shrunk as a scroll. . . . The Reformation had an invisible, mystic, and ideal aim: the result was indeed to be embodied in external things; but its spirit, its worth, was internal, invisible, infinite. Our English Revolution, too, originated in Religion. Men did battle, even in those days, not for Purse sake, but for Conscience sake. Nay, in our own days, it is no way different. The French Revolution itself had something higher in it than cheap bread and a Habeas-corpus act. Here, too, was an Idea; a Dynamic, not a Mechanic force. It was a struggle, though a blind and at last an insane one, for the infinite, divine nature of Right, of Freedom, of Country.

Thus does man, in every age, vindicate, consciously or unconsciously, his celestial birthright. Thus does nature hold on her wondrous, unquestionable course; and all our systems and theories are but so many froth-eddies or sand-banks, which from time to time she casts up and washes away. When we can drain the Ocean into our mill-ponds, and bottle up the Force of Gravity, to be sold by retail, in our gas-jars; then may we hope to comprehend the infinitudes of man's soul under formulas of Profit and Loss; and rule over this too, as over a patent engine, by checks, and valves, and balances.

Nay, even with regard to Government itself, can it be necessary to remind any one that Freedom, without which indeed all spiritual life is impossible, depends on infinitely more complex influences than either the extension or the curtailment of the 'democratic interest?' Who is there that 'taking the high *priori* road,' shall point out what these influences are; what deep, subtle, inextricably entangled influences they have been, and may be? For man is not the creature and product of Mechanism; but, in a far truer sense, its creator and producer: it is the noble people that makes the noble Government; rather than conversely. . . .

These and the like facts are so familiar, the truths which they preach so obvious, and have in all past times been so universally believed and acted on, that we should almost feel ashamed for repeating them; were it not that, on every hand, the memory of them seems to have passed away, or at best died into a faint tradition, of no value as a practical principle. To judge by the loud clamour of our Constitution-builders, Statists, Economists, directors, creators, reformers of Public Societies; in a word, all manner of Mechanists, from the Cartwright up to the Code-maker; and by the nearly total silence of all Preachers and Teachers who should give a voice to Poetry, Religion, and Morality, we might fancy either that man's Dynamical nature was, to all spiritual intents, extinct—or else so perfected, that nothing more was to be made of it by the old means; and henceforth only in his Mechanical contrivances did any hope exist for him.

To define the limits of these two departments of man's activity, which work into one another, and by means of one another, so intricately and inseparably, were by its nature an impossible attempt. Their relative importance, even to the wisest mind, will vary in different times, according to the special wants and dispositions of these times. Meanwhile, it seems clear enough that only in the right coordination of the two, and the vigorous forwarding of *both*, does our true line of action lie. Undue cultivation of the inward or Dynamical province leads to idle, visionary, impracticable courses, and especially in rude eras, to Superstition and Fanaticism, with their long train of baleful and well-known evils. Undue cultivation of the outward, again, though less immediately prejudicial, and even for the time productive of many palpable benefits, must, in the long run, by destroying Moral Force, which is the parent of all other Force, prove not less certainly, and perhaps still more hopelessly, pernicious. This, we take it, is the grand characteristic of our age. By our skill in Mechanism, it has come to pass that, in the management of external things, we excel all other ages; while in whatever respects the pure moral nature, in true dignity of soul and character, we are perhaps inferior to most civilized ages.

In fact, if we look deeper, we shall find that this faith in Mechanism has now struck its roots deep into men's most intimate, primary sources of conviction; and is thence sending up, over his whole life and activity, innumerable stems—fruit-bearing and poison-bearing. The truth is, men have lost their belief in the Invisible, and believe, and hope, and work only in the Visible; or, to speak it in other words, This is not a Religious age. Only the material, the immediately practical, not the divine and spiritual, is important to us. The infinite, absolute character of Virtue has passed into a finite, conditional one; it is no longer a worship of the Beautiful and Good; but a calculation of the Profitable. Worship, indeed, in any sense, is not recognised among us, or is mechanically explained into Fear of pain, or Hope of pleasure. Our true Deity is Mechanism. It has subdued external Nature for us, and, we think, it will do all other things. We are Giants in physical power: in a deeper than a metaphorical sense, we are Titans, that strive, by heaping mountain on mountain, to conquer Heaven also.

The strong mechanical character, so visible in the spiritual pursuits and methods of this age, may be traced much farther into the condition and prevailing disposition of our spiritual nature itself. Consider, for example, the general fashion of Intellect in this era. Intellect, the power man has of knowing and believing, is now nearly synonymous with Logic, or the mere power of arranging and communicating. Its implement is not Meditation, but Argument. 'Cause and effect' is almost the only category under which we look at, and work with, all Nature. Our first question with regard to any object is not, What is it? but, How is it? We are no longer instinctively driven to apprehend, and lay to heart, what is Good and Lovely, but rather to enquire, as onlookers, how it is produced, whence it comes, whither it goes? Our favourite Philosophers have no love and no hatred; they stand among us not to do, or to create any thing, but as a sort of Logic-mills to grind out the true causes and effects of all that is done and created. To the eye of a Smith, a Hume, or a Constant, all is well that works quietly. An Order of Ignatius Loyola, a Presbyterianism of John Knox, a Wickliffe, or a Henry the Eighth, are simply so many mechanical phenomena, caused or causing.

. . . Wonder, indeed, is, on all hands, dying out: it is the sign of uncultivation to wonder. Speak to any small man of a high, majestic Reformation, of a high, majestic Luther to lead it, and forthwith he sets about 'accounting' for it! how the 'circumstances of the time' called for such a character, and found him, we suppose, standing girt and road-ready, to do its errand; how the 'circumstances of the time' created, fashioned, floated him quietly along into the result; how, in short, this small man, had he been there, could have performed the like himself! For it is the 'force of circumstances' that does every thing; the force of one man can do nothing. Now all this is grounded on little more than a metaphor. We figure Society as a 'Machine,' and that mind is opposed to mind, as body is to body; whereby two, or at most ten, little minds must be stronger than one great mind. Notable

absurdity! For the plain truth, very plain, we think, is, that minds
are opposed to minds in quite a different way; and *one* man that has
a higher Wisdom, a hitherto unknown spiritual Truth in him, is
stronger, not than ten men that have it not, or than ten thousand, but
than *all* men, that have it not; and stands among them with a quite
ethereal, angelic power, as with a sword out of Heaven's own armoury,
sky-tempered, which no buckler, and no tower of brass, will finally
withstand.

.   .   .   .

To what extent theological Unbelief, we mean intellectual dissent
from the Church, in its view of Holy Writ, prevails at this day, would
be a highly important, were it not, under any circumstances, an almost
impossible enquiry. But the Unbelief, which is of a still more fundamental character, every man may see prevailing, with scarcely any but
the faintest contradiction, all around him; even in the Pulpit itself.
Religion, in most countries, more or less in every country, is no longer
what it was, and should be—a thousand-voiced psalm from the heart
of Man to his invisible Father, the fountain of all Goodness, Beauty,
Truth, and revealed in every revelation of these; but for the most part,
a wise prudential feeling grounded on mere calculation; a matter, as all
others now are, of Expediency and Utility; whereby some smaller
quantum of earthly enjoyment may be exchanged for a far larger
quantum of celestial enjoyment. Thus Religion, too, is Profit; a working for wages; not Reverence, but vulgar Hope or Fear. Many, we
know, very many, we hope, are still religious in a far different sense;
were it not so, our case were too desperate: But to witness that such
is the temper of the times, we take any calm observant man, who
agrees or disagrees in our feeling on the matter, and ask him whether
our view of it is not in general well-founded.

Literature, too, if we consider it, gives similar testimony. At no
former era has Literature, the printed communication of Thought,
been of such importance as it is now. We often hear that the Church
is in danger; and truly so it is—in a danger it seems not to know of:
For, with its tithes in the most perfect safety, its functions are becoming more and more superseded. The true Church of England, at
this moment, lies in the Editors of its Newspapers. These preach to
the people daily, weekly; admonishing kings themselves; advising peace
or war, with an authority which only the first Reformers, and a
long-past class of Popes, were possessed of; inflicting moral censure;
imparting moral encouragement, consolation, edification; in all ways,
diligently 'administering the Discipline of the Church.' It may be

said, too, that in private disposition, the new Preachers somewhat resemble the Mendicant Friars of old times: outwardly full of holy zeal; inwardly not without stratagem, and hunger for terrestrial things. But omitting this class, and the boundless host of watery personages who pipe, as they are able, on so many scrannel straws, let us look at the higher regions of Literature, where, if anywhere, the pure melodies of Poesy and Wisdom should be heard. Of natural talent there is no deficiency: one or two richly-endowed individuals even give us a superiority in this respect. But what is the song they sing? Is it a tone of the Memnon Statue, breathing music as the *light* first touches it? a 'liquid wisdom,' disclosing to our sense the deep, infinite harmonies of Nature and man's soul? Alas, no! It is not a matin or vesper hymn to the Spirit of all Beauty, but a fierce clashing of cymbals, and shouting of multitudes, as children pass through the fire to Molech! Poetry itself has no eye for the Invisible. Beauty is no longer the god it worships, but some brute image of Strength; which we may well call an idol, for true Strength is one and the same with Beauty, and its worship also is a hymn. The meek, silent Light can mould, create, and purify all nature; but the loud Whirlwind, the sign and product of Disunion, of Weakness, passes on, and is forgotten. How widely this veneration for the physically Strongest has spread itself through Literature, any one may judge, who reads either criticism or poem.[14] We praise a work, not as 'true,' but as 'strong;' our highest praise is that it has 'affected' us, has 'terrified' us. All this, it has been well observed, is the 'maximum of the Barbarous,' the symptom, not of vigorous refinement, but of luxurious corruption. It speaks much, too, for men's indestructible love of truth, that nothing of this kind will abide with them; that even the talent of a Byron cannot permanently seduce us into idol-worship; but that he, too, with all his wild syren charming, already begins to be disregarded and forgotten.

Again, with respect to our Moral condition: here also, he who runs may read that the same physical, mechanical influences are everywhere busy. For the 'superior morality,' of which we hear so much, we, too, would desire to be thankful: at the same time, it were but blindness to deny that this 'superior morality' is properly rather an 'inferior criminality' produced not by greater love of Virtue, but by greater perfection of Police; and of that far subtler and stronger Police, called Public Opinion. This last watches over us with its Argus eyes

14. Carlyle has himself been justly accused of excessive veneration of the physically strong. See, especially, Eric Bentley, *A Century of Hero-Worship* (1957). The fact that here Carlyle attacks this veneration of strength indicates the wide difference between his early and late writings.

more keenly than ever; but the 'inward eye' seems heavy with sleep.
Of any belief in invisible, divine things, we find as few traces in our
Morality as elsewhere. It is by tangible, material considerations that
we are guided, not by inward and spiritual. Self-denial, the parent of
all virtue, in any true sense of that word, has perhaps seldom been
rarer: so rare is it, that the most, even in their abstract speculations,
regard its existence as a chimera. Virtue is Pleasure, is Profit; no
celestial, but an earthly thing. Virtuous men, Philanthropists, Martyrs,
are happy accidents; their 'taste' lies the right way! In all senses, we
worship and follow after Power; which may be called a physical
pursuit. No man now loves Truth, as Truth must be loved, with an
infinite love; but only with a finite love, and as it were *par amours*.
Nay, properly speaking, he does not *believe* and know it, but only
'*thinks*' it, and that 'there is every probability!' He preaches it aloud,
and rushes courageously forth with it—if there is a multitude huzzaing
at his back! yet ever keeps looking over his shoulder, and the instant
the huzzaing languishes, he too stops short. In fact, what morality we
have takes the shape of Ambition, of Honour; beyond money and
money's worth, our only rational blessedness is Popularity. It were but
a fool's trick to die for conscience. Only for 'character,' by duel, or, in
case of extremity, by suicide, is the wise man bound to die. By arguing
on the 'force of circumstances,' we have argued away all force from
ourselves; and stand leashed together, uniform in dress and movement,
like the rowers of some boundless galley. This and that may be right
and true; *but* we must not do it. Wonderful 'Force of Public Opinion!'
We must act and walk in all points as it prescribes; follow the traffic
it bids us, realize the sum of money, the degree of 'influence' it expects
of us, or we shall be lightly esteemed; certain mouthfuls of articulate
wind will be blown at us, and this what mortal courage can front?
Thus, while civil Liberty is more and more secured to us, our moral
Liberty is all but lost. Practically considered, our creed is Fatalism; and,
free in hand and foot, we are shackled in heart and soul, with far
straiter than feudal chains. Truly may we say, with the Philosopher,
'the deep meaning of the Laws of Mechanism lies heavy on us;' and
in the closet, in the marketplace, in the temple, by the social hearth,
encumbers the whole movements of our mind, and over our noblest
faculties is spreading a nightmare sleep.

These dark features, we are aware, belong more or less to other
ages, as well as to ours. This faith in Mechanism, in the all-importance
of physical things, is in every age the common refuge of Weakness and
blind Discontent; of all who believe, as many will ever do, that man's

true good lies without him, not within. We are aware also, that, as applied to ourselves in all their aggravation, they form but half a picture; that in the whole picture there are bright lights as well as gloomy shadows. If we here dwell chiefly on the latter, let us not be blamed: it is in general more profitable to reckon up our defects than to boast of our attainments.

Neither, with all these evils more or less clearly before us, have we at any time despaired of the fortunes of society. Despair, or even despondency, in that respect, appears to us, in all cases, a groundless feeling. We have a faith in the imperishable dignity of man; in the high vocation to which, throughout this his earthly history, he has been appointed. However it may be with individual nations, whatever melancholic speculators may assert, it seems a well-ascertained fact that, in all times, reckoning even from those of the Heraclides and Pelasgi, the happiness and greatness of mankind at large has been continually progressive. Doubtless this age also is advancing. Its very unrest, its ceaseless activity, its discontent, contains matter of promise. Knowledge, education, are opening the eyes of the humblest—are increasing the number of thinking minds without limit. This is as it should be; for, not in turning back, not in resting, but only in resolutely struggling forward, does our life consist. Nay, after all, our spiritual maladies are but of Opinion; we are but fettered by chains of our own forging, and which ourselves also can rend asunder. This deep, paralysed subjection to physical objects comes not from nature, but from our own unwise mode of *viewing* Nature. . . .

Meanwhile that great outward changes are in progress can be doubtful to no one. The time is sick and out of joint. Many things have reached their height; and it is a wise adage that tells us, 'the darkest hour is nearest the dawn.' Whenever we can gather any indication of the public thought, whether from printed books, as in France or Germany, or from Carbonari's rebellions and other political tumults, as in Spain, Portugal, Italy, and Greece, the voice it utters is the same. The thinking minds of all nations call for change. There is a deep-lying struggle in the whole fabric of society; a boundless, grinding collision of the New with the Old. The French Revolution, as is now visible enough, was not the parent of this mighty movement, but its offspring. Those two hostile influences, which always exist in human things, and on the constant intercommunion of which depends their health and safety, had lain in separate masses accumulating through

15. The Carbonari were members of secret revolutionary societies in the nineteenth century. The name has been carelessly applied to almost any such society since.

generations, and France was the scene of their fiercest explosion; but the final issue was not unfolded in that country; nay, it is not yet anywhere unfolded. Political freedom is hitherto the object of these efforts; but they will not and cannot stop there. It is towards a higher freedom than mere freedom from oppression by his fellow-mortal, that man dimly aims. Of this higher, heavenly freedom, which is 'man's reasonable service,' all his noble institutions, his faithful endeavours and loftiest attainments, are but the body, and more and more approximated emblem.

On the whole, as this wondrous planet, Earth, is journeying with its fellows through infinite space, so are the wondrous destinies embarked on it journeying through infinite time, under a higher guidance than ours. For the present, as our Astronomy informs us, its path lies towards *Hercules*, the constellation of *Physical Power:* But that is not our most pressing concern. Go where it will, the deep HEAVEN will be around it. Therein let us have hope and sure faith. To reform a world, to reform a nation, no wise man will undertake; and all but foolish men know that the only solid, though a far slower reformation, is what each begins and perfects on *himself*.

THOMAS CARLYLE

# Characteristics*

The healthy know not of their health, but only the sick: this is the
Physician's Aphorism; and applicable in a far wider sense than he gives
it. We may say, it holds no less in moral, intellectual, political, poetical, than in merely corporeal therapeutics; that wherever, or in what
shape soever, powers of the sort which can be named *vital* are at work,
herein lies the test of their working right or working wrong.

In the Body, for example, as all doctors are agreed, the first condition of complete health is, that each organ perform its function
unconsciously, unheeded; let but any organ announce its separate
existence, were it even boastfully, and for pleasure, not for pain, then
already has one of those unfortunate 'false centres of sensibility'
established itself, already is derangement there. The perfection of
bodily wellbeing is, that the collective bodily activities seem one; and
be manifested, moreover, not in themselves, but in the action they
accomplish. If a Dr Kitchener[1] boast that his system is in high order,

* From *Edinburgh Review*, LIV (December, 1831), 351–83.
    1. Dr. William Kitchener (1775–1827) was convinced that health de-
pends to a great extent on the proper preparation of food. He was himself

Dietetic Philosophy may indeed take credit; but the true Peptician was that Countryman who answered that, 'for his part, he had no system.' In fact, unity, agreement, is always silent, or soft-voiced; it is only discord that loudly proclaims itself. So long as the several elements of Life, all fitly adjusted, can pour forth their movement like harmonious tuned strings, it is a melody and unison; Life, from its mysterious fountains, flows out as in celestial music and diapason—which also, like that other music of the spheres, even because it is perennial and complete, without interruption and without imperfection, might be fabled to escape the ear. Thus, too, in some languages, is the state of health well denoted by a term expressing unity; when we feel ourselves as we wish to be, we say that we are *whole*.

Few mortals, it is to be feared, are permanently blessed with that felicity of 'having no system:' nevertheless, most of us, looking back on young years, may remember seasons of a light, aerial translucency and elasticity, and perfect freedom; the body had not yet become the prison-house of the soul, but was its vehicle and implement, like a creature of the thought, and altogether pliant to its bidding. We knew not that we had limbs, we only lifted, hurled, and leapt; through eye and ear, and all avenues of sense, came clear unimpeded tidings from without, and from within issued clear victorious force; we stood as in the centre of Nature, giving and receiving, in harmony with it all; unlike Virgil's Husbandmen, 'too happy *because* we did not know our blessedness.' In those days, health and sickness were foreign traditions that did not concern us; our whole being was as yet One, the whole man like an incorporated Will. Such, were Rest or ever-successful Labour the human lot, might our life continue to be: a pure, perpetual, unregarded music; a beam of perfect white light, rendering all things visible, but itself unseen, even because it was of that perfect whiteness, and no irregular obstruction had yet broken it into colours. The beginning of Inquiry is Disease: all Science, if we consider well, as it must have originated in the feeling of something being wrong, so it is and continues to be but Division, Dismemberment, and partial healing of the wrong. Thus, as was of old written, the Tree of Knowledge springs from a root of evil, and bears fruits of good and evil. Had Adam remained in Paradise, there had been no Anatomy and no Metaphysics.

But, alas, as the Philosopher declares, 'Life itself is a disease; a

---

an epicure and a skilled cook, noted for the elaborate dinners he gave. Carlyle was plagued from his youth with dyspepsia, and his writings are filled with half-comical allusions to the importance of good digestion to moral and spiritual health.

working incited by suffering'; action from passion! The memory of
that first state of Freedom and paradisiac Unconsciousness has faded
away into an ideal poetic dream. We stand here too conscious of many
things: with Knowledge, the symptom of Derangement, we must
even do our best to restore a little Order. Life is, in few instances, and
at rare intervals, the diapason of a heavenly melody; oftenest the fierce
jar of disruptions and convulsions, which, do what we will, there is
no disregarding. Nevertheless such is still the wish of Nature on our
behalf; in all vital action, her manifest purpose and effort is, that we
should be unconscious of it, and, like the peptic Countryman, never
know that we 'have a system.' For indeed vital action every where is
emphatically a means, not an end; Life is not given us for the mere
sake of Living, but always with an ulterior external Aim: neither is it
on the process, on the means, but rather on the result, that Nature, in
any of her doings, is wont to intrust us with insight and volition.
Boundless as is the domain of man, it is but a small fractional proportion of it that he rules with Consciousness and by Forethought: what
he can contrive, nay, what he can altogether know and comprehend,
is essentially the mechanical, small; the great is ever, in one sense or
other, the vital, it is essentially the mysterious, and only the surface of
it can be understood. But Nature, it might seem, strives, like a kind
mother, to hide from us even this, that she is a mystery: she will have
us rest on her beautiful and awful bosom as if it were our secure home;
on the bottomless boundless Deep, whereon all human things fearfully
and wonderfully swim, she will have us walk and build, as if the film
which supported us there (which any scratch of a bare bodkin will
rend asunder, any sputter of a pistol-shot instantaneously burn up)
were no film, but a solid rock-foundation. For ever in the neighbourhood of an inevitable Death, man can forget that he is born to die; of
his Life, which, strictly meditated, contains in it an Immensity and
an Eternity, he can conceive lightly, as of a simple implement wherewith to do day-labour and earn wages. So cunningly does Nature, the
mother of all highest Art, which only apes her from afar, 'body forth
the Finite from the Infinite;' and guide man safe on his wondrous
path, not more by endowing him with vision, than, at the right place,
with blindness! Under all her works, chiefly under her noblest work,
Life, lies a basis of Darkness, which she benignantly conceals; in Life,
too, the roots and inward circulations which stretch down fearfully to
the regions of Death and Night, shall not hint of their existence, and
only the fair stem with its leaves and flowers, shone on by the fair sun,
disclose itself, and joyfully grow.

However, without venturing into the abstruse, or too eagerly ask-

ing Why and How, in things where our answer must needs prove, in
great part, an echo of the question, let us be content to remark farther,
in the merely historical way, how that Aphorism of the bodily Physician holds good in quite other departments. Of the Soul, with her
activities, we shall find it no less true than of the Body: nay, cry the
Spiritualists, is not that very division of the unity, Man, into a
dualism of Soul and Body, itself the symptom of disease; as, perhaps,
your frightful theory of Materialism, of his being but a Body, and
therefore, at least, once more a unity, may be the paroxysm which was
critical, and the beginning of cure! But omitting this, we observe, with
confidence enough, that the truly strong mind, view it as Intellect, as
Morality, or under any other aspect, is nowise the mind acquainted
with its strength; that here as before the sign of health is Unconsciousness. In our inward, as in our outward world, what is mechanical lies
open to us; not what is dynamical and has vitality. Of our Thinking,
we might say, it is but the mere upper surface that we shape into
articulate Thoughts;—underneath the region of argument and conscious discourse, lies the region of meditation; here, in its quiet
mysterious depths, dwells what vital force is in us; here, if aught is
to be created, and not merely manufactured and communicated, must
the work go on. Manufacture is intelligible, but trivial; Creation is
great, and cannot be understood. Thus, if the Debater and Demon-
strator, whom we may rank as the lowest of true thinkers, knows what
he has done, and how he did it, the Artist, whom we rank as the
highest, knows not; must speak of Inspiration, and in one or the other
dialect, call his work the gift of a divinity.

But, on the whole, 'genius is ever a secret to itself;' of this old
truth we have, on all sides, daily evidence. The Shakespeare takes no
airs for writing *Hamlet* and the *Tempest*, understands not that it is
any thing surprising: Milton, again, is more conscious of his faculty,
which accordingly is an inferior one. On the other hand, what cackling
and strutting must we not often hear and see, when, in some shape of
academical prolusion, maiden speech, review article, this or the other
well-fledged goose has produced its goose-egg, of quite measurable
value, were it the pink of its whole kind; and wonders why all mortals
do not wonder!

Foolish enough, too, was the College Tutor's surprise at Walter
Shandy: how, though unread in Aristotle, he could nevertheless argue;
and not knowing the name of any dialectic tool, handled them all to
perfection. Is it the skilfullest Anatomist that cuts the best figure at
Sadler's Wells? or does the Boxer hit better for knowing that he has
a flexor longus and a flexor brevis? But, indeed, as in the higher case

of the Poet, so here in that of the Speaker and Inquirer, the true force is an unconscious one. The healthy Understanding, we should say, is not the Logical, argumentative, but the Intuitive; for the end of Understanding is not to prove, and find reasons, but to know and believe. Of Logic, and its limits, and uses and abuses, there were much to be said and examined; one fact, however, which chiefly concerns us here, has long been familiar: that the man of logic and the man of insight; the Reasoner and the Discoverer, or even Knower, are quite separable,—indeed, for most part, quite separate characters. In practical matters, for example, has it not become almost proverbial that the man of logic cannot prosper? This is he whom business people call Systematic and Theorizer and Word-monger; his *vital* intellectual force lies dormant or extinct, his whole force is mechanical, conscious: of such a one it is foreseen that, when once confronted with the infinite complexities of the real world, his little compact theorem of the world will be found wanting; that unless he can throw it overboard, and become a new creature, he will necessarily founder. Nay, in mere Speculation itself, the most ineffectual of all characters, generally speaking, is your dialectic man-at-arms; were he armed cap-a-pie in syllogistic mail of proof, and perfect master of logic-fence, how little does it avail him! Consider the old Schoolmen, and their pilgrimage towards Truth: the faithfullest endeavour, incessant unwearied motion, often great natural vigour; only no progress: nothing but antic feats of one limb poised against the other; there they balanced, somersetted, and made postures; at best gyrated swiftly, with some pleasure, like Spinning Dervishes, and ended where they began. So is it, so will it always be, with all System-makers and builders of logical card-castles; of which class a certain remnant must, in every age, as they do in our own, survive and build. Logic is good, but it is not the best. The Irrefragable Doctor, with his chains of induction, his corollaries, dilemmas, and other cunning logical diagrams and apparatus, will cast you a beautiful horoscope, and speak reasonable things; nevertheless your stolen jewel, which you wanted him to find you, is not forthcoming. Often by some winged word, winged as the thunderbolt is, of a Luther, a Napoleon, a Goethe, shall we see the difficulty split asunder, and its secret laid bare; while the Irrefragable, with all his logical roots, hews at it, and hovers round it, and finds it on all hands too hard for him.

Again, in the difference between Oratory and Rhetoric, as indeed every where in that superiority of what is called the Natural over the Artificial, we find a similar illustration. The Orator persuades and carries all with him, he knows not how; the Rhetorician can prove

that he ought to have persuaded and carried all with him: the one
is in a state of healthy unconsciousness, as if he 'had no system;' the
other, in virtue of regimen and dietetic punctuality, feels at best that
'his system is in high order.' So stands it, in short, with all forms of
Intellect, whether as directed to the finding of Truth, or to the fit
imparting thereof; to Poetry, to Eloquence, to depth of Insight, which
is the basis of both these; always the characteristic of right performance
is a certain spontaneity, an unconsciousness; 'the healthy know not of
their health, but only the sick.' So that the old percept of the critic, as
crabbed as it looked to his ambitious disciple, might contain in it a
most fundamental truth, applicable to us all, and in much else than
Literature: 'Whenever you have written any sentence that looks
particularly excellent, be sure to blot it out.' In like manner,
under milder phraseology, and with a meaning purposely much wider,
a living Thinker has taught us: 'Of the Wrong we are always conscious, of the Right never.'

But if such is the law with regard to Speculation and the Intellectual power of man, much more is it with regard to Conduct, and
the power, manifested chiefly therein, which we name Moral. 'Let not
thy left hand know what thy right hand doeth:' whisper not to thy
own heart, How worthy is this action; for then it is already becoming
worthless. The good man is he who *works* continually in well-doing; to
whom well-doing is as his natural existence, awakening no astonishment, requiring no commentary; but there, like a thing of course, and
as if it could not but be so. Self-contemplation, on the other hand, is
infallibly the symptom of disease, be it or be it not the sign of cure:
an unhealthy Virtue is one that consumes itself to leanness in repent-
ing and anxiety; or, still worse, that inflates itself into dropsical
boastfulness and vain glory: either way, it is a self-seeking; an unprofitable looking behind us to measure the way we have made:
whereas the sole concern is to walk continually forward, and make
more way. If in any sphere of Man's Life, then in the moral sphere, as
the inmost and most vital of all, it is good that there be wholeness;
that there be unconsciousness, which is the evidence of this. Let the
free reasonable Will, which dwells in us, as in our Holy of Holies, be
indeed free, and obeyed like a Divinity, as is its right and its effort: the
perfect obedience will be the silent one. Such perhaps were the sense
of that maxim, enunciating, as is usual, but the half of a truth: 'To
say that we have a clear conscience is to utter a solecism; had we never
sinned, we should have had no conscience.' Were defeat unknown,
neither would victory be celebrated by songs of triumph.

This, true enough, is an ideal, impossible state of being; yet ever

the goal towards which our actual state of being strives; which it is the
more perfect the nearer it can approach. Nor, in our actual world,
where Labour must often prove ineffectual, and thus in all senses
Light alternate with Darkness, and the nature of an ideal Morality be
much modified, is the case, thus far, materially different. It is a fact
which escapes no one, that, generally speaking, whoso is acquainted
with his worth has but a little stock to cultivate acquaintance with.
Above all, the public acknowledgment of such acquaintance, indicating
that it has reached quite an intimate footing, bodes ill. Already, to the
popular judgment, he who talks much about Virtue in the abstract,
begins to be suspicious; it is shrewdly guessed that where there is
great preaching, there will be little almsgiving. Or again, on a wider
scale, we can remark that ages of Heroism are not ages of Moral
Philosophy; Virtue, when it can be philosophized of, has become
aware of itself, is sickly, and beginning to decline. A spontaneous
habitual all-pervading spirit of Chivalrous Valour shrinks together, and
perks itself up into shriveled Points of Honour; humane Courtesy and
Nobleness of mind dwindle into punctilious Politeness, 'avoiding
meats;' 'paying tithe of mint and anise, neglecting the weightier
matters of the law.' Goodness, which was a rule to itself, must appeal
to Precept, and seek strength from Sanctions; the Freewill no longer
reigns unquestioned and by divine right, but like a mere earthly
sovereign, by expediency, by Rewards and Punishments: or rather, let
us say, the Freewill, so far as may be, has abdicated and withdrawn into
the dark, and a spectral nightmare of a Necessity usurps its throne; for
now that mysterious Self-impulse of the whole man, heaven-inspired
and in all senses partaking of the Infinite, being captiously questioned
in a finite dialect, and answering, as it needs must, by silence,—is
conceived as non-extant, and only the outward Mechanism of it remains acknowledged: of Volition, except as the synonym of Desire,
we hear nothing; of 'Motives,' without any Mover, more than enough.

So, too, when the generous Affections have become wellnigh
paralytic, we have the reign of Sentimentality. The greatness, the
profitableness, at any rate the extremely ornamental nature of high
feeling, and the luxury of doing good; charity, love, self-forgetfulness,
devotedness, and all manner of godlike magnanimity, are every where
insisted on, and pressingly inculcated in speech and writing, in prose
and verse; Socinian Preachers[2] proclaim 'Benevolence' to all the four

2. Socinianism was the belief named after Faustus Socinus (1539–1604)
and his uncle Laelius Socinus (1525–63). They were anti-trinitarians who
thought the only solid basis for protestantism was human reason. What contradicted reason must be regarded as incredible.

winds, and have TRUTH engraved on their watch-seals: unhappily with little or no effect. Were the Limbs in right walking order, why so much demonstrating of Motion? The barrenest of all mortals is the Sentimentalist. Granting even that he were sincere, and did not wilfully deceive us, or without first deceiving himself, what good is in him? Does he not lie there as a perpetual lesson of despair, and type of bedrid valetudinarian impotence? His is emphatically a Virtue that has become, through every fibre, conscious of itself; it is all sick, and feels as if it were made of glass, and durst not touch or be touched: in the shape of work, it can do nothing; at the utmost, by incessant nursing and caudling, keep itself alive. As the last stage of all, when Virtue, properly so called, has ceased to be practised, and become extinct, and a mere remembrance, we have the era of Sophists, descanting of its existence, proving it, denying it, mechanically 'accounting' for it;—as dissectors and demonstrators cannot operate till once the body be dead.

Thus is true Moral genius, like true Intellectual, which indeed is but a lower phasis thereof, 'ever a secret to itself.' The healthy moral nature loves Goodness, and without wonder wholly lives in it: the unhealthy makes love to it, and would fain get to live in it; or, finding such courtship fruitless, turns round, and not without contempt abandons it. These curious relations of the Voluntary and Conscious to the Involuntary and Unconscious, and the small proportion which, in all departments of our life, the former bears to the latter—might lead us into deep questions of Psychology and Physiology: such, however, belong not to our present object. Enough, if the fact itself become apparent, that Nature so meant it with us; that in this wise we are made. We may now say, that view man's individual Existence under what aspect we will, under the highest Spiritual, as under the merely Animal aspect, every where the grand vital energy, while in its sound state, is an unseen unconscious one; or, in the words of our old Aphorism, 'the healthy know not of their health, but only the sick.'

To understand man, however, we must look beyond the individual man and his actions or interests, and view him in combination with his fellows. It is in Society that man first feels what he is; first becomes what he can be. In Society an altogether new set of spiritual activities are evolved in him, and the old immeasurably quickened and strengthened. Society is the genial element wherein his nature first lives and grows; the solitary man were but a small portion of himself, and must continue for ever folded in, stunted, and only half alive. 'Already,' says a deep Thinker, with more meaning than will disclose itself at once, 'my opinion, my conviction, gains *infinitely* in strength and sureness, the moment a second mind has adopted it.' Such, even in its simplest form, is association; so wondrous the communion of soul with soul as directed to the mere act of Knowing! In other higher acts, the wonder is still more manifest; as in that portion of our being which we name the Moral: for properly, indeed, all communion is of a moral sort, whereof such intellectual communion (in the act of knowing) is itself an example. But with regard to Morals strictly so called, it is in Society, we might almost say, that Morality begins; here at least it takes an altogether new form, and on every side, as in living growth, expands itself. The Duties of Man to himself, to what is Highest in himself, make but the First Table of the Law: to the First Table is now superadded a Second, with the Duties of Man to his Neighbour; whereby also the significance of the First now assumes its true importance. Man has joined himself with man; soul acts and reacts on soul; a mystic miraculous unfathomable Union establishes itself; Life, in all its elements, has become intensated, consecrated. The lightning-spark of Thought, generated, or say rather heaven-kindled, in the solitary mind, awakens its express likeness in another mind, in a thousand other minds, and all blaze up together in combined fire; reverberated from mind to mind, fed also with fresh fuel in each, it acquires incalculable new Light as Thought, incalculable new Heat as converted into Action. By and by, a common store of Thought can accumulate, and be transmitted as an everlasting possession: Literature, whether as preserved in the memory of Bards, in Runes and Hiero-glyphs engraved on stone, or in Books of written or printed paper, comes into existence, and begins to play its wondrous part. Polities are formed; the weak submitting to the strong; with a willing loyalty, giving obedience that he may receive guidance: or say rather, in honour of our nature, the ignorant submitting to the wise; for so it is in all even the rudest communities, man never yields himself wholly to brute Force, but always to moral Greatness; thus the universal title of respect, from the Oriental *Scheik*, from the *Sachem* of the red Indians, down to our English *Sir*, implies only that he whom we mean to honour is our *senior*. Last, as the crown and all-supporting keystone of the fabric, Religion arises. The devout Meditation of the isolated man, which flitted through his soul, like a transient tone of Love and Awe from unknown lands, acquires certainty, continuance, when it is shared in by his brother men. 'Where two or three are gathered together' in the name of the Highest, then first does the Highest, as it is written, 'appear among them to bless them;' then first does an Altar and act of united Worship open a way from Earth to Heaven; whereon, were it but a simple Jacob's-ladder, the heavenly Messengers will travel, with

glad tidings and unspeakable gifts for men. Such is Society, the vital
articulation of many individuals into a new collective individual:
greatly the most important of man's attainments on this earth; that in
which, and by virtue of which, all his other attainments and attempts
find their arena, and have their value. Considered well, Society is the
standing wonder of our existence; a true region of the Supernatural; as
it were, a second all-embracing Life, wherein our first individual Life
becomes doubly and trebly alive, and whatever of Infinitude was in
us bodies itself forth, and becomes visible and active.

To figure Society as endowed with Life is scarcely a metaphor;
but rather the statement of a fact by such imperfect methods as
language affords. Look at it closely, that mystic Union, Nature's
highest work with man, wherein man's volition plays an indispensable
yet so subordinate a part, and the small Mechanical grows so mysteriously and indissolubly out of the infinite Dynamical, like Body out
of Spirit—is truly enough vital, what we can call vital, and bears the
distinguishing character of life. In the same style also, we can say that
Society has its periods of sickness and vigour, of youth, manhood,
decrepitude, dissolution, and new-birth; in one or other of which stages
we may, in all times, and all places where men inhabit, discern it; and
do ourselves, in this time and place, whether as co-operating or as
contending, as healthy members or as diseased ones, to our joy and
sorrow, form part of it. The question, What is the actual condition of
Society? has in these days unhappily become important enough. No
one of us is unconcerned in that question; but for the majority of
thinking men a true answer to it, such is the state of matters, appears
almost as the one thing needful. Meanwhile as the true answer, that is
to say, the complete and fundamental answer and settlement, often as
it has been demanded, is nowhere forthcoming, and indeed by its
nature is impossible, any honest approximation towards such is not
without value. The feeblest light, or even so much as a more precise
recognition of the darkness, which is the first step to attainment of
light, will be welcome.

This once understood, let it not seem idle if we remark that here
too our old Aphorism holds; that again in the Body Politic, as in the
animal body, the sign of right performance is Unconsciousness. Such
indeed is virtually the meaning of that phrase 'artificial state of
Society,' as contrasted with the natural state, and indicating something so inferior to it. For, in all vital things, men distinguish an
Artificial and a Natural; founding on some dim perception or sentiment of the very truth we here insist on: the Artificial is the conscious,
mechanical; the Natural is the unconscious, dynamical. Thus as we

have an artificial Poetry, and prize only the natural; so likewise we have an artificial Morality, an artificial Wisdom, an artificial Society. The artificial Society is precisely one that knows its own structure, its own internal functions; not in watching, not in knowing which, but in working outwardly to the fulfilment of its aim, does the wellbeing of a Society consist. Every Society, every Polity, has a spiritual principle; is the embodyment, tentative, and more or less complete, of an Idea: all its tendencies of endeavour, specialities of custom, its laws, politics, and whole procedure (as the glance of some Montesquieu[3] across innumerable superficial entanglements can partly decipher) are prescribed by an Idea, and flow naturally from it, as movements from the living source of motion. This Idea, be it of devotion to a Man or class of Men, to a Creed, to an Institution, or even, as in more ancient times, to a piece of Land, is ever a true Loyalty; has in it something of a religious, paramount, quite infinite character; it is properly the Soul of the State, its Life; mysterious as other forms of Life, and like these working secretly, and in a depth beyond that of consciousness.

Accordingly, it is not in the vigorous ages of a Roman Republic that Treatises of the Commonwealth are written: while the Decii are rushing with devoted bodies on the enemies of Rome, what need of preaching Patriotism? The virtue of Patriotism has already sunk from its pristine, all-transcendent condition, before it has received a name. So long as the Commonwealth continues rightly athletic, it cares not to dabble in anatomy. Why teach Obedience to the sovereign; why so much as admire it, or separately recognize it, while a divine idea of Obedience perennially inspires all men? Loyalty, like Patriotism, of which it is a form, was not praised till it had begun to decline; the *Preux Chevaliers*[4] first became rightly admirable, when 'dying for their king,' had ceased to be a habit with chevaliers. For if the mystic significance of the State, let this be what it may, dwells vitally in every heart, encircles every life as with a second higher life, how should it stand self-questioning? It must rush outward, and express itself by works. Besides, if perfect, it is there as by necessity, and does not excite inquiry: it is also by nature, infinite, has no limits;

3. Charles de Secondat Montesquieu (1689–1755) was the author of the famous *Spirit of Laws*. He put the study of laws on a new footing, relating them to the time and conditions in which they originate, rather than subjecting each to an abstract system of "Right & Wrong."

4. These were the Nine Worthies, embodiments of the qualities of chivalry. Traditionally, they were Hector, Alexander, Caesar, Joshua, David, Judas Macabeus, Arthur, Charlemagne, and Godfrey of Bouillon.

therefore can be circumscribed by no conditions and definitions; cannot be reasoned of; except *musically*, or in the language of Poetry, cannot yet so much as be spoken of.

In those days, Society was what we name healthy, sound at heart. Not, indeed, without suffering enough; not without perplexities, difficulty on every side: for such is the appointment of man; his highest and sole blessedness is, that he toil, and know what to toil at: not in ease, but in united victorious labour, which is at once evil and the victory over evil, does his Freedom lie. Nay, often, looking no deeper than such superficial perplexities of the early Time, historians have taught us that it was all one mass of contradiction and disease; and in the antique Republic, or feudal Monarchy, have seen only the confused chaotic quarry, not the robust labourer, or the stately edifice he was building of it. If Society, in such ages, had its difficulty, it had also its strength; if sorrowful masses of rubbish so encumbered it, the tough sinews to hurl them aside, with indomitable heart, were not wanting. Society went along without complaint; did not stop to scrutinize itself, to say, How well I perform, or, Alas, how ill! Men did not yet feel themselves to be 'the envy of surrounding nations;' and were enviable on that very account. Society was what we can call *whole*, in both senses of the word. The individual man was in himself a whole, or complete union; and could combine with his fellows as the living member of a greater whole. For all men, through their life, were animated by one great Idea; thus all efforts pointed one way, every where there was *wholeness*. Opinion and Action had not yet become disunited; but the former could still produce the latter, or attempt to produce it, as the stamp does its impression while the wax is not hardened. Thought, and the Voice of thought, were also a unison; thus, instead of Speculation we had Poetry; Literature, in its rude utterance, was as yet a heroic Song, perhaps, too, a devotional Anthem. Religion was everywhere; Philosophy lay hid under it, peacefully included in it. Herein, as in the life-centre of all, lay the true health and oneness. Only at a later era must Religion split itself into Philosophies; and thereby the vital union of Thought being lost, disunion and mutual collision in all provinces of Speech and of Action more and more prevail. For if the Poet, or Priest, or by whatever title the inspired thinker may be named, is the sign of vigour and wellbeing; so likewise is the Logician, or uninspired thinker, the sign of disease, probably of decrepitude and decay. Thus, not to mention other instances, one of them much nearer hand,—so soon as Prophecy among the Hebrews had ceased, then did the reign of Argumentation begin; and the ancient Theocracy, in its Sadduceeisms and Phariseeisms, and vain jangling of sects and doctors, give token that the *soul* of it had fled, and that the *body* itself, by natural dissolution, 'with the old forces still at work, but working in reverse order,' was on the road to final disappearance.

We might pursue this question into innumerable other ramifications; and every where, under new shapes, find the same truth, which we here so imperfectly enunciate, disclosed: that throughout the whole world of man, in all manifestations and performances of his nature, outward and inward, personal and social, the Perfect, the Great is a mystery to itself, knows not itself; whatsoever does know itself is already little, and more or less imperfect. Or otherwise, we may say, Unconsciousness belongs to pure unmixed Life; Consciousness to a diseased mixture and conflict of Life and Death: Unconsciousness is the sign of Creation; Consciousness at best, that of Manufacture. So deep, in this existence of ours, is the significance of Mystery. Well might the Ancients make Silence a god; for it is the element of all godhood, infinitude, or transcendental greatness; at once the source and the ocean wherein all such begins and ends. In the same sense too, have Poets sung 'Hymns to the Night;' as if Night were nobler than Day; as if Day were but a small motley-coloured veil spread transiently over the infinite bosom of Night, and did but deform and hide from us its purely transparent, eternal deeps. So likewise have they spoken and sung as if Silence were the grand epitome and complete sum-total of all Harmony; and Death, what mortals call Death, properly the beginning of Life. Under such figures, since except in figures there is no speaking of the Invisible, have men endeavoured to express a great Truth;—a Truth, in our times, as nearly as is perhaps possible, forgotten by the most; which nevertheless continues for ever true, for ever all-important, and will one day, under new figures, be again brought home to the bosoms of all.

But, indeed, in a far lower sense, the rudest mind has still some intimation of the greatness there is in Mystery. If Silence was made a god of by the Ancients, he still continues a government clerk among us Moderns. To all Quacks, moreover, of what sort soever, the effect of Mystery is well known: here and there some Cagliostro,[5] even in latter days, turns it to notable account: the Blockhead also, who is

5. Alexandre, Comte de Cagliostro (1745–95), was one of the most famous charlatans in history. His real name was Joseph Balsamo and he made his fortune by assuming innumerable identities in travels around Europe. He was particularly successful as a spiritualist. The inquisition finally sentenced him and he died in prison. Carlyle's essay, "Cagliostro," treats him as the great symbol of contemporary Quackery.

ambitious, and has no talent, finds sometimes in 'the talent of silence,' a kind of succedaneum. Or again, looking on the opposite side of the matter, do we not see, in the common understanding of mankind, a certain distrust, a certain contempt of what is altogether self-conscious and mechanical? As nothing that is wholly seen through has other than a trivial character; so any thing professing to be great, and yet wholly to see through itself, is already known to be false, and a failure. The evil repute your 'theoretical men' stand in, the acknowledged inefficiency of 'Paper Constitutions', and all that class of objects, are instances of this. Experience often repeated, and perhaps a certain instinct of something far deeper that lies under such experiences, has taught men so much. They know, beforehand, that the loud is generally the insignificant, the empty. Whatsoever can proclaim itself from the housetops may be fit for the hawker, and for those multitudes that must needs buy of him; but for any deeper use, might as well continue unproclaimed. Observe, too, how the converse of the proposition holds; how the insignificant, the empty, is usually the loud; and, after the manner of a drum, is loud even because of its emptiness. The uses of some Patent Dinner Calefactor can be bruited abroad over the whole world in the course of the first winter; those of the Printing Press are not so well seen into for the first three centuries: the passing of the Select Vestries Bill[6] raises more noise and hopeful expectancy among mankind, than did the promulgation of the Christian Religion. Again, and again, we say, the great, the creative and enduring, is ever a secret to itself; only the small, the barren and transient, is otherwise.

If we now, with a practical medical view, examine, by this same test of Unconsciousness, the Condition of our own Era, and of man's Life therein, the diagnosis we arrive at is nowise of a flattering sort. The state of Society, in our days, is of all possible states the least an unconscious one: this is specially the Era when all manner of Inquiries into what was once the unfelt, involuntary sphere of man's existence, find their place, and as it were occupy the whole domain of thought. What, for example, is all this that we hear, for the last generation or two, about the Improvement of the Age, the Spirit of the Age, Destruction of Prejudice, Progress of the Species, and the March of Intellect, but an unhealthy state of self-sentience, self-survey; the precursor and prognostic of still worse health? That Intellect do march, if possible at double-quick time, is very desirable; nevertheless why should she turn round at every stride, and cry: See you what a stride

6. For a discussion of this bill, see Cobbett's lecture on the French Revolution in this volume.

I have taken! Such a marching of Intellect is distinctly of the spavined kind; what the Jockeys call 'all action and no go.' Or at best, if we examine well, it is the marching of that gouty Patient, whom his Doctors had clapt on a metal floor artificially heated to the searing point, so that he was obliged to march, and marched with a vengeance —no-whither. Intellect did not awaken for the first time yesterday; but has been under way from Noah's Flood downwards: greatly her best progress, moreover, was in the old times, when she said nothing about it. In those same 'dark ages,' Intellect (metaphorically as well as literally) could invent *glass*, which now she has enough ado to grind into *spectacles*. Intellect built not only Churches, but a Church, *the* Church, based on this firm Earth, yet reaching up, and leading up, as high as Heaven; and now it is all she can do to keep its doors bolted, that there be no tearing of the Surplices, no robbery of the Alms-box. She built a Senate-house likewise, glorious in its kind; and now it costs her a wellnigh mortal effort to sweep it clear of vermin, and get the roof made rain-tight.

But the truth is, with Intellect, as with most other things, we are now passing from that first or boastful stage of Self-sentience into the second or painful one: out of these often asseverated declarations that 'our system is in high order,' we come now, by natural sequence, to the melancholy conviction that it is altogether the reverse. Thus, for instance, in the matter of Government, the period of the 'Invaluable Constitution' must be followed by a Reform Bill; to laudatory De Lolmes succeed objurgatory Benthams. At any rate, what Treatises on the Social Contract, on the Elective Franchise, the Rights of Man, the Rights of Property, Codifications, Institutions, Constitutions, have we not, for long years, groaned under! Or again, with a wider survey, consider those Essays on Man, Thoughts on Man, Inquiries concerning Man; not to mention Evidences of the Christian Faith, Theories of Poetry, Considerations on the Origin of Evil, which during the last century have accumulated on us to a frightful extent. Never since the beginning of Time, was there, that we hear or read of, so intensely self-conscious a Society. Our whole relations to the Universe and to our fellow man have become an Inquiry, a Doubt: nothing will go on of its own accord, and do its function quietly; but all things must be probed into, the whole working of man's world be anatomically studied. Alas, anatomically studied, that it may be medically aided! Till at length, indeed, we have come to such a pass, that except in this same Medicine, with its artifices and appliances, few can so much as imagine any strength or hope to remain for us. The whole Life of Society must now be carried on by drugs: doctor after doctor appears with his nostrum, of Co-operative Societies, Universal Suffrage, Cottage-and-Cow systems, Repression of Population, Vote by Ballot. To such height has the dyspepsia of Society reached; as indeed the constant grinding internal pain, or from time to time the mad spasmodic throes, of all Society do otherwise too mournfully indicate.

Far be it from us to attribute, as some unwise persons do, the disease itself to this unhappy sensation that there is a disease! The Encyclopedists did not produce the troubles of France; but the troubles of France produced the Encyclopedists, and much else. The Self-consciousness is the symptom merely; nay, it is also the attempt towards cure. We record the fact, without special censure; not wondering that Society should feel itself, and in all ways complain of aches and twinges, for it has suffered enough. Napoleon was but a Job's-comforter, when he told his wounded Staff-officer, twice unhorsed by cannon balls, and with half his limbs blown to pieces: *Vous vous écoutez trop!*[7]

On the outward, or as it were Physical diseases of Society, it were beside our purpose to insist here. These are diseases which he who runs may read; and sorrow over, with or without hope. Wealth has accumulated itself into masses; and Poverty, also in accumulation enough, lies impassably separated from it; opposed, uncommunicating, like forces in positive and negative poles. The gods of this lower world sit aloft on glittering thrones, less happy than Epicurus' gods, but as indolent, as impotent; while the boundless living chaos of Ignorance and Hunger welters terrific, in its dark fury, under their feet. How much among us might be likened to a whited sepulchre; outwardly all Pomp and Strength; but inwardly full of horror and despair and dead men's bones! Iron highways, with their wains fire-winged, are uniting all ends of the firm Land; quays and moles, with their innumerable stately fleets, tame the Ocean into our pliant bearer of burdens; Labour's thousand arms, of sinew and of metal, all-conquering, every where, from the tops of the mountain down to the depths of the mine and the caverns of the sea, ply unweariedly for the service of man: Yet man remains unserved. He has subdued this Planet, his habitation and inheritance, yet reaps no profit from the victory. Sad to look upon, in the highest stage of civilisation, nine-tenths of mankind must struggle in the lowest battle of savage or even animal man, the battle against Famine. Countries are rich, prosperous in all manner of increase, beyond example: but the Men of those countries are poor, needier than ever of all sustenance outward and inward; of

7. "You obey too well."

Belief, of Knowledge, of Money, of Food. The rule *Sic vos non vobis*,[8] never altogether to be got rid of in men's Industry, now presses with such incubus weight, that Industry must shake it off, or utterly be strangled under it; and, alas, can as yet but grasp and rave, and aimlessly struggle, like one in the final deliration. Thus Change, or the inevitable approach of Change, is manifest every where. In one Country we have seen lava-torrents of fever-frenzy envelope all things; Government succeed Government, like the fantasms of a dying brain: in another Country, we can even now see, in maddest alternation, the Peasant governed by such guidance as this: To labour earnestly one month in raising wheat, and the next month labour earnestly in burning it. So that Society, were it not by nature immortal, and its death ever a new-birth, might appear, as it does in the eyes of some, to be sick to dissolution, and even now writhing in its last agony. Sick enough we must admit it to be, with disease enough, a whole nosology of diseases; wherein he perhaps is happiest that is not called to prescribe as physician;—wherein, however, one small piece of policy, that of summoning the Wisest in the Commonwealth, by the sole method yet known or thought of, to come together and with their whole soul consult for it, might, but for late tedious experiences, have seemed unquestionable enough.

But leaving this, let us rather look within, into the Spiritual condition of Society, and see what aspects and prospects offer themselves there. For, after all, it is there properly that the secret and origin of the whole is to be sought: the Physical derangements of Society are but the image and impress of its Spiritual; while the heart continues sound, all other sickness is superficial, and temporary. False Action is the fruit of false Speculation; let the spirit of Society be free and strong, that is to say, let true Principles inspire the members of Society, then neither can disorders accumulate in its Practice; each disorder will be promptly, faithfully inquired into, and remedied as it arises. But alas, with us the Spiritual condition of Society is no less sickly than the Physical. Examine man's internal world, in any of its social relations and performances, here too all seems diseased self-consciousness, collision, and mutually-destructive struggle. Nothing acts from within outwards in undivided healthy force; every thing lies impotent, lamed, its force turned inwards, and painfully 'listens to itself.'

To begin with our highest Spiritual function, with Religion, we might ask, whither has Religion now fled? Of Churches and their

8. The whole quotation reads, *Sic vos non vobis mellificates apes*, i.e., so do you bees make honey not for yourselves.

establishments we here say nothing; nor of the unhappy domains of Unbelief, and how innumerable men, blinded in their minds, must 'live without God in the world:' but, taking the fairest side of the matter, we ask, What is the nature of that same Religion, which still lingers in the hearts of the few who are called, and call themselves, specially the Religious? Is it a healthy Religion, vital, unconscious of itself; that shines forth spontaneously in doing of the Work, or even in preaching of the Word? Unhappily, no. Instead of heroic martyr Conduct, and inspired and soul-inspiring Eloquence, whereby Religion itself were brought home to our living bosoms, to live and reign there, we have 'Discourses on the Evidences,' endeavouring, with smallest result, to make it probable that such a thing as Religion exists. The most enthusiastic Evangelicals do not preach a Gospel, but keep describing how it should and might be preached; to awaken the sacred fire of Faith, as by a sacred contagion, is not their endeavour; but, at most, to describe how Faith shows and acts, and scientifically distinguish true Faith from false. Religion, like all else, is conscious of itself, listens to itself; it becomes less and less creative, vital; more and more mechanical. Considered as a whole, the Christian Religion, of late ages, has been continually dissipating itself into Metaphysics; and threatens now to disappear, as some rivers do, in deserts of barren sand.

Of Literature, and its deep-seated, wide-spread maladies, why speak? Literature is but a branch of Religion, and always participates in its character: However, in our time, it is the only branch that still shows any greenness; and, as some think, must one day become the main stem. Now, apart from the subterranean and tartarean regions of Literature;—leaving out of view the frightful, scandalous statistics of Puffing, the mystery of Slander, Falsehood, Hatred, and other convulsion-work of rabid Imbecility, and all that has rendered Literature on that side a perfect 'Babylon the mother of Abominations,' in very deed, making the world 'drunk' with the wine of her iniquity;—forgetting all this, let us look only to the regions of the upper air; to such Literature as can be said to have some attempt towards truth in it, some tone of music, and if it be not poetical, to hold of the poetical. Among other characteristics, is not this manifest enough: that it knows itself? Spontaneous devotedness to the object, being wholly possessed by the object, what we can call Inspiration, has wellnigh ceased to appear in Literature. Which melodious Singer forgets that he is singing melodiously? We have not the love of greatness, but the love of the love of greatness. Hence infinite Affectations, Distractions; in every case inevitable Error. Consider, for one example, this peculiarity of modern Literature, the sin that has been named View-hunting. In our elder writers, there are no paintings of scenery for its own sake; no euphuistic gallantries with Nature, but a constant heart-love for her, a constant dwelling in communion with her. View-hunting, with so much else that is of kin to it, first came decisively into action through the *Sorrows of Werter;*[9] which wonderful Performance, indeed, may in many senses be regarded as the progenitor of all that has since become popular in Literature; whereof, in so far as concerns spirit and tendency, it still offers the most instructive image; for nowhere, except in its own country, above all in the mind of its illustrious Author, has it yet fallen wholly obsolete. Scarcely ever, till that late epoch, did any worshipper of Nature become entirely aware that he was worshipping, much to his own credit, and think of saying to himself: Come let us make a description! Intolerable enough: when every puny whipster draws out his pencil, and insists on painting you a scene; so that the instant you discern such a thing as 'wavy outline,' 'mirror of the lake,' 'stern headland,' or the like, in any Book, you must timorously hasten on; and scarcely the Author of Waverley himself can tempt you not to skip.

Nay, is not the diseased self-conscious state of Literature disclosed in this one fact, which lies so near us here, the prevalence of Reviewing! Sterne's wish for a reader 'that would give up the reins of his imagination into his author's hands, and be pleased he knew not why, and cared not wherefore,' might lead him a long journey now. Indeed, for our best class of readers, the chief pleasure, a very stinted one, is this same knowing of the Why; which many a Kames and Bossu[10] has been, ineffectually enough, endeavouring to teach us: till at last these also have laid down their trade; and now your Reviewer is a mere *taster;* who tastes, and says, by the evidence of such palate, such tongue, as he has got—It is good; it is bad. Was it thus that the French carried out certain inferior creatures on their Algerine Expedition, to taste the wells for them, and try whether they were poisoned? Far be it from us to disparage our own craft, whereby we have·our living! Only we must note these things: that Reviewing spreads with

9. Goethe's *Sorrows of Young Werther* (1774), the portrait of a passionately romantic and self-destructive young lover, was an immediate sensation throughout Europe. Carlyle, like many before him, took it as a great expression of the spiritual malaise of the time. But he felt it was a stage which Goethe had to outgrow, and which he did outgrow, notably in his *Wilhelm Meister,* which Carlyle himself translated in 1824.

10. Henry Home, Lord Kames (1696–1782), was a Scottish judge and an anti-Humean metaphysician. Bossu might have been N. Bossu, a French sailor of the eighteenth century, who was one of the first to describe Louisiana and who described his discoveries in travel books.

strange vigour; that such a man as Byron reckons the Reviewer and
the Poet equal; that, at the last Leipsic Fair, there was advertised a
Review of Reviews. By and by it will be found that 'all Literature has
become one boundless self-devouring Review; and as in London routs,
we have to *do* nothing, but only to *see* others do nothing.'—Thus
does Literature also, like a sick thing, superabundantly 'listen to itself.'

No less is this unhealthy symptom manifest, if we cast a glance
on our Philosophy, on the character of our speculative Thinking. Nay
already, as above hinted, the mere existence and necessity of a Philosophy is an evil. Man is sent hither not to question, but to work: 'the
end of man,' it was long ago written, 'is an Action, not a Thought.'
In the perfect state, all Thought were but the Picture and inspiring
Symbol of Action; Philosophy, except as Poetry and Religion, had no
being. And yet how, in this imperfect state, can it be avoided, can it
be dispensed with? Man stands as in the centre of Nature; his fraction
of Time encircled by Eternity, his handbreadth of Space encircled by
Infinitude: how shall he forbare asking himself, What am I; and
Whence; and Whither? How too, except in slight partial hints, in
kind asseverations and assurances such as a mother quiets her fretfully
inquisitive child with, shall he get answer to such inquiries?

The disease of Metaphysics, accordingly, is a perennial one. In
all ages, those questions of Death and Immortality, Origin of Evil,
Freedom and Necessity, must, under new forms, anew make their
appearance; ever, from time to time, must the attempt to shape for
ourselves some Theorem of the Universe be repeated. And ever unsuc-
cessfully: for what Theorem of the Infinite can the Finite render complete? We, the whole species of Mankind, and our whole existence
and history, are but a floating speck in the illimitable ocean of the
All; yet *in* that ocean; indissoluble portion thereof; partaking of its
infinite tendencies; borne this way and that by its deep-swelling tides,
and grand ocean currents;—of which what faintest chance is there that
we should ever exhaust the significance, ascertain the goings and com-
ings? A region of Doubt, therefore, hovers for ever in the background;
in Action alone can we have certainty. Nay properly Doubt is the indispensable, inexhaustible material whereon Action works, which
Action has to fashion into Certainty and Reality; only on a canvass
of Darkness, such is man's way of being, could the many-coloured
picture of our Life paint itself and shine.

. . . It is a chronic malady that of Metaphysics, as we said, and
perpetually recurs on us. At the utmost, there is a better and a worse
in it; a stage of convalescence, and a stage of relapse with new sickness: these for ever succeed each other, as is the nature of all Life-

movement here below. The first, or convalescent stage, we might also name that of Dogmatical or Constructive Metaphysics; when the mind constructively endeavours to scheme out, and assert for itself an actual Theorem of the Universe, and therewith for a time rests satisfied. The second or sick stage might be called that of Sceptical or Inquisitory Metaphysics; when the mind having widened its sphere of vision, the existing Theorem of the Universe no longer answers the phenomena, no longer yields contentment; but must be torn in pieces, and certainty anew sought for in the endless realms of Denial. All Theologies and sacred Cosmogonies belong, in some measure, to the first class: in all Pyrrhonism from Pyrrho down to Hume[11] and the innumerable disciples of Hume, we have instances enough of the second. In the former, so far as it affords satisfaction, a temporary anodyne to Doubt, an arena for wholesome Action, there may be much good; indeed, in this case, it holds rather of Poetry than of Metaphysics, might be called Inspiration rather than Speculation. The latter is Metaphysics proper; a pure, unmixed, though from time to time a necessary evil.

For truly, if we look into it, there is no more fruitless endeavour than this same, which the Metaphysician proper toils in: to deduce Conviction out of Negation. How, by merely testing and rejecting what is not, shall we ever attain knowledge of what is? Metaphysical Speculation, as it begins in No or Nothingness, so it must needs end in Nothingness; circulates and must circulate in endless vortices; creating, swallowing—itself. Our being is made up of Light and Darkness, the Light resting on the Darkness, and balancing it; every where there is Dualism, Equipoise; a perpetual Contradiction dwells in us: 'where shall I place myself to escape from my own shadow?' Consider it well, Metaphysics is the attempt of the mind to rise above the mind; to environ, and shut in, or as we say, comprehend the mind. Hopeless struggle, for the wisest, as for the foolishest! What strength of sinew, or athletic skill, will enable the stoutest athlete to fold his own body in his arms, and, by lifting, lift up himself? The Irish Saint swam the Channel 'carrying his head in his teeth:' but the feat has never been imitated.

11. A habit of thought, named after the philosopher Pyrrhon (365–275 B.C.), which entailed a total scepticism about the possibility of knowing anything. According to this view, one must suspend all judgment and live in calm because all things are in a state of flux. Hume was not, in this sense, a pure Pyrrhonist because his own scepticism did not lead him personally to this sort of negative stoicism. But Hume's sceptical philosophy became for almost a century the target of philosophers—especially the German romantics from whom Carlyle learned—who tried to re-establish the possibility of belief.

That this is the age of Metaphysics, in the proper, or sceptical Inquisitory sense; that there was a necessity for its being such an age, we regard as our indubitable misfortune. From many causes, the arena of free Activity has long been narrowing, that of sceptical Inquiry becoming more and more universal, more and more perplexing. The Thought conducts not to the Deed; but in boundless chaos, self-devouring, engenders monstrosities, fantasms, fire-breathing chimeras. Profitable Speculation were this: What is to be done; and How is it to be done? But with us not so much as the What can be got sight of. For some generations, all Philosophy has been a painful, captious, hostile question towards every thing in the Heaven above, in the Earth beneath: Why art thou there? Till at length it has come to pass that the worth and authenticity of all things seems dubitable or deniable: our best effort must be unproductively spent not in working, but in ascertaining our mere Whereabout, and so much as whether we are to work at all. Doubt, which, as was said, ever hangs in the background of our world, has now become our middle-ground and foreground; whereon, for the time, no fair Life-picture can be painted, but only the dark air-canvass itself flow round us, bewildering and benighting.

Nevertheless, doubt as we will, man is actually Here; not to ask questions, but to do work: in this time, as in all times, it must be the heaviest evil for him, if his faculty of Action lie dormant, and only that of sceptical Inquiry exert itself. Accordingly, whoever looks abroad upon the world, comparing the Past with the Present, may find that the practical condition of man, in these days, is one of the saddest; burdened with miseries which are in a considerable degree peculiar. In no time was man's life what he calls a happy one; in no time can it be so. A perpetual dream there has been of Paradises, and some luxurious Lubberland, where the brooks should run wine, and the trees bend with ready-baked viands; but it was a dream merely, an impossible dream. Suffering, Contradiction, Error, have their quite perennial, and even indispensable, abode in this Earth. Is not Labour the inheritance of man? And what Labour for the present is joyous, and not grievous? Labour, Effort, is the very interruption of that Ease, which man foolishly enough fancies to be his Happiness: and yet without Labour there were no Ease, no Rest, so much as conceivable. Thus Evil, what we call Evil, must ever exist while man exists: Evil, in the widest sense we can give it, is precisely the dark, disordered material out of which man's Freewill has to create an edifice of order, and Good. Ever must Pain urge us to Labour; and only in free Effort can any blessedness be imagined for us.

But if man has, in all ages, had enough to encounter, there has, in most civilized ages, been an inward force vouchsafed him, whereby the pressure of things outward might be withstood. Obstruction abounded; but Faith also was not wanting. It is by Faith that man removes mountains: while he had Faith, his limbs might be wearied with toiling, his back galled with bearing; but the heart within him was peaceable and resolved. In the thickest gloom there burnt a lamp to guide him. If he struggled and suffered, he felt that it even should be so; knew for what he was suffering and struggling. Faith gave him an inward Willingness; a world of Strength wherewith to front a world of Difficulty. The true wretchedness lies here: that the Difficulty remain and the Strength be lost; that Pain cannot relieve itself in free Effort; that we have the Labour, and want the Willingness. Faith strengthens us, enlightens us, for all endeavours and endurances; with Faith we can do all, and dare all, and life itself has a thousand times been joyfully given away. But the sum of man's misery is even this, that he feel himself crushed under the Juggernaut wheels, and know that Juggernaut is no divinity, but a dead mechanical idol.

Now this is specially the misery which has fallen on man in our Era. Belief, Faith has wellnigh vanished from the world. The youth on awakening in this wondrous Universe, no longer finds a competent theory of its wonders. Time was, when if he asked himself: What is man; what are the duties of man? the answer stood ready written for him. But now the ancient 'ground-plan of the All' belies itself when brought into contact with reality; Mother Church has, to the most, become a superannuated Stepmother, whose lessons go disregarded; or are spurned at, and scornfully gainsayed. For young Valour and thirst of Action no ideal Chivalry invites to heroism, prescribes what is heroic: the old ideal of Manhood has grown obsolete, and the new is still invisible to us, and we grope after it in darkness, one clutching this phantom, another that; Werterism, Byronism, even Brummelism, each has its day. For Contemplation and love of Wisdom no Cloister now opens its religious shades; the Thinker must, in all senses, wander homeless, too often aimless, looking up to a Heaven which is dead for him, round to an Earth which is deaf. Action, in those old days, was easy, was voluntary, for the divine worth of human things lay acknowledged; Speculation was wholesome, for it ranged itself as the handmaid of Action; what could not so range itself died out by its natural death, by neglect. Loyalty still hallowed obedience, and made rule noble; there was still something to be loyal to: the Godlike stood embodied under many a symbol in men's interests and business; the Finite shadowed forth the Infinite; Eternity looked through Time. The

Life of man was encompassed and overcanopied by a glory of Heaven, even as his dwelling-place by the azure vault.

How changed in these new days! Truly may it be said, the Divinity has withdrawn from the Earth; or veils himself in that wide-wasting Whirlwind of a departing Era, wherein the fewest can discern his goings. Not Godhood, but an iron, ignoble circle of Necessity embraces all things; binds the youth of these times into a sluggish thrall, or else exasperates him into a rebel. Heroic Action is paralysed; for what worth now remains unquestionable with him? At the fervid period when his whole nature cries aloud for Action, there is nothing sacred under whose banner he can act; the course and kind and conditions of free Action are all but undiscoverable. Doubt storms in on him through every avenue; inquiries of the deepest, painfullest sort must be engaged with; and the invincible energy of young years waste itself in sceptical, suicidal cavillings; in passionate 'questionings of Destiny,' whereto no answer will be returned.

For men, in whom the old perennial principle of Hunger (be it Hunger of the poor Day-drudge who stills it with eighteen-pence a-day, or of the ambitious Place-hunter who can nowise still it with so little) suffices to fill up existence, the case is bad, but not the worst. These men have an aim, such as it is; and can steer towards it, with chagrin enough truly; yet, as their hands are kept full, without desperation. Unhappier are they to whom a higher instinct has been given; who struggle to be persons, not machines; to whom the Universe is not a warehouse, or at best fancy-bazaar, but a mystic temple and hall of doom. For such men there lie properly two courses open. The lower, yet still an estimable class, take up with worn-out Symbols of the Godlike; keep trimming and trucking between these and Hypocrisy, purblindly enough, miserably enough. A numerous intermediate class end in Denial; and form a theory that there is no theory; that nothing is certain in the world, except this fact of Pleasure being pleasant; so they try to realize what trifling modicum of Pleasure they can come at, and to live contented therewith, winking hard. Of these we speak not here; but only of the second nobler class, who also have dared to say No, and cannot yet say Yea; but feel that in the No they dwell as in a Golgotha, where life enters not, where peace is not appointed them. Hard, for most part, is the fate of such men; the harder the nobler they are. In dim forecastings, wrestles within them the 'Divine Idea of the World,' yet will nowhere visibly reveal itself. They have to realise a Worship for themselves, or live unworshipping. The Godlike has vanished from the world; and they, by the strong cry of their soul's agony, like true wonder-workers, must again evoke its presence.

This miracle is their appointed task; which they must accomplish, or die wretchedly: this miracle has been accomplished by such; but not in our land; our land yet knows not of it. . . .

To the better order of such minds any mad joy of Denial has long since ceased: the problem is not now to deny, but to ascertain and perform. Once in destroying the False, there was a certain inspiration; but now the genius of Destruction has done its work, there is now nothing more to destroy. The doom of the Old has long been pronounced, and irrevocable; the Old has passed away: but, alas, the New appears not in its stead; the Time is still in pangs of travail with the New. Man has walked by the light of conflagrations, and amid the sound of falling cities; and now there is darkness, and long watching till it be morning. . . .

Such being the condition, temporal and spiritual, of the world at our Epoch, can we wonder that the world 'listens to itself,' and struggles and writhes, every where externally and internally, like a thing in pain? Nay, is not even this unhealthy action of the world's Organization, if the symptom of universal disease, yet also the symptom and sole means of restoration and cure? The effort of Nature, exerting her medicative force to cast out foreign impediments, and once more become One, become whole? In Practice, still more in Opinion, which is the precursor and prototype of Practice, there must needs be collision, convulsion; much has to be ground away. Thought must needs be Doubt and Inquiry, before it can again be Affirmation and Sacred Precept. Innumerable 'Philosophies of Man,' contending in boundless hubbub, must annihilate each other, before an inspired Poesy and Faith for Man can fashion itself together.

. . . . .

. . . Unhappy who, in such a time, felt not, at all conjunctures, ineradicably in his heart the knowledge that a God made this Universe, and a Demon not! And shall Evil always prosper, then? Out of all Evil comes Good; and no Good that is possible but shall one day be real. Deep and sad as is our feeling that we stand yet in the bodeful Night; equally deep, indestructible is our assurance that the Morning also will not fail. Nay, already, as we look round, streaks of a dayspring are in the east: it is dawning; when the time shall be fulfilled, it will be day. The progress of man towards higher and nobler Developments of whatever is highest and noblest in him, lies not only prophesied to Faith, but now written to the eye of Observation, so that he who runs may read.

One great step of progress, for example, we should say, in actual circumstances, was this same; the clear ascertainment that we are in

progress. About the grand Course of Providence, and his final Purposes with us, we can know nothing, or almost nothing: man begins
in darkness, ends in darkness; mystery is every where around us and
in us, under our feet, among our hands. Nevertheless so much has
become evident to every one, that this wondrous Mankind is advancing
somewhither; that at least all human things are, have been, and for
ever will be, in Movement and Change;—as, indeed, for beings that
exist in Time, by virtue of Time, and are made of Time, might have
been long since understood. In some provinces, it is true, as in Experimental Science, this discovery is an old one; but in most others
it belongs wholly to these latter days. How often, in former ages, by
eternal Creeds, eternal Forms of Government, and the like, has it
been attempted, fiercely enough, and with destructive violence, to
chain the Future under the Past; and say to the Providence, whose ways
with man are mysterious, and through the great Deep: Hitherto shalt
thou come, but no farther! A wholly insane attempt; and for man
himself, could it prosper, the frightfullest of all enchantments, a very
Life-in-Death. Man's task here below, the destiny of every individual
man, is to be in turns Apprentice and Workman; or say rather, Scholar,
Teacher, Discoverer: by nature he has a strength for learning, for
imitating; but also a strength for acting, for knowing on his own
account. Are we not in a World seen to be Infinite; the relations
lying closest together modified by those latest-discovered, and lying
farthest asunder? Could you ever spell-bind man into a Scholar merely,
so that he had nothing to discover, to correct; could you ever establish
a Theory of the Universe that were entire, unimprovable, and which
needed only to be got by heart; man then were spiritually defunct, the
species We now name Man had ceased to exist. But the gods, kinder
to us than we are to ourselves, have forbidden such suicidal acts. As
Phlogiston is displaced by Oxygen, and the Epicycles of Ptolemy by
the Ellipses of Kepler; so does Paganism give place to Catholicism,
Tyranny to Monarchy, and Feudalism to Representative Government,
—where also the process does not stop. Perfection of Practice, like
completeness of Opinion, is always approaching, never arrived; Truth,
in the words of Schiller, *immer wird, nie ist*; never *is*, always *is a-being*.

Sad, truly, were our condition did we know but this, that Change
is universal and inevitable. Launched into a dark shoreless sea of
Pyrrhonism, what would remain for us but to sail aimless, hopeless;
or make madly merry, while the devouring Death had not yet engulfed
us? As, indeed, we have seen many, and still see many do. Nevertheless
so stands it not. The venerator of the Past (and to what pure heart
is the Past, in that 'moonlight of memory,' other than sad and holy?)

sorrows not over its departure, as one utterly bereaved. The true Past departs not, nothing that was worthy in the Past departs; no Truth or Goodness realized by man ever dies, or can die; but is all still here, and, recognised or not, lives and works through endless changes. If all things, to speak in the German dialect, are discerned by us, and exist for us, in an element of Time, and therefore of Mortality and Mutability; yet Time itself reposes on Eternity: the truly Great and Transcendental has its basis and substance in Eternity; stands revealed to us as Eternity in a vesture of Time. Thus in all Poetry, Worship, Art, Society, as one form passes into another, nothing is lost: it is but the superficial, as it were the *body* only, that grows obsolete and dies; under the mortal body lies a *soul* that is immortal; that anew incarnates itself in fairer revelation; and the Present is the living sum-total of the whole Past.

In Change, therefore, there is nothing terrible, nothing supernatural: on the contrary, it lies in the very essence of our lot, and life in this world. To-day is not yesterday: we ourselves change; how can our Works and Thoughts, if they are always to be the fittest, continue always the same? Change, indeed, is painful; yet ever needful: and if Memory have its force and worth, so also has Hope. Nay, if we look well to it, what is all Derangement, and necessity of great Change, in itself such an evil, but the product simply of *increased resources* which the old *methods* can no longer administer; of new wealth which the old coffers will no longer contain? What is it, for example, that in our own day bursts asunder the bonds of ancient Political Systems, and perplexes all Europe with the fear of Change, but even this: the increase of social resources, which the old social methods will no longer sufficiently administer? The new omnipotence of the Steam-engine is hewing asunder quite other mountains than the physical. Have not our economical distresses, those barnyard Conflagrations[12] themselves, the frightfullest madness of our mad epoch, their rise also in what is a real increase: increase of Men; of human Force; properly, in such a Planet as ours, the most precious of all increases? It is true again, the ancient methods of administration will no longer suffice. Must the indomitable millions, full of old Saxon energy and fire, lie cooped up in this Western Nook, choking one another, as in a Blackhole of Calcutta, while a whole fertile untenanted Earth, desolate for want of the ploughshare, cries: Come and till me, come and

12. The traditional form of protest among agricultural workers against hardships imposed, as they thought, by landowners and government, was the burning of hayricks. Such demonstrations became particularly frequent in bad times, and they greatly frightened landowners, who insisted on severe penalties.

reap me? If the ancient Captains can no longer yield guidance, new must be sought after: for the difficulty lies not in nature, but in artifice: the European Calcutta-Blackhole has no walls but air ones, and paper ones.—So too, Scepticism itself, with its innumerable mischiefs, what is it but the sour fruit of a most blessed increase, that of Knowledge; a fruit, too, that will not always continue sour?

In fact, much as we have said and mourned about the unproductive prevalence of Metaphysics, it was not without some insight into the use that lies in them. Metaphysical Speculation, if a necessary evil, is the forerunner of much good. The fever of Scepticism must needs burn itself out, and burn out thereby the Impurities that caused it; then again will there be clearness, health. The principle of Life, which now struggles painfully, in the outer, thin, and barren domain of the Conscious or Mechanical, may then withdraw into its inner Sanctuaries, its abysses of mystery and miracle: withdraw deeper than ever into that domain of the Unconscious, by nature infinite and inexhaustible; and creatively work there. From that mystic region, and from that alone, all wonders, all Poesies, and Religions, and Social Systems have proceeded: the like wonders, and greater and higher, lie slumbering there; and, brooded on by the spirit of the waters, will evolve themselves, and rise like exhalations from the Deep.

Of our modern Metaphysics, accordingly, may not this already be said, that if they have produced no Affirmation, they have destroyed much Negation? It is a disease expelling a disease: the fire of Doubt, as above hinted, consuming away the Doubtful; that so the Certain come to light, and again lie visible on the surface. English or French Metaphysics, in reference to this last stage of the speculative process, are not what we allude to here; but only the Metaphysics of the Germans. In France or England, since the days of Diderot and Hume, though all thought has been of a sceptico-metaphysical texture, so far as there were any Thought,—we have seen no Metaphysics; but only more or less ineffectual questionings whether such could be. In the Pyrrhonism of Hume and the Materialism of Diderot, Logic had, as it were, overshot itself, overset itself. Now, though the athlete, to use our old figure, cannot, by much lifting, lift up his own body, he may shift it out of a laming posture, and get to stand in a free one. Such a service have German Metaphysics done for man's mind. The second sickness of Speculation has abolished both itself and the first. Friedrich Schlegel complains much of the fruitlessness, the tumult and transiency of German as of all Metaphysics; and with reason: yet in that wide-spreading, deep-whirling vortex of Kantism, so soon metamorphosed into Fichteism, Schellingism, and then as Hegelism, and

Cousinism, perhaps finally evaporated, is not this issue visible enough, that Pyrrhonism and Materialism, themselves necessary phenomena in European culture, have disappeared; and a Faith in Religion has again become possible and inevitable for the scientific mind; and the word *Free*-thinker no longer means the Denier or Caviller, but the Believer, or the Ready to believe? Nay, in the higher Literature of Germany, there already lies, for him that can read it, the beginning of a new revelation of the Godlike; as yet unrecognized by the mass of the world; but waiting there for recognition, and sure to find it when the fit hour comes. This age also is not wholly without its Prophets.

Again, under another aspect, if Utilitarianism, or Radicalism, or the Mechanical Philosophy, or by whatever name it is called, has still its long task to do; nevertheless we can now see through it and beyond it: in the better heads, even among us English, it has become obsolete; as in other countries, it has been, in such heads, for some forty or even fifty years. What sound mind among the French, for example, now fancies that men can be governed by 'Constitutions;' by the never so cunning mechanizing of Self-interests, and all conceivable adjustments of checking and balancing; in a word, by the best possible solution of this quite insoluble and impossible problem, *Given a world of Knaves, to produce an Honesty from their united action?* Were not experiments enough of this kind tried before all Europe, and found wanting, when, in that doomsday of France, the infinite gulf of human Passion shivered asunder the thin rinds of Habit; and burst forth all-devouring, as in seas of Nether Fire? Which cunningly-devised 'Constitution,' constitutional, republican, democratic, sans-cullotic, could bind that raging chasm together? Were they not all burnt up, like Paper as they were, in its molten eddies; and still the fire-sea raged fiercer than before? It is not by Mechanism, but by Religion; not by Self-interest, but by Loyalty, that men are governed or governable.

Remarkable it is, truly, how every where the eternal fact begins again to be recognised, that there is a Godlike in human affairs; that God not only made us and beholds us, but is in us and around us; that the Age of Miracles, as it ever was, now is. Such recognition we discern on all hands, and in all countries: in each country after its own fashion. In France, among the younger nobler minds, strangely enough; where, in their loud contention with the Actual and Conscious, the Ideal or Unconscious is, for the time, without exponent; where Religion means not the parent of Polity, as of all that is highest, but Polity itself; and this and the other earnest man has not been wanting, who could whisper audibly: 'Go to, I will make a Religion.' In England still more strangely; as in all things, worthy England will have its way: by the shrieking of hysterical women, casting out of devils, and other 'gifts of the Holy Ghost.' Well might Jean Paul say, in this his twelfth hour of the Night, 'the living dream;' well might he say, ' the dead walk.' Meanwhile let us rejoice rather that so much has been seen into, were it through never so diffracting media, and never so madly distorted; that in all dialects, though but half-articulately, this high Gospel begins to be preached: 'Man is still Man.' The genius of Mechanism, as was once before predicted, will not always sit like a choking incubus on our soul; but at length when by a new magic Word the old spell is broken, become our slave, and as familiar-spirit do all our bidding. 'We are near awakening when we dream that we dream.'

He that has an eye and a heart can even now say: Why should I falter? Light has come into the world; to such as love Light, so as Light must be loved, with a boundless all-doing, all-enduring love. For the rest, let that vain struggle to read the mystery of the Infinite cease to harass us. It is a mystery which, through all ages, we shall only read here a line of, there another line of. Do we not already know that the name of the Infinite is GOOD, is GOD? Here on Earth we are as Soldiers, fighting in a foreign land; that understand not the plan of the campaign, and have no need to understand it; seeing well what is at our hand to be done. Let us do it like Soldiers, with submission, with courage, with a heroic joy. 'Whatsoever thy hand findeth to do, do it with all thy might.' Behind us, behind each one of us, lie Six Thousand Years of human effort, human conquest: before us is the boundless Time, with its as yet uncreated and unconquered Continents and Eldorados, which we, even we, have to conquer, to create; and from the bosom of Eternity shine for us celestial guiding stars.

My inheritance how wide and fair!
Time is my fair seed-field, of Time I'm heir.

JOHN STUART MILL

# The Spirit of the Age*

JOHN STUART MILL (1806–73) WAS PERHAPS
the most important philosopher of the Victorian period, although
his stock in this capacity has fallen considerably in the twentieth
century. In his *Autobiography* (1873), he dismisses *The Spirit of
the Age* as an unimportant essay, and he did not reprint it in the
collection of his miscellaneous essays, *Dissertations and Discussions* (1859–76). But the essay is nevertheless of great interest: it
reveals a good deal about the period with which this volume is
concerned, and it represents (with the essay *Civilization*) an aspect of Mill's thought which tends to be overlooked. In this connection, see Gertrude Himmelfarb's introduction to her collection
of Mill's *Essays on Politics and Culture* (1962).

* From *Examiner* (January 9, 23, 1831), 20–21; 50–52. Four other
sections, omitted here for the sake of economy, are also interesting, especially
as they spell out the important distinction between the "natural" and the
"transitional" states of society. SEE *Examiner* (February 6; April 3; May 15,
29, 1831).

Although in his early years Mill was almost exclusively an expounder of the rigid utilitarian ideas of his father, James Mill, and of Jeremy Bentham, by the time of this essay he had come under other influences. By 1826 he was going through the "mental crisis" described in the fifth chapter of his autobiography, and this crisis led him to reshape many of his ideas. He was learning from Coleridge and some of his disciples the inadequacy of Bentham's view of human nature and of history, and he was influenced, as well, by the Saint-Simonians and Auguste Comte, whose systems entailed not only a complete reconstruction of society but also a systematic theory of history. Some of that theory can be discerned in the two essays included here.

The notion of a *Zeitgeist* (a "spirit of the age") entered English thought from many directions. Carlyle, who borrowed it from the Germans, recognized in Mill's *Spirit of the Age* attitudes not very different from his own. Ironically, he described the then unknown to him author of the essay as a "new Mystic." Mill, however, so far from being a mystic, was to be known later as the "Saint of Rationalism"; Carlyle, for his part, later lost faith in Mill and described the *Autobiography* as the "autobiography of a steam engine." But Mill, especially after reading Alexis de Tocqueville's *Democracy in America* (1835), consistently maintained reservations about pure democracy. He was capable, as demonstrated here, of tempering his radicalism with an intelligent conservatism and even of entertaining ideas not apparently altogether rational.

I

The "spirit of the age" is in some measure a novel expression. I do not believe that it is to be met with in any work exceeding fifty years in antiquity. The idea of comparing one's own age with former ages, or with our notion of those which are yet to come, had occurred to philosophers; but it never before was itself the dominant idea of any age.

It is an idea essentially belonging to an age of change. Before men begin to think much and long on the peculiarities of their own times, they must have begun to think that those times are, or are destined to be, distinguished in a very remarkable manner from the times which preceded them. Mankind are then divided, into those who are still what they were, and those who have changed: into the men of the present age, and the men of the past. To the former, the spirit of the age is a subject of exultation; to the latter, of terror; to both, of eager and anxious interest. The wisdom of ancestors, and the march of intellect, are bandied from mouth to mouth; each phrase originally an expression of respect and homage, each ultimately usurped by the partisans of the opposite catch-word, and in the bitterness of their spirit, turned into the sarcastic jibe of hatred and insult.

The present times possess this character. A change has taken place in the human mind; a change which, being effected by insensible gradations, and without noise, had already proceeded far before it was generally perceived. When the fact disclosed itself, thousands awoke as from a dream. They knew not what processes had been going on in the minds of others, or even in their own, until the change began to invade outward objects; and it became clear that those were indeed new men, who insisted upon being governed in a new way.

But mankind are now conscious of their new position. The conviction is already not far from being universal, that the times are pregnant with change; and that the nineteenth century will be known to posterity as the era of one of the greatest revolutions of which history has preserved the remembrance, in the human mind, and in the whole constitution of human society. Even the religious world teems with new interpretations of the Prophecies, foreboding mighty changes near at hand. It is felt that men are henceforth to be held together by new ties, and separated by new barriers; for the ancient bonds will now no longer unite, nor the ancient boundaries confine. Those men who carry their eyes in the back of their heads and can see no other portion of the destined track of humanity than that which it has already travelled, imagine that because the old ties are severed mankind henceforth are not to be connected by any ties at all; and hence their affliction, and their awful warnings. For proof of this assertion, I may refer to the gloomiest book ever written by a cheerful man—Southey's "Colloquies on the Progress and Prospects of Society;" a very curious and not uninstructive exhibition of one of the points of view from which the spirit of the age may be contemplated. They who prefer the ravings of a party politician to the musings of a recluse, may consult a late article in Blackwood's Magazine,[1] under

1. [David Robinson], "Letter to Christopher North, Esquire, on the Spirit of the Age, By One of the Democracy," *Blackwood's Edinburgh Magazine*, XXVIII (December, 1830), 900–20.

the same title which I have prefixed to this paper. For the reverse of the picture, we have only to look into any popular newspaper or review.

Amidst all this indiscriminate eulogy and abuse, these undistinguishing hopes and fears, it seems to be a very fit subject for philosophical inquiry, what the spirit of the age really is; and how or wherein it differs from the spirit of any other age. The subject is deeply important: for, whatever we may think or affect to think of the present age, we cannot get out of it; we must suffer with its sufferings, and enjoy with its enjoyments; we must share in its lot, and, to be either useful or at ease, we must even partake its character. No man whose good qualities were mainly those of another age, ever had much influence on his own. And since every age contains in itself the germ of all future ages as surely as the acorn contains the future forest, a knowledge of our own age is the fountain of prophecy—the only key to the history of posterity. It is only in the present that we can know the future; it is only through the present that it is in our power to influence that which is to come.

Yet, because our own age is *familiar* to us, we are presumed, if I may judge from appearances, to know it by nature. A statesman, for example, if it be required of him to have studied any thing at all (which, however, is more than I would venture to affirm) is supposed to have studied history—which is at best the spirit of ages long past, and more often the mere inanimate carcass without the spirit: but is it ever asked (or to whom does the question ever occur?) whether he understands his own age? Yet that also is history, and the most important part of history, and the only part which a man may know and understand, with absolute certainty, by using the proper means. He may learn in a morning's walk through London more of the history of England during the nineteenth century, than all the professed English histories in existence will tell him concerning the other eighteen: for, the obvious and universal facts, which every one sees and no one is astonished at, it seldom occurs to any one to place upon record; and posterity, if it learn the rule, learns it, generally, from the notice bestowed by contemporaries on some accidental exception. Yet are politicians and philosophers perpetually exhorted to judge of the present by the past, when the present alone affords a fund of materials for judging, richer than the whole stores of the past, and far more accessible.

But it is unadvisable to dwell longer on this topic, lest we should be deemed studiously to exaggerate that want, which we desire that the reader should think ourselves qualified to supply. It were better, without further preamble, to enter upon the subject, and be tried by our ideas themselves, rather than by the need of them.

The first of the leading peculiarities of the present age is, that it is an age of transition. Mankind have outgrown old institutions and old doctrines, and have not yet acquired new ones. When we say outgrown, we intend to prejudge nothing. A man may not be either better or happier at six-and-twenty, than he was at six years of age: but the same jacket which fitted him then, will not fit him now.

The prominent trait just indicated in the character of the present age, was obvious a few years ago only to the more discerning: at present it forces itself upon the most inobservant. Much might be said, and shall be said on a fitting occasion, of the mode in which the old order of things has become unsuited to the state of society and of the human mind. But when almost every nation on the continent of Europe has achieved, or is in the course of rapidly achieving, a change in its form of government; when our own country, at all former times the most attached in Europe to its old institutions, proclaims almost with one voice that they are vicious both in the outline and in the details, and that they *shall* be renovated, and purified, and made fit for civilized man, we may assume that a part of the effects of the cause just now pointed out, speak sufficiently loudly for themselves. To him who can reflect, even these are but indications which tell of a more vital and radical change. Not only, in the conviction of almost all men, things as they are, are wrong—but, according to that same conviction, it is not by remaining in the old ways that they can be set right. Society demands, and anticipates, not merely a new machine, but a machine constructed in another manner. Mankind will not be led by their old maxims, nor by their old guides; and they will not choose either their opinions or their guides as they have done heretofore. The ancient constitutional texts were formerly spells which would call forth or allay the spirit of the English people at pleasure: what has become of the charm? Who can hope to sway the minds of the public by the old maxims of law, or commerce, or foreign policy, or ecclesiastical policy? Whose feelings are now roused by the mottoes and watchwords of Whig and Tory? And what Whig or Tory could command ten followers in the warfare of politics by the weight of his own personal authority? Nay, what landlord could call forth his tenants, or what manufacturer his men? Do the poor respect the rich, or adopt their sentiments? Do the young respect the old, or adopt their sentiments? Of the feelings of our ancestors it may almost be said that we retain only such as are the natural and necessary growth of a state of human society, however constituted; and I only adopt the energetic expression of a member of the House of Commons, less than two years ago, in saying of the young men, even of that rank in society, that they are ready to advertise for opinions.

Since the facts are so manifest, there is the more chance that a few reflections on their causes, and on their probable consequences, will receive whatever portion of the reader's attention they may happen to deserve.

With respect, then, to the discredit into which old institutions and old doctrines have fallen, I may premise, that this discredit is, in my opinion, perfectly deserved. Having said this, I may perhaps hope, that no perverse interpretation will be put upon the remainder of my observations, in case some of them should not be quite so conformable to the sentiments of the day as my commencement might give reason to expect. The best guide is not he who, when people are in the right path, merely praises it, but he who shows them the pitfalls and the precipices by which it is endangered; and of which, as long as they were in the wrong road, it was not so necessary that they should be warned.

There is one very easy, and very pleasant way of accounting for this general departure from the modes of thinking of our ancestors: so easy, indeed, and so pleasant, especially to the hearer, as to be very convenient to such writers for hire or for applause, as address themselves not to the men of the age that is gone by, but to the men of the age which has commenced. This explanation is that which ascribes the altered state of opinion and feeling to the growth of the human understanding. According to this doctrine, we reject the sophisms and prejudices which misled the uncultivated minds of our ancestors, because we have learnt too much, and have become too wise, to be imposed upon by such sophisms and such prejudices. It is our knowledge and our sagacity which keep us free from these gross errors. We have now risen to the capacity of perceiving our true interests; and it is no longer in the power of impostors and charlatans to deceive us.

I am unable to adopt this theory. Though a firm believer in the improvement of the age, I do not believe that its improvement has been of this kind. The grand achievement of the present age is the *diffusion* of *superficial* knowledge; and that surely is no trifle, to have been accomplished by a single generation. The persons who are in possession of knowledge adequate to the formation of sound opinions by their own lights, form also a constantly increasing number, but hitherto at all times a small one. It would be carrying the notion of the march of intellect too far, to suppose that an average man of the present day is superior to the greatest men of the beginning of the eighteenth century; yet they *held* many opinions which we are fast renouncing. The intellect of the age, therefore, is not the cause which we are in search of. I do not perceive that, in the mental training which has been received by the immense majority of the reading and thinking part of my countrymen, or in the kind of knowledge and other intellectual aliment which has been supplied to them, there is any thing likely to render them much less accessible to the influence of imposture and charlatanerie than there ever was. The Dr. Eadys still dupe the lower classes, the St. John Longs[2] the higher: and it would not be difficult to produce the political and literary antitypes of both. Neither do I see, in such observations as I am able to make upon my contemporaries, evidence that they have any principle within them which renders them much less liable now than at any former period to be misled by sophisms and prejudices. All I see is, that the opinions which have been transmitted to them from their ancestors, are not the kind of sophisms and prejudices which are fitted to possess any considerable ascendancy in their altered frame of mind. And I am rather inclined to account for this fact in a manner not reflecting such extraordinarily great honour upon the times we live in, as would result from the theory by which all is ascribed to the superior expansion of our understandings.

The intellectual tendencies of the age, considered both on the favourable and on the unfavourable side, it will be necessary, in the prosecution of the present design, to review and analyse in some detail. For the present it may be enough to remark, that it is seldom safe to ground a positive estimate of a character upon mere negatives: and that the faults or the prejudices, which a person, or an age, or a nation *has not*, go but a very little way with a wise man towards forming a high opinion of them. A person may be without a single prejudice, and yet utterly unfit for every purpose in nature. To have erroneous convictions is one evil; but to have no strong or deep-rooted convictions at all, is an enormous one. Before I compliment either a man or a generation upon having got rid of their prejudices, I require to know what they have substituted in lieu of them.

Now, it is self-evident that no fixed opinions have yet generally

2. I cannot identify Dr. Eady. St. John Long (1798–1834) was a doctor who achieved great success through an original method of treating rheumatism, consumption, and other ailments—the application of corrosive liniments and friction. When one of his patients died, he was tried, found guilty, and fined 250 pounds sterling. He died of consumption, after refusing to be treated by his own method.

established themselves in the place of those which we have abandoned;
that no new doctrines, philosophical or social, as yet command, or
appear likely soon to command, an assent at all comparable in unanimity to that which the ancient doctrines could boast of while they
continued in vogue. So long as this intellectual anarchy shall endure,
we may be warranted in believing that we are in a fair way to become
wiser than our forefathers; but it would be premature to affirm that we
are already wiser. We have not yet advanced beyond the unsettled
state, in which the mind is, when it has recently found itself out in a
grievous error, and has not yet satisfied itself of the truth. The men
of the present day rather incline to an opinion than embrace it; few,
except the very penetrating, or the very presumptuous, have full
confidence in their own convictions. This is not a state of health, but,
at the best, of convalescence. It is a necessary stage in the progress of
civilization, but it is attended with numerous evils; as one part of a
road may be rougher or more dangerous than another, although every
step brings the traveller nearer to his desired end.

Not increase of wisdom, but a cause of the reality of which we
are better assured, may serve to account for the decay of prejudices;
and this is, increase of discussion. Men may not reason, better, concerning the great questions in which human nature is interested, but
they reason more. Large subjects are discussed more, and longer, and
by more minds. Discussion has penetrated deeper into society; and if
no greater numbers than before have attained the higher degrees of
intelligence, fewer grovel in that state of abject stupidity, which can
only co-exist with utter apathy and sluggishness.

The progress which we have made, is precisely that sort of progress which increase of discussion suffices to produce, whether it be
attended with increase of wisdom or no. To discuss, and to question
established opinions, are merely two phrases for the same thing. When
all opinions are questioned, it is in time found out what are those
which will not bear a close examination. Ancient doctrines are then
put upon their proofs; and those which were originally errors, or have
become so by change of circumstances, are thrown aside. Discussion
does this. It is by discussion, also, that true opinions are discovered and
diffused. But this is not so certain a consequence of it as the weakening of error. To be rationally assured that a given doctrine is *true*, it is
often necessary to examine and weigh an immense variety of facts. One
single well-established fact, clearly irreconcilable with a doctrine, is
sufficient to prove that it is *false*. Nay, opinions often upset themselves
by their own incoherence; and the impossibility of their being well-
founded may admit of being brought home to a mind not possessed

of so much as one positive truth. All the inconsistencies of an opinion with itself, with obvious facts, or even with other prejudices, discussion evolves and makes manifest: and indeed this mode of refutation, requiring less study and less real knowledge than any other, is better suited to the inclination of most disputants. But the moment, and the mood of mind, in which men break loose from an error, is not, except in natures very happily constituted, the most favourable to those mental processes which are necessary to the investigation of truth. What led them wrong at first, was generally nothing else but the incapacity of seeing more than one thing at a time; and that incapacity is apt to stick to them when they have turned their eyes in an altered direction. They usually resolve that the new light which has broken in upon them shall be the sole light; and they wilfully and passionately blew out the ancient lamp, which, though it did not show them what they now see, served very well to enlighten the objects in its immediate neighbourhood. Whether men adhere to old opinions or adopt new ones, they have in general an invincible propensity to split the truth, and take half, or less than half of it; and a habit of erecting their quills and bristling up like a porcupine against any one who brings them the other half, as if he were attempting to deprive them of the portion which they have.

I am far from denying, that, besides getting rid of error, we are also continually enlarging the stock of positive truth. In physical science and art, this is too manifest to be called in question; and in the moral and social sciences, I believe it to be as undeniably true. The wisest men in every age generally surpass in wisdom the wisest of any preceding age, because the wisest men possess and profit by the constantly increasing accumulation of the ideas of all ages: but the multitude (by which I mean the majority of all ranks) have the ideas of their own age, and no others: and if the multitude of one age are nearer to the truth than the multitude of another, it is only in so far as they are guided and influenced by the authority of the wisest among them.[3]

This is connected with certain points which, as it appears to me, have not been sufficiently adverted to by many of those who hold, in common with me, the doctrine of the indefinite progressiveness of the human mind; but which must be understood, in order correctly to

3. The distance between this view and that of Carlyle, which eventually turned into "hero-worship," is not great. One of the central problems of the great Victorian writers was to find some source of authority that would counteract what they felt to be the increasing disintegration of "received values."

appreciate the character of the present age, as an age of moral and political transition. These, therefore, I shall attempt to enforce and illustrate in the next paper.

II

I have said that the present age is an age of transition: I shall now attempt to point out one of the most important consequences of this fact. In all other conditions of mankind, the uninstructed have faith in the instructed. In an age of transition, the divisions among the instructed nullify their authority, and the uninstructed lose their faith in them. The multitude are without a guide; and society is exposed to all the errors and dangers which are to be expected when persons who have never studied any branch of knowledge comprehensively and as a whole attempt to judge for themselves upon particular parts of it.

That this is the condition we are really in, I may spare myself the trouble of attempting to prove: it has become so habitual, that the only difficulty to be anticipated is in persuading any one that this is not our natural state, and that it is consistent with any good wishes towards the human species, to pray that we may come safely out of it. The longer any one observes and meditates, the more clearly he will see, that even wise men are apt to mistake the almanack of the year for a treatise on chronology; and as in an age of transition the source of all improvement is the exercise of private judgment, no wonder that mankind should attach themselves to that, as to the ultimate refuge, the last and only resource of humanity. In like manner, if a caravan of travellers had long been journeying in an unknown country under a blind guide, with what earnestness would the wiser among them exhort the remainder to use their own eyes, and with what disfavour would any one be listened to who should insist upon the difficulty of finding their way, and the necessity of procuring a guide after all. He would be told with warmth, that they had hitherto missed their way solely from the fatal weakness of allowing themselves to be guided, and that they never should reach their journey's end until each man dared to think and see for himself. And it would perhaps be added (with a smile of contempt), that if he were sincere in doubting the capacity of his fellow-travellers to see their way, he might prove his sincerity by presenting each person with a pair of spectacles, by means whereof their powers of vision might be strengthened, and all indistinctness removed.

The men of the past, are those who continue to insist upon our still adhering to the blind guide. The men of the present, are those who bid each man look about for himself, with or without the promise of spectacles to assist him.

While these two contending parties are measuring their sophistries against one another, the man who is capable of other ideas than those of his age, has an example in the present state of physical science, and in the manner in which men shape their thoughts and their actions within its sphere, of what is to be hoped for and laboured for in all other departments of human knowledge; and what, beyond all possibility of doubt, will one day be attained.

We never hear of the right of private judgment in physical science; yet it exists; for what is there to prevent any one from denying every proposition in natural philosophy, if he be so minded? The physical sciences however have been brought to so advanced a stage of improvement by a series of great men, and the methods by which they are cultivated so entirely preclude the possibility of material error when due pains are taken to arrive at the truth, that all persons who have studied those subjects have come to a nearly unanimous agreement upon them. Some minor differences doubtless exist; there are points on which the opinion of the scientific world is not finally made up. But these are mostly questions rather of curiosity than of use, and it is seldom attempted to thrust them into undue importance, nor to remove them, by way of appeal from the tribunal of the specially instructed to that of the public at large. The compact mass of authority thus created overawes the minds of the uninformed: and if here and there a wrong-headed individual, like Sir Richard Phillips,[4] impugns Newton's discoveries, and revives the long-forgotten sophisms of the Cartesians, he is not regarded. Yet the fallacies which at one time enthralled the subtlest understandings, might find, we suspect, in the present day, some intellects scarcely strong enough to resist them: but no one dares to stand up against the scientific world, until he too has qualified himself to be named as a man of science: and no one does this without being forced, by irresistible evidence, to adopt the received opinion. The physical sciences, therefore, (speaking of them

4. Richard Phillips (1767–1840) was an author, publisher, and bookseller who distinguished himself with his argument against the law of gravitation. He was also a radical democrat from whose shop was distributed advanced democratic literature. Although he was jailed for selling Paine's *Rights of Man*, he later became editor of the *Monthly Magazine*, then Sheriff of London, and was finally knighted in 1807.

generally) are continually *growing*, but never *changing*: in every age they receive indeed mighty improvements, but for them the age of transition is past.

It is almost unnecessary to remark in how very different a condition from this, are the sciences which are conversant with the moral nature and social condition of man. In those sciences, this imposing unanimity among all who have studied the subject does not exist; and every dabbler, consequently, thinks his opinion as good as another's. Any man who has eyes and ears shall be judge whether, in point of fact, a person who has never studied politics, for instance, or political economy systematically, regards himself as any-way precluded thereby from promulgating with the most unbounded assurance the crudest opinions, and taxing men who have made those sciences the occupation of a laborious life, with the most contemptible ignorance and imbecility. It is rather the person who *has* studied the subject systematically that is regarded as disqualified. He is a *theorist*: and the word which expresses the highest and noblest effort of human intelligence is turned into a bye-word of derision. People pride themselves upon taking a "plain, matter-of-fact" view of a subject. I once heard of a book entitled "Plain Politics for Plain People." I well remember the remark of an able man on that occasion: "What would be thought of a work with such a title as this, Plain Mathematics for Plain People?" The parallel is most accurate. The nature of the evidence on which these two sciences rest, is different, but both are systems of connected truth: there are very few of the practical questions of either, which can be discussed with profit unless the parties are agreed on a great number of preliminary questions: and accordingly, most of the political discussions which one hears and reads are not unlike what one would expect if the binomial theorem were propounded for argument in a debating society none of whose members had completely made up their minds upon the Rule of Three. Men enter upon a subject with minds in no degree fitted, by previous acquirements, to understand and appreciate the true arguments: yet they lay the blame on the arguments, not on themselves: truth, they think, is under a peremptory obligation of being intelligible to them, whether they take the right means of understanding it or no. Every mode of judging, except from first appearances, is scouted as false refinement. If there were a party among philosophers who still held to the opinion that the sun moves round the earth, can any one doubt on which side of the question the vulgar would be? What terms could express their contempt for those who maintained the contrary! Men form their opinions according to natural shrewdness, without any of the advantages of study. Here and there a hardheaded man, who sees farther into a mill-stone than his neighbours, and takes it into his head that thinking on a subject is one way of understanding it, excogitates an entire science, and publishes his volume; in utter unconsciousness of the fact, that a tithe of his discoveries were known a century ago, and the remainder (supposing them not too absurd to have occurred to anybody before) have been refuted in any year which you can mention, from that time to the present.

This is the state we are in; and the question is, how we are to get out of it. As I am unable to take the view of this matter which will probably occur to most persons as being the most simple and natural, I shall state in the first instance what this is, and my reasons for dissenting from it.

A large portion of the talking and writing common in the present day, respecting the instruction of the people, and the diffusion of knowledge, appears to me to conceal, under loose and vague generalities, notions at bottom altogether fallacious and visionary.

I go, perhaps, still further than most of those to whose language I so strongly object, in the expectations which I entertain of vast improvements in the social condition of man, from the growth of intelligence among the body of the people; and I yield to no one in the degree of intelligence of which I believe them to be capable. But I do not believe that, along with this intelligence, they will ever have sufficient opportunities of study and experience, to become themselves familiarly conversant with all the inquiries which lead to the truths by which it is good that they should regulate their conduct, and to receive into their own minds the whole of the evidence from which those truths have been collected, and which is necessary for their establishment. If I thought all this indispensable, I should despair of human nature. As long as the day consists but of twenty-four hours, and the age of man extends but to threescore and ten, so long (unless we expect improvements in the arts of production sufficient to restore the golden age) the great majority of mankind will need the far greater part of their time and exertions for procuring their daily bread. Some few remarkable individuals will attain great eminence under every conceivable disadvantage; but for men in general, the principal field for the exercise and display of their intellectual faculties is, and ever will be, no other than their own particular calling or occupation. This does not place any limit to their possible intelligence; since the mode of learning, and the mode of practising, that occupation itself, might be made one of the most valuable of all exercises of intelligence: especially when, in all the occupations in which man is a mere machine, his agency is so rapidly becoming superseded by real machinery. But what sets no limit to the *powers* of the mass of mankind, nevertheless limits greatly their possible *acquirements*. Those persons whom the circumstances of society, and their own position in it, permit to dedicate themselves to the investigation and study of physical, moral, and social truths, as their peculiar calling, can alone be expected to make the evidences of such truths a subject of profound meditation, and to make themselves thorough masters of the philosophical grounds of those opinions of which it is desirable that all should be firmly *persuaded*, but which they alone can entirely and philosophically *know*. The remainder of mankind must, and, except in periods of transition like the present, always do, take the far greater part of their opinions on all extensive subjects upon the authority of those who have studied them.

It does not follow that all men are not to inquire and investigate. The only complaint is, that most of them are precluded by the nature of things from ever inquiring and investigating enough. It is right that they should acquaint themselves with the evidence of the truths which are presented to them, to the utmost extent of each man's intellects, leisure, and inclination. Though a man may never be able to understand Laplace, that is no reason he should not read Euclid. But it by no means follows that Euclid is a blunderer, or an arrant knave, because a man who begins at the forty-seventh proposition cannot understand it: and even he who begins at the beginning, and is stopped by the *pons asinorum*,[5] is very much in the wrong if he swears he will navigate his vessel himself, and not trust to the non-sensical calculations of mathematical land-lubbers. Let him learn what he can, and as well as he can—still however bearing in mind, that there are others who probably know much with which he not only is unacquainted, but of the evidence of which, in the existing state of his knowledge, it is impossible that he should be a competent judge.

It is no answer to what has just been observed, to say that the grounds of the most important moral and political truths are simple and obvious, intelligible to persons of the most limited faculties, with moderate study and attention; that all mankind, therefore, may master the evidences, and none need take the doctrines upon trust. The matter of fact upon which this objection proceeds, is happily true. The proofs of the moral and social truths of greatest importance to mankind, are few, brief, and easily intelligible; and happy will be the day on which these shall begin to be circulated among the people,

5. The "asses' bridge," that is, the fifth proposition of Euclid's First Book, so called because it contains a diagram that looks like a bridge.

instead of second-rate treatises on the Polarization of Light, and on the Rigidity of Cordage. But, in the first place, it is not every one— and there is no one at a very early period of life—who has had sufficient experience of mankind in general, and has sufficiently re- flected upon what passes in his own mind, to be able to appreciate the force of the reasons when laid before him. There is, however, a great number of important truths, especially in Political Economy, to which, from the particular nature of the evidence on which they rest, this difficulty does not apply. The proofs of these truths may be brought down to the level of even the uninformed multitude, with the most complete success. But, when all is done, there still remains something which they must always and inevitably take upon trust: and this is, that the arguments really are as conclusive as they appear; that there exist no considerations relevant to the subject which have been kept back from them; that every objection which can suggest itself has been duly examined by competent judges, and found immaterial. It is easy to say that the truth of certain propositions is obvious to *common sense*. It may be so: but how am I assured that the conclusions of common sense are confirmed by accurate knowledge? Judging by com- mon sense is merely another phrase for judging by first appearances; and every one who has mixed among mankind with any capacity for observing them, knows that the men who place implicit faith in their own common sense are, without any exception, the most wrong- headed, and impracticable persons with whom he has ever had to deal. The maxim of pursuing truth without being biassed by authority, does not state the question fairly; there is no person who does not prefer truth to authority—for authority is only appealed to as a voucher for truth. The real question, to be determined by each man's own judgment, is, whether most confidence is due in the particular case, to his own understanding, or to the opinion of his authority? It is there- fore obvious, that there are some persons in whom disregard of authority is a virtue, and others in whom it is both an absurdity and a vice. The presumptuous man needs authority to restrain him from error: the modest man needs it to strengthen him in the right. What truths, for example, can be more obvious, or can rest upon considera- tions more simple and familiar, than the first principles of morality? Yet we know that extremely ingenious things may be said in opposi- tion to the plainest of them—things which the most highly-instructed men, though never for a single moment misled by them, have had no small difficulty in satisfactorily answering. Is it to be imagined that if these sophisms had been referred to the verdict of the half-instructed —and we cannot expect the majority of every class to be any thing more—the solution of the fallacy would always have been found and understood? notwithstanding which, the fallacy would not, it is most probable, have made the slightest impression upon them:—and why? Because the judgment of the multitude would have told them, that their own judgment was not a decision in the last resort; because the conviction of their understandings going along with the moral truth, was sanctioned by the authority of the best-informed; and the objection, though insoluble by their own understandings, was not supported but contradicted by the same imposing authority. But if you once persuade an ignorant or a half-instructed person, that he ought to assert his liberty of thought, discard all authority, and—I do not say use his own judgment, for that he never can do too much—but *trust* solely to his own judgment, and receive or reject opinions according to his own views of the evidence;—if, in short, you teach to all the lesson of *indifferency*, so earnestly, and with such admirable effect, inculcated by Locke upon *students*, for whom alone that great man wrote, the merest trifle will suffice to unsettle and perplex their minds. There is not a truth in the whole range of human affairs, however obvious and simple, the evidence of which an ingenious and artful sophist may not succeed in rendering doubtful to minds not very highly cultivated, if those minds insist upon judging of all things exclusively by their own lights. The presumptuous man will dogmatize, and rush headlong into opinions, always shallow, and as often wrong as right; the man who sets only the just value upon his own moderate powers, will scarcely ever feel more than a half-conviction. You may prevail on them to repudiate the authority of the best-instructed, but each will full surely be a mere slave to the authority of the person next to him, who has greatest facilities for continually forcing upon his attention considerations favourable to the conclusion he himself wishes to be drawn.

It is, therefore, one of the necessary conditions of humanity, that the majority must either have wrong opinions, or no fixed opinions, or must place the degree of reliance warranted by reason, in the authority of those who have made moral and social philosophy their peculiar study. It is right that every man should attempt to understand his interest and his duty. It is right that he should follow his reason as far as his reason will carry him, and cultivate the faculty as highly as possible. But reason itself will teach most men that they must, in the last resort, fall back upon the authority of still more cultivated minds, as the ultimate sanction of the convictions of their reason itself.

But where is the authority which commands this confidence, or deserves it? Nowhere: and here we see the peculiar character, and at the same time the peculiar inconvenience, of a period of moral and social transition. At all other periods there exists a large body of received doctrine, covering nearly the whole field of the moral relations of man, and which no one thinks of questioning, backed as it is by the authority of all, or nearly all, persons, supposed to possess knowledge enough to qualify them for giving an opinion on the subject. This state of things does not now exist in the civilized world—except, indeed, to a certain limited extent in the United States of America. The progress of inquiry has brought to light the insufficiency of the ancient doctrines; but those who have made the investigation of social truths their occupation, have not yet sanctioned any new body of doctrine with their unanimous, or nearly unanimous, consent. The true opinion is recommended to the public by no greater weight of authority than hundreds of false opinions; and, even at this day, to find any thing like a united body of grave and commanding authority, we must revert to the doctrines from which the progressiveness of the human mind, or, as it is more popularly called, the improvement of the age, has set us free.

In the mean time, as the old doctrines have gone out, and the new ones have not yet come in, every one must judge for himself as he best may. Learn, and think for yourself, is reasonable advice for the day: but let not the business of the day be so done as to prejudice the work of the morrow. "Les supériorités morales," to use the words of Fiévée,[6] "finiront par s'entendre"; the first men of the age will one day join hands and be agreed: and then there is no power in itself, on earth or in hell, capable of withstanding them.

But ere this can happen there must be a change in the whole framework of society, as at present constituted. Worldly power must pass from the hands of the stationary part of mankind into those of the progressive part. There must be a moral and social revolution, which shall, indeed, take away no men's lives or property, but which shall leave to no man one fraction of unearned distinction or unearned importance.

That man cannot achieve his destiny but through such a transformation, and that it will and *shall* be effected, is the conclusion of every man who can *feel the wants of his own age*, without hankering after past ages. Those who may read these papers, and in particular

6. Joseph Fiévée (1767–1839), a writer of drama and fiction. Although imprisoned in France during the Reign of Terror, he was later freed and became successful politically and diplomatically. His *Lettres sur l'Angleterre* (1802) evoked a violent review from the *Edinburgh*.

the next succeeding one, will find there an attempt, how far successful others must judge, to set forth the grounds of this belief.

For mankind to change their institutions while their minds are unsettled, without fixed principles, and unable to trust either themselves or other people, is, indeed, a fearful thing. But a bad way is often the best, to get out of a bad position. Let us place our trust for the future, not in the wisdom of mankind, but in something far surer—the force of circumstances—which makes men see that, when it is near at hand, which they could not foresee when it was at a distance, and which so often and so unexpectedly makes the right course, in a moment of emergency, at once the easiest and the most obvious.

JOHN STUART MILL

# Civilization:
# Signs of the Times[*]

The word civilization, like many other terms of the philosophy of
human nature, is a word of double meaning. It sometimes stands for
*human improvement* in general, and sometimes for *certain kinds* of
improvement in particular.

We are accustomed to call a country more civilized if we think it
more improved; more eminent in the best characteristics of Man and
Society; further advanced in the road to perfection; happier, nobler,
wiser. This is one sense of the word civilization. But in another sense
it stands for that kind of improvement only which distinguishes a
wealthy and populous nation from savages or barbarians. It is in this
sense that we may speak of the vices or the miseries of civilization; and
that the question has been seriously propounded, whether civilization
is on the whole a good or an evil? Assuredly we entertain no doubt on
this point; we hold that civilization is a good, that it is the cause of

[*] From *The Westminster Review*, XXV (April, 1836), 1–28.

much good, and is not incompatible with any; but we think there
is other good, much even of the highest good, which civilization in
this sense does not provide for, and some which it has a tendency
(though that tendency may be counteracted) to impede.

The inquiry, into which these considerations would lead us, is
calculated to throw light upon many of the characteristic features of
our time. The present era is pre-eminently the era of civilization, in
the narrow sense; whether we consider what has already been achieved,
or the rapid advances making towards still greater achievements. We
do not regard the age as either equally advanced or equally progressive
in many of the other kinds of improvement. In some it appears to us
stationary, in some even retrograde. Moreover, the consequences, the
irresistible consequences of a state of advancing civilization; the new
position in which that advance has placed, and is every day more and
more placing mankind; the entire inapplicability of old rules to this
new position, and the necessity, if we would either realize the benefits
of the new state or preserve those of the old, that we should adopt
many new rules, and new courses of action; are topics which seem to
require a more comprehensive examination than they have usually
received.

We shall in the present article invariably use the word civilization
in the narrow sense: not that in which it is synonymous with improvement, but that in which it is the direct converse or contrary of
rudeness or barbarism. Whatever be the characteristics of what we call
savage life, the contrary of these, or rather the qualities which society
puts on as it throws off these, constitute civilization. Thus, a savage
tribe consists of a handful of individuals, wandering or thinly scattered
over a vast tract of country: a dense population, therefore, dwelling in
fixed habitations, and largely collected together in towns and villages,
we term civilized. In savage life there is no commerce, no manufactures, no agriculture, or next to none; a country rich in the fruits of
agriculture, commerce, and manufactures, we call civilized. In savage
communities each person shifts for himself; except in war (and even
then very imperfectly) we seldom see any joint operations carried on
by the union of many; nor do savages find much pleasure in each
other's society. Wherever, therefore, we find human beings acting
together for common purposes in large bodies, and enjoying the
pleasures of social intercourse, we term them civilized. In savage life
there is little or no law, or administration of justice; no systematic
employment of the collective strength of society, to protect individuals
against injury from one another; every one trusts to his own strength

or cunning, and where that fails, he is without resource. We accordingly call a people civilized, where the arrangements of society, for protecting the persons and property of its members, are sufficiently perfect to maintain peace among them; *i.e.* to induce the bulk of the community to rely for their security mainly upon the social arrangements, and renounce for the most part, and in ordinary circumstances, the vindication of their interests (whether in the way of aggression or of defence) by their individual strength or courage.

These ingredients of civilization are various, but consideration will satisfy us that they are not improperly classed together. History, and their own nature, alike show, that they begin together, always coexist, and accompany each other in their growth. Wherever there has introduced itself sufficient knowledge of the arts of life, and sufficient security of property and person, to render the progressive increase of wealth and population possible, the community becomes and continues progressive in all the elements which we have just enumerated. All these elements exist in modern Europe, and especially in Great Britain, in a more eminent degree, and in a state of more rapid progression, than at any other place or time. We shall attempt to point out some of the consequences which that high and progressive state of civilization has already produced, and of the further ones which it is hastening to produce.

The most remarkable of those consequences of advancing civilization, which the state of the world is now forcing upon the attention of thinking minds, is this: that power passes more and more from individuals, and small knots of individuals, to masses: that the importance of the masses becomes constantly greater, that of individuals less.

The causes, evidences, and consequences of this law of human affairs, well deserve attention.

There are two elements of importance and influence among mankind: the one is, property; the other, powers and acquirements of mind. Both of these, in an early stage of civilization, are confined to a few persons. In the beginnings of society, the power of the masses does not exist; because property and intelligence have no existence beyond a very small portion of the community, and even if they had, those who possessed the smaller portions would be, from their incapacity of co-operation, unable to cope with those who possessed the larger.

First, as to property: In the more backward countries of the present time, and in all Europe at no distant date, we see property

entirely concentrated in a small number of hands; the remainder of
the people being, with few exceptions, either the military retainers
and dependents of the possessors of property, or serfs, stripped and
tortured at pleasure by one master, and pillaged by a hundred. At no
period could it be said that there was literally no middle class—but
that class was extremely feeble, both in numbers and in power: while
the labouring people, absorbed in manual toil, with difficulty earned,
by the utmost excess of exertion, a more or less scanty and always
precarious subsistence. The character of this state of society was the
utmost excess of poverty and impotence in the masses; the most
enormous importance and uncontrollable power of a small number of
individuals, each of whom, within his own sphere, knew neither law
nor superior.

We must leave to history to unfold the gradual rise of the trading
and manufacturing classes, the gradual emancipation of the agricultural, the tumults and *bouleversements* which accompanied these
changes in their course, and the extraordinary alterations in institutions, opinions, habits, and the whole of social life, which they brought
in their train. We need only ask the reader to form a conception of
the vastness of all that is implied in the words, growth of a middle
class; and then bid him reflect upon the immense increase of the
numbers and property of that class throughout Great Britain, France,
Germany, and other countries in every successive generation, and the
novelty of a labouring class receiving such wages as are now commonly
earned by nearly the whole of the manufacturing, that is, of the most
numerous portion of the operative classes of this country—and ask
himself whether, from causes so unheard of, unheard of effects ought
not to be expected to flow. It must at least be evident, that if, as
civilization advances, property and intelligence become thus widely
diffused among the millions, it must also be an effect of civilization,
that the portion of either of these which can belong to an individual
must have a tendency to become less and less influential, and all results
must more and more be decided by the movements of masses; provided
that the power of combination among the masses keeps pace with the
progress of their resources. And that it does so who can doubt? There
is not a more accurate test of the progress of civilization than the
progress of the power of co-operation.

Look at the savage: he has bodily strength, he has courage, enterprise, and is often not without intelligence; what makes all savage
communities poor and feeble? The same cause which prevented the
lions and tigers from long ago extirpating the race of men—incapacity
of co-operation. It is only civilized beings who can combine. All

combination is compromise: it is the sacrifice of some portion of individual will, for a common purpose. The savage cannot bear to sacrifice, for any purpose, the satisfaction of his individual will. His impulses cannot bend to his calculations. Look again at the slave: he is used indeed to make his will give way; but to the commands of a master, not to a superior purpose of his own. He is wanting in intelligence to form such a purpose; above all, he cannot frame to himself the conception of a fixed rule: nor if he could, has he the capacity to adhere to it; he is habituated to control, but not to self-control; when a driver is not standing over him with a cart-whip, he is found more incapable of withstanding any temptation, or constraining any inclination, than the savage himself.

We have taken extreme cases, that the fact we seek to illustrate might stand out more conspicuously. But the remark itself applies universally. As any people approach to the condition of savages or of slaves, so are they incapable of acting in concert. Look even at war, the most serious business of a barbarous people; see what a figure rude nations, or semicivilized and enslaved nations, have made against civilized ones, from Marathon downwards. Why? Because discipline is more powerful than numbers, and discipline, that is, perfect co-operation, is an attribute of civilization. To come to our own times, read Napier's History of the Peninsular War;[1] see how incapable half-savages are of co-operation. Amidst all the enthusiasm of the Spanish people struggling against Napoleon, no one leader, military or political, could act in concert with another; no one would sacrifice one iota of his consequence, his authority, or his opinion, to the most obvious demands of the common cause; neither generals nor soldiers could observe the simplest rules of the military art. . . .

It is not difficult to see why this incapacity of organized combination characterizes savages, and disappears with the growth of civilization. Co-operation, like other difficult things, can be learnt only by practice: and to be capable of it in great things, a people must be gradually trained to it in small. Now the whole course of advancing civilization is a series of such training. The labourer in a rude state of society works singly, or if several are brought to work together by the will of a master, they work side by side, but not in concert; one man digs his piece of ground, another digs a similar piece of ground

1. William Francis Patrick Napier (1785–1860) was a general who fought with Wellington in Spain and Portugal during the Peninsular War. His *History of the War in the Peninsula and in the South of France from the Year 1807 to the Year 1814*, 6 vols. (1828–40), was widely regarded as the best on the subject.

close by him. In the situation of an ignorant labourer, tilling even his own field, with his own hand, and seeing no one except his wife and his children, what is there that can teach him to co-operate? The division of employments—the accomplishment by the combined labour of several, of tasks which could not be achieved by any number of persons singly—is the great school of co-operation. What a lesson, for instance, is navigation, as soon as it passes out of its first simple stage—the safety of all, constantly depending upon the vigilant performance by each, of the part peculiarly allotted to him in the common task. Military operations, when not wholly undisciplined, are a similar school; so are all the operations of commerce and manufactures which require the employment of many hands upon the same thing at the same time. By these operations, mankind learn the value of combination; they see how much and with what ease it accomplishes, which never could be accomplished without it; they learn a practical lesson of submitting themselves to guidance, and subduing themselves to act as interdependent parts of a complex whole. A people thus progressively trained to combination by the business of their lives, become capable of carrying the same habits into new things. For it holds universally, that the one only mode of learning to do anything, is actually doing something of the same kind under easier circumstances. Habits of discipline once acquired, qualify human beings to accomplish all other things for which discipline is needed. No longer either spurning control, or being incapable of seeing its advantages, whenever any object presents itself which can be attained by co-operation, and which they see or believe to be beneficial, they are ripe for attaining it.

The characters, then, of a state of high civilization being the diffusion of property and intelligence, and the power of co-operation; the next thing to observe is the astonishing development which all these elements have assumed of late years.

The rapidity with which property has accumulated and is accumulating in the principal countries of Europe, but especially in this island, is obvious to every one. The capital of the industrious classes overflows into foreign countries, and into all kinds of wild speculations. The amount of capital annually exported from Great Britain alone, surpasses probably the whole wealth of the most flourishing commercial republics of antiquity. But the capital, collectively so vast, is composed almost entirely of small portions; very generally so small, that the owners cannot, without other means of livelihood, subsist upon the profits of them. While such is the growth of property in the hands of the mass, the circumstances of the higher classes have undergone nothing like a corresponding improvement. Many large fortunes have, it is true, been accumulated, but many others have been wholly or partially dissipated; for the inheritors of immense fortunes, as a class, always live at least up to their incomes when at the highest, and the unavoidable vicissitudes of those incomes are always sinking them deeper and deeper into debt. The English landlords, as they themselves are constantly telling us, are a bankrupt body, and the real owners of the bulk of their estates are the mortgagees. In other countries the large properties have very generally been broken down; in France, by revolution, and the revolutionary law of inheritance; in Prussia, by successive edicts of that substantially democratic, though nominally absolute government.

With respect to knowledge and intelligence, it is the truism of the age, that the masses, both of the middle and even of the working classes, are treading upon the heels of their superiors.

If we now consider the progress made by those same masses in the capacity and habit of co-operation, we find it equally surprising. At what period were the operations of productive industry carried on upon anything like their present scale? Were so many hands ever before employed at the same time upon the same work, as now in all the principal departments of manufactures and commerce? To how enormous an extent is business now carried on by joint stock companies—in other words, by many small capitals thrown together to form one great one. The country is covered with associations. There are societies for political, societies for religious, societies for philanthropic purposes. But the greatest novelty of all is the spirit of combination which has gone forth among the working classes. The present age has seen the commencement of benefit societies; and they now, as well as the more questionable Trades' Unions, overspread the whole country. A more powerful, though not so ostensible, instrument of combination than any of these, has but lately become universally accessible—the newspaper. The newspaper carries the voice of the many home to every individual among them; by the newspaper, each learns that all others are feeling as he feels, and that if he is ready, he will find them also prepared to act upon what they feel. The newspaper is the telegraph which carries the signal throughout the country, and the flag round which it rallies. Hundreds of newspapers, speaking in the same voice at once, and the rapidity of communication afforded by improved means of locomotion, were what enabled the whole country to combine in that simultaneous, energetic demonstration of determined will which carried the Reform Act. Both these facilities are on the increase, every one may see how rapidly; and they will enable the people on all decisive occasions to form a collective will, and render that collective will irresistible.

To meet this wonderful development of physical and intellectual power on the part of the masses, can it be said that there has been any corresponding quantity of intellectual power or moral energy unfolded among those individuals or classes who have enjoyed superior advantages? No one, we think, will affirm it. There is a great increase of humanity, a decline of bigotry, and of many of the repulsive qualities of aristocracy, among our conspicuous classes; but there is, to say the least, no increase of shining ability, and a very marked decrease of vigour and energy. With all the advantages of this age, its facilities for mental cultivation, the incitements and the rewards which it holds out to exalted talents, there can scarcely be pointed out in the European annals any stirring times, which have brought so little that is distinguished, either morally or intellectually, to the surface.

That this, too, is no more than was to be expected from the tendencies of civilization, when no attempt is made to correct them, we shall have occasion to show presently. But even if civilization did nothing to lower the eminences, it would produce an exactly similar effect by raising the plains. When the masses become powerful, an individual, or a small band of individuals, can be nothing except by influencing the masses; and to do this becomes daily more difficult, and requires higher powers, from the constantly increasing number of those who are vying with one another to attract the public attention. Our position, therefore, is established, that by the natural growth of civilization, power passes from individuals to masses, and the weight and importance of an individual, as compared with the mass, sink into greater and greater insignificance.

The change which is thus in progress, and to a great extent consummated, is the greatest ever recorded in human affairs; the most complete, the most fruitful in consequences, and the most irrevocable. Whoever can meditate upon it, and not see that so great a revolution vitiates all existing rules of government and policy, and renders all practice and all predictions grounded only upon prior experience worthless, is wanting in the very first and most elementary principle of statesmanship in these times.

'Il faut,' as M. de Tocqueville has said, 'une science politique nouvelle à un monde tout nouveau.'[2] The whole face of society is reversed—all the natural elements of power have definitively changed places, and there are people who talk to us of standing up for ancient

2. "A new political science is necessary in a completely new world."

institutions, and the duty of sticking to the British Constitution settled in 1688! What is still more extraordinary, these are the people
who accuse others of disregarding variety of circumstances, and
imposing their abstract theories upon all states of society without
discrimination.

We put it to those who call themselves Conservatives, whether,
when the whole power in society is passing into the hands of the
masses, they really think it possible to prevent the masses from making
that power predominant as well in the government as elsewhere? The
triumph of democracy, or, in other words, of the government of public
opinion, does not depend upon the opinion of any individual or set
of individuals that it ought to triumph, but upon the natural laws
of the progress of wealth, upon the diffusion of reading, and the increase of the facilities of human intercourse. If Lord Kenyon or the
Duke of Newcastle[3] could stop these, they might accomplish something. There is no danger of the prevalence of democracy in Syria or
Timbuctoo. But he must be a poor politician who does not know, that
whatever is the growing power in society will force its way into the
government, by fair means or foul. The distribution of constitutional
power cannot long continue very different from that of real power,
without a convulsion. Nor, if the institutions which impede the progress of democracy could be by any miracle preserved, could even they
do more than render that progress a little slower. Were the constitution of Great Britain to remain henceforth unaltered, we are not the
less under the dominion, becoming every day more irresistible, of
public opinion.

With regard to the advance of democracy, there are two different
positions which it is possible for a rational person to take up, according as he thinks the masses prepared, or unprepared, to exercise the
control which they are acquiring over their destiny, in a manner which
would be an improvement upon what now exists. If he thinks them
prepared, he will aid the democratic movement; or if he deem it to
be proceeding fast enough without him, he will at all events refrain
from resisting it. If, on the contrary, he thinks the masses unprepared
for complete control over their government—seeing at the same

3. George Kenyon (1776–1855) was the son of the first Lord Kenyon,
a famous judge and master of the rolls. Kenyon was a rigid Tory. Henry Pelham Fiennes Pelham Clinton, Fourth Duke of Newcastle (1785–1851) was
also a rigid conservative who violently opposed all reforms. He provoked a
riot and the burning of his mansion when, in Parliament, he defended the
ejection from his land of some tenants by saying, "Is it not lawful for me to
do what I please with mine own?"

time that, prepared or not, they cannot be prevented from acquiring it—he will exert his utmost efforts in contributing to prepare them; using all means, on the one hand, for making the masses themselves wiser and better; on the other, for so rousing the slumbering energy of the opulent and lettered classes, so storing the youth of those classes with the profoundest and most valuable knowledge, so calling forth whatever of individual greatness exists or can be raised up in the country, as to create a power which might partially rival the mere power of the masses, and might exercise the most salutary influence over them for their own good. When engaged earnestly in works like these, one can understand how a rational person might think that in order to give more time for the performance of them, it were well if the current of democracy, which can in no sort be stayed, could be prevailed upon for a time to flow less impetuously. With Conservatives of this sort, all Radicals of corresponding enlargement of view, could fraternize as frankly and cordially as with many of their own friends: and we speak from an extensive knowledge of the wisest and most high-minded of that body, when we take upon ourselves to answer for them, that they would never push forward their own political projects in a spirit or with a violence which could tend to frustrate any rational endeavours towards the object nearest their hearts, the instruction of the understandings and the elevation of the characters of all classes of their countrymen.

But who is there among the political party calling themselves Conservatives, that professes to have any such object in view? Is there one who seeks to employ the interval of respite which he might hope to gain by withstanding democracy, in qualifying the people to wield the democracy more wisely when it comes? Is there one who would not far rather resist any such endeavour, on the principle that knowledge is power, and that its further diffusion would make the dreaded evil come sooner? Again, is there a Conservative in either house of parliament who feels that the character of the higher classes needs renovating, to qualify them for a more arduous task and a keener strife than has yet fallen to their lot? Is not the character of a Tory lord or country gentleman, or a Church of England parson, perfectly satisfactory to them? Is not the existing constitution of the two Universities—those bodies whose especial duty it was to counteract the debilitating influence of the circumstances of the age upon individual character, and to send forth into society a succession of minds, not the creatures of their age, but capable of being its improvers and regenerators—the Universities, by whom this their especial duty has been basely neglected, until, as is usual with all neglected duties, the

very consciousness of it as a duty has faded from their remembrance,—
is not, we say, the existing constitution, and the whole existing system
of these Universities, down to the smallest of their abuses, the exclusion of Dissenters, a thing for which every Tory, though he may
not as he pretends die in the last ditch, will at least vote in the last
division? The Church, professedly the other great instrument of national culture, long since perverted (we speak of rules, not exceptions)
into the great instrument of preventing all culture, except the inculcation of obedience to established maxims and constituted authorities
—what Tory has a scheme in view for any changes in this body, but
such as may pacify assailants, and make the institution wear a less
disgusting appearance to the eye? What political Tory will not resist
to the very last moment any alteration in that Church, which will
prevent its livings from being the provisions for a family, its dignities
the reward of political or of private services? The Tories, those at
least connected with parliament or office, do not aim at having good
institutions, or even at preserving the present ones: their object is to
profit by them while they exist.

We scruple not to express our belief that a truer spirit of Conservation, as to everything good in the principles and professed objects of our old institutions, lives in many who are determined
enemies of those institutions in their present state, than in most of
those who call themselves Conservatives. But there are many well-
meaning people who always confound attachment to an end, with
blind adherence to any set of means by which it either is, or is pretended to be, already pursued; and have yet to learn, that bodies of
men who live in honour and importance upon the pretence of fulfill-
ing ends which they never honestly seek, are the great hinderance to
the attainment of those ends; and whoever has the attainment really
at heart, must begin by sweeping them from his path.

Thus far as to the political effects of Civilization. Its moral
effects, which as yet we have only glanced at, demand further elucidation. They may be considered under two heads: the direct influence
of Civilization itself upon individual character, and the moral effects
produced by the insignificance into which the individual falls in
comparison with the masses.

One of the effects of a high state of civilization upon character,
is a relaxation of individual energy: or rather the concentration of it
within the narrow sphere of the individual's money-getting pursuits.
As civilization advances, every person becomes dependent, for more
and more of what most nearly concerns him, not upon his own

exertions, but upon the general arrangements of society. In a rude state, each man's personal security, the protection of his family, his property, his liberty itself, depends greatly upon his bodily strength and his mental energy or cunning: in a civilized state, all this is secured to him by causes extrinsic to himself. The growing mildness of manners is a protection to him against much that he was before exposed to, while for the remainder he may rely with constantly increasing assurance upon the soldier, the policeman, and the judge; and (where the efficiency or purity of those instruments, as is usually the case, lags behind the general march of civilization) upon the advancing strength of public opinion. There remains, as inducements to call forth energy of character, the desire of wealth or of personal aggrandizement, the passion of philanthropy, and the love of active virtue. But the objects to which these various feelings point are matters of choice, not of necessity, nor do the feelings act with anything like equal force upon all minds. The only one of them which can be considered as anything like universal, is the desire of wealth; and wealth being, in the case of the majority, the most accessible means of gratifying all their other desires, nearly the whole of the energy of character which exists in highly civilized societies concentrates itself in the pursuit of that object. In the case, however, of the most influential classes—those whose energies, if they had them, might be exercised on the greatest scale and with the most considerable result —the desire of wealth is already sufficiently satisfied to render them averse to suffer pain or incur voluntary labour for the sake of any further increase. The same classes also enjoy, from their station alone, a high degree of personal consideration. Except the high offices of the state, there is hardly anything to tempt the ambition of men in their circumstances. Those offices, when a great nobleman could have them for asking for, and keep them with less trouble than he could manage his private estate, were, no doubt, desirable enough possessions for such persons; but, when they become posts of labour, vexation, and anxiety, and besides cannot be had without paying the price of some previous toil, experience shows that among men unaccustomed to sacrifice their amusements and their ease, the number upon whom these high offices operate as incentives to activity, or in whom they call forth any vigour of character, is extremely limited. Thus it happens, that in highly civilized countries, and particularly among ourselves, the energies of the middle classes are almost confined to money-getting, and those of the higher classes are nearly extinct.

There is another circumstance to which we may trace much both of the good and of the bad qualities which distinguish our civiliza-

tion from the rudeness of former times. One of the effects of civilization (not to say one of the ingredients in it) is, that the spectacle, and
even the very idea of pain, is kept more and more out of the sight
of those classes who enjoy in their fulness the benefits of civilization.
The state of perpetual personal conflict, rendered necessary by the circumstances of all former times, and from which it was hardly possible
for any person, in whatever rank of society, to be exempt, necessarily
habituated every one to the spectacle of harshness, rudeness, and
violence, to the struggle of one indomitable will against another,
and to the alternate suffering and infliction of pain. These things,
consequently, were not as revolting even to the best and most actively
benevolent men of former days, as they are to our own; and we find
the recorded conduct of those men frequently such as would be
universally considered very unfeeling in a person of our own day.
They, however, thought less of the infliction of pain, because they
thought less of pain altogether. When we read of actions of the
Greeks and Romans, or our own ancestors, denoting callousness to
human suffering, we must not think that those who committed these
actions were as cruel as we must become before we could do the like.
The pain which they inflicted, they were in the habit of voluntarily
undergoing from slight causes; it did not appear to them as great an
evil, as it appears, and as it really is, to us, nor did it in any way
degrade their minds. In our own time, the necessity of personal collision between one person and another is, comparatively speaking,
almost at an end. All those necessary portions of the business of
society which oblige any person to be the immediate agent or ocular
witness of the infliction of pain, are delegated by common consent to
peculiar and narrow classes: to the judge, the soldier, the surgeon, the
butcher, and the executioner. To most people in easy circumstances,
any pain, except that inflicted upon the body by accident or disease,
and the more delicate and refined griefs of the imagination and the
affections, is rather a thing known of than actually experienced. This
is much more emphatically true in the more refined classes, and as
refinement advances: for it is in keeping as far as possible out of sight,
not only actual pain, but all that can be offensive or disagreeable to
the most sensitive person, that refinement consists. We may remark
too, that this is possible only by a perfection of mechanical arrangements impracticable in any but a high state of civilization. Now, most
kinds of pain and annoyance appear much more unendurable to those
who have little experience of them, than to those who have much.
The consequence is that, compared with former times, there is in the
refined classes of modern civilized communities much more of the

amiable and humane, and much less of the heroic. The heroic essentially consists in being ready, for a worthy object, to do and to suffer, but especially to do, what is painful or disagreeable: and whoever does not early learn to do this, will never be a great character. There has crept over the refined classes, over the whole class of gentlemen in England, a moral effeminacy, an inaptitude for every kind of struggle. . . .

If the source of great virtues thus dries up, great vices are placed, no doubt, under considerable restraint. The *régime* of public opinion is adverse to at least the indecorous vices: and as that restraining power gains strength, and certain classes or individuals cease to possess a virtual exemption from it, the change is highly favourable to the outward decencies of life. Nor can it be denied that the diffusion of even such knowledge as civilization naturally brings, has no slight tendency to rectify, though it be but partially, the standard of public opinion; to undermine many of those prejudices and superstitions which make mankind hate each other for things not really odious; to make them take a juster measure of the tendencies of actions, and weigh more correctly the evidence on which they condemn or applaud their fellow-creatures; to make, in short, their approbation direct itself more correctly to good actions, and their disapprobation to bad. What are the limits to this natural improvement in public opinion, when there is no other sort of cultivation going on than that which is the accompaniment of civilization, we need not at present inquire. It is enough that within those limits there is an extensive range; that as much of improvement in the general understanding, softening of the feelings, and decay of pernicious errors, as naturally attends the progress of wealth and the spread of reading, suffices to render the judgment of the public upon actions and persons, so far as evidence is before them, much more discriminating and correct.

But here presents itself another ramification of the effects of civilization, which it has often surprised us to find so little attended to. The individual becomes so lost in the crowd, that though he depends more and more upon opinion, he is apt to depend less and less upon well-grounded opinion: upon the opinion of those who know him. And established character becomes at once more difficult to gain, and more easily to be dispensed with.

It is in a small society, where everybody knows everybody, that public opinion, when well directed, exercises its most salutary influence. Take the case of a tradesman in a small country town: to every one of his customers he is long and intimately known; their opinion of him has been formed after repeated trials; if he could deceive them once, he cannot hope to go on deceiving them in the quality of his goods; he has no other customers to look to if he loses these, while, if his goods are really what they pretend to be, he may hope among so few competitors that this also will be known and recognised, and that he will acquire the character, as a man and a tradesman, which his conduct entitles him to. Far different is the case of a man setting up in business in the crowded streets of a great city. If he trust solely to the quality of his goods, to the honesty and faithfulness with which he performs what he undertakes, he may remain ten years without a customer: be he ever so honest, he is driven to cry out on the housetops that his wares are the best of wares, past, present, and to come; while if he proclaim this, true or false, with sufficient loudness to excite the curiosity of passers by, and can give his commodities a gloss, a saleable look, not easily to be seen through at a superficial glance, he may drive a thriving trade although no customer ever enter his shop twice. There has been much complaint of late years, of the growth, both in the world of trade and in that of intellect, or quackery, and especially of puffing: but nobody seems to have remarked, that these are the inevitable outgrowth of immense competition; of a state of society where any voice, not pitched in an exaggerated key, is lost in the hubbub. Success, in so crowded a field, depends not upon what a person is, but upon what he seems: mere marketable qualities become the object instead of substantial ones, and a man's labour and capital are expended less in *doing* anything than in persuading other people that he has done it. Our own age has seen this evil brought to its consummation. Quackery there always was, but it once was a test of the absence of sterling qualities: there was a proverb that good wine needed no bush. It is our own age which has seen the honest dealer driven to quackery, by hard necessity, and the certainty of being undersold by the dishonest. For the first time, arts for attracting public attention form a necessary part of the qualifications even of the deserving; and skill in these, goes farther than any other quality towards ensuring success. The same intensity of competition drives the trading public more and more to play high for success, to throw for all or nothing; and this, together with the difficulty of sure calculations in a field of commerce so widely extended, renders bankruptcy no longer disgraceful, because no longer a presumption either of dishonesty or imprudence: the discredit which it still incurs belongs to it, alas! mainly as an indication of poverty. Thus public opinion loses another of those simple criteria of desert, which, and which alone, it is capable of correctly applying; and the very cause which has rendered it omnipotent in the gross, weakens the precision and force with which its judgment is brought home to individuals.

It is not solely on the private virtues, that this growing insignificance of the individual in the mass, is productive of mischief. It corrupts the very fountain of the improvement of public opinion itself; it corrupts public teaching; it weakens the influence of the more cultivated few over the many. Literature has suffered more than any other human production by the common disease. When there were few books, and when few read at all save those who had been accustomed to read the best authors, books were written with the well-grounded expectation that they would be read carefully, and if they deserved it, would be read often. A book of sterling merit, when it came out, was sure to be heard of, and might hope to be read, by the whole reading class; it might succeed by its real excellencies, although not got up to strike at once; and even if so got up, unless it had the support of genuine merit, it fell into oblivion. The rewards were then for him who wrote *well*, not *much*; for the laborious and learned, not the crude and ill-informed writer. But now the case is reversed.

. . . .

Hence we see that literature is becoming more and more ephemeral: books, of any solidity, are actually gone by; even reviews are not now considered sufficiently light; the attention cannot sustain itself on any serious subject, even for the space of a review-article. In the more attractive kinds of literature, the novel and the magazine, although the demand has so greatly increased, the supply has so outstripped it, that even a novel is seldom a lucrative speculation. It is only under circumstances of rare attraction that a bookseller will now give anything to an author for copyright. As the difficulties of success thus progressively increase, all other ends are more and more sacrificed for the attainment of it; literature becomes more and more a mere reflection of the current sentiments, and has almost entirely abandoned its mission as an enlightener and improver of them.

There are now in this country, we may say, but two modes left, in which an individual mind can hope to produce much direct effect upon the minds and destinies of his countrymen generally; as a member of parliament, or an editor of a London newspaper. In both these capacities much may still be done by an individual, because, while the power of the collective body is very great, the number of participants in it does not admit of much increase. One of these monopolies will be opened to competition when the newspaper stamp is taken off;[4] whereby the importance of the newspaper press in the aggregate, considered as the voice of public opinion, will be much increased, and the influence of any one writer in helping to form that opinion greatly diminished. This we might regret, did we not remember to what ends that influence is now used, and is sure to be so while newspapers are a mere investment of capital for the sake of mercantile profit.

Is there, then, no remedy? Are the decay of individual energy, the weakening of the influence of superior minds over the multitude, the growth of *charlatanerie*, and the diminished efficacy of public opinion as a restraining power—are these the price we necessarily pay for the benefits of civilization, and can they only be avoided by checking the diffusion of knowledge, discouraging the spirit of combination, prohibiting improvements in the arts of life, and repressing the further increase of wealth and of production? Assuredly not. Those advantages which civilization cannot give—which in its uncorrected influence it has even a tendency to destroy—may yet coexist with civilization; and it is only when joined to civilization that they can produce their fairest fruits. All that we are in danger of losing we may preserve, all that we have lost we may regain, and bring to a perfection hitherto unknown; but not by slumbering, and leaving things to themselves, no more than by ridiculously trying our strength against their irresistible tendencies: only by establishing counter-tendencies, which may combine with those tendencies, and modify them.

The evils are, that the individual is lost and becomes impotent in the crowd, and that individual character itself becomes relaxed and

4. In the eighteenth century, the Government imposed a tax on newspapers (the Stamp Tax) in order to control the entrance of the newly developed periodical press into political questions. In addition, it imposed an advertising tax (originally one shilling per insertion). The Stamp Tax continued to grow, but it did not manage to impede the growth of circulation. In 1789, the tax went to two pence, the Advertising Tax, to three shillings. And in 1815, the Stamp Tax rose to a forbidding four pence (in itself more than a member of the poorer classes could afford for a newspaper). The tax applied, however, only to papers reporting the news, and a popular press, concentrating on opinion rather than news, grew up—led by William Cobbett and his two-penny *Political Register*. The Six Acts of 1819 attempted to crush these "opinion" newspapers, and only willingness on the part of editors to struggle and face imprisonment made it possible for the radical press to grow. Most liberals and radicals argued strenuously against the Stamp Tax, but it was not completely removed until 1855. In the period with which this volume is concerned, a radical and independent press was beginning, for the first time, to develop.

enervated. For the first evil, the remedy is, greater and more perfect combination among individuals; for the second, national institutions of education, and forms of polity, calculated to invigorate the individual character.

The former of these *desiderata*, as its attainment depends upon a change in the habits of society itself, can only be realized by degrees, as the necessity becomes felt; but circumstances are even now to a certain extent forcing it on. In Great Britain especially (which so far surpasses the rest of the world in the extent and rapidity of the accumulation of wealth) the fall of profits, consequent upon the vast increase of population and capital, is rapidly extinguishing the class of small dealers and small producers, from the impossibility of living on their diminished profits, and is throwing business of all kinds more and more into the hands of large capitalists—whether these be rich individuals, or joint stock companies formed by the aggregation of many small capitals. We are not among those who believe that this progress is tending to the complete extinction of individual competition, or that the entire productive resources of the country will within any assignable number of ages, if ever, be administered by, and for the benefit of, a general association of the whole community. But we believe that the multiplication of competitors in all branches of business and in all professions—which renders it more and more difficult to obtain success by merit alone, more and more easy to obtain it by plausible pretence—will find a limiting principle in the progress of the spirit of co-operation; that in every overcrowded department there will arise a tendency among individuals so to unite their labours or their capitals, that the purchaser or employer will have to choose, not among innumerable individuals, but among a few groups. Competition will be as active as ever, but the number of competitors will be brought within manageable bounds.

Such a spirit of co-operation is most of all wanted among the intellectual classes and professions. The amount of human labour, and labour of the most precious kind, now wasted, and wasted too in the cruelest manner, for want of combination, is incalculable. What a spectacle, for instance, does the medical profession present! One successful practitioner, burthened with more work than mortal man can perform, and which he performs so summarily that it were often better let alone;—in the surrounding streets twenty unhappy men, each of whom has been as laboriously and expensively trained as he has, to do the very same thing, and is possibly as well qualified, wasting their capabilities and starving for want of work. Under better arrangements these twenty would form a corps of subalterns marshalled under their more successful leader; who (granting him to be really the ablest physician of the set, and not merely the most successful impostor) is wasting time in physicking people for headaches and heartburns, which he might with better economy of mankind's resources turn over to his subordinates, while he employed his maturer powers and greater experience in studying and treating those more obscure and difficult cases, upon which science has not yet thrown sufficient light, and to which ordinary knowledge and abilities would not be adequate. By such means every person's capacities would be turned to account, and the highest minds being kept for the highest things, these would make progress while ordinary occasions would be no losers.

But it is in literature, above all, that a change of this sort is of most pressing urgency. There the system of individual competition has fairly worked itself out, and things cannot continue much longer as they are. Literature is a province of exertion upon which more, of the first value of human nature, depends, than upon any other; a province in which the highest and most valuable order of works, those which most contribute to form the opinions and shape the characters of subsequent ages, are, more than in any other class of productions, placed beyond the possibility of appreciation by those who form the bulk of the purchasers in the book-market; insomuch that, even in ages when these were a far less numerous and more select class than now, it was an admitted point that the only success which writers of the first order could look to was the verdict of posterity. That verdict could, in those times, be confidently expected by whoever was worthy of it; for the good judges, though few in number, were sure to read every work of merit which appeared; and as the recollection of one book was not in those days immediately obliterated by a hundred others, they remembered it, and kept alive the knowledge of it to subsequent ages. But in our day, from the immense multitude of writers (which is now not less remarkable than the multitude of readers), and from the manner in which the people of this age are obliged to read, it is difficult for what does not strike during its novelty, to strike at all: a book either misses fire altogether, or is so read as to make no permanent impression; and the best equally with the worst are forgotten by the next day.

For this there is no remedy, while the public have no guidance beyond booksellers' advertisements, and the venal paragraphs of newspapers and small periodicals, to direct them in distinguishing what is not worth reading from what is. The resource must in time be, some organized co-operation among the leading intellects of the age, whereby works of first-rate merit, of whatever class, and of whatever tendency in point of opinion, might come forth with the stamp on them, from the first, of the approval of those whose name would carry authority. There are many causes why we must wait long for such a combination; but (with enormous defects, both in plan and in execution) the Society for the Diffusion of Useful Knowledge was as considerable a step towards it as could be expected in the present state of men's minds, and in a first attempt. Literature has had in this country two ages; it must now have a third. The age of patronage, as Johnson a century ago proclaimed, is gone. The age of booksellers, it has been proclaimed in our own time, has now well nigh died out. In the first there was nothing intrinsically base, nor in the second any thing inherently independent and liberal. Each has done great things; both have had their day. The time is coming when authors, as a collective guild, must be their own patrons and their own booksellers.

These things must bide their time. But the other of the two great *disiderata*, the regeneration of individual character among our lettered and opulent classes, by the adaptation to that purpose of our institutions, and, above all, of our educational institutions, is an object of more urgency, and for which more might be immediately accomplished if the will and the understanding were not alike wanting.

This, unfortunately, is a subject on which, for the inculcation of rational views, everything is yet to be done; for, all that we would inculcate, all that we deem of vital importance, all upon which we conceive the salvation of the next and all future ages to rest, has the misfortune to be almost equally opposed to the most popular doctrines of our own time, and to the prejudices of those who cherish the empty husk of what has descended from ancient times. We are at issue equally with the admirers of Oxford and Cambridge, Eton and Westminster, and with the generality of their professed reformers. We regard the system of those institutions, as actually administered, with sentiments little short of utter abhorrence. But we do not conceive that their vices would be cured by bringing their studies into a closer connection with what it is the fashion to term "the business of the world," by dismissing the logic and classics which are still nominally taught, to substitute modern languages and experimental physics. We would have classics and logic taught far more really and deeply than at present, and we would add to them other studies more alien than any which yet exist to the "business of the world," but more

germane to the great business of every rational being, the strengthening
and enlarging of his own intellect and character. The empirical knowledge which the world demands, which is the stock in trade of money-
getting life, we would leave the world to provide for itself; content
with infusing into the youth of our country a spirit, and training them
to habits, which would ensure their acquiring such knowledge easily,
and using it well. These, we know, are not the sentiments of the
vulgar; but we believe them to be those of the best and wisest of all
parties. . . .

. . . The difficulty, the all but insuperable difficulty, which continues to oppose either . . . reform of our old academical institutions,
or the establishment of . . . new ones, as shall give us an education
capable of forming great minds, is, that in order to do so it is necessary to begin by eradicating the idea which nearly all the upholders
and nearly all the impugners of the Universities rootedly entertain, as
to the objects not merely of academical education, but of education
itself. What is this idea?—That the object of education is, not to
qualify the pupil for judging what is true or what is right, but to
provide that he shall think true what we think true, and right what
we think right—that not the spirit in which the person's opinions are
arrived at and held, but the opinions themselves, are the main point.
This is the deep-seated error, the inveterate prejudice, which the real
reformer of English education has to struggle against. Is it astonishing
that great minds are not produced, in a country where the test of a
great mind is, agreeing in the opinions of the small minds? where
every institution for spiritual culture which the country has—the
church, the universities, and almost every dissenting community—are
constituted on the following as their avowed principle: that the object
is, *not* that the individual should go forth determined and qualified
to seek truth ardently, vigorously, and disinterestedly; *not* that he be
furnished at setting out with the needful aids and facilities, the needful materials and instruments for that search, and then left to the
unshackled use of them; *not* that, by a free communion with the
thoughts and deeds of the great minds which preceded him, he be
inspired at once with the courage to dare all which truth and his
conscience require, and the modesty to weigh well the grounds of
what others think, before adopting contrary opinions of his own:
*not* this—no; but that the triumph of the system, the merit, the
excellence in the sight of God which it possesses, or which it can
impart to its pupil, is, that his speculations shall terminate in the
adoption, in words, of a particular set of opinions. That provided he

adhere to these opinions, it matters little whether he receive them from authority or from examination; and worse, that it matters little by what temptations of interest or vanity, by what voluntary or involuntary sophistication with his intellect, and deadening of his noblest feelings, that result is arrived at; that it even matters comparatively little whether to his mind the words are mere words, or the representatives of realities—in what sense he receives the favoured set of propositions, or whether he attaches to them any sense at all. Were ever great minds thus formed? Never! The few great minds which this country has produced have been formed in spite of nearly every thing which could be done to stifle their growth. And all thinkers, much above the common order, who have grown up in the Church of England, or in any other Church, have been produced in latitudinarian epochs, or while the impulse of intellectual emancipation which gave existence to the Church had not quite spent itself. The flood of burning metal which issued from the furnace flowed on a few paces before it congealed.

That the English Universities have, throughout, proceeded upon the principle, that the intellectual association of mankind must be founded upon articles, i.e., upon a promise of belief in certain opinions; that the scope of all they do is to prevail upon their pupils, by fair means or foul, to acquiesce in the opinions which are set down for them; that the abuse of the human faculties so forcibly denounced by Locke under the name of "principling" their pupils is their sole method in religion, politics, morality, or philosophy—is vicious indeed, but the vice is equally prevalent without and within their pale, and is no farther disgraceful to them than inasmuch as a better doctrine has been taught for a century past by the superior spirits, with whom in point of intelligence it was their duty to maintain themselves on a level. But, that when this object was attained they cared for no other; that if they could make churchmen, they cared not to make religious men; that if they could make Tories, whether they made patriots was indifferent to them; that if they could prevent heresy, they cared not if the price paid were stupidity—this constitutes the peculiar baseness of those bodies. Look at them. While their sectarian character, while the exclusion of all who will not sign away their freedom of thought, is contended for as if life depended upon it, there is not a trace in the system of the Universities that any other object whatever is seriously cared for. Nearly all the professorships have degenerated into sinecures. Few of the professors ever deliver a lecture. One of the few great scholars who have issued from either University for a century (and he was such before he went thither), the Rev.

Connop Thirlwall,[5] has published to the world that in his University at least, even religion—even what the Church of England terms religion —is not taught; and his dismissal, for this piece of honesty, from the tutorship of his college, is one among the daily proofs how much safer it is for twenty men to neglect their duty, than for one man to impeach them of the neglect. The only studies really encouraged are classics and mathematics; neither of them a useless study, though the last, as an instrument for fashioning the mental powers, greatly overrated; but Mr. Whewell,[6] a high authority against his own University, has just published a pamphlet, chiefly to prove that the kind of mathematical attainment by which Cambridge honours are gained, expertness in the use of the calculus, is not that kind which has any tendency to produce superiority of intellect. The mere shell and husk of the syllogistic logic at the one University, the wretchedest smattering of Locke and Paley[7] at the other, are all of moral or psychological science that is taught at either. As a means of educating the many, the Universities are absolutely null. The youth of England are not educated. . . .

Are these the places which are to send forth minds capable of maintaining a victorious struggle with the debilitating influences of the age, and strengthening the weak side of Civilization by the support of a higher Cultivation? This, however, is what we require from these institutions; or, in their default, from others which must take their place. And the very first step towards their reform, must be to unsectarianize them wholly—not by the paltry measure of allowing Dissenters to come and be taught orthodox sectarianism, but by putting an end to sectarian teaching altogether. The principle itself of dogmatic religion, dogmatic morality, dogmatic philosophy, is what

5. Connop Thirlwall (1797–1875) was a liberal clergyman who became Bishop of St. David's. A child prodigy, he was regarded by Mill as the best speaker he ever heard. His defence of an act to admit dissenters to Cambridge forced him to resign his fellowship. His humanity, brilliance, and energy earned him widespread respect.

6. William Whewell (1794–1866) was a scientist who became the respected master of Trinity College, Cambridge. After writing his *Philosophy of the Inductive Sciences*, he turned his attention almost exclusively to moral philosophy. He was responsible for valuable reform in his College.

7. William Paley (1743–1805) was for some time regarded as one of the most important theologians and moral philosophers in England. In his *Evidences of Christianity* (1794) and his *Principles of Moral and Political Philosophy* (1785), he argued the existence of God from design. He insisted (a) that God wishes his creatures to be happy, and (b) that motives must be supplied to virtue by means of a system of rewards and punishments.

requires to be rooted out; not any particular manifestation of that principle.

The very corner-stone of an education intended to form great minds must be the recognition of the principle, that the object is to call forth the greatest possible quantity of intellectual *power*, and to inspire the intensest *love of truth*; and this without a particle of regard to the results to which the exercise of that power may lead, even though it should conduct the pupil to opinions diametrically opposite to those of his teachers. We say this not because we think opinions unimportant, but precisely because of the immense importance which we attach to them; for in proportion to the degree of intellectual power and love of truth which we succeed in creating, is the certainty that (whatever may happen in any one particular instance) in the aggregate of instances true opinions will be the result; and intellectual power and practical love of truth are alike impossible where the reasoner is shown his conclusions, and informed beforehand that he is expected to arrive at them.

We are not so absurd as to propose that the teacher should not inculcate his own opinions as the true ones, and exert his utmost powers to exhibit their truth in the strongest light. To abstain from this would be to nourish the worst intellectual habit of all, that of not finding, and not looking for, certainty in anything. But the teacher himself should not be held to any creed; nor should the question be whether the opinions he inculcates are the true ones, but whether he knows all creeds, and, in enforcing his own, states the arguments for all conflicting opinions fairly. In this spirit it is that all the great subjects are taught from the chairs of the German and French Universities. The most distinguished teacher is selected, whatever be his particular views, and he consequently teaches in the spirit of free inquiry, not of dogmatic imposition. Were such the practice here, we believe that the results would greatly eclipse France and Germany, because we believe that when the restraints on free speculation and free teaching were taken off, there would be found in many individual minds among us, a vein of solid and accurate thought, as much superior in variety and sterling value to any which has yet manifested itself in those countries (except in one or two distinguished instances) as the present tone of our national mind is in many important points inferior.

. . . .

We have dwelt so long on the reforms in education necessary for regenerating the character of the higher classes, that we have not space remaining to state what changes in forms of polity and social arrangements we conceive to be required for the same purpose. We can only just indicate the leading idea. Civilization has brought about a degree of security and fixity in the possession of all advantages once acquired, which has rendered it, for the first time in Europe, possible for a rich man to lead the life of a Sybarite, and nevertheless enjoy throughout life a degree of power and consideration which could formerly be earned or retained only by personal activity. We cannot undo what civilization has done, and again stimulate the energy of the higher classes by insecurity of property, or danger of life or limb. The only adventitious motive it is in the power of society to hold out is reputation and consequence, and of this as much use as possible should be made for the encouragement of desert. The main thing which social changes can do for the improvement of the higher classes—and it is what the progress of democracy is insensibly but certainly accomplishing—is gradually to put an end to every kind of unearned distinction, and let the only road open to honour and ascendancy be that of personal qualities.

ROBERT SOUTHEY

# State and Prospects
# of the Country*

ROBERT SOUTHEY (1774–1843) WAS, WITH
Wordsworth and Coleridge, one of the Lake Poets. Like them, he
greeted the French Revolution with radical enthusiasm, but his
disillusionment with it set in rather early and he lived to turn violently against it as against almost every one of his youthful political
principles. After helping to set up the Tory *Quarterly Review* in
1809, he became poet laureate in 1813.

Perhaps the most interesting aspect of his career is his turn
to Toryism and to a defense of the political and religious establishment. From Macaulay's review of his *Sir Thomas More; or
Colloquies on the Progress and Prospects of Society*, 2 vols.
(1829), one can learn what the Whig attitude was toward Southey.
But, as one can infer from some of the things Southey says in the

* From *Quarterly Review*, XXXIX (April, 1829), 475–520.

present essay (probably written at the same time as the *Colloquies*), Macaulay was not altogether fair to him. Curiously, Macaulay's liberalism now reads in many instances like conservatism. His distrust of the state and his reliance on private property and completely free enterprize frequently contrast unfavorably with Southey's apparently greater concern for the individual and for a more equitable distribution of wealth (to be brought about with the aid of the state). Southey, moreover, shows an awareness of the inevitability of the growth in power of the lower classes which Macaulay refuses to allow him. In the present essay, his analysis of the state of society is at least as just as Macaulay's.

It should be noted that in a short review of Carlyle's *Signs of the Times* in the *Examiner* (October 4, 1829), Albany Fonblanque, that journal's radical editor, treated Southey's essay very favorably while attacking Carlyle's vigorously. The essay itself gives some idea, even in abridged form, of the *Quarterly's* slow-moving, fact-laden manner, although Southey's crispness of style is rather superior to the general *Quarterly* tone. His essay is also striking in the absence of the obvious and insistent political bias that tends to mar a large proportion of *Quarterly* contributions.

We shall now proceed to notice some of the most striking peculiarities which the social condition of the present time exhibits. In contrasting the present state of European society with the past, one of the first circumstances which strikes us is the improvement which has taken place in its communications. There was no part of the Roman policy which so effectually promoted the good of mankind, or which has transmitted such exalted ideas of the imperial grandeur, as the number and magnificence of their roads. Though constructed principally for military purposes, they were of vast utility to the districts which they traversed, and proved the most efficacious means of promoting the comfort and civilization of the conquered peoples. As an instance of the extraordinary celerity in travelling which occasionally took place in ancient times, we are informed by Pliny, that Tiberius travelled two hundred Roman miles in a day and a night, on being despatched by Augustus to console his sick brother Germanicus. But the ordinary rate of travelling even in those days was slow in comparison of what it is at present. Cicero speaks of a messenger coming from Rome to his government of Cilicia, in Asia Minor, in forty-seven days. . . . As the empire declined, the roads gradually fell into neglect; and, during the dark ages, their ruinous condition rendered communication difficult beyond what we can now find it easy to conceive. It is not easy to ascertain, from one period to another, what the state of the roads was, but they must have improved as trade increased. We know that the amelioration of them was slow; that the arts of constructing and directing them were for a long time understood very imperfectly; and that the first kingdom in which the condition of the great roads at all approached the present standard of excellence was Sweden—where, from its want of wealth, and remote situation, no such occurrence could reasonably have been looked for.

The new arrangement for the arrival and departure of mails which took place in England in 1793, greatly forwarded that improvement of the principal roads which had been going on through the eighteenth century; and, from 1793 to the present moment, the highways, crossroads, bridges, and ferries, throughout the whole extent of this country, are decidedly superior to those which are to be seen anywhere else. There are few places where the materials for making roads are so excellent and plentiful as in England; and as good roads conduce so much to the comfort as well as profit of those who use them, it is probable this is an advantage which the inhabitants of this country will for a long period possess in greater perfection than their neighbours.

A remarkable improvement has, however, recently taken place in roads and bridges all over Europe. Materials for road-making have been found where formerly they were not believed to exist, and the skill with which they are employed is surprising. Neither clay, sand, morasses, torrents, precipices, nor any other obstacles, are deemed insurmountable. . . . The traveller can nowhere direct his steps without seeing bridges building, and roads opening, widening, levelling, and repairing; and it is difficult to determine what states or districts at present show most zeal and judgment in this branch of national improvement.

The progress lately made in water conveyance is still more remarkable. The first canals known in this part of the world, were those which were formed in Italy and the Low Countries, and served in several cases both to drain the ground and for the conveyance of merchandise. France followed their example, and, by means of the canal of Languedoc, (which is now acknowledged to have failed in the objects for which it was constructed,) joined the Channel and the Mediterranean. Several others have since been completed, and others are in progress; but that country is never likely to place much dependance on its canal communications. About the middle of the last century, the commercial prosperity of this country induced it to turn its attention to canals; and from its abundance of water, and the moderate elevation of its surface, it has now pushed canal navigation beyond every other country. Austria has now got rail-roads, and it, as well as Prussia, and Sweden, possesses canals; and Russia, both within her old limits and in Poland, is zealously encouraging canals to connect her rivers, and transport the produce of the soil. The application of steam to shipping, which deserves to be ranked among the greatest discoveries, theoretical or practical, which ever were made, has, however, done more within the last twenty years to facilitate the communication between different places by water, than all the contrivances that went before it. Steam-vessels are now found permanently or occasionally plying from the bottom of the Mediterranean all round to the top of the Baltic. No place in this part of the world has derived so great advantage from the discovery of steam-vessels as England. Its situation, coal, and commerce, enable it to shoot forth these vessels in every direction; and, by means of the certainty and celerity of their passage, they have diminished its distance, and multiplied its means of access to every part of the European continent. To these accommodations in travelling must be added the variety, excellence, and cheapness, of public conveyances, and the quick and secure transmission of letters by post. The combination of these discoveries and improved arrangements has produced an ease, certainty, and rapidity of intercourse, exceeding all past experience or imagination. We are, perhaps, not far enough removed from these changes to estimate them at their proper value. Though few in number and simple in their operation, they have yet done more to change the face and multiply the comforts of society, than all the inventions which have taken place from the earliest ages to the present day.

The increase in the number of travellers, which these facilities have caused, is another of the chief peculiarities of the present period. The inhabitants of every country, but particularly of England, who travel for their improvement or gratification, have multiplied fifty or a hundred fold, and their numbers are continually augmenting. One now thinks as little of going into another kingdom, as fifty years ago he would have done of going into a neighbouring county. In time of peace, Europe may now be said to compose but one family: and

whenever a stranger of established character or extensive information
is received abroad under a hospitable roof, instead of fruitlessly endeavouring to overcome the obstacles which the want of community
of manners, language, and ideas presented in former times to all easy
and agreeable intercourse, he finds himself engaged at once in animated conversation with persons of congenial habits, on topics of
mutual and equal interest. It is scarcely possible to estimate these
advantages too highly. They break down the artificial distinctions
which separate one man from another, remove misapprehension, ignorance, and prejudice, and bind together the inhabitants of different
countries by endearing ties of recollection. On the other hand, it must
be acknowledged that the simplicity of heart and the earnestness of
kindness, which were among the most engaging characteristics of
former days, have almost wholly disappeared. "Ce peuple," said Mar-
montel of the inhabitants of his native village, "qui depuis s'est laissé
dénaturer comme tant d'autres, était alors la bonté même,"[1] and the
observation is now-a-days far more extensively true. The warm and
tender feelings which riveted each man so firmly to his kindred,
friends, and neighbours, have now lost much of their former vigour.
They were the securities which each man gave and received for the
amiableness and integrity of his conduct; and could not be forfeited
without reducing him to the condition of a stranger or an outcast. But
little of any such check on irregularity now exists. The bonds of society
now sit so loose, and connexions are contracted and dissolved with so
much ease and indifference, that persons of almost every rank may
float along the stream of life, without taking or exciting much real
interest in a single human being. Attachment to place has nearly
become extinct also. That rush of recollection, which made the tear
start and the heart throb on revisiting the scenes of infancy or youth,
is felt no more, or has degenerated into a transient and almost im-
perceptible agitation. All deep impressions are obliterated by perpetual
change of company and abode, and their place is supplied by pliability
of disposition, civility of manners, and a sort of indiscriminate and
inactive good-will towards all mankind.

   We neither desire to elevate past times, nor to depreciate the
present. The object is simply to point out one of the most universal
and essential changes in society which the age exhibits. The change
itself may be unavoidable, but its consequences are inevitable also.
They have long been felt, and now begin to be acknowledged and
deplored in the ordinary intercourse of social, as well as in the closest

   1. "These people, who have since allowed themselves to lose touch with
nature like so many others, were then goodness itself."

relations of domestic life. We possess the external means of enjoyment to a degree which our ancestors never dreamed of, but they are counterbalanced by much of that selfishness and that indifference which have been ranked among the most fatal destroyers of human happiness in the last stages of social luxury and national degeneracy.

Another characteristic of the present time is the extraordinary increase of education and knowledge which has taken place within the last forty years. That a much larger proportion of the people of Europe now read and write than formerly, is indisputable. Those parts of it which are Protestant were early distinguished from those which continued Roman Catholics, in respect of education; and they have ever since retained their superiority. But, with the exception of Spain and Portugal, it is impossible not to perceive that the means and habit of reading have of late increased everywhere. The multiplication of newspapers and periodical publications; the number of booksellers' shops; and the profusion of literary institutions and circulating libraries, are infallible indications of the extraordinary spread of education and reading. What effect this change may eventually produce on society it is too soon to decide; but we cannot help expressing an apprehension, that both education and reading have been pushed too far among the lower classes, and that, among the higher, they are not taking a very desirable direction. With regard to labourers and mechanics, experience has already proved to demonstration, that the instruction which consists merely in being taught to read and write, will by no means insure that proper regulation of the mind and conduct which some enthusiastic friends of education expected from it. To render reading and writing really useful, that moral and religious discipline which parents, pastors, masters, and relatives can alone bestow, must be superadded; and yet, strangely enough, this is a branch of education which those who are most solicitous about mere reading and writing have almost totally neglected. It will also, in all likelihood, become manifest ere long, that the labouring classes will not permanently devote a large proportion of their leisure time to the acquisition of knowledge, either by means of reading or any other sort of application. Novelty and vanity may give a temporary impulse, and the curiosity which is natural to man may prolong the exertion; but in no age or country can a large proportion of those whose lot it is to earn their bread by the sweat of their brows, be prevailed upon regularly to begin intellectual exertion when their daily task is ended. The body then requires repose; domestic concerns demand attention; and if the few hours which remain are applied to that which with all men ought to be the chief concern—the improvement of the heart—

it would probably be found the surest means of advancing the improvement of the head also. If mechanics and labourers could be persuaded to make a study of the Bible, it would be found to convey more useful knowledge, for this world as well as the next, than all the volumes and lectures which are likely to be prepared for their edification. Let it not be understood that we are hostile to the instruction of any order of society. There can be no doubt that the facilities afforded to those among the lower orders, who really have a love of learning, and the zeal which has been shown to improve them, are among the most signal peculiarities of the present day, and deserving of all commendation; but we confess we are not satisfied, that the rage for education and reading—the cheapness of books—the multitude of teachers—and the spare time created by the extension of machinery,—will produce ultimately that practical good which some philanthropists anticipate. That the present course promotes refinement, is indisputable; but whether it is to render those classes between the high and the low, which now form so large a part of the community, more able and willing to discharge the relative duties of life,— (which, after all, it is the chief business of education to teach,)—is a great deal more doubtful. Whatever opinion may be formed on this subject, the existence of an unprecedented desire of knowledge among the middling ranks cannot be called in question. It presses itself upon the notice of the traveller in the remotest districts of Europe; is discernible in the contents of the school-books of children; in the daily intercourse of life; and in the philosophical words and phrases which now form part of the language of ordinary conversation.

Let us now examine the progress which education and reading have made among the higher orders. Books are found in every house and on every table, and are resorted to on all occasions when there is nothing else to do. But, though the stream of knowledge has become wider, it has not always become deeper, or more fructifying as it flows. It must be confessed that the present age is unfavourable to severe or persevering study. The Greeks had no other literature than their own, enriched with the little they had gleaned from Egypt; the Romans had no other than that of Greece; and, till within the last fifty years, the learning of a well read person was confined to that of Greece and Rome, a few of the most celebrated Italian, French, and Spanish writers, and a limited selection from the works published in our own language. To these languages, German must now be added; and in each of them, a list of authors of celebrity might be drawn up, whose works it would require the lifetime of a laborious student to digest. In addition to this, the sciences of agriculture, natural history in all its branches, mechanics, chemistry, mineralogy, and geology, have either been created or exceedingly extended. To master all this is impossible. No perseverance can toil through such a mass, nor memory retain it. Besides this, the press teems with new systems, manuals, and abridgments, many of them excellent in their kind, and conveying knowledge more easily, simply, or compendiously than before, but certainly not exercising the powers of the mind so effectually as the original authors would do from whose works they are compiled. Feeling themselves without time or strength to embrace the vast field of knowledge now expanded before them, readers give up profound and systematic application in despair, and betake themselves to works of a subordinate character, which furnish them with what information they immediately want, or which present science or literature in a ready and familiar form. However convenient this sort of reading may be, it has little tendency to strengthen and enlarge the understanding. A person becomes a mere living dictionary, unless the acquisition of knowledge has been accompanied with that exertion of his own faculties, by which alone it can be turned to profit. It is the substitution of mere knowledge, for the power of saying and doing that which is fit, which, more than anything besides, contributes to stamp this the age of moderate men, and to render the existing state of society so unfavourable to every sort of extraordinary excellence. Every one is expected to know so much, and go so much into company, in order either to rise in the world or become known—and such encroachments are made upon every one's leisure by his family and friends—that few have the opportunity of making great acquirements, and fewer still have the power of turning these to profit. By these means, the qualifications of readers are reduced below their former standard, and they bring to the perusal of a book neither the taste nor the judgment of which authors, in former days, had the fear before their eyes. No person willingly sits down to a piece of close or continued reasoning. It is not thought necessary to be oppressed with too many facts at once, and, unless argument is conveyed in an entertaining form, it will not be listened to at all.

We should be sorry to incur the charge of depreciating the merit of daily and periodical publications, of which so much of the literature of the present day consists. Within certain limits, and under proper management, they are eminently qualified to promote information and inquiry; but when they become excessive in number, as they now certainly are; intemperate or over-bearing in their language or spirit; or support one side of a cause and oppose another, merely to serve the purposes of a party or the interests of individuals, they are among the most formidable adversaries to sound judgment and literature, which the course of events has ever raised up. Yet the desultory, defective, and often erroneous and inconsistent intelligence conveyed in these publications, constitutes half the stock of knowledge of a considerable portion of the reading world throughout Europe—and novels, books of travels, and memoirs, make up the remainder. That well written novels may occasionally form a proper recreation from severe occupations, may very safely be admitted; but, at present, even very middling performances of this class enjoy a circulation which the very best of them ought hardly to have attained; and no where more largely than in England has the spread of this idle appetite tended to interfere with the perusal of better books, and to withdraw the young of both sexes from the discharge of sacred obligations. The most popular novels either undertake to paint historical personages and occurrences, which the progress of the story, or the ignorance of the writers, often leads them to exaggerate or misrepresent; or well-known living characters are described under feigned names, in order that a sum of money may be obtained by the author for the exhibition of a friend or acquaintance, and idle curiosity be gratified by the detail of scandalous or unfounded anecdotes.

We own we are astonished that books of this sort should continue to be read with such avidity. The mind of the public cannot be more effectually abused and unsettled, than by the systematic conversion of history, private life, religion, and morality, into themes for works of fiction, and the full extent of the mischief will only be seen when it is too late. Some of the memoirs that have been lately published are highly valuable both in point of substance and composition, but the greater part of them are little superior to novels on the score of authenticity, and inferior to them in every other quality. Some of the travels which have appeared are also excellent; but by far the largest portion have been written hastily and with imperfect information, and are spun out to a length bearing no proportion to the importance of the facts communicated. It is an ungracious task to speak harshly of the taste or fashion of the day, or to find fault with the manner in which time is spent by the affluent and idle; but we are fully persuaded that it would be better for many persons never to open a book at all, than that the mind should be corrupted or enfeebled by the constant perusal of works of whatever kind which reduce it to a state of inactivity or indolent enjoyment. . . .

A change similar to that which has taken place among readers has taken place among authors also. Most of the class are so impatient to reap the reward of their labours, or so apprehensive of being supplanted by competitors for public favour, that few are willing to bestow the time and trouble which are necessary for the composition of a standard work. Nor when such works happen to be produced, do the writers of them obtain that eminent and permanent place in public estimation which they have fairly earned. In the eyes of a refined judge, the distance between a first and a second-rate performance is equal probably to that between a second-rate one and the lowest of all; but by the mass of what is called the literary world, it is scarcely seen and less regarded. Whoever, therefore, endeavours to rival the best models of ancient or modern times, must be sustained by his own inherent love of excellence, without depending upon any other support. He must be satisfied to sink in a short time into the crowd of men who have printed books, and give place to others whom novelty, absurdity, politics, or any silly caprice of that very small, and not very wise, circle which calls itself *the world*, may have raised into unmerited celebrity. This has sensibly degraded the whole body of those who write for public amusement or instruction; and literature, instead of being the noblest and purest of all pursuits, adopted in youth and adhered to in age, for its own sake, and in the generous devotion of a love and a passion, has sunk into a trade, which hundreds take up, exactly as they would cotton-spinning or coach-building. The consequence is, that books are written not in the manner that is best fitted to enlighten and amend the public, but to flatter it; and arts are employed for this purpose, to which, in better times, it would neither have been thought creditable nor necessary to resort. When a book has attained a little ephemeral notoriety, or when the private or political object has been gained, it has fully served its end; and if any one will look over the list of books which have issued from the press within the last ten or twenty years, he will be astonished how small a portion of them deserves to be rescued from that oblivion to which they are inevitably destined. We appeal to the judgment of our readers, whether we have been guilty of any mistatement or exaggeration in these observations, and whether the present state of European literature, and especially of the English, tends not rather to reduce authors to the level of ordinary readers, than to elevate readers to the level on which authors ought to stand. There is one remedy for this growing evil which may come: a time may arrive, when all classes of the community shall be able to read less and obliged to think more. The books read will then become more select; the perusal of them more profitable; and those authors who by their gifts and attainments are really qualified to improve or enlighten mankind, will be restored to that pre-eminence of which they never ought to have been dispossessed.

Another striking peculiarity of the present times is the improvement which has taken place in the outward condition of all ranks of society. Many shocking and painful disorders have almost wholly disappeared; and others, which flesh must still be heir to, have by superior treatment been rendered less violent and dangerous. The cruelties and calamities of war have been mitigated; the plague, except in Turkey and some other countries bordering on the Mediterranean, is almost unknown; and famines, arising either from cold or heat, are now of much less frequent occurrence than they formerly were. While these scourges of the human race have been removed or diminished, inventions of every sort, conducing to personal enjoyment, have been multiplied or brought to perfection. In houses, dress, furniture, horses, roads, conveyances, and every thing which can minister to the ease and gratification of mind or body; in the number and refinement of the sources of amusement; and in all articles of domestic luxury and convenience; the progress that has lately been made is unprecedented either for extent or rapidity. There is not a district to be found in any European state, in which the traveller is not struck with the taste and magnificence displayed in the architecture of public and private buildings, the multiplication and commodiousness of bathing and watering places, hotels, coffee-houses, and reading-rooms; the exquisite arrangement of gardens, grounds, and villas; and the neatness of cottages, shops, and manufactories. In England, above all, this alteration is conspicuous. In the most unfrequented corners of the country, and among all sorts and conditions of people, the comforts of life appear to be scattered with a profusion, of which in ancient or modern times there is no example. It furnishes a picture as beautiful as any which the pencil of the painter or pen of the poet can describe; and no native or foreigner can travel fifty or sixty miles along a public road, without being lost in wonder and astonishment. Towns, villages, hamlets, mansions, farm-houses, and cottages, are everywhere scattered about in the most pleasing and romantic situations; and the whole population appears to be rejoicing in unbounded fulness and repose. Would that the reality corresponded in every respect with appearances, and that these appearances were likely to last!

As a consequence of this improvement in the physical circumstances of the people, the population of Europe has increased, and is increasing, with a rapidity wholly unexampled. In a few places, such as Rome, Venice, Bologna, Genoa, Verona, Seville, Barcelona, Cadiz, Lubec, Bremen, Ghent, Bruges, Cologne, Strasburg, Nuremberg, and Augsburg, political revolutions, or the different channels which trade has taken, may have caused numbers to diminish; but these towns are exceptions to the rule, and only render more conspicuous the rate at which population generally is advancing. The capitals of Petersburg, Berlin, Vienna, Brussels, Paris, Hamburg, Frankfort, Milan, Munich, Stuttgard, Stockholm, and the territories to which they belong, are all swelling in extent and numbers. New habitations everywhere strike the eye; fresh manufactories and establishments are springing up; and if one pays a second visit to almost any district of Europe a few years after the first, the multiplication of the human species becomes almost as obvious to the eye, as the inspection of statistical tables makes it to the understanding. In this respect England has, within the last thirty or forty years, outstripped all the countries of the continent. London has increased to a size which nearly rivals the populousness of Babylon, Nineveh, Rome, Pekin, and Canton. Glasgow has advanced from 60 or 70,000 to 170,000; Liverpool from 50 or 60,000 to 160,000; and Edinburgh, Manchester, Paisley, Birmingham, Norwich, Brighton, Cork, Belfast, and some other places, have increased nearly in the same proportion. The population of England, Wales, and Scotland was, in

| | |
|---|---|
| 1801 | 10,942,646 |
| 1811 | 12,596,803 |
| 1821 | 14,391,631 |

The population of Ireland was estimated in

| | |
|---|---|
| 1672, by Sir Wm. Petty, at | 1,320,000 |
| 1695, by Capt. Smith | 1,034,102 |
| 1712, by Thomas Dobbs, Esq. | 2,099,094 |
| 1726 | 2,309,106 |
| 1754, by Hearth Money Collectors | 2,372,634 |
| 1785 | 2,845,932 |
| 1792, by Rev. Dr. Beaufort | 4,088,226 |
| 1805, by T. Newenham, Esq. | 5,395,456 |
| 1814, by incomplete Census of 1812 | 5,937,856 |
| 1821, Return under the Population Act | 6,801,827 |

By the last census then, it appears that the population of Great Britain and Ireland together amounted to 21,193,458; and, probably, at this moment, it approaches to 25,000,000. At no period in the annals of Europe has the augmentation of its numbers made such advances; and it is still advancing with undiminished activity. Whether this rate of acceleration can be or ought to be stopped; and if it cannot, what the consequences are to be; are questions upon which it is not now necessary to enter. They are not matter of speculation, but of the deepest practical concern, and, unless we are mistaken, will more and more force themselves upon the attention of every reflecting individual in the kingdom. They are here introduced merely as links in the great chain of events which have brought about that state of society in which we now live.

The last point to which we shall here advert, is the tendency of all the changes now going on in society, to approximate the lower classes to the higher. That there is an approximation he that has eyes to see and ears to hear must admit. The only question is, to what extent it has proceeded. It is obvious in dress, manners, and acquirements; and has been greatly encouraged by the improvement which has taken place in manufactures, and by the substitution of machinery for manual labour. Most mechanical employments are now carried on with so much neatness and dexterity that they scarcely affect the external garb, person, or appearance; and all articles of dress have become so cheap, that the same sort, if not the same quality, of the material of which it is composed, is within the reach of almost all ranks and conditions. The fashion of male and female dress has also become so nearly alike all over Europe, that its air and appearance alone would be an unsafe test of the rank or country of those who wear it. Nearly as great a change has taken place in manners as in dress. Distinctions between the language and address of the various classes of society will always be perceptible to refined judges, but those wide intervals with which former times were familiar, exist no longer. There are few persons of good sense, above the lowest rank, who do not speak and act, in these days, with ease and propriety. The extraordinary intercourse which has taken place, has brought about an universal polish. Persons placed far apart in wealth and station often approach each other so nearly in air and demeanour, and so difficult is it to excel in refinement, that those who take the lead in rank and fashion, occasionally seek for distinction in an entirely opposite direction. The assimilation now mentioned is seen every where, and is fully as remarkable in the other parts of Europe, as in England. The lower classes have also gained upon the higher with respect to the conveniences of life. Enter into any house, of which the occupier is above the condition of a common labourer, and the profusion of comforts, beyond what were known twenty or thirty years ago, almost exceeds belief. Through every step of the ascending series, scarcely any distinction exists between those who are more or less wealthy, than in the scale of their establishments. The same taste and elegance reign in their houses, furniture, and grounds,—at their tables,—and in every other part of their household arrangements. There is a wide distinction as to the size and number of the apartments in the house, and one still wider with respect to the number of servants, carriages and horses. But there the distinction ends, and never could persons of moderate means, by the help of taste and judgment, place themselves so nearly on a level with the most exalted.

The most essential point, however, in which the lower classes have advanced upon the higher, is that of personal acquirements. It is not in early life that the education of the lower orders is better than that of their superiors. There is generally great anxiety manifested, on the part of the higher orders, that the attainments of their sons and daughters should correspond with their station in society, and the wish of the parent is usually seconded by the talents and disposition of the child. It is before and after they have reached maturity, that the youth of the aristocracy begin to lose ground in the race of emulation. The sons of the nobility and great landed proprietors are no longer required to discharge various public functions which, in ruder periods, they were wont to do; while such numbers of them are everywhere to be seen, that their rank alone does not place them on that eminence which it formerly commanded. Their ardour is thus damped for honourable exertion on the one hand, while the blandishments of ease and luxury allure them on the other. As they advance in life, the management of property, the cares of a family, and the various duties of society, demand so much of their time, that it requires extraordinary skill and resolution to reserve any considerable portion of it at their own disposal. In the mean while, art and science are daily diminishing that proportion of the community which subsists by mere manual labour. Books, instruction, and travelling, are more within the reach of all, and those who must live by their own exertions, or whose means debar them from expensive pleasures, are induced and compelled to improve themselves with unremitting assiduity. The result of this indolence on the one hand, and diligence on the other, is, that, in nine out of ten occasions, where extraordinary proficiency or information really is demanded, the higher classes are surpassed by those who were originally their inferiors, not only in birth, but in education, and perhaps also in capacity.

This procession in society has extended to attainments of every kind, and to none more visibly than matters of state and legislation. Wherever limited governments exist, all subjects connected with the good of the community are discussed with a degree of intelligence and freedom unknown at any antecedent period. It being now the general practice to print and circulate all papers and documents relating to measures of foreign or domestic policy, official men are deprived of the exclusive means of information to which they were accustomed to attach so much importance, and all classes feel themselves more competent to think and speak upon them. Votes and resolutions of legislative bodies are therefore regarded with diminished reverence; and whenever public opinion has once been strongly expressed, it is much more likely to press legislative assemblies in it than to be driven back by them. . . . The increased influence of this *opinion* is in part, no doubt, owing to increasing kindness and consideration shewn by those who are in authority, but we are bound to confess that we ascribe it principally to the additional attention which the mass of the people insist on being paid to their interests and views. No fact in history is more striking than the indifference with which even the lives of common men were formerly regarded; but now they, and all other classes and bodies of men, have become better acquainted with their own power and consequence, and are daily bringing forward fresh pretensions. How long this approximation of the lower classes to the higher may continue or increase, or in what it may eventually issue, are questions upon which we presume to offer no opinion. The present state of society in Europe is altogether unexampled. With a marked and growing spirit of resistance on the part of the people, there is, on the part of their rulers, a want of corresponding energy and judgment to command them. To whatever good or evil this disposition may be found to lead, it will be the business of every wise and good man, in his proper sphere and on all proper occasions, to discourage the industrious classes of society from entertaining expectations of arriving at a degree of happiness and perfection which, in this state of existence, it is impossible to reach.

THOMAS BABINGTON MACAULAY

# Southey's Colloquies
# on Society*

THOMAS BABINGTON MACAULAY (1800–1859)
was one of the most successful men of his time, as a politician,
diplomat, and writer. The son of Zachary Macaulay, an Evangelical
crusader against slavery and one of the inner circle of the Clapham
Sect, he grew out of Evangelicalism without ever losing the prejudices—moral and political—that it entailed. A prodigious reader
and fine classical scholar with a memory almost photographic, he
became the star writer for the *Edinburgh Review* just when the
first generation of writers who gave that journal its fame were
beginning to lose their freshness or die out. From the point of view
of literature, his life seems a long apprenticeship for the writing of
his famous *History of England*, 5 vols. (1848–61), the last volume
of which is incomplete and appeared after his death.

* From *Edinburgh Review*, L (January, 1830), 528–65.

But Macaulay's was a life of action as well as of study. Committed absolutely to Whig principles, he became one of their finest spokesmen in Parliament. His tenure as a member of the Supreme Council of India earned him a fortune and profoundly influenced the future of India, especially with regard to education. From the point of view of history, he seems to have been excessively committed to party, naively optimistic, and rather facile as a writer.

His essay on Southey's *Colloquies* has all his representative virtues and shortcomings. His commitment to party and the resultant bias is clear. His optimism, in the face of the views of his contemporaries represented in this section, and of the subsequent catastrophes of the twentieth century, is painfully obvious. But there is a third consideration, for in this essay Macaulay usefully reminds us of something that, in our jeremiads as critics of culture, we tend to forget. The condition of England was fast improving in many ways, at least materially, and Macaulay's vision of the 1930s, if we put aside for a moment the Nazi holocaust, was remarkably prescient. If we emphasize the horrors of the industrial revolution, we must nevertheless recognize that we act as though its gains were worth the expense. It is probably true that freedom means little to people too hungry to enjoy it, and that richness of spirit is only thoroughly meaningful in a world where people have genuine options.

It would be scarcely possible for a man of Mr Southey's talents and acquirements to write two volumes so large as those before us, which should be wholly destitute of information and amusement. Yet we do not remember to have read with so little satisfaction any equal quantity of matter, written by any man of real abilities. We have, for some time past, observed with great regret the strange infatuation which leads the Poet-laureate to abandon those departments of literature in which he might excel, and to lecture the public on sciences of which he has still the very alphabet to learn. He has now, we think, done his worst. The subject which he has at last undertaken to treat is one which demands all the highest intellectual and moral qualities of a philosophical statesman,—an understanding at once comprehensive and acute,—a heart at once upright and charitable. Mr Southey brings to the task two faculties which were never, we believe, vouchsafed in measure so copious to any human being,—the faculty of believing without a reason, and the faculty of hating without a provocation.

It is, indeed, most extraordinary that a mind like Mr Southey's, —a mind richly endowed in many respects by nature, and highly cultivated by study,—a mind which has exercised considerable influence on the most enlightened generation of the most enlightened people that ever existed—should be utterly destitute of the power of discerning truth from falsehood. Yet such is the fact. Government is to Mr Southey one of the fine arts. He judges of a theory or a public measure, of a religion, a political party, a peace or a war, as men judge of a picture or a statue, by the effect produced on his imagination. A chain of associations is to him what a chain of reasoning is to other men; and what he calls his opinions, are in fact merely his tastes.

.  .  .  .

Now, in the mind of Mr Southey, reason has no place at all, as either leader or follower, as either sovereign or slave. He does not seem to know what an argument is. He never uses arguments himself. He never troubles himself to answer the arguments of his opponents. It has never occurred to him, that a man ought to be able to give some better account of the way in which he has arrived at his opinions than merely that it is his will and pleasure to hold them,—that there is a difference between assertion and demonstration,—that a rumour does not always prove a fact,—that a fact does not always prove a theory, —that two contradictory propositions cannot be undeniable truths, —that to beg the question, is not the way to settle it,—or that when an objection is raised, it ought to be met with something more convincing, than "scoundrel" and "blockhead."

It would be absurd to read the works of such a writer for political instruction. The utmost that can be expected from any system promulgated by him is that it may be splendid and affecting,—that it may suggest sublime and pleasing images. His scheme of philosophy is a mere day-dream, a poetical creation, like the Domdaniel caverns, the Swerga, or Padalon; and indeed, it bears no inconsiderable resemblance to those gorgeous visions. Like them, it has something of invention, grandeur, and brilliancy. But like them, it is grotesque and extravagant,

and perpetually violates that conventional probability which is essential
to the effect even of works of art.

.    .    .    .

We have always heard, and fully believe, that Mr Southey is
a very amiable and humane man; nor do we intend to apply to him
personally any of the remarks which we have made on the spirit of his
writings. Such are the caprices of human nature. . . . The only
opponents to whom he gives quarter are those in whom he finds
something of his own character reflected. He seems to have an in-
stinctive antipathy for calm, moderate men—for men who shun
extremes and who render reasons. He has treated Mr Owen of Lanark,[1]
for example, with infinitely more respect than he has shown to
Mr Hallam or to Dr Lingard;[2] and this for no reason that we can
discover, except that Mr Owen is more unreasonably and hopelessly
in the wrong than any speculator of our time.

Mr Southey's political system is just what we might expect from
a man who regards politics, not as a matter of science, but as a matter
of taste and feeling. All his schemes of government have been inconsistent with themselves. In his youth he was a republican; yet, as he

1. Robert Owen (1771–1858) was an extremely important figure in the
development of cooperative and socialist activities in early Victorian England.
Essentially a utopian theoretician, he was nevertheless a practical and successful
businessman. As manager and then owner of the cotton mills at New Lanark,
he established an entirely new kind of working community. He discouraged
employment of children, established schools for them, set up low-priced
company stores, and improved workers' housing and machinery. In his *New
View of Society* (1813) he laid out his main ideas. He assumed that character
is wholly created by circumstance and that labor is the natural standard of
value. He attempted to establish completely self-contained cooperative communities, including his most famous experiment at New Harmony, Indiana, in
1825. He also attempted to push legislation on labor reform through Parliament. He was not, however, a democrat, and wished to establish a paternalistic relation with workers; he was therefore left behind when the labor movement began to develop seriously. Some of his views can be found in the essay
included in this volume by William Thompson, one of his more practical
and independent disciples. It should be noted here that the liberal Whig
Macaulay is completely out of sympathy with Owen's theories of reform,
while the conservative Tory Southey is sympathetic toward them.
    2. Henry Hallam (1777–1851) was the father of Arthur Henry Hallam,
celebrated in Tennyson's *In Memoriam*. Hallam wrote an important *History
of England from the Accession of Henry VII to the Death of George II*
(1827), also from a Whig point of view. John Lingard (1771–1851) was a
Catholic historian who was concerned to demonstrate to Protestants that
Catholicism did not entail bigotry and fanaticism. His *History of England*,
which appeared between 1819 and 1830, was relatively moderate and objective, and designed not to offend Protestants.

tells us in his preface to these Colloquies, he was even then opposed to the Catholic claims. He is now a violent Ultra-Tory. Yet while he maintains, with vehemence approaching to ferocity, all the sterner and harsher parts of the Ultra-Tory theory of government, the baser and dirtier part of that theory disgusts him. Exclusion, persecution, severe punishments for libellers and demagogues, proscriptions, massacres, civil war, if necessary, rather than any concession to a discontented people,—these are the measures which he seems inclined to recommend. A severe and gloomy tyranny—crushing opposition—silencing remonstrance—drilling the minds of the people into unreasoning obedience,—has in it something of grandeur which delights his imagination. But there is nothing fine in the shabby tricks and jobs of office. And Mr Southey, accordingly, has no toleration for them. When a democrat, he did not perceive that his system led logically, and would have led practically, to the removal of religious distinctions. He now commits a similar error. He renounces the abject and paltry part of the creed of his party, without perceiving that it is also an essential part of that creed. He would have tyranny and purity together; though the most superficial observation might have shown him that there can be no tyranny without corruption.

It is high time, however, that we should proceed to the consideration of the work, which is our more immediate subject, and which, indeed, illustrates in almost every page our general remarks on Mr Southey's writings. In the preface, we are informed that the author, notwithstanding some statements to the contrary, was always opposed to the Catholic Claims. We fully believe this; both because we are sure that Mr Southey is incapable of publishing a deliberate falsehood, and because his averment is in itself probable. It is exactly what we should have expected that, even in his wildest paroxysms of democratic enthusiasm, Mr Southey would have felt no wish to see a simple remedy applied to a great practical evil; that the only measure which all the great statesmen of two generations have agreed with each other in supporting, would be the only measure which Mr Southey would have agreed with himself in opposing. He has passed from one extreme of political opinion to another, as Satan in Milton went round the globe, contriving constantly to "ride with darkness." Wherever the thickest shadow of the night may at any moment chance to fall, there is Mr Southey. It is not every body who could have so dexterously avoided blundering on the daylight in the course of a journey to the Antipodes.

Mr Southey has not been fortunate in the plan of any of his fictitious narratives. But he has never failed so conspicuously, as in the work before us; except, indeed, in the wretched Vision of Judgment. In November 1817, it seems, the Laureate was sitting over his newspaper, and meditating about the death of the Princess Charlotte. An elderly person, of very dignified aspect, makes his appearance, announces himself as a stranger from a distant country, and apologises very politely for not having provided himself with letters of introduction. Mr Southey supposes his visitor to be some American gentleman, who has come to see the lakes and the lake-poets, and accordingly proceeds to perform, with that grace which only long experience can give, all the duties which authors owe to starers. He assures his guest that some of the most agreeable visits which he has received have been from Americans, and that he knows men among them whose talents and virtues would do honour to any country. . . .

. . . The visitor informs the hospitable poet that he is not an American, but a spirit. Mr Southey, with more frankness than civility, tells him that he is a very queer one. The stranger holds out his hand. It has neither weight nor substance. Mr Southey upon this becomes more serious; his hair stands on end; and he adjures the spectre to tell him what he is, and why he comes. The ghost turns out to be Sir Thomas More. The traces of martyrdom, it seems, are worn in the other world, as stars and ribbands are worn in this. Sir Thomas shows the poet a red streak round his neck, brighter than a ruby, and informs him that Cranmer wears a suit of flames in paradise,—the right hand glove, we suppose, of peculiar brilliancy.

Sir Thomas pays but a short visit on this occasion, but promises to cultivate the new acquaintance which he has formed, and, after begging that his visit may be kept secret from Mrs Southey, vanishes into air.

The rest of the book consists of conversations between Mr Southey and the spirit about trade, currency, Catholic emancipation, periodical literature, female nunneries, butchers, snuff, book-stalls, and a hundred other subjects. Mr Southey very hospitably takes an opportunity to lionize the ghost round the lakes, and directs his attention to the most beautiful points of view. Why a spirit was to be evoked for the purpose of talking over such matters, and seeing such sights— why the vicar of the parish, a blue-stocking from London, or an American, such as Mr Southey supposed his aerial visitor to be, might not have done as well—we are unable to conceive. Sir Thomas tells Mr Southey nothing about future events, and indeed absolutely disclaims the gift of prescience. He has learned to talk modern English: he has read all the new publications, and loves a jest as well as when he jested with the executioner, though we cannot say that the quality of his wit has materially improved in Paradise. His powers of reasoning, too, are by no means in as great vigour as when he sate on the woolsack;[3] and though he boasts that he is "divested of all those passions which cloud the intellects and warp the understandings of men," we think him—we must confess—far less stoical than formerly. As to revelations, he tells Mr Southey at the outset to expect none from him. The Laureate expresses some doubts, which assuredly will not raise him in the opinion of our modern millennarians, as to the divine authority of the Apocalypse. But the ghost preserves an impenetrable silence. As far as we remember, only one hint about the employments of disembodied spirits escapes him. He encourages Mr Southey to hope that there is a Paradise Press, at which all the valuable publications of Mr Murray and Mr Colburn[4] are reprinted as regularly as at Philadelphia; and delicately insinuates, that Thalaba and the Curse of Kehama are among the number. What a contrast does this absurd fiction present to those charming narratives which Plato and Cicero prefixed to their dialogues! What cost in machinery, yet what poverty of effect! A ghost brought in to say what any man might have said! The glorified spirit of a great statesman and philosopher dawdling, like a bilious old Nabob at a watering-place, over quarterly reviews and novels—dropping in to pay long calls—making excursions in search of the picturesque! . . .

We now come to the conversations which pass between Mr Southey and Sir Thomas More, or rather between two Southeys, equally eloquent, equally angry, equally unreasonable, and equally given to talking about what they do not understand. Perhaps we could not select a better instance of the spirit which pervades the whole book than the discussion touching butchers. These persons are represented as castaways, as men whose employment hebetates the faculties and hardens the heart;—not that the poet has any scruples about the use of animal food. He acknowledges that it is for the good of the animals themselves that men should feed upon them. "Nevertheless," says he, "I cannot but acknowledge, like good old John Fox, that the sight of a slaughter-house or shambles, if it does not disturb

3. The Lord-Chancellor (the highest judicial officer) traditionally sits in the House of Lords on a woolsack.
4. John Murray (1778–1843) was a Tory publisher. He first suggested a Tory periodical to counter the Edinburgh Review, and he got, among others, Scott and Southey to join in founding the Quarterly Review in 1809. Henry Colburn (d. 1855) was an enterprising and very successful publisher. He started several journals, published the diaries of Evelyn and Pepys, and a series called Modern Standard Novelists.

this clear conviction, excites in me uneasiness and pain, as well as loathing. And that they produce a worse effect upon the persons employed in them, is a fact acknowledged by that law or custom which excludes such persons from sitting on juries upon cases of life and death."

This is a fair specimen of Mr Southey's mode of looking at all moral questions. Here is a body of men engaged in an employment, which, by his own account, is beneficial, not only to mankind, but to the very creatures on whom we feed. Yet he represents them as men who are necessarily reprobates—as men who must necessarily be reprobates, even in the most improved state of society—even, to use his own phrase, in a Christian Utopia. And what reasons are given for a judgment so directly opposed to every principle of sound and manly morality? Merely this, that he cannot abide the sight of their apparatus—that, from certain peculiar associations, he is affected with disgust when he passes by their shops. He gives, indeed, another reason; a certain law or custom, which never existed but in the imaginations of old women, and which, if it had existed, would have proved just as much against butchers as the ancient prejudice against the practice of taking interest for money, proves against the merchants of England. Is a surgeon a castaway? We believe that nurses, when they instruct children in that venerable law or custom which Mr Southey so highly approves, generally join the surgeon to the butcher. A dissecting-room would, we should think, affect the nerves of most people as much as a butcher's shambles. But the most amusing circumstance is, that Mr Southey, who detests a butcher, should look with special favour on a soldier. . . . Human blood, indeed, is by no means an object of so much loathing to Mr Southey, as the hides and paunches of cattle. In 1814, he poured forth poetical maledictions on all who talked of peace with Buonaparte. He went over the field of Waterloo,—a field, beneath which twenty thousand of the stoutest hearts that ever beat are mouldering,—and came back in an ecstasy, which he mistook for poetical inspiration. . . . We do not, however, blame Mr Southey for exulting, even a little ferociously, in the brave deeds of his countrymen, or for finding something "comely and reviving" in the bloody vengeance inflicted by an oppressed people on its oppressors. Now, surely, if we find that a man whose business is to kill Frenchmen may be humane, we may hope that means may be found to render a man humane whose business is to kill sheep. . . . Mr Southey's feeling, however, is easily explained. A butcher's knife is by no means so elegant as a sabre, and a calf does not bleed with half the grace of a poor wounded hussar.

It is in the same manner that Mr Southey appears to have formed his opinion of the manufacturing system. There is nothing which he hates so bitterly. It is, according to him, a system more tyrannical than that of the feudal ages,—a system of actual servitude,—a system which destroys the bodies and degrades the minds of those who are engaged in it. He expresses a hope that the competition of other nations may drive us out of the field; that our foreign trade may decline, and that we may thus enjoy a restoration of national sanity and strength. But he seems to think that the extermination of the whole manufacturing population would be a blessing, if the evil could be removed in no other way.

Mr Southey does not bring forward a single fact in support of these views, and, as it seems to us, there are facts which lead to a very different conclusion. In the first place, the poor-rate is very decidedly lower in the manufacturing than in the agricultural districts. If Mr Southey will look over the Parliamentary returns on this subject, he will find that the amount of parish relief required by the labourers in the different counties of England, is almost exactly in inverse proportion to the degree in which the manufacturing system has been introduced into those counties. . . .

As to the effect of the manufacturing system on the bodily health, we must beg leave to estimate it by a standard far too low and vulgar for a mind so imaginative as that of Mr Southey—the proportion of births and deaths. We know that, during the growth of this atrocious system—this new misery,—(we use the phrases of Mr Southey,)—this new enormity—this birth of a portentous age—this pest, which no man can approve whose heart is not seared, or whose understanding has not been darkened—there has been a great diminution of mortality—and that this diminution has been greater in the manufacturing towns than anywhere else. The mortality still is, as it always was, greater in towns than in the country. But the difference has diminished in an extraordinary degree. There is the best reason to believe, that the annual mortality of Manchester, about the middle of the last century, was one in twenty-eight. It is now reckoned at one in forty-five. In Glasgow and Leeds a similar improvement has taken place. Nay, the rate of mortality in those three great capitals of the manufacturing districts, is now considerably less than it was fifty years ago over England and Wales taken together—open country and all. We might with some plausibility maintain, that the people live longer because they are better fed, better lodged, better clothed, and better attended in sickness; and that these improvements are owing to that increase of national wealth which the manufacturing system has produced.

Much more might be said on this subject. But to what end? It is not from bills of mortality and statistical tables that Mr Southey has learned his political creed. He cannot stoop to study the history of the system which he abuses—to strike the balance between the good and evil which it has produced—to compare district with district, or generation with generation. We will give his own reason for his opinion—the only reason which he gives for it—in his own words:

> We remained awhile in silence, looking upon the assemblage of dwellings below. Here, and in the adjoining hamlet of Mill-beck, the effects of manufactures and of agriculture may be seen and compared. The old cottages are such as the poet and the painter equally delight in beholding. Substantially built of the native stone without mortar, dirtied with no white lime, and their long, low roofs covered with slate, if they had been raised by the magic of some indigenous Amphion's music, the materials could not have adjusted themselves more beautifully in accord with the surrounding scene; and time has still further harmonized them with weather-stains, lichens, and moss, short grasses, and short fern, and stone-plants of various kinds. The ornamented chimneys, round or square, less adorned than those which, like little turrets, crest the houses of the Portuguese peasantry; and yet not less happily suited to their place, the hedge of clipt box beneath the windows, the rose-bushes beside the door, the little patch of flower-ground, with its tall hollyocks in front; the garden beside, the bee-hives, and the orchard with its bank of daffodils and snow-drops, the earliest and the profusest in these parts, indicate in the owners some portion of ease and leisure, some regard to neatness and comfort, some sense of natural, and in-nocent, and healthful enjoyment. The new cottages of the manu-facturers are upon the manufacturing pattern—naked, and in a row.
>
> How is it, said I, that every thing which is connected with manufactures presents such features of unqualified deformity? From the largest of Mammon's temples down to the poorest hovel in which his helotry are stalled, these edifices have all one character. Time will not mellow them; nature will neither clothe nor conceal them; and they will remain always as offensive to the eye as to the mind.

Here is wisdom. Here are the principles on which nations are to be governed. Rose-bushes and poor-rates, rather than steam-engines and independence. Mortality and cottages with weather-stains, rather than health and long life with edifices which time cannot mellow. We are told, that our age has invented atrocities beyond the imagination of our fathers; that society has been brought into a state, compared with which extermination would be a blessing;—and all because the dwellings of cotton-spinners are naked and rectangular. Mr Southey has found out a way, he tells us, in which the effects of manufactures and agriculture may be compared. And what is this way? To stand on a hill, to look at a cottage and a manufactory, and to see which is the prettier. Does Mr Southey think that the body of the English peasantry live, or ever lived, in substantial and ornamented cottages, with box-hedges, flower-gardens, beehives, and orchards? If not, what is his parallel worth? We despise those *filosofastri*, who think that they serve the cause of science by depreciating literature and the fine arts. But if any thing could excuse their narrowness of mind, it would be such a book as this. It is not strange that when one enthusiast makes the picturesque the test of political good, another should feel inclined to proscribe altogether the pleasures of taste and imagination.

. . . .

There is, we have said, no consistency in Mr Southey's political system. But if there be in it any leading principle, if there be any one error which diverges more widely and variously than any other, it is that of which his theory about national works is a ramification. He conceives that the business of the magistrate is, not merely to see that the persons and property of the people are secure from attack, but that he ought to be a perfect jack-of-all-trades,—architect, engineer, schoolmaster, merchant, theologian,—a Lady Bountiful in every parish, —a Paul Pry in every house, spying, eaves-dropping, relieving, admonishing, spending our money for us, and choosing our opinions for us. His principle is, if we understand it rightly, that no man can do any thing so well for himself, as his rulers, be they who they may, can do it for him; that a government approaches nearer and nearer to perfection, in proportion as it interferes more and more with the habits and notions of individuals.

He seems to be fully convinced, that it is in the power of government to relieve the distresses under which the lower orders labour. Nay, he considers doubt on this subject as impious. We cannot refrain from quoting his argument on this subject. It is a perfect jewel of logic.

"Many thousands in your metropolis," says Sir Thomas More, "rise every morning without knowing how they are to subsist during the day; as many of them, where they are to lay their

heads at night. All men, even the vicious themselves, know that
wickedness leads to misery; but many, even among the good and
the wise, have yet to learn that misery is almost as often the
cause of wickedness."

"There are many," says Montesinos, "who know this, but
believe that it is not in the power of human institutions to prevent this misery. They see the effect, but regard the causes as
inseparable from the condition of human nature."

"As surely as God is good," replies Sir Thomas, "so surely
there is no such thing as necessary evil. For, by the religious-
mind, sickness, and pain, and death, are not to be accounted
evils."

Now, if sickness, pain, and death, are not evils, we cannot understand why it should be an evil that thousands should rise without
knowing how they are to subsist. The only evil of hunger is, that it
produces first pain, then sickness, and finally death. If it did not
produce these it would be no calamity. If these are not evils, it is no
calamity. We cannot conceive why it should be a greater impeachment
of the Divine goodness, that some men should not be able to find
food to eat, than that others should have stomachs which derive no
nourishment from food when they have eaten it. Whatever physical
effects want produces may also be produced by disease. Whatever
salutary effects disease may produce, may also be produced by want. If
poverty makes men thieves, disease and pain often sour the temper
and contract the heart.

We will propose a very plain dilemma: Either physical pain is
an evil, or it is not an evil. If it is an evil, then there is necessary evil
in the universe: If it is not, why should the poor be delivered from it?

Mr Southey entertains as exaggerated a notion of the wisdom
of governments as of their power. He speaks with the greatest disgust
of the respect now paid to public opinion. That opinion is, according
to him, to be distrusted and dreaded; its usurpation ought to be
vigorously resisted; and the practice of yielding to it is likely to ruin
the country. To maintain police is, according to him, only one of the
ends of government. Its duties are patriarchal and paternal. It ought
to consider the moral discipline of the people as its first object, to
establish a religion, to train the whole community in that religion, and
to consider all dissenters as its own enemies.

"Nothing," says Sir Thomas, "is more certain, than that
religion is the basis upon which civil government rests; that from
religion power derives its authority, laws their efficacy, and both

their zeal and sanction; and it is necessary that this religion be established as for the security of the state, and for the welfare of the people, who would otherwise be moved to and fro with every wind of doctrine. A state is secure in proportion as the people are attached to its institutions; it is, therefore, the first and plainest rule of sound policy, that the people be trained up in the way they should go. The state that neglects this prepares its own destruction; and they who train them in any other way are undermining it. Nothing in abstract science can be more certain than these positions are."

"All of which," answers Montesinos, "are nevertheless denied by our professors of the arts Babblative and Scribblative; some in the audacity of evil designs, and others in the glorious assurance of impenetrable ignorance."

The greater part of the two volumes before us is merely an amplification of these absurd paragraphs. What does Mr Southey mean by saying, that religion is demonstrably the basis of civil government? He cannot surely mean that men have no motives except those derived from religion for establishing and supporting civil government, that no temporal advantage is derived from civil government, that man would experience no temporal inconvenience from living in a state of anarchy? If he allows, as we think he must allow, that it is for the good of mankind in this world to have civil government, and that the great majority of mankind have always thought it for their good in this world to have civil government, we then have a basis for government quite distinct from religion. It is true, that the Christian religion sanctions government, as it sanctions every thing which promotes the happiness and virtue of our species. But we are at a loss to conceive in what sense religion can be said to be the basis of government, in which it is not also the basis of the practices of eating, drinking, and lighting fires in cold weather. Nothing in history is more certain than that government has existed, has received some obedience and given some protection, in times in which it derived no support from religion,—in times in which there was no religion that influenced the hearts and lives of men. It was not from dread of Tartarus, or belief in the Elysian fields, that an Athenian wished to have some institutions which might keep Orestes from filching his cloak, or Midias from breaking his head. "It is from religion," says Mr Southey, "that power derives its authority, and laws their efficacy." From what religion does our power over the Hindoos derive its authority, or the law in virtue of which we hang Brahmins its efficacy? For thousands of years civil government has existed in almost every corner of the world,—in ages of priestcraft,—in ages of fanaticism,—in ages of Epicurean indifference,—in ages of enlightened piety. However pure or impure the faith of the people might be, whether they adored a beneficent or a malignant power, whether they thought the soul mortal or immortal, they have, as soon as they ceased to be absolute savages, found out their need of civil government, and instituted it accordingly. It is as universal as the practice of cookery. Yet, it is as certain, says Mr Southey, as any thing in abstract science, that government is founded on religion. We should like to know what notion Mr Southey has of the demonstrations of abstract science. But a vague one, we suspect.

The proof proceeds. As religion is the basis of government, and as the state is secure in proportion as the people are attached to its institutions, it is therefore, says Mr Southey, the first rule of policy, that the government should train the people in the way in which they should go; and it is plain, that those who train them in any other way, are undermining the state.

Now it does not appear to us to be the first object that people should always believe in the established religion, and be attached to the established government. A religion may be false. A government may be oppressive. And whatever support government gives to false religions, or religion to oppressive governments, we consider as a clear evil.

The maxim, that governments ought to train the people in the way in which they should go, sounds well. But is there any reason for believing that a government is more likely to lead the people in the right way, than the people to fall into the right way of themselves? Have there not been governments which were blind leaders of the blind? Are there not still such governments? Can it be laid down as a general rule that the movement of political and religious truth is rather downwards from the government to the people, than upwards from the people to the government? These are questions which it is of importance to have clearly resolved. Mr. Southey declaims against public opinion, which is now, he tells us, usurping supreme power. Formerly, according to him, the laws governed; now public opinion governs. What are laws but expressions of the opinion of some class which has power over the rest of the community? By what was the world ever governed, but by the opinion of some person or persons? By what else can it ever be governed? What are all systems, religious, political, or scientific, but opinions resting on evidence more or less satisfactory? The question is not between human opinion, and some higher and more certain mode of arriving at truth, but between opinion and opinion,—between the opinion of one man and another, or of one class and another, or of one generation and another. Public opinion is not infallible; but can Mr Southey construct any institutions which shall secure to us the guidance of an infallible opinion? Can Mr Southey select any family,—any profession—any class, in short, distinguished by any plain badge from the rest of the community, whose opinion is more likely to be just than this much-abused public opinion? Would he choose the peers, for example? Or the two hundred tallest men in the country? Or the poor Knights of Windsor? Or children who are born with cawls, seventh sons of seventh sons? We cannot suppose that he would recommend popular elections; for that is merely an appeal to public opinion. And to say that society ought to be governed by the opinion of the wisest and best, though true, is useless. Whose opinion is to decide, who are the wisest and best?

Mr Southey and many other respectable people seem to think that when they have once proved the moral and religious training of the people to be a most important object, it follows, of course, that it is an object which the government ought to pursue. They forget that we have to consider, not merely the goodness of the end, but also the fitness of the means. Neither in the natural nor in the political body have all members the same office. There is surely no contradiction in saying that a certain section of the community may be quite competent to protect the persons and property of the rest, yet quite unfit to direct our opinions, or to superintend our private habits.

So strong is the interest of a ruler, to protect his subjects against all depredations and outrages except his own,—so clear and simple are the means by which this end is to be effected, that men are probably better off under the worst governments in the world, than they would be in a state of anarchy. Even when the appointment of magistrates has been left to chance, as in the Italian Republics, things have gone on better than they would have done, if there had been no magistrates at all, and every man had done what seemed right in his own eyes. But we see no reason for thinking that the opinions of the magistrate are more likely to be right than those of any other man. None of the modes by which rulers are appointed,—popular election, the accident of the lot, or the accident of birth,—afford, as far as we can perceive, much security for their being wiser than any of their neighbours. The chance of their being wiser than all their neighbours together is still smaller. Now we cannot conceive how it can be laid down, that it is the duty and the right of one class to direct the opinions of another, unless it can be proved that the former class is more likely to form just opinions than the latter.

The duties of government would be, as Mr Southey says that they are, paternal, if a government were necessarily as much superior in wisdom to a people, as the most foolish father, for a time, is to the most intelligent child, and if a government loved a people as fathers generally love their children. But there is no reason to believe, that a government will either have the paternal warmth of affection or the paternal superiority of intellect. Mr Southey might as well say, that the duties of the shoemaker are paternal, and that it is an usurpation in any man not of the craft to say that his shoes are bad, and to insist on having better. The division of labour would be no blessing, if those by whom a thing is done were to pay no attention to the opinion of those for whom it is done. The shoemaker, in the Relapse, tells Lord Foppington, that his lordship is mistaken in supposing that his shoe pinches. "It does not pinch—it cannot pinch—I know my business—and I never made a better shoe." This is the way in which Mr Southey would have a government treat a people who usurp the privilege of thinking. Nay, the shoemaker of Vanburgh has the advantage in the comparison. He contented himself with regulating his customer's shoes, about which he knew something, and did not presume to dictate about the coat and hat. But Mr Southey would have the rulers of a country prescribe opinions to the people, not only about politics, but about matters concerning which a government has no peculiar sources of information,—concerning which any man in the streets may know as much, and think as justly, as a king,—religion and morals.

Men are never so likely to settle a question rightly, as when they discuss it freely. A government can interfere in discussion, only by making it less free than it would otherwise be. Men are most likely to form just opinions, when they have no other wish than to know the truth, and are exempt from all influence, either of hope or fear. Government, as government, can bring nothing but the influence of hopes and fears to support its doctrines. It carries on controversy, not with reasons, but with threats and bribes. If it employs reasons, it does so not in virtue of any powers which belong to it as a government. Thus, instead of a contest between argument and argument, we have a contest between argument and force. Instead of a contest in which truth, from the natural constitution of the human mind, has a decided advantage over falsehood, we have a contest, in which truth can be victorious only by accident.

And what, after all, is the security which this training gives to governments? . . . Let us take that form of religion, which he holds to be the purest, the system of the Arminian[5] part of the Church of England. Let us take the form of government which he most admires and regrets, the government of England in the time of Charles the First. Would he wish to see a closer connexion between church and state than then existed? Would he wish for more powerful ecclesiastical tribunals? for a more zealous king? for a more active primate? Would he wish to see a more complete monopoly of public instruction given to the Established Church? Could any government do more to train the people in the way in which he would have them go? And in what did all this training end? The Report of the State of the Province of Canterbury, delivered by Laud to his Master at the close of 1639, represents the Church of England as in the highest and most palmy state. So effectually had the government pursued that policy which Mr Southey wishes to see revived, that there was scarcely the least appearance of dissent. Most of the bishops stated that all was well among their flocks. Seven or eight persons in the diocese of Peterborough had seemed refractory to the church, but had made ample submission. In Norfolk and Suffolk all whom there had been reason to suspect had made profession of conformity, and appeared to observe it strictly. It is confessed that there was a little difficulty in bringing some of the vulgar in Suffolk to take the sacrament at the rails in the chancel. This was the only open instance of non-conformity which the vigilant eye of Laud could find in all the dioceses of his twenty-one suffragans, on the very eve of a revolution, in which primate and church, and monarch and monarchy, were to perish together.

At which time would Mr Southey pronounce the constitution more secure; in 1639, when Laud presented this Report to Charles, or now, when thousands of meetings openly collect millions of dissenters, when designs against the tithes are openly avowed, when books attacking not only the Establishment, but the first principles of Christianity, are openly sold in the streets? The signs of discontent, he tells us, are stronger in England now than in France when the States-General met; and hence he would have us infer that a revolution like that of France may be at hand. Does he not know that the danger of states is to be estimated, not by what breaks out of the public mind, but by what stays in it? Can he conceive any thing more terrible than the situation

5. Arminianism is a kind of rationalist Christianity, which assumes that election and condemnation are determined by rational faith, and that it is possible to fall from grace. Methodist Arminians believed that "God willeth all men to be saved by speaking the truth in love" but that man might or might not accept salvation.

of a government which rules without apprehension over a people of hypocrites,—which is flattered by the press, and cursed in the inner chambers—which exults in the attachment and obedience of its subjects, and knows not that those subjects are leagued against it in a freemasonry of hatred, the sign of which is every day conveyed in the glance of ten thousand eyes, the pressure of ten thousand hands, and the tone of ten thousand voices? Profound and ingenious policy! Instead of curing the disease, to remove those symptoms by which alone its nature can be known! To leave the serpent his deadly sting, and deprive him only of his warning rattle!

When the people whom Charles had so assiduously trained in the good way had rewarded his paternal care by cutting off his head, a new kind of training came into fashion. Another government arose, which, like the former, considered religion as its surest basis, and the religious discipline of the people as its first duty. Sanguinary laws were enacted against libertinism; profane pictures were burned; drapery was put on indecorous statues; the theatres were shut up; fast-days were numerous; and the Parliament resolved that no person should be admitted into any public employment, unless the House should be first satisfied of his vital godliness. We know what was the end of this training. We know that it ended in impiety, in filthy and heartless sensuality, in the dissolution of all ties of honour and morality. We know that at this very day scriptural phrases, scriptural names, perhaps some scriptural doctrines, excite disgust and ridicule, solely because they are associated with the austerity of that period.

Thus has the experiment of training the people in established forms of religion been twice tried in England on a large scale; once by Charles and Laud, and once by the Puritans. The High Tories of our time still entertain many of the feelings and opinions of Charles and Laud, though in a mitigated form; nor is it difficult to see that the heirs of the Puritans are still amongst us. It would be desirable that each of these parties should remember how little advantage or honour it formerly derived from the closest alliance with power,—that it fell by the support of rulers, and rose by their opposition,—that of the two systems, that in which the people were at any time being drilled, was always at that time the unpopular system,—that the training of the High Church ended in the reign of the Puritans, and the training of the Puritans in the reign of the harlots.

This was quite natural. Nothing is so galling and detestable to a people not broken in from the birth, as a paternal, or, in other words, a meddling government,—a government which tells them what to read, and say, and eat, and drink, and wear. Our fathers could not bear it two hundred years ago; and we are not more patient than they. Mr Southey thinks that the yoke of the church is dropping off, because it is loose. We feel convinced that it is borne only because it is easy, and that, in the instant in which an attempt is made to tighten it, it will be flung away. It will be neither the first nor the strongest yoke that has been broken asunder and trampled under foot in the day of the vengeance of England.

How far Mr Southey would have the government carry its measures for training the people in the doctrines of the church, we are unable to discover. In one passage Sir Thomas More asks with great vehemence,

"Is it possible that your laws should suffer the unbelievers to exist as a party?"

"Vetitum est adeo sceleris nihil?"[6]

Montesinos answers. "They avow themselves in defiance of the laws. The fashionable doctrine which the press at this time maintains is, that this is a matter in which the laws ought not to interfere, every man having a right, both to form what opinion he pleases upon religious subjects, and to promulgate that opinion."

It is clear, therefore, that Mr Southey would not give full and perfect toleration to infidelity. In another passage, however, he observes, with some truth, though too sweepingly, that "any degree of intolerance short of that full extent which the Papal Church exercises where it has the power, acts upon the opinions which it is intended to suppress, like pruning upon vigorous plants; they grow the stronger for it." These two passages, put together, would lead us to the conclusion that, in Mr Southey's opinion, the utmost severity ever employed by the Roman Catholic Church in the days of its greatest power ought to be employed against unbelievers in England; in plain words, that Carlile[7] and his shopmen ought to be burned in Smithfield, and that every person who, when called upon, should decline to make a solemn profession of Christianity, ought to suffer the same fate. We do not, however, believe that Mr Southey would recommend such a course, though his language would, in the case of any other writer, justify us in supposing this to be his meaning. His opinions form no system at all. He never sees, at one glance, more of a question than will furnish

6. "Is there no crime forbidden?"
7. Richard Carlile (1790–1843), a brave and frequently imprisoned freethinker, was influenced deeply by Paine's *Rights of Man*. He published and sold many journals, pamphlets, and books which were outspokenly opposed to the government and to religion. He kept going to prison on principle, and frequently edited antigovernment journals from his cell.

matter for one flowing and well-turned sentence; so that it would be
the height of unfairness to charge him personally with holding a
doctrine, merely because that doctrine is deducible, though by the
closest and most accurate reasoning, from the premises which he has
laid down. We are, therefore, left completely in the dark as to Mr
Southey's opinions about toleration. Immediately after censuring the
government for not punishing infidels, he proceeds to discuss the
question of the Catholic disabilities—now, thank God, removed—and
defends them on the ground that the Catholic doctrines tend to
persecution, and that the Catholics persecuted when they had power.

"They must persecute," says he, "if they believe their own creed,
for conscience-sake; and if they do not believe it, they must persecute
for policy; because it is only by intolerance that so corrupt and injurious a system can be upheld."

That unbelievers should not be persecuted, is an instance of
national depravity at which the glorified spirits stand aghast. Yet a sect
of Christians is to be excluded from power, because those who
formerly held the same opinions were guilty of persecution. We have
said that we do not very well know what Mr Southey's opinion about
toleration is. But, on the whole, we take it to be this, that everybody
is to tolerate him, and that he is to tolerate nobody.

We will not be deterred by any fear of misrepresentation from
expressing our hearty approbation of the mild, wise, and eminently
Christian manner, in which the Church and the Government have
lately acted with respect to blasphemous publications. We praise them
for not having thought it necessary to encircle a religion pure, merciful,
and philosophical,—a religion to the evidences of which the highest
intellects have yielded,—with the defences of a false and bloody superstition. The ark of God was never taken till it was surrounded by the
arms of earthly defenders. In captivity, its sanctity was sufficient to
vindicate it from insult, and to lay the hostile fiend prostrate on the
threshold of his own temple. The real security of Christianity is to
be found in its benevolent morality, in its exquisite adaptation to the
human heart, in the facility with which its scheme accommodates
itself to the capacity of every human intellect, in the consolation
which it bears to the house of mourning, in the light with which it
brightens the great mystery of the grave. To such a system it can bring
no addition of dignity or of strength, that it is part and parcel of the
common law. It is not now for the first time left to rely on the force
of its own evidences, and the attractions of it own beauty. . . .
The whole history of the Christian Religion shows, that she is in far
greater danger of being corrupted by the alliance of power, than of
being crushed by its opposition. Those who thrust temporal sovereignty

upon her, treat her as their prototypes treated her author. They bow the knee, and spit upon her; they cry Hail! and smite her on the cheek; they put a sceptre into her hand, but it is a fragile reed; they crown her, but it is with thorns; they cover with purple the wounds which their own hands have inflicted on her; and inscribe magnificent titles over the cross on which they have fixed her to perish in ignominy and pain.

The general view which Mr Southey takes of the prospects of society is very gloomy; but we comfort ourselves with the consideration that Mr Southey is no prophet. He foretold, we remember, on the very eve of the abolition of the Test and Corporation Acts, that these hateful laws were immortal, and that pious minds would long be gratified by seeing the most solemn religious rite of the Church profaned, for the purpose of upholding her political supremacy. In the book before us, he says that Catholics cannot possibly be admitted into Parliament until those whom Johnson called "the bottomless Whigs," come into power. While the book was in the press, the prophecy was falsified, and a Tory of the Tories, Mr Southey's own favourite hero, won and wore that noblest wreath, "*Ob cives servatos.*"[8]

The signs of the times, Mr Southey tells us, are very threatening. His fears for the country would decidedly preponderate over his hopes, but for his firm reliance on the mercy of God. Now, as we know that God has once suffered the civilised world to be overrun by savages, and the Christian religion to be corrupted by doctrines which made it, for some ages, almost as bad as Paganism, we cannot think it inconsistent with his attributes that similar calamities should again befal mankind.

We look, however, on the state of the world, and of this kingdom in particular, with much greater satisfaction, and with better hopes. Mr Southey speaks with contempt of those who think the savage state happier than the social. On this subject, he says, Rousseau never imposed on him even in his youth. But he conceives that a community which has advanced a little way in civilisation is happier than one which has made greater progress. The Britons in the time of Caesar were happier, he suspects, than the English of the nineteenth century. On the whole, he selects the generation which preceded the Reformation as that in which the people of this country were better off than at any time before or since.

This opinion rests on nothing, as far as we can see, except his

8. "Because of the citizens he had served." Macaulay refers here to the great Duke of Wellington, Arthur Wellesley (1769–1852), who became a hero during the Napoleonic wars and who was Prime Minister in 1829 when Catholic Emancipation passed Parliament.

own individual associations. He is a man of letters; and a life destitute
of literary pleasures seems insipid to him. He abhors the spirit of the
present generation, the severity of its studies, the boldness of its
enquiries, and the disdain with which it regards some old prejudices
by which his own mind is held in bondage. He dislikes an utterly
unenlightened age; he dislikes an investigating and reforming age.
The first twenty years of the sixteenth century would have exactly
suited him. They furnished just the quality of intellectual excitement
which he requires. The learned few read and wrote largely. A scholar
was held in high estimation; but the rabble did not presume to think;
and even the most enquiring and independent of the educated classes
paid more reverence to authority, and less to reason, than is usual in
our time. This is a state of things in which Mr Southey would have
found himself quite comfortable; and, accordingly, he pronounces it
the happiest state of things ever known in the world.

The savages were wretched, says Mr Southey; but the people in
the time of Sir Thomas More were happier than either they or we.
Now, we think it quite certain that we have the advantage over the
contemporaries of Sir Thomas More, in every point in which they
had any advantage over savages.

Mr Southey does not even pretend to maintain that the people
in the sixteenth century were better lodged or clothed than at present.
He seems to admit that in these respects there has been some little
improvement. It is indeed a matter about which scarcely any doubt
can exist in the most perverse mind, that the improvements of machinery have lowered the price of manufactured articles, and have
brought within the reach of the poorest some conveniencies which Sir
Thomas More or his master could not have obtained at any price.

The labouring classes, however, were, according to Mr Southey,
better fed three hundred years ago than at present. We believe that he
is completely in error on this point. The condition of servants in
noble and wealthy families, and of scholars at the Universities, must
surely have been better in those times than that of common day-
labourers; and we are sure that it was not better than that of our
workhouse paupers. From the household book of the Northumberland
family, we find that in one of the greatest establishments of the
kingdom the servants lived almost entirely on salt meat, without any
bread at all. A more unwholesome diet can scarcely be conceived. In
the reign of Edward the Sixth, the state of the students at Cambridge
is described to us, on the very best authority, as most wretched. Many
of them dined on pottage made of a farthing's worth of beef with a
little salt and oatmeal, and literally nothing else. This account we have
from a contemporary master of St Johns. Our parish poor now eat

wheaten bread. In the sixteenth century the labourer was glad to get barley, and was often forced to content himself with poorer fare. In Harrison's introduction to Holinshed we have an account of the state of our working population in the "golden days," as Mr Southey calls them, of good Queen Bess. "The gentilitie," says he, "commonly provides themselves sufficiently of wheat for their own tables, whylest their household and poore neighbours in some shires are inforced to content themselves with rice or barleie; yea, and in time of dearth, many with bread made eyther of beanes, peason, or otes, or of altogether, and some acornes among. I will not say that this extremity is oft so well to be seen in time of plentie as of dearth; but if I should I could easily bring my trial: for albeit there be much more grounde eared nowe almost in everye place then hath beene of late yeares, yet such a price of corne continueth in eache towne and markete, without any just cause, that the artificer and poore labouring man is not able to reach unto it, but is driven to content himself with horse-corne; I mean beanes, peason, otes, tares, and lintelles." We should like to see what the effect would be of putting any parish in England now on allowance of "horse-corne." The helotry of Mammon are not, in our day, so easily enforced to content themselves as the peasantry of that happy period, as Mr Southey considers it, which elapsed between the fall of the feudal and the rise of the commercial tyranny.

"The people," says Mr Southey, "are worse fed than when they were fishers." And yet in another place he complains that they will not eat fish. "They have contracted," says he, "I know not how, some obstinate prejudice against a kind of food at once wholesome and delicate, and everywhere to be obtained cheaply and in abundance, were the demand for it as great as it ought to be." It is true that the lower orders have an obstinate prejudice against fish. But hunger has no such obstinate prejudices. If what was formerly a common diet is now eaten only in times of severe pressure, the inference is plain. The people must be fed with what they at least think better food than that of their ancestors.

The advice and medicine which the poorest labourer can now obtain, in disease or after an accident, is far superior to what Henry the Eighth could have commanded. Scarcely any part of the country is out of the reach of practitioners, who are probably not so far inferior to Sir Henry Halford as they are superior to Sir Anthony Denny.[9] That there has been a great improvement in this respect Mr Southey allows. Indeed he could not well have denied it. "But," says he,

9. Sir Henry Halford (1766–1844) was physician extraordinary to the king in 1795 and the head of London medical practice. Sir Anthony Denny probably is the zealous promoter of the Reformation (1501–49).

"the evils for which these sciences are the palliative, have increased since the time of the Druids, in a proportion that heavily overweighs the benefit of improved therapeutics." We know nothing either of the diseases or the remedies of the Druids. But we are quite sure that the improvement of medicine has far more than kept pace with the increase of disease during the last three centuries. This is proved by the best possible evidence. The term of human life is decidedly longer in England than in any former age, respecting which we possess any information on which we can rely. All the rants in the world about picturesque cottages and temples of Mammon will not shake this argument. No test of the state of society can be named so decisive as that which is furnished by bills of mortality. That the lives of the people of this country have been gradually lengthening during the course of several generations, is as certain as any fact in statistics, and that the lives of men should become longer and longer, while their physical condition, during life, is becoming worse and worse, is utterly incredible.

Let our readers think over these circumstances. Let them take into the account the sweating sickness and the plague. Let them take into the account that fearful disease which first made its appearance in the generation to which Mr Southey assigns the palm of felicity, and raged through Europe with a fury at which the physician stood aghast, and before which the people were swept away by thousands. Let them consider the state of the northern counties, constantly the scene of robberies, rapes, massacres, and conflagrations. Let them add to all this the fact that seventy-two thousand persons suffered death by the hands of the executioner during the reign of Henry the Eighth, and judge between the nineteenth and the sixteenth century.

We do not say that the lower orders in England do not suffer severe hardships. But, in spite of Mr Southey's assertions, and in spite of the assertions of a class of politicians, who, differing from Mr Southey in every other point, agree with him in this, we are inclined to doubt whether they really suffer greater physical distress than the labouring classes of the most flourishing countries of the Continent.

It will scarcely be maintained that the lazzaroni who sleep under the porticos of Naples, or the beggars who besiege the convents of Spain, are in a happier situation than the English commonalty. The distress which has lately been experienced in the northern part of Germany, one of the best governed and most prosperous districts of Europe, surpasses, if we have been correctly informed, any thing which has of late years been known among us. In Norway and Sweden the peasantry are constantly compelled to mix bark with their bread, and even this expedient has not always preserved whole families and neighbourhoods from perishing together of famine. An experiment has lately been tried in the kingdom of the Netherlands, which has been cited to prove the possibility of establishing agricultural colonies on the waste-lands of England; but which proves to our minds nothing so clearly as this, that the rate of subsistence to which the labouring classes are reduced in the Netherlands is miserably low, and very far inferior to that of the English paupers. No distress which the people here have endured for centuries, approaches to that which has been felt by the French in our own time. The beginning of the year 1817, was a time of great distress in this island. But the state of the lowest classes here was luxury compared with that of the people of France. We find in Magendie's *Journal de Physiologe Expermentale*, a paper on a point of physiology connected with the distress of that season. It appears that the inhabitants of six departments, Aix, Jura, Doubs, Haute Saone, Vosges, and Saone et Loire, were reduced first to oatmeal and potatoes, and at last to nettles, bean-stalks, and other kinds of herbage fit only for cattle; that when the next harvest enabled them to eat barley-bread, many of them died from intemperate indulgence in what they thought an exquisite repast; and that a dropsy of a peculiar description was produced by the hard fare of the year. Dead bodies were found on the rocks and in the fields. A single surgeon dissected six of these, and found the stomach shrunk, and filled with the unwholesome aliment which hunger had driven men to share with beasts. Such extremity of distress as this is never heard of in England, or even in Ireland. We are, on the whole, inclined to think, though we would speak with diffidence on a point on which it would be rash to pronounce a positive judgment without a much longer and closer investigation than we have bestowed upon it, that the labouring classes of this island, though they have their grievances and distresses, some produced by their own improvidence, some by the errors of their rulers, are on the whole better off as to physical comforts, than the inhabitants of any equally extensive district of the old world. On this very account, suffering is more acutely felt and more loudly bewailed here than elsewhere. We must take into the account the liberty of discussion, and the strong interest which the opponents of a ministry always have to exaggerate the extent of the public disasters. There are many parts of Europe in which the people quietly endure distress that here would shake the foundations of the state,—in which the inhabitants of a whole province turn out to eat grass with less clamour than one Spitalfields weaver would make here, if the overseers were to put him on barley-bread. In those new countries in which a civilized population has at its command a boundless extent of the richest soil, the condition of the labourer is probably happier than in any society which has lasted for many centuries. But in the old world we must confess ourselves unable to find any satisfactory record of any great nation, past or present, in which the working classes have been in a more comfortable situation than in England during the last thirty years. When this island was thinly peopled, it was barbarous. There was little capital; and that little was insecure. It is now the richest and the most highly civilized spot in the world; but the population is dense. Thus we have never known that golden age, which the lower orders in the United States are now enjoying. We have never known an age of liberty, of order, and of education, an age in which the mechanical sciences were carried to a great height, yet in which the people were not sufficiently numerous to cultivate even the most fertile valleys. But, when we compare our own condition with that of our ancestors, we think it clear that the advantages arising from the progress of civilisation have far more than counterbalanced the disadvantages arising from the progress of population. While our numbers have increased tenfold, our wealth has increased a hundred fold. Though there are so many more people to share the wealth now existing in the country than there were in the sixteenth century, it seems certain, that a greater share falls to almost every individual, than fell to the share of any of the corresponding class in the sixteenth century. The King keeps a more splendid court. The establishments of the nobles are more magnificent. The esquires are richer, the merchants are richer, the shopkeepers are richer. The serving-man, the artisan, and the husbandman, have a more copious and palatable supply of food, better clothing, and better furniture. This is no reason for tolerating abuses, or for neglecting any means of ameliorating the condition of our poorer countrymen. But it is a reason against telling them, as some of our philosophers are constantly telling them, that they are the most wretched people who ever existed on the face of the earth.

We have already adverted to Mr Southey's amusing doctrine about national wealth. A state, says he, cannot be too rich; but a people may be too rich. His reason for thinking this, is extremely curious.

A people may be too rich, because it is the tendency of the commercial, and more especially, of the manufacturing system, to collect wealth rather than to diffuse it. Where wealth is necessarily employed in any of the speculations of trade, its increase is in proportion to its amount. Great capitalists become like pikes in a fish-pond, who devour the weaker fish; and it is but too certain, that the poverty of one part of the people seems to increase in the same ratio as the riches of another. There are examples of this in history. In Portugal, when the high tide of wealth flowed in from the conquests in Africa and the East, the effect of that great influx was not more visible in the augmented splendour of the court, and the luxury of the higher ranks, than in the distress of the people.

Mr Southey's instance is not a very fortunate one. The wealth which did so little for the Portuguese was not the fruit, either of manufactures or of commerce carried on by private individuals. It was the wealth, not of the people, but of the government and its creatures, of those who, as Mr. Southey thinks, can never be too rich. The fact is, that Mr Southey's proposition is opposed to all history, and to the phenomena which surround us on every side. England is the richest country in Europe, the most commercial, and the most manufacturing. Russia and Poland are the poorest countries in Europe. They have scarcely any trade, and none but the rudest manufactures. Is wealth more diffused in Russia and Poland than in England? There are individuals in Russia and Poland, whose incomes are probably equal to those of our richest countrymen. It may be doubted, whether there are not, in those countries, as many fortunes of eighty thousand a-year, as here. But are there as many fortunes of five thousand a-year, or of one thousand a-year? There are parishes in England, which contain more people of between five hundred and three thousand pounds a-year, than could be found in all the dominions of the Emperor Nicholas. The neat and commodious houses which have been built in London and its vicinity, for people of this class, within the last thirty years, would of themselves form a city larger than the capitals of some European kingdoms. And this is the state of society in which the great proprietors have devoured the smaller!

The cure which Mr Southey thinks that he has discovered is worthy of the sagacity which he has shown in detecting the evil. The calamities arising from the collection of wealth in the hands of a few capitalists are to be remedied by collecting it in the hands of one great capitalist, who has no conceivable motive to use it better than other capitalists,—the all-devouring state.

It is not strange that, differing so widely from Mr Southey as to the past progress of society, we should differ from him also as to its probable destiny. He thinks, that to all outward appearance, the country is hastening to destruction; but he relies firmly on the goodness of God. We do not see either the piety, or the rationality, of thus confidently expecting that the Supreme Being will interfere to disturb the common succession of causes and effects. We, too, rely on his goodness,—on his goodness as manifested, not in extraordinary inter-positions, but in those general laws which it has pleased him to establish in the physical and in the moral world. We rely on the natural tendency of the human intellect to truth, and on the natural tendency of society to improvement. We know no well-authenticated instance of a people which has decidedly retrograded in civilisation and prosperity, except from the influence of violent and terrible calamities,—such as those which laid the Roman Empire in ruins, or those which, about the beginning of the sixteenth century, desolated Italy. We know of no country which, at the end of fifty years of peace and tolerably good government, has been less prosperous than at the beginning of that period. The political importance of a state may decline, as the balance of power is disturbed by the introduction of new forces. Thus the influence of Holland and of Spain is much diminished. But are Holland and Spain poorer than formerly? We doubt it. Other countries have outrun them. But we suspect that they have been positively, though not relatively, advancing. We suspect that Holland is richer than when she sent her navies up the Thames,— that Spain is richer than when a French king was brought captive to the footstool of Charles the Fifth.

History is full of the signs of this natural progress of society. We see in almost every part of the annals of mankind how the industry of individuals, struggling up against wars, taxes, famines, conflagra-tions, mischievous prohibitions, and more mischievous protections, creates faster than government can squander, and repairs whatever invaders can destroy. We see the capital of nations increasing, and all the arts of life approaching nearer and nearer to perfection, in spite of the grossest corruption and the wildest profusion on the part of rulers.

The present moment is one of great distress. But how small will that distress appear when we think over the history of the last forty years;—a war, compared with which, all other wars sink into in-significance;—taxation, such as the most heavily taxed people of former times could not have conceived;—a debt larger than all the public debts that ever existed in the world added together;—the food of the people studiously rendered dear;—the currency imprudently debased, and imprudently restored. Yet is the country poorer than in 1790? We fully believe that, in spite of all the misgovernment of her rulers, she has been almost constantly becoming richer and richer.

Now and then there has been a stoppage, now and then a short retrogression; but as to the general tendency there can be no doubt. A single breaker may recede, but the tide is evidently coming in.

If we were to prophesy that in the year 1930, a population of fifty millions, better fed, clad, and lodged than the English of our time, will cover these islands,—that Sussex and Huntingdonshire will be wealthier than the wealthiest parts of the West-Riding of Yorkshire now are,—that cultivation, rich as that of a flower-garden, will be carried up to the very tops of Ben Nevis and Helvellyn,—that machines, constructed on principles yet undiscovered, will be in every house,—that there will be no highways but rail-roads, no travelling but by steam,—that our debt, vast as it seems to us, will appear to our great-grandchildren a trifling encumbrance, which might easily be paid off in a year or two,—many people would think us insane. We prophesy nothing; but this we say—If any person had told the Parliament which met in perplexity and terror after the crash in 1720, that in 1830 the wealth of England would surpass all their wildest dreams—that the annual revenue would equal the principal of that debt which they considered as an intolerable burden—that for one man of L.10,000 then living, there would be five men of L.50,000; that London would be twice as large and twice as populous, and that nevertheless the mortality would have diminished to one-half what it then was,—that the postoffice would bring more into the exchequer than the excise and customs had brought in together under Charles II,—that stagecoaches would run from London to York in twenty-four hours—that men would sail without wind, and would be beginning to ride without horses—our ancestors would have given as much credit to the prediction as they gave to Gulliver's Travels. Yet the prediction would have been true; and they would have perceived that it was not altogether absurd, if they had considered that the country was then raising every year a sum which would have purchased the fee-simple of the revenue of the Plantagenets—ten times what supported the government of Elizabeth—three times what, in the time of Oliver Cromwell, had been thought intolerably oppressive. To almost all men the state of things under which they have been used to live seems to be the necessary state of things. We have heard it said, that five per cent is the natural interest of money, that twelve is the natural number of a jury, that forty shillings is the natural qualification of a county voter. Hence it is, that though, in every age, every body knows that up to his own time progressive improvement has been taking place, nobody seems to reckon on any improvement during the next generation. We cannot absolutely prove that those are in error who tell us that society has reached a turning point—that we have seen our best days. But so said all who came before us, and with just as much apparent reason. . . . On what principle is it, that when we see nothing but improvement behind us, we are to expect nothing but deterioration before us?

It is not by the intermeddling of Mr Southey's idol—the omniscient and omnipotent State—but by the prudence and energy of the people, that England has hitherto been carried forward in civilisation; and it is to the same prudence and the same energy that we now look with comfort and good hope. Our rulers will best promote the improvement of the people by strictly confining themselves to their own legitimate duties—by leaving capital to find its most lucrative course, commodities their fair price, industry and intelligence their natural reward, idleness and folly their natural punishment—by maintaining peace, by defending property, by diminishing the price of law, and by observing strict economy in every department of the state. Let the Government do this—the people will assuredly do the rest.

# II

# THE MARCH OF MIND

Liberty, in our opinion, is but a modern invention (the growth of books and printing), and whether new or old, is not the less desirable.

WILLIAM HAZLITT,
*The Spirit of the Age*

THOMAS LOVE PEACOCK

# Crotchet Castle*

THOMAS LOVE PEACOCK (1785–1866), A CLOSE
friend of Shelley and a thoroughly literary man, gave up his career
as a poet (a decidedly minor poet) upon entering the East India
Company in 1819. His literary work after that date consists largely
in satirical-romantic novels, of which Crotchet Castle (1831) is
one, though not at all the best. In these novels, he was interested
in ideas rather than in people. But despite the clarity with which
his characters express ideas, despite his known opposition to tyranny and his decidedly anticlerical bent, it is difficult to determine
from his books precisely what his other personal views were.

The second chapter of Crotchet Castle is specifically concerned
with the contemporary increase in the diffusion of knowledge; but
it is not certain that Peacock accepts unqualified the views of the
cynical Dr. Folliott. Folliott expresses with considerable satirical

* From Thomas Love Peacock, Crochet Castle, First Edition (London:
T. Hookham, 1831), pp. 19–38.

force an attitude central among the well-educated and conservative toward the spread of knowledge. But since Peacock was both intelligent and opposed to tyranny, the book will suggest that blind and ignorant reactionaries were not alone in feeling that to spread knowledge might also be to dissipate it, and that to educate people in technical matters that they are unequipped to use or pursue might even be dangerous.

## THE MARCH OF MIND

Quoth Ralpho: nothing but the abuse
Of human learning you produce.

BUTLER

"GOD bless my soul, sir!" exclaimed the Reverend Doctor Folliott, bursting, one fine May morning, into the breakfast-room at Crotchet Castle, I am out of all patience with this march of mind. Here has my house been nearly burned down, by my cook taking it into her head to study Hydrostatics, in a six-penny tract, published by the Steam Intellect Society, and written by a learned friend[1] who is for doing all the world's business as well as his own, and is equally well qualified to handle every branch of human knowledge. I have a great abomination of this learned friend; as author, lawyer, and politician, he is *triformis*, like Hecate: and in every one of his three forms he is *bifrons*,[2] like Janus; the true Mr. Facing-both-ways of Vanity Fair. My cook must read his rubbish in bed; and as might naturally be expected, she dropped suddenly fast asleep, overturned the candle, and set the curtains in a blaze. Luckily, the footman went into the room at the moment, in time to tear down the curtains and throw them into the chimney, and a pitcher of water on her nightcap extinguished her wick: she is a greasy subject, and would have burned like a short mould."

The reverend gentleman exhaled his grievance without looking

1. Probably Lord Brougham.
2. "Three-formed" and "two-faced."

to the right or to the left; at length, turning on his pivot, he perceived that the room was full of company, consisting of young Crotchet and some visitors whom he had brought from London. The Reverend Doctor Folliott was introduced to Mr. Mac Quedy, the economist; Mr. Skionar,[3] the transcendental poet; Mr. Firedamp, the meteorologist; and Lord Bossnowl, son of the Earl of Foolincourt, and member for the borough of Rogueingrain.

The divine took his seat at the breakfast-table, and began to compose his spirits by the gentle sedative of a large cup of tea, the demulcent of a well-buttered muffin, and the tonic of a small lobster.

THE REV. DR. FOLLIOTT: You are a man of taste, Mr. Crotchet. A man of taste is seen at once in the array of his breakfast-table. It is the foot of Hercules, the far-shining face of the great work, according to Pindar's doctrine: ἀρχομένου ἔργου πρόσωπον χρὴ θέμεν τηλαυγές.[4] The breakfast is the πρόσωπον of the great work of the day. Chocolate, coffee, tea, cream, eggs, ham, tongue, cold fowl, all these are good, and bespeak good knowledge in him who sets them forth: but the touchstone is fish: anchovy is the first step, prawns and shrimps the second; and I laud him who reaches even to these: potted char and lampreys are the third, and a fine stretch of progression; but lobster is, indeed, matter for a May morning, and demands a rare combination of knowledge and virtue in him who sets it forth.

MR. MAC QUEDY: Well sir, and what say you to a fine fresh trout, hot and dry, in a napkin? or a herring out of the water into the frying pan, on the shore of Loch Fyne?

THE REV. DR. FOLLIOTT: Sir, I say every nation has some eximious virtue; and your country is pre-eminent in the glory of fish for breakfast. We have much to learn from you in that line at any rate.

MR. MAC QUEDY: And in many others, sir, I believe. Morals and metaphysics, politics and political economy, the way to make the most of all the modifications of smoke; steam, gas, and paper currency; you have all these to learn from us; in short, all the arts and sciences. We are the modern Athenians.

THE REV. DR. FOLLIOTT: I, for one, sir, am content to learn

3. It is not clear that these characters are modelled on any particular persons. But the greatest propagandists for political economy were frequently Scots (e.g., J. R. MacCulloch); and Mr. Skionar represents Coleridgean metaphysicians who were influenced by German Romantic philosophy. Peacock footnotes Mac Quedy as "Quasi Mac Q. E. D., son of a demonstration;" and Skionar as Greek for the Latin "*Umbrae somnium*," i.e., "the shadows of sleep."

4. "Far-shining be the face/ Of a great work begun" (Peacock's note).

nothing from you but the art and science of fish for breakfast. Be content, sir, to rival the Bœotians, whose redeeming virtue was in fish, touching which point you may consult Aristophanes and his scholiast in the passage of Lysistrata, ἀλλ᾽ ἄφελε τὰς ἐγχέλεις,[5] and leave the name of Athenians to those who have a sense of the beautiful, and a perception of metrical quantity.

MR. MAC QUEDY: Then, sir, I presume you set no value on the right principles of rent, profit, wages, and currency?

THE REV. DR. FOLLIOTT: My principles, sir, in these things are, to take as much as I can get, and to pay no more than I can help. These are every man's principles, whether they be the right principles or no. There, sir, is political economy in a nutshell.

MR. MAC QUEDY: The principles, sir, which regulate production and consumption are independent of the will of any individual as to giving or taking, and do not lie in a nutshell by any means.

THE REV. DR. FOLLIOTT: Sir, I will thank you for a leg of that capon.

LORD BOSSNOWL: But, sir, by the by, how come your footman to be going into your cook's room? It was very providential to be sure, but—

THE REV. DR. FOLLIOTT: Sir, as good came of it, I shut my eyes, and asked no questions. I suppose he was going to study hydrostatics, and he found himself under the necessity of practising hydraulics.

MR. FIREDAMP: Sir, you seem to make very light of science.

THE REV. DR. FOLLIOTT: Yes, sir, such science as the learned friend deals in: every thing for every body, science for all, schools for all, rhetoric for all, law for all, physic for all, words for all, and sense for none. I say, sir, law for lawyers, and cookery for cooks: and I wish the learned friend, for all his life, a cook that will pass her time in studying his works; then every dinner he sits down to at home, he will sit on the stool of repentance.

LORD BOSSNOWL: Now really that would be too severe: my cook should read nothing but Ude.

THE REV. DR. FOLLIOTT: No, sir! let Ude and the learned friend singe fowls together; let both avaunt from my kitchen. θύρας δ᾽ ἐπίθεσθε βεβήλοις.[6] Ude says an elegant supper may be given with sandwiches. *Horresco referens.*[7] An elegant supper, *Dî meliora piis.*[8]

---

5. "Calonice wishes destruction to all Boeotians. Lysistrata answers, 'Except the eels' " (Peacock's note).

6. "Shut the doors against the profane." (Peacock's note).

7. "I tremble as I speak it."

8. "God [gives] the best things to pious men."

No Ude for me. Conviviality went out with punch and suppers. I cherish their memory. I sup when I can, but not upon sandwiches. To offer me a sandwich, when I am looking for a supper, is to add insult to injury. Let the learned friend, and the modern Athenians, sup upon sandwiches.

MR. MAC QUEDY: Nay, sir; the modern Athenians know better than that. A literary supper in sweet Edinbroo' would cure you of the prejudice you seem to cherish against us.

THE REV. DR. FOLLIOTT: Well, sir, well; there is cogency in a good supper; a good supper in these degenerate days, bespeaks a good man; but much more is wanted to make up an Athenian. Athenians, indeed! where is your theatre? who among you has written a comedy? where is your attic salt? which of you can tell who was Jupiter's great grandfather? or what metres will successively remain, if you take off the three first syllables, one by one, from a pure antispastic acatalectic tetrameter? Now, sir, there are three questions for you; theatrical, mythological, and metrical; to every one of which an Athenian would give an answer that would lay me prostrate in my own nothingness.

MR. MAC QUEDY: Well, sir, as to your metre and your mythology, they may e'en wait a wee. For your comedy, there is the Gentle Shepherd of the divine Allan Ramsay.[9]

THE REV. DR. FOLLIOTT: The Gentle Shepherd! It is just as much a comedy as the book of Job.

MR. MAC QUEDY: Well, sir, if none of us have written a comedy, I cannot see that it is any such great matter, any more than I can conjecture what business a man can have at this time of day with Jupiter's great grandfather.

THE REV. DR. FOLLIOTT: The great business is, sir, that you call yourselves Athenians, while you know nothing that the Athenians thought worth knowing, and dare not show your noses before the civilized world in the practice of any one art in which they were excellent. Modern Athens, sir! the assumption is a personal affront to every man who has a Sophocles in his library. I will thank you for an anchovy.

MR. MAC QUEDY: Metaphysics, sir; metaphysics. Logic and moral philosophy. There we are at home. The Athenians only sought the way, and we have found it; and to all this we have added political economy, the science of sciences.

THE REV. DR. FOLLIOTT: A hyperbarbarous technology, that no Athenian ear could have borne. Premises assumed without evidence, or

9. Allan Ramsay (1686–1758) was a Scotsman who developed a great reputation as pastoral poet.

in spite of it; and conclusions drawn from them so logically, that they must necessarily be erroneous.

MR. SKIONAR: I cannot agree with you, Mr. Mac Quedy, that you have found the true road of metaphysics, which the Athenians only sought. The Germans have found it, sir: the sublime Kant, and his disciples.

MR. MAC QUEDY: I have read the sublime Kant, sir, with an anxious desire to understand him, and I confess I have not succeeded.

THE REV. DR. FOLLIOTT: He wants the two great requisites of head and tail.

MR. SKIONAR: Transcendentalism is the philosophy of intuition, the development of universal convictions; truths which are inherent in the organization of mind, which cannot be obliterated, though they may be obscured, by superstitious prejudice on the one hand, and by the Aristotelian logic on the other.

MR. MAC QUEDY: Well, sir, I have no notion of logic obscuring a question.

MR. SKIONAR: There is only one true logic, which is the transcendental; and this can prove only the one true philosophy, which is also the transcendental. The logic of your Modern Athens can prove every thing equally; and that is, in my opinion, tantamount to proving nothing at all.

MR. CROTCHET: The sentimental against the rational, the intuitive against the inductive, the ornamental against the useful, the intense against the tranquil, the romantic against the classical; these are great and interesting controversies, which I should like, before I die, to see satisfactorily settled.

MR. FIREDAMP: There is another great question, greater than all these, seeing that it is necessary to be alive in order to settle any question; and this is the question of water against human life. Wherever there is water, there is *malaria*, and wherever there is *malaria*, there are the elements of death. The great object of a wise man should be to live on a gravelly hill, without so much as a duck-pond within ten miles of him, eschewing cisterns and waterbutts, and taking care that there be no gravel-pits for lodging the rain. The sun sucks up infection from water, wherever it exists on the face of the earth.

THE REV. DR. FOLLIOTT: Well, sir, you have for you the authority of the ancient mystagogue, who said: Ἔστιν ὕδωρ ψυχῇ θάνατος.[10] For my part I care not a rush (or any other aquatic and inesculent vegetable) who or what sucks up either the water or the infection. I

10. "Literally, which is sufficient for the present purpose, 'Water is death to the soul.'" (Peacock's note).

think the proximity of wine a matter of much more importance than the longinquity of water. You are here within a quarter of a mile of the Thames, but in the cellar of my friend, Mr. Crotchet, there is the talismanic antidote of a thousand dozen of old wine; a beautiful spectacle, I assure you, and a model of arrangement.

MR. FIREDAMP: Sir, I feel the malignant influence of the river in every part of my system. Nothing but my great friendship for Mr. Crotchet would have brought me so nearly within the jaws of the lion.

THE REV. DR. FOLLIOTT: After dinner, sir, after dinner, I will meet you on this question. I shall then be armed for the strife. You may fight like Hercules against Achelous, but I shall flourish the Bacchic thyrsus, which changed rivers into wine: as Nonnus sweetly sings, Οἴνῳ κυματόεντι μέλας κελάρυζεν Ὑδάσπης.[11]

MR. CROTCHET, JUN: I hope, Mr. Firedamp, you will let your friendship carry you a little closer into the jaws of the lion. I am fitting up a flotilla of pleasure-boats, with spacious cabins, and a good cellar, to carry a choice philosophical party up the Thames and Severn, into the Ellesmere canal, where we shall be among the mountains of North Wales; which we may climb or not, as we think proper; but we will, at any rate, keep our floating hotel well provisioned, and we will try to settle all the questions over which a shadow of doubt yet hangs in the world of philosophy.

MR. FIREDAMP: Out of my great friendship for you, I will certainly go; but I do not expect to survive the experiment.

THE REV. DR. FOLLIOTT: *Alter erit tum Tiphys, et altera quæ vehat Argo Delectos Heroas.*[12] I will be of the party, though I must hire an officiating curate, and deprive poor dear Mrs. Folliott, for several weeks, of the pleasure of combing my wig.

LORD BOSSNOWL: I hope, if I am to be of the party, our ship is not to be the ship of fools: He! He!

THE REV. DR. FOLLIOTT: If you are one of the party, sir, it most assuredly will not: Ha! Ha!

LORD BOSSNOWL: Pray sir, what do you mean by Ha! Ha!?

THE REV. DR. FOLLIOTT: Precisely, sir, what you mean by He! He!

MR. MAC QUEDY: You need not dispute about terms; they are two modes of expressing merriment, with or without reason; reason being in no way essential to mirth. No man should ask another why he laughs, or at what, seeing that he does not always know, and that,

11. "Hydaspes gurgled, dark with billowy wine" (Peacock's note).
12. "Another Tiphys on the waves shall float,/ And chosen heroes freight his glorious boat" (Peacock's note).

if he does, he is not a responsible agent. Laughter is an involuntary action of certain muscles, developed in the human species by the progress of civilization. The savage never laughs.

THE REV. DR. FOLLIOTT: No, sir, he has nothing to laugh at. Give him Modern Athens, the "learned friend," and the Steam Intellect Society.[13] They will develope his muscles.

13. This is Peacock's comic name for The Society for the Diffusion of Useful Knowledge, which was founded in 1826 by Lord Brougham.

WILLIAM HAZLITT

# The Life of
# Napoleon Bonaparte*

WILLIAM HAZLITT (1778–1830) IS MOST
widely known as an essayist and critic of literature and the arts. He
was, however, a brilliant and divers writer, whose career began not
in criticism but in philosophy, law, and politics. He was even something of a painter and grammarian.

Hazlitt's political views were central to his whole career, and
from the point of view of this volume are the most important
aspect of his writings. His attitudes were shaped, along with those
of the Lake Poets, by the French Revolution. But unlike Wordsworth, Coleridge, and Southey, and, indeed, most of his contemporaries, he remained loyal to the commitments of his youth. He
remained a bitter enemy of tyranny in any shape and a passionate

* From William Hazlitt, The Life of Napoleon Bonaparte, 4 vols., First
Edition (London: Hunt and Clarke, 1828–30), from Chapter III.

defender of freedom. Napoleon's tyranny and the destruction of all revolutionary hopes at Waterloo came to him as a terrible shock. Late in his career, however, he returned to Napoleon and the events which created his great hopes for human freedom, and he rejoiced once again in the overthrow of the tyrannical Bourbons by the Revolution.

For various reasons, political and personal, Hazlitt was widely disliked and distrusted, even by the friends of his youth. But his writing demonstrates not only the clarity and brilliance of his mind, but a courageous personal integrity. In the material included here the intensity of his commitment to the popular cause is apparent, especially the commitment to the need for free discussion and for the diffusion of knowledge beyond the establishment to the people.

### THE FRENCH REVOLUTION— PRELIMINARY REMARKS

The French Revolution might be described as a remote but inevitable result of the invention of the art of printing. The gift of speech, or the communication of thought by words, is that which distinguishes man from other animals. But this faculty is limited and imperfect without the intervention of books, which render the knowledge possessed by every one in the community accessible to all. There is no doubt, then, that the press (as it has existed in modern times) is the great organ of intellectual improvement and civilisation. It was impossible in this point of view, that those institutions, which were founded in a state of society and manners long anterior to this second breathing of understanding into the life of man, should remain on the same proud footing after it, with all their disproportions and defects. Many of these, indeed, must be softened by the lapse of time and influence of opinion, and give way of their own accord: but others are too deeply rooted in the passions and interests of men to be wrenched asunder without violence, or by the mutual consent of the parties concerned; and it is this which makes revolutions necessary, with their train of lasting good and present evil. When a government, like an old-fashioned building, has become crazy and rotten, stops the way of improvement, and only serves to collect diseases and corruption, and the proprietors refuse to come to any compromise, the community proceed in this as in some other cases; they set summarily to work—"they pull down the house, they abate the nuisance." All other things had changed: why then should governments remain the same, an excrescence and an incumbrance on the state? It is only because they have most power and most interest to continue their abuses. This circumstance is a reason why it is doubly incumbent on those who are aggrieved by them to get rid of them; and makes the shock the greater, when opinion at last becomes a match for arbitrary power.

The feudal system was in full vigour almost up to the period of the discovery of printing. Much had been done since that time: but it was the object of the French Revolution to get rid at one blow of the frame-work and of the last relics of that system. Before the diffusion of knowledge and inquiry, governments were for the most part the growth of brute force or of barbarous superstition. Power was in the hands of a few, who used it only to gratify their own pride, cruelty, or avarice, and who took every means to extend and cement it by fear and favour. The lords of the earth, disdaining to rule by the choice or for the benefit of the mass of the community, whom they regarded and treated as no better than a herd of cattle, derived their title from the skies, pretending to be accountable for the exercise or abuse of their authority to God only—the throne rested on the altar, and every species of atrocity or wanton insult having power on its side, received the sanction of religion, which it was thenceforth impiety and rebellion against the will of Heaven to impugn. This state of things continued and grew worse and worse, while knowledge and power were confined within mere local and personal limits. Each petty sovereign shut himself up in his castle or fortress, and scattered havoc and dismay over the unresisting country around him. In an age of ignorance and barbarism, when force and interest decided every thing, and reason had no means of making itself heard, what was to prevent this or act as a check upon it? The lord himself had no other measure of right than his own will: his pride and passions would blind him to every consideration of conscience or humanity; he would regard every act of disobedience as a crime of the deepest die, and to give unbridled sway to his lawless humours, would become the ruling passion and sole study of his life. How would it stand with those within the immediate circle of his influence or his vengeance? Fear would make them cringe, and lick the feet of their haughty and capricious oppressor: the hope of reward or the dread of punishment would stifle the sense of justice or pity; despair of success would make them cowards, habit would confirm them into slaves, and they would look up with bigotted devotion (the boasted *loyalty* of the good old times) to the right of the strongest as the only law. A king would only be the head of a confederation of such petty despots, and the happiness or rights of the people would be equally disregarded by them both. Religion, instead of curbing this state of rapine and licentiousness, became an accomplice and a party in the crime; gave absolution and plenary indulgence for all sorts of enormities; granting the forgiveness of Heaven in return for a rich jewel or fat abbey-lands, and setting up a regular (and what in the end proved an intolerable) traffic in violence, cruelty, and lust. As to the restraints of law, there was none but what resided in the breast of the *Grand Seigneur*, who hung up in his court-yard, without judge or jury, any one who dared to utter the slightest murmur against the most flagrant wrong. Such must be the consequence, as long as there was no common standard or impartial judge to appeal to; and this could only be found in public opinion, the offspring of books. As long as any unjust claim or transaction was confined to the knowledge of the parties concerned, the tyrant and the slave, which is the case in all unlettered states of society, *might* must prevail over *right;* for the strongest would bully, and the weakest must submit, even in his own defence, and persuade himself that he was in the wrong, even in his own despite: but the instant the world (that dread jury) are impannelled, and called to look on and be umpires in the scene, so that nothing is done by connivance or in a corner, then reason mounts the judgment-seat in lieu of passion or interest, and opinion becomes law, instead of arbitrary will; and farewell feudal lord and sovereign king!

From the moment that the press opens the eyes of the community beyond the actual sphere in which each moves, there is from that time inevitably formed the germ of a body of opinion directly at variance with the selfish and servile code that before reigned paramount, and approximating more and more to the manly and disinterested standard of truth and justice. Hitherto force, fraud, and fear decided every question of individual right or general reasoning; the possessor of rank and influence, in answer to any censure or objection to his conduct, appealed to God and to his sword:—now a new principle is brought into play which had never been so much as dreamt of, and before which he must make good his pretensions, or it will shatter his strongholds of pride and prejudice to atoms, as the pent-up air shatters whatever resists its expansive force. This power is public opinion, exercised upon men, things, and general principles, and to which mere physical power must conform, or it will crumble it to powder. Books alone teach us to judge of truth and good in the abstract: without a knowledge of things at a distance from us, we judge like savages or animals from our senses and appetites only; but by the aid of books and of an intercourse with the world of ideas, we are purified, raised, ennobled from savages into intellectual and rational beings. Our impressions of what is near to us are false, of what is distant feeble; but the last gaining strength from being united in public opinion, and expressed by the public voice, are like the congregated roar of many waters, and quail the hearts of princes. Who but the tyrant does not hate the tyrant? Who but the slave does not despise the slave? The first of these looks upon himself as a God, upon his vassal as a clod of the earth, and forces him to be of the same opinion: the philosopher looks upon them both as men, and instructs the world to do so. While they had to settle their pretensions by themselves, and in the night of ignorance, it is no wonder no good was done; while pride intoxicated the one, and fear stupefied the other. But let them be brought out of that dark cave of despotism and superstition, and let a thousand other persons, who have no interest but that of truth and justice, be called on to determine between them, and the plea of the lordly oppressor to make a beast of burden of his fellow-man becomes as ridiculous as it is odious. All that the light of philosophy, the glow of patriotism, all that the brain wasted in midnight study, the blood poured out upon the scaffold or in the field of battle can do or have done, is to take this question in all cases from before the first gross, blind and iniquitous tribunal, where power insults over weakness, and place it before the last more just, disinterested, and in the end more formidable one, where each individual is tried by his peers, and according to rules and principles which have received the common examination and the common consent. A public sense is thus formed, free from slavish awe or the traditional assumption of insolent superiority, which the more it is exercised becomes the more enlightened and enlarged, and more and more requires equal rights and equal laws. This new sense acquired by the people, this new organ of opinion and feeling, is like bringing a battering-train to bear upon some old Gothic castle, long the den of rapine and crime, and must finally prevail against all absurd and antiquated institutions, unless it is violently suppressed, and this engine of political reform turned by bribery and terror against itself. Who in reading history, where the characters are laid open and the circumstances fairly stated, and where he himself has no false bias to mislead him, does not take part with the oppressed against the oppressor? Who is there that admires Nero at

the distance of two thousand years? Did not the *Tartuffe* in a manner
hoot religious hypocrisy out of France; and was it not on this account
constantly denounced by the clergy? What do those, who read the
annals of the Inquisition, think of that dread tribunal? And what has
softened its horrors but those annals being read? What figure does the
massacre of St. Bartholomew make in the eyes of posterity? But books
anticipate and conform the decision of the public, of individuals, and
even of the actors in such scenes, to that lofty and irrevocable standard,
mould and fashion the heart and inmost thoughts upon it, so that
something manly, liberal, and generous grows out of the fever of passion and the palsy of base fear; and this is what is meant by the progress of modern civilisation and modern philosophy. An individual in
a barbarous age and country throws another who has displeased him
(without other warrant than his will) into a dungeon, where he pines
for years, and then dies; and perhaps only the mouldering bones of
the victim, discovered long after, disclose his fate: or if known at the
time, the confessor gives absolution, and the few who are let into the
secret are intimidated from giving vent to their feelings, and hardly
dare disapprove in silence. Let this act of violence be repeated afterwards in story, and there is not an individual in the whole nation
whose bosom does not swell with pity, or whose blood does not curdle
within him at the recital of so foul a wrong. Why then should there
be an individual in a nation privileged to do what no other individual
in the nation can be found to approve? But he has the power, and
will not part with it in spite of public opinion. Then that public
opinion must become active, and break the moulds of prescription in
which his right derived from his ancestors is cast, and this will be a
Revolution. Is that a state of things to regret or bring back, the bare
mention of which makes one shudder? But the form, the shadow of
it only was left: then why keep up that form, or cling to a shadow of
injustice, which is no less odious than contemptible, except to make
an improper use of it? Let all the wrongs public and private produced
in France by arbitrary power and exclusive privileges for a thousand
years be collected in a volume, and let this volume be read by all who
have hearts to feel or capacity to understand, and the strong, stifling
sense of oppression and kindling burst of indignation that would
follow will be that impulse of public opinion that led to the French
Revolution. Let all the victims that have perished under the mild,
paternal sway of the ancient *régime*, in dungeons, and in agony,
without a trial, without an accusation, without witnesses, be assembled
together, and their chains struck off, and the shout of jubilee and
exultation they would make, or that nature would make at the sight,

will be the shout that was heard when the Bastille fell! The dead pause that ensued among the Gods of the earth, the rankling malice, the panic-fear, when they saw law and justice raised to an equality with their sovereign will, and mankind no longer doomed to be their sport, was that of fiends robbed of their prey: their struggles, their arts, their unyielding perseverance, and their final triumph was that of fiends when it is restored to them!

It has been sometimes pretended as if the French Revolution burst out like a volcano, without any previous warning, only to alarm and destroy—or was one of those comet-like appearances, the approach of which no one can tell till the shock and conflagration are felt. What is the real state of the case? There was not one of those abuses and grievances which the rough grasp of the Revolution shook to air, that had not been the butt of ridicule, the theme of indignant invective, the subject of serious reprobation for near a century. They had been held up without ceasing and without answer to the derision of the gay, the scorn of the wise, the sorrow of the good. The most witty, the most eloquent, the most profound writers were unanimous in their wish to remove or reform these abuses, and the most dispassionate and well-informed part of the community joined in the sentiment: it was only the self-interested or the grossly ignorant who obstinately clung to them. Every public and private complaint had been subjected to the touchstone of inquiry and argument; the page of history, of fiction, of the drama, of philosophy had been laid open, and their contents poured into the public ear, which turned away disgusted from the arts of sophistry or the menace of authority. It was this operation of opinion, enlarging its circle, and uniting nearly all the talents, the patriotism, and the independence of the country in its service, that brought about the events which followed. Nothing else did or could. It was not a dearth of provisions, the loss of the queen's jewels, that could overturn all the institutions and usages of a great kingdom—it was not the Revolution that produced the change in the face of society, but the change in the texture of society that produced the Revolution, and brought its outward appearance into a nearer correspondence with its inward sentiments. There is no other way of accounting for so great and sudden a transition. Power, prejudice, interest, custom, ignorance, sloth, and cowardice were against it: what then remained to counterbalance this weight, and to overturn all obstacles, but reason and conviction which were for it? *Magna est veritas, et prevalebit.*[1]

1. "Truth is great, and will prevail."

JAMES MILL

# Periodical Literature*

JAMES MILL (1772–1836), FATHER OF JOHN
Stuart Mill, was perhaps the single most important figure in the
spread of Benthamite, utilitarian doctrines in the first decades of
the nineteenth century. Although the amount of his writing is
relatively small, all that he wrote was enormously influential. He
was one of the guiding spirits behind the founding of the radical
*Westminster Review* in 1824, and although he did not become
editor and eventually lost all patience with the journal's adminis-
trative policies, his contributions to it were very important.

Mill's writing is not very attractive; it has little of the flexibil-
ity found in that of his son, largely because the elder's mind was
more dogmatic and rationalistic. In his *Analysis of the Human
Mind* (1829), for instance, he intended to make the workings of
the mind "as clear as the road to Charing Cross." In keeping with

* From *Edinburgh Review*, I (January, 1824), 206–22.

Bentham's method, Mill insisted on returning to the most elementary assumptions, questioning them, and building systematically (and, perhaps, pedantically) upon them. It is difficult to overestimate the importance of his views, however, both in the minds of his contemporaries and in the movements to reform which followed upon his principles. Carlyle, Coleridge, and indeed many others (including, to a certain extent, John Stuart Mill himself) felt that utilitarianism was a dehumanizing, mechanical doctrine. But behind Mill's intellectual rigor and the coldness of his style lay a strong passion for justice and human improvement.

The present essay was designed as the first in a series of essays exposing the biases and defects of the other major quarterlies. It is interesting as a criticism of the *Edinburgh Review,* and especially as a demonstration of the typical utilitarian style and assumptions of Mill.

I f periodical criticism is good for any thing, it cannot be less needed in the case of periodical literature, than of any other class of the productions of the press. It is indeed a subject of wonder, that periodical publications should have existed so long, and have come at last to occupy so great a portion of the time and attention of the largest class of readers, without having become subject to a regular and systematic course of criticism. We trust it will appear that we shall have rendered an important service to the progress of the human mind, in setting at least an example of this species of control; in showing how great has been the need of it before it existed, how much of evil it is calculated to prevent, and how much of positive advantage it cannot fail to secure.

Periodical literature is so wide a field, that though we shall not interdict ourselves from any part of it, we shall select for our province more particularly that portion, with respect to which the demand for the service which we thus desire to see rendered, will, to every intelligent mind, appear to be the strongest. The review of books, with the influence which it has in giving direction to the taste for reading, has long been a department of literature the effect of which has been very imperfectly appreciated. For a considerable number of years this field has been to such a degree occupied by two rival, celebrated, and successful publications, that the old have sunk into insignificance: the attempt to elevate new ones, has hitherto proved abortive; and it will hardly be incumbent on us, unless with casual exceptions, to bestow much of our attention upon the rest.

Another circumstance renders criticism peculiarly necessary in the case of the publications to which we have alluded; we mean, the Edinburgh and Quarterly Reviews: under the guise of reviewing books, these publications have introduced the practice of publishing dissertations, not only upon the topics of the day, but upon all the most important questions of morals and legislation, in the most extensive acceptation of these terms. Whatever occasion, therefore, there can be for that species of censorship which criticism exercises over those who assume the task of supplying nourishment to the human mind, it is presented by the publications in question, and with peculiar circumstances of aggravation.

Of these circumstances, some they have in common with other periodical publications; some are peculiar to themselves. One law to which periodical literature is subject is attended with consequences, the good and evil of which have never yet been sufficiently analysed, though it is of the highest importance that they should be familiarised to the public mind. If a work is published, not periodical, and possesses real merit, it can afford to be overlooked for a time; and though it may be little noticed for the first year, or years, may count with tolerable certainty upon that degree of ultimate fame to which it is entitled. Not so with periodical literature. That must have immediate success, to secure so much as existence. A periodical production must sell immediately, at least to a certain extent, otherwise it cannot be carried on. A periodical production must be read the next day, or month, or quarter, otherwise it will not be read at all. Every motive, therefore, which prompts to the production of any thing periodical, prompts to the study of immediate effect, of unpostponed popularity, of the applause of the moment. To catch at this applause is then to be regarded as a grand characteristic of periodical literature; and the good and evil consequences which arise from it deserve to be diligently traced, and correctly estimated.

On the favourable side it may be affirmed, that as the diffusion of all the good which is derived from reading, must be in proportion to the diffusion of this which is its instrument, this peculiarity in periodical literature is an eminent advantage. By consulting the public taste with continual anxiety, the pleasures of reading are perpetually supplied to the greatest possible number. The number of those who love reading and the number of those who derive pleasure from periodical literature, are the same. To it, therefore, we are, it may be said, indebted, for the grand source of general intelligence; that is, the grand source of the greatest possible good.

The most effectual mode of doing good to mankind by reading, is, to correct their errors; to expose their prejudices; to refute opinions which are generated only by partial interests, but to which men are, for that reason, so much the more attached; to censure whatever is mean and selfish in their behaviour, and attach honour to actions solely in proportion to their tendency to increase the sum of happiness, lessen the sum of misery.

But this is a course which periodical literature cannot pursue. To please the great body of men, which is the object of the periodical writer, he must flatter their prejudices. Instead of calling in question the opinions to which they are wedded, he must applaud them; and the more he can furnish such men with reasons for being more in love with their opinions than before, the more he is sure of commanding their approbation, and of increasing their zeal to promote the reputation of his work.

The most mischievous of all erroneous opinions are those which lead to the injury of the great number of mankind, for the benefit of the small number; which tend to make it the interest of the small number, by giving them the power, to oppress the great number in all practicable ways, and to brutalise them for the purpose of rendering the oppression more easy, and more secure. That these are the most mischievous of all opinions, is proved by merely telling what they are. That literature is useful only as it contributes to the extirpation of these detestable opinions, is so far true, that deprive it of this tendency, and it is doubtful whether it would not be more of a curse than a blessing. These, however, are the very opinions which periodical literature is under the strongest inducements to promote, and the discouragement of which it is utterly unsafe to undertake. It is obvious what is the general course it will pursue.

The opinions, on the propagation of which the success of periodical writings depends,—immediate success, that success which is essential to their existence,—are the opinions in vogue; the opinions of those whose influence is the most extensive, who can go farthest in creating or hindering a reputation. But what is the class most instrumental in setting the fashion, which exercises the greatest control over the opinions of other men? The answer is not uncertain. The people of power compose it. The favourite opinions of people in power are the opinions which favour their own power; those opinions which we have already characterised as being the grand instruments of evil in this world, the ultimate and real cause of the degradation and misery of the great mass of mankind. To these opinions periodical literature is under a sort of necessity, under an inducement which generally operates as necessity, of serving as a pandar.

It is a common observation, that notwithstanding the influence of error in the world, arising partly from ignorance, partly from the influence of interested opinions in high quarters, the opinion of the wise and disinterested, though they are small in number, always, or at least generally, prevails at last, and becomes the opinion of the world. That there is this tendency in the opinions of the wise, is certain; and it is the ground of all our hopes for the amelioration of mankind. When an opinion, founded on truth, and tending to good, is once declared, and when there is the means of making it generally known, and of calling to it continually the attention of mankind, it is sure to make its way, and by degrees to bear down all that opposes it.

Here, however, the characteristic malady of periodical literature is most clearly seen. Instead of aiding this beneficent progress, it is opposed to it. The success of those important opinions, the progress of which involves the overthrow of the opinions which are dearest to the classes by whom power is exercised for their own benefit over the rest of the community, and dear to them for this reason, that they tend to the support of the power which they so employ, is *slow*. Periodical literature depends upon *immediate* success. It must, therefore, patronise the opinions which are now in vogue, the opinions of those who are now in power. It will obtain applause, and will receive reward, in proportion as it is successful in finding plausible reasons for the maintenance of the favourite opinions of the powerful classes, and plausible reasons for the discountenance and rejection of the opinions which tend to rescue the interests of the greater number from the subjection under which they lie to the interests of the small number. In this view, it is evident, that, so long as the interest of the smaller number is the predominating interest in any community; so long periodical literature is the natural enemy of the most important and beneficent class of opinions, and so long may the balance of its effects be expected to be decidedly in opposition to them. We say the balance of its effects, because there is no doubt that occasionally, from various motives, the more important of which we shall think it expedient to describe, the periodical press displays exertions both in opposition to the opinions which tend to confirm abusive powers in the hands of the few, and in favour of the opinions which tend to rescue from these powers the interests of the greater number.

After the mass of the people have become a reading people, a reward is held out for writings addressed peculiarly to them. The opinions of the people will, of course, be consulted in such writings; and those opinions which are peculiarly recommended to the powerful classes by the circumstances of their favouring the existence of those powers of theirs, which may be used for their personal purposes, will not be the peculiar objects of applause. But it is with the more numerous, as it is with the less numerous classes; they have some opinions which are just as well as important, and they have others which are erroneous.

It is of very little importance, in addressing the people, to continue recommending to them right opinions, which they already possess. Labour of such a kind is labour thrown away. The really useful effort, in the case of the people, as in the case of any other class, is to contend against erroneous opinions, and introduce to them ideas which, though full of important consequences, are as yet strange, and perhaps revolting, to their minds. From this undertaking it is now sufficiently evident to our readers that the periodical press is debarred. It cannot wait for that success which depends upon the slow progress of just opinions, and the slow removal of prevalent errors. It must aim at that immediate applause which is bestowed only for immediate pleasure; for gratification administered to the mind in its present state; for encouragement of the favourite idea, flattery of the reigning prejudice.

We have seen, during some late years, in this country, since the talent of reading has become more general, periodical publications, addressed in a particular manner to the more numerous class. They are cheap publications, from the circumstances of the purchasers; and they have been worse than they otherwise might have been, from the characters of those who have been the principal instruments in their production, and who, had they been wiser and better men (for, with little exception, they have been very defective in one or other, or both, of these requisites), might have obtained as much success, with less subservience to the errors of those whom they have addressed. It is abundantly apparent, however, even on a cursory inspection of the writings to which we have thus alluded, that the principal influence to which they bend is that of the favourite opinions, right or wrong, of those to whom they look for their reward. That writings produced under this influence can hardly fail, where men are as ill instructed as they still are in this country, and where partial and sinister interests so greatly preponderate, to have a greater tendency to evil than good, we imagine cannot, after what we have stated, be regarded as matter of doubt.

The two publications which we have already pointed out as destined to be the principal objects of our attention in this department, are addressed to the aristocratical classes. From the circumstances belonging to them it will appear that they may be regarded as almost exclusively addressed to those classes. To what degree they have been subservient to the interests of those classes, in other words, hostile to the interests of the more numerous class, it would be premature in us, and perhaps hardly fair, as yet, to pronounce. That can be properly determined only by evidence adduced; and that evidence will be among the results of the examination to which we mean to subject them. It is enough in the meantime to estimate correctly the inducements to this fatal subserviency under which they have been placed.

Assuming that they agree in this main and characteristic circumstance, of being addressed to the aristocratical classes, upon what principle, we may be asked, do we account for the great diversity which appears in their tone and character; a diversity so remarkable, that they are not regarded as competitors, but as enemies, as tending not to the same, but to opposite ends; as promoting irreconcilable opinions, the one upholding what the other endeavours to destroy? The elucidation of this point is of great importance, in laying the ground-work to our future labours in this department. It is in fact a point, the elucidation of which goes far into the philosophy of British history, and will therefore, if we can perform it satisfactorily, demand a rather more than ordinary portion of attention, on the part both of our readers and of ourselves.

We use the term "aristocracy" in a somewhat extended signification; and as we shall for the most part adhere to that use of it, we are under the necessity of expounding somewhat carefully the sense we thus attach to it, and of requesting our readers to bestow attention enough upon this explanation to retain it in their memory for future purposes. We do not use it in the mere sense of a titled nobility; nor in that of the families possessed of large fortunes. These are connected circumstances, but of secondary, rather than primary import. Wherever a government is not so constituted as to exist solely for the good of the community, aggregately considered, its powers are distributed into a certain number of hands, in some cases bearing a greater, in some a less proportion to the whole community; but a number always small in comparison with the population at large. This body, sharing among them the powers of government, and sharing among themselves also the profits of misrule, we denominate the aristocratical body; and by this term, or the aristocratical class, or in one word, the aristocracy, we shall be careful to distinguish them. The comparatively small number possessing political power compose the real aristocracy, by whatever circumstances, birth, or riches, or other accident, the different portions of them become possessed of it.

The aristocracy in some countries consists almost entirely of the lords of the soil. This in former times was the case in almost all the countries of Europe. And in those which have made the smallest progress in knowledge and civilisation, it is to a great degree the case at the present moment. In countries still more sunk in barbarism, as in Turkey, and in most Asiatic countries, the military hordes compose almost the whole of the efficient aristocracy, and are not hereditary. In our own country, the aristocracy is a motley body; and it imports us to be familiarly acquainted with the ingredients of the compound. If we assent to the doctrine of the Edinburgh Review,—and we are willing, for the present, to take it upon their showing,—we must conclude that the powers of government are centered in the House of Commons, and are there substantially and ultimately exercised. If this be the case, it is only necessary to enquire, of whom the House of Commons is composed, and by whom the members are sent there; because in their hands, of course, the powers of government are efficiently lodged. It will not be necessary for us to go into the minute details, or indeed into any disputed subjects. For the conclusions which concern our present purpose the broad and incontrovertible matters of fact will suffice. The owners of the great landed estates have the principal influence in sending members into the House of Commons. They possess the representation of the counties exclusively. The members for the counties (Middlesex has more of the nature of a town) are returned by a combination among the leading families, and commonly by a compromise between the two parties, the one being a Whig and the other a Tory. In respect to the boroughs it is not necessary that we should descend to a particular enumeration. Mere notoriety will suffice for our present purpose. That a large proportion of them are in the hands of the same great families, either to nominate or effectually to influence the return of the members, will not be denied; because men in their senses do not make affirmations with respect to matters of fact which every body who knows them possesses sufficient grounds to deny.

There is a certain number of the boroughs, the constitution of which is such, that the electors find it for their interest to sell their votes on each occasion to the highest bidder. It is proper, though it is somewhat of a deviation from the present purpose, to remark, that this class of the boroughs is a general subject of vituperation, to those who, from their influence as landed proprietors, determine the election in counties, and in the boroughs over which their influence extends. Unhappily their influence sets the fashion in morality as well as in dress; and their long-continued cries have made it be regarded as peculiarly infamous in the electors in boroughs to sell their votes. But why should it be more infamous in a poor elector to sell his vote in a borough, than for a rich lord of the soil to sell his vote in parliament? "Why is the one traffic infamous, the other honourable?" For this reason, and this alone, that the great men influence public opinion more than the little men: the case would otherwise have been directly the reverse; the conduct of the rich lord would have been the most infamous, as in degree it is unquestionably the most highly mischievous. The case of the elector in the borough who sells his vote to the highest bidder, and that of the man who in a borough or a county gives it habitually to the lord, are essentially the same. Each, with little or no regard to the fitness of the man for whom the vote is given, follows his own interest. The elector who places his vote habitually at the disposal of his landlord, does so because his landlord could, and he fears would, do him injury, if he acted otherwise. The elector who takes money for his vote, does so for the immediate benefit which it yields. It is the part of men who are not legislators, but drivellers, to whine against people for following their interest. In legislation the only enquiry is, how to make the interest of men and their duty coincide. What we desire is, to place the right of voting for members of parliament on such a footing, that it shall not be for the interest of the voter to give his suffrage from any other motive than the verdict of his conscience, preferring the fittest man. And for that we are called Radicals, and other names intended to be opprobrious, by those whose interest it is that the right of voting should never be placed on any better than the present foundation.

To return to the mode in which the boroughs, so constituted as to make it the interest of the electors to sell their votes to the highest bidder, affect the composition of the British aristocracy;—it is evident that they open a door of admission into the governing body to monied men. Such men, in considerable numbers, do by such means, as well as by what is called the purchase of a borough, that is, of the means of intimidation over the wretched electors, originally possessed by some neighbouring lord of the soil, become members of the House of Commons; and thus the class of monied men become sharers in the possession of the powers of government, and form a portion, though a minor, and hence a subordinate, portion, of the aristocracy of England.

In the composition of the aristocracy of England, the importance of its two props deserves much and careful consideration. Its two props are, the Church, and the Law; by the Law, we mean here the professional body.

We need not lengthen our investigation by representing the influence which religion exercises over the minds of men. It will be allowed to be great. It is evident of what importance it is to an aristocracy, that is, a small number, exercising, and for their own advantage, power over the great number, to be able to turn this influence, the influence of religion, to their own purposes. It is manifest how great a support to their power they may derive from it. Now it is obvious, that the short and effectual method of being able to turn the influence of religion to their own purposes, is to obtain an influence over the teachers of religion. It is equally easy to discover a sure expedient for their obtaining an influence over the teachers of religion. It is to form them into a corporate and dependent body, with gradation of emoluments and power, from something small, to something very great; retaining the nomination to the enjoyment of those emoluments principally in their hands, and admitting the body to a share in the power and profits of the aristocracy. In the aristocracy of England, accordingly, the church, or the organised priesthood of the state, is to be regarded as a real and efficient part. Of the mode in which it acts as a portion of the aristocracy, and receives its share of the profits of misrule, the details must be left for future opportunities.

As the security for person and property, the things most dear to men, depends upon the law, to be sure of possessing the requisite knowledge of the law, is to every individual a matter of the last importance. If the law were as simple and clear as it might be made, every man of competent understanding might have all the knowledge of it requisite for his guidance and security. But where the law has been rendered exceedingly complex and obscure, nobody understands it but those who devote themselves professionally to the study of it. The class of lawyers become, in such circumstances, a class of very great importance. Men look to their knowledge as the principal ground of their security; they acquire a habit of trusting to them in almost every important transaction of their lives. In proportion as they have much to risk, that is, in proportion as they are rich; and in proportion as they are timid, that is, averse to run risks;—they fall into a state of absolute dependance upon the lawyers. It is evident from this explanation, that as it is of great importance to the aristocracy to be able to use the influence of the teachers of religion for their own purposes, it is of great importance to them also, to be able to use the influence of the lawyers for their own purposes. To this end they are obliged to admit them to a requisite share in all the advantages of the aristocracy. It is known to every body how unintelligible a mass the English law is; how extensive a sway the tribe of lawyers exercise over the actions of their countrymen; and to how considerable a share in all the distinctions of the aristocracy, and all the profits of misrule, they are admitted. Details we reserve for occasions as they arise. The general facts, as we have stated them, are too notorious to admit of dispute. Accordingly, the share, which the Church and the Law are treated with, in the good things of the aristocracy, inures their strenuous exertions in its support; and, at all times, whatever is noxious in aristocratical opinions and prejudices has had the great majority of both those bodies for its zealous supporters: all those doctrines which have for their object to secure the interests of the great number against the usurpations of the small number, and all the individuals who promote those doctrines, have been, at all times, to the great majority of lawyers and churchmen, the objects of the most bitter persecution.

From the developments which we have thus afforded, we think a pretty clear conception of what is meant by the aristocracy of this country, politically considered, may easily be drawn. The more efficient part of it is undoubtedly that small number of leading families, probably not two hundred in all, which return a majority of the members of the House of Commons. This oligarchy is really and truly the governing power of the country. This governing power, like other governing powers, is obliged to make sacrifices to convenience; and in order to have instruments, and secure the services of those who would be dangerous enemies, is constrained to make a partnership concern, and to deal out certain minor shares: those are the shares of the monied interest, the church, and the law. Men of talent, as a class, have been sometimes represented as a constituent part of the House of Commons, and thence of the aristocracy; but, we think, erroneously. If they come in independently, by the purchase of a seat, they come in as monied men. If they come in as the nominees of this or the other great landlord, they come in as mere attorneys of the aristocracy. They are servants in an office; they are not a part of the aristocracy, any more than their butlers or stewards.

We are now drawing to a close with that development which we have deemed necessary, as enabling us to characterise two publications which are addressed to the aristocracy of this country, and which, notwithstanding their agreement in this leading circumstance, exhibit so much diversity in their more obvious appearances.

There is only one particular more into the analysis of which, as a preliminary explanation, it will be necessary for us to enter. The aristocracy of this country are naturally, in their political proceedings, divided, under the guidance of their interests, into two sections. The Quarterly Review follows the one section: the Edinburgh Review follows the other. The one of these sections is commonly known under the title of the ministerial party. The other is known under that of the opposition party. What are the interests which preside over the formation of the ministerial party are sufficiently obvious; and as they are in general correctly estimated, we are under no inducement to spend many words in explaining them.

As the benefits, periodically arising from the engrossment of the powers of government in the hands of the few and the consequent employment of them for the benefit of that few, have to be divided; and as the division in this country is confided to a fixed individual, called the King, who thus acts as the head of the aristocratical and governing body to whose interest it is more conducive to give up the division to such a functionary, than to run the risk of those destructive contests, which, but for such an expedient, it would be apt to occasion; —all that part of the aristocracy, who either are satisfied with the share which they receive, or think they have a better chance of such a share by meriting the favour of the present distributors than by any other course they can pursue, range themselves under the King's immediate advisers, and lend their influence to the promotion of all their designs. This class of motives is so obvious, and the operation of them so well understood, that we may now pass to the consideration of the interests which operate to the formation of the other section of the British aristocracy.

To all candid and intelligent readers it is unnecessary to remark, that we are here tracing the interests which predominate in the several situations which it is our object to explain. It is obvious, that all enlightened legislation proceeds upon a calculation of those interests, and that it is the business of true philosophy to form that calculation exactly. It is not therefore necessary for us here to enter into the motives of a different sort, which may bear a share in ranging this or that individual in the one or the other party. One man may adhere to the ministry, because he approves of their conduct; another may join the opposition, because the conduct of the ministry appears to him to be wrong. All that is necessary here is, to caution unwary reasoners against allowing those motives which may predominate in the breast of individuals, from occupying that place in their reasonings which belongs to those motives which act upon the class as a class, and by which, as a class, they must be governed. It would be absurd to say that a comparatively small number of men formed into a class by possessing all the powers of government over the great number, and the means of using those powers for their own advantage, will not, as a class, be actuated by the desire to render that advantage as great as possible. This being admitted, and it being clear that a man would render himself contemptible by denying it, the only care of the rational man is, to ascertain the course of action to which that desire must conduct the class; and having done so, to make it known to others. This is the course which it is now our endeavour to pursue; and our anxiety is to guard our readers against the delusion which is so often practised, of turning away the attention from the consideration of the motives which must govern the class, by holding up to attention the other motives, which always may, and very often do, actuate individuals. There is not a more fertile source of false reasoning, in matters of government, than this.

If, in the class who share among them the powers of government, there is one part who are pleased with the share which they receive of the advantages, or prefer the prospect which they have of sharing under the favour of the existing distributors; there is also, naturally, a part who are not pleased with the share which they receive, and who are willing to prefer any tolerable chance of sharing by other hands. These are they who, in this country, form themselves into what is called the opposition. The interest which actuates the conduct of this section of the aristocracy, are somewhat less obvious, from the modifications they undergo, than those which actuate the ministerial section. The immediate object of the opposition is to effect a change of the hands by which the distribution of the advantages is made—to obtain hands through which their share will be enlarged. The means which these interests prescribe to them for the attainment of this object, afford a clue to the labyrinth of their conduct. The grand expedient for driving a minister from his situation is, to deprive him of support in the House of Commons; to lessen as much as possible the number of those who vote for, increase as much as possible the number of those who vote against him. There are minor expedients, court intrigues, and others, but this is so much the leading and established course, that we may, for the present purpose, overlook the remainder. The plan, therefore, is, to excite disapprobation of the principles and conduct of those who retain the distribution, and to excite approbation of the principles and conduct of those whom they wish to hold it in their stead. In this the Opposition are under the necessity of endeavouring to reconcile courses which are rather opposed to one another.

The primary object, of course, is, to discredit the ministry, and augment the favour of their own leaders with the aristocratical class. But in order to do this the more effectually, it is expedient to produce as much as possible of the same effects upon the public at large, including the middling and lower classes. Public opinion operates in various ways upon the aristocratical class, partly by contagion, partly by conviction, partly by intimidation: and the principal strength of that current is derived from the greatness of the mass by which it is swelled. It is the interest of the Opposition, therefore, to act, in such a manner, or rather to speak,—for speaking is their action,—so as to gain favour from both the few and the many. This they are obliged to endeavour by a perpetual system of compromise, a perpetual trimming between the two interests. To the aristocratical class they aim at making it appear, that the conduct of their leaders would be more advantageous even to that class, than the conduct of the ministry, which they paint in colours as odious to the aristocracy as they can. On the other hand, to gain the favour of the popular class, they are obliged to put forth principles which appear to be favourable to their interests, and to condemn such measures of conduct as tend to injure the many for the benefit of the few. In their speeches and writings, therefore, we commonly find them playing at seesaw. If a portion of the discourse has been employed in recommending the interests of the people, another must be employed in recommending the interests of the aristocracy. Having spoken a while on the one side, they must speak a while on the other. Having written a few pages on the one side, they must write as many on the other. It matters not how much the one set of principles are really at variance with the other, provided the discordance is not very visible, or not likely to be clearly seen by the party on whom it is wished that the delusion should pass.

In this game, of aristocratical, and popular, it is sufficiently evident on which side, at last, the winnings remain. There are two sufficient reasons which determine the point. In the first place, it is the aristocracy through whose decision exclusively the object of the Opposition must be attained,—that of ejecting the ministerial party, and giving possession to them. They must, therefore, be very careful not to excite any suspicion that they are in reality less favourable to the aristocratical side of the account than those whom they wish to supplant. And, therefore, whatever the zeal of which they make show in favour of the people, it must still appear to the aristocracy, that it bears upon no points of which they have any occasion to be afraid; that it leads to the diminution of none of the advantages which the monopoly of the powers of government bestows upon them. There is another, and a perfectly sufficient reason in favour of the same tendency, that the opposition themselves are a section of the aristocracy; a section that wishes, and hopes, to be the leading section; and which, therefore, cannot be expected to aim at the diminution of advantages which are its own.

From this development of the interests and views of the two sections of the aristocracy in this country, it is clearly seen what may be expected to be the aim and tendency of the publications, particularly periodical, which look for success to the favour and applause of the one or the other. Those on the ministerial side have, as far as the interests of the aristocracy are concerned, a more simple course to pursue. They advocate them directly, and with enthusiasm, affected, or real. The aristocracy are spoken of as the country. Whenever the interests of the country are named, it is the interests of the aristocracy that are meant. The aristocracy are all in all. Compared with them, every thing is of trifling importance. With respect to the interests of the ministerial section, the business of the writers on that side is, to beat down the pretensions both of the opposition section of the aristocracy, and of the people. The people are represented as altogether vile, and any desires which they may exhibit to see the powers of government so disposed of, that they may have some security that these powers shall not be employed for the benefit of the aristocracy at their expense, as inconceivably wicked; as contrary, above all things, to religion; also contrary to law, and to order. The opposition section of the aristocracy are arraigned on two accounts; first, as attaching blame to the ministers for factious purposes, namely, to put their leaders in, and the ministers out, without being able to show, that the conduct of the ministers is not as good for the country, that is, the aristocracy, as that of the opposition leaders would be; and secondly, a still more dreadful odium is endeavoured to be cast upon them, by representing the professions which they are obliged to make in favour of the people as acts of support to these hideous pretensions of the people about securities for good government, which tend to the overthrow of the church and the state.

The course which is necessary to be pursued, by such periodical publications as adopt the vocation of promoting the cause of the opposition section of the aristocracy, will be easily understood, after what has been already said, without many words for its elucidation. The seesaw of the party must be recommended; and the more of skill and pains is bestowed upon this object, the more of approbation may be expected. It is called the middle course. Every art is used to gain it reputation, under the title of moderation, and by the application of bad names to the two sets of opinions, between which the party oscillates, and which it is in reality putting forward by turns. The set of opinions, purely on the side of aristocratical power, are called despotical. Those which support the demand of effectual securities in favour of the people are declared anarchical, and are commonly stigmatised by some nickname in the slang of the day; jacobinical, for instance, at one time; radical, at another. They have a method worth observing, by which they prove that the party holds a middle course; by which term *middle* they always desire to be understood *wise*. When the people blame the party as aristocratical, and produce actual declarations of opinion on the part of its leaders which go the full length of the aristocratical pretensions, the writers ask how you can misinterpret their words so far, when they can produce you other declarations of opinion which go to as great an extent in favour of the popular demands. This proceeding they reverse, when charged as democratical, on the part of the aristocracy. They do not allow that two contradictory opinions on one and the same point, destroy one another, and should be regarded as no opinion at all. They hold that two contradictory opinions are good for nothing, each of them by itself; but that, both together, they form another nice opinion, exactly in the middle way between both.

It is essential, in writing upon this plan, to deal as much as possible in vague language, and cultivate the skilful use of it. Words which appear to mean much, and may by those to whom they are addressed be interpreted to mean much, but which may also, when it suits the convenience of those who have used them, be shown to mean little or nothing, are of singular importance to those whose business it is to play the game of compromise, to trim between irreconcilable interests, to seesaw between contradictory opinions.

Language of this description is peculiarly needed in making declarations which are meant to gain favour with the people. A party which is itself a section of the aristocracy, which desires to please the aristocracy, and by means of pleasing them to become the distributors of the good things which the possession of the powers of the government bestows upon the aristocracy, risk nothing by speaking explicitly in favour of their privileges. What is requisite is to have vague terms at command, when it is necessary to speak in opposition to these privileges. Aristocratical domination, in the abstract, may be spoken of as something exceedingly hateful, or pregnant with the worst of consequences. The people may be exhorted to be on their guard against it. They may even be told that the ministers have no other object than to introduce it; and that this alone is a sufficient reason for hating them, and for using every exertion to turn them out. In the meantime, great care must be used not to remove any part of the veil which conceals from the view of the people, the real amount of aristocratical power in this country. When any specific measure is proposed, which would really operate to the diminution of that power, —choosing the members of parliament by ballot, for instance,—it must be loudly decried, and every thing must be done to attach to it, if possible, the apprehension of evil consequences. On the other hand, if a measure is proposed which has the appearance of being calculated to diminish the power of the aristocracy, but which in reality has no such tendency, perhaps the very reverse, such as the disfranchisement of the boroughs called rotten, giving the representation to the counties, then the epithets of praise must be collected. The man who brings forward such a measure as this, must be hailed as the first of men; the man who should accomplish it, must be described as the most happy.

One important part of the business of writers on the side of the opposition section of the aristocracy, one of the qualities by which they can most effectually recommend themselves, is, being ingenious in the invention of schemes of this description; schemes which may have the appearance to the people of being calculated to add to their securities, but which would, even if accomplished, leave the power of the aristocracy untouched. Of this class of plans one example is seen in that which we have already mentioned, diminishing the number of borough members to augment that of county members. Another example is seen in the doctrine about representation by classes; by which it is attempted to persuade the people, that they have securities enough, provided every class is represented in the House of Commons; that is to say, the landed interest represented, the mercantile interest represented, the army, the navy, the law, the people represented; though it should appear that the people have no real, efficient control over one man in this composition; that they have not the choice of so much as six, out of six hundred; and that even a bare majority, chosen and influenced by the aristocracy, would determine in the long run, and on the real balance of the account the nature of the government.

Having thus seen what are the motives which operate upon the two sets of periodical writers who address themselves to the two sections of the aristocracy, we have anticipated much of the general matter which will be applicable in criticising, in detail, the Edinburgh and the Quarterly Reviews. We have already stated, that the Edinburgh Review is addressed to the aristocracy on the side of the opposition section; the Quarterly Review is addressed to it on the side of the ministerial section. We shall see in our progress how truly they have obeyed the springs which we have represented as operating generally upon the conduct of publications produced in similar circumstances.

It will be understood that we have been speaking of the political part of these two publications; including, in the political pale, the two props of the aristocratical polity, the political religion of the country, and the law, in both senses of the term. As to the literature of the Quarterly and Edinburgh Reviews, in the more confined sense of the term,—the poetry, and other works of imagination and entertainment, the mathematics, chemistry, and so on,—these publications have lain under no peculiar bias from situation; and the goodness or badness of their articles on these subjects must be ascribed to the accidental qualities, moral or intellectual, of the writers. As far as their criticisms on these subjects may appear worthy of notice, they will be reviewed in other departments of this section of our work.

One word of a personal nature seems to be required. We have described the interests which operate to withdraw periodical writers from the line of utility, and we have represented it as nearly impossible for them to keep true to it. What! Are we, it may be asked, superior to seducements to which all other men succumb? If periodical writing is by its nature so imbued with evil, why is it that we propose to add to the supply of a noxious commodity? Do we promise to keep out the poison which all other men yield to the temptation of putting in? If we made such a pretension, our countrymen would do right in laughing it to scorn; and we hope they would not fail to adopt so proper a course. We have no claim to be trusted, any more than any one among our contemporaries: but we have a claim to be tried. Men have diversities of taste; and it is not impossible that a man should exist who really has a taste for the establishment of the securities for good government, and would derive more pleasure from the success of this pursuit, than of any other pursuit in which he could engage, wealth or power not excepted. All that we desire is, that it may not be reckoned impossible that we may belong to a class of this description.

There is another motive, as selfish as that which we ascribe to any body, by which we may be actuated. We may be sanguine enough, or silly enough, or clear-sighted enough, to believe, that intellectual and moral qualities have made a great progress among the people of this country; and that the class who will really approve endeavours, in favour of good government, and of the happiness and intelligence of men, are a class sufficiently numerous to reward our endeavours. . . .

CHARLES KNIGHT

# The Penny Magazine

CHARLES KNIGHT (1791–1873), AN EXTRAOR-
dinarily busy publisher, editor, and writer, devoted the greater part
of his life to popular instruction. The bibliography of works he
wrote and edited is enormous, and almost every entry was originally
directed at the poor and the partially educated.

In 1828, he took over superintendence of the publications of
The Society for the Diffusion of Useful Knowledge, and in 1832
he began publication of *Knight's Penny Magazine* for the Society.
(In 1832, two other penny magazines of the same kind also began
publication—*Chambers' Edinburgh Journal*, edited by William
Chambers [1800–1883], equally industrious in the cause of providing reading for the poor, actually sold for one pence halfpenny;
and the *Saturday Magazine*, published for The Society for the Promotion of Christian Knowledge. Penny journals were possible
because of the great technological developments in printing, about
which Knight speaks, and because they did not print news and
thus avoided the Stamp Tax.

Unfortunately, though probably well-intentioned, many penny journals were painfully condescending. *The Penny Magazine* was particularly guilty in this respect, as this grotesquely patronizing essay on the British Museum shows. Many intelligent people among the lower classes recognized and were offended by the tone, feeling that the knowledge being dispensed in *The Penny Magazine* was anything but "useful." Such views were well summed up in a book called *Junius Redivivus: The Producing Man's Companion; an Essay on the Present State of Society, Moral, Political, and Physical in England* (1833), by W. B. Adams. Adams, a radical contributor to *The Monthly Repository* (a unitarian-utilitarian journal), wrote:

A Penny Magazine has been established by the Society, from which they or their agents derive a large profit, to the mischief of private traders in the same articles. This one would not grumble at; it might perhaps be only fair competition, but what is the matter contained in the works? The people wish to know what is the cause they are reduced to live, in many cases, in wretched dwellings devoid of comforts; and by way of answer, they are treated to a dissertation on the Pyramids. They wish to know why a large number of them are reduced to a short supply of food, and others are starved to death; and they are furnished with an essay on the mode of cultivating sugar or coffee in the West Indies. Anything and everything but really needful knowledge is supplied to the people, but moral and political knowledge is altogether withheld, as if from a fear that they would become wiser than their rulers. Nay, lest they should by accident acquire useful modern books, they are carefully admonished to buy up old copies of the Spectator at book-stalls. The Society has been named in scorn "The Useless."

## PREFACE*

Upon the completion of the First Volume of the "Penny Magazine," it may not be inexpedient to offer a few observations to the purchasers of this little work, whose sale has been justly regarded as one of the most remarkable indications of the extent to which the desire for knowledge has reached in the United Kingdom.

It was considered by Edmund Burke, about forty years ago, that there were eighty thousand *readers* in this country. In the present year it has been shown, by the sale of the "Penny Magazine," that there are two hundred thousand *purchasers* of one periodical work. It may be fairly calculated that the number of readers of that single work amounts to a million.

If this incontestable evidence of the spread of the ability to read be most satisfactory, it is still more satisfactory to consider the species of reading which has had such an extensive and increasing popularity. In this work there has never been a single sentence that could inflame a vicious appetite; and not a paragraph that could minister to prejudices and superstitions which a few years since were common. There have been no excitements for the lovers of the marvellous—no tattle or abuse for the gratification of a diseased taste for personality—and, above all, no party politics. The subjects which have uniformly been treated have been of the broadest and simplest character. Striking points of Natural History—Accounts of the great Works of Art in

* From *The Penny Magazine*, I (1832), iii–iv.

Sculpture and Painting—Descriptions of such Antiquities as possess historical interest—Personal Narratives of Travellers—Biographies of Men who have had a permanent influence on the condition of the world—Elementary Principles of Language and Numbers—established facts in Statistics and Political Economy—these have supplied the materials for exciting the curiosity of a million of readers. This consideration furnishes the most convincing answer to the few (if any there now remain) who assert that General Education is an evil. The people will not abuse the power they have acquired to read, and therefore to think. Let them be addressed in the spirit of sincerity and respect, and they will prove that they are fully entitled to the praise which Milton bestowed upon their forefathers, as "a nation not slow and dull, but of a quick, ingenious, and piercing spirit,—acute to invent, subtile and sinewy to discourse, not beneath the reach of any point the highest that human capacity can soar to."

It must not, however, be forgotten that some of the unexampled success of this little work is to be ascribed to the liberal employment of illustrations, by means of Wood-cuts. At the commencement of the publication, before the large sale which it has reached could at all have been contemplated, the cuts were few in number, and partly selected from another work of the Society—the "Library of Entertaining Knowledge." But as the public encouragement enabled the conductors to make greater exertions to give permanency to the success which the "Penny Magazine" had attained, it became necessary to engage artists of eminence, both as draughtsmen and wood-engravers, to gratify a proper curiosity, and cultivate an increasing taste, by giving representations of the finest Works of Art, of Monuments of Antiquity, and of subjects of Natural History, in a style that had been previously considered to belong only to expensive books. In the prosecution of this undertaking there have been great mechanical difficulties. The wood-cuts, as well as the text, are transferred to stereotype plates—and the impressions are rapidly printed from these plates by machinery. In this process there can of course be no delicate and careful adjustment, such as is found necessary in printing wood-cuts by the common press. The average number of the "Penny Magazine," printed *daily* from two sets of stereotype plates, is sixteen thousand, on both sides;—at the common printing press, one thousand impressions, on both sides, can only be obtained, even where particular care is not required. Seeing, therefore, that the speed with which the "Penny Magazine" is printed, is sixteen times greater than in ordinary printing, some indulgence must be made for defects in the wood-cuts, as they appeared in a few of the early numbers. Those defects have been now almost entirely overcome, by the talent of the engravers, adapting their art to a new process.

It may not be uninteresting to mention two or three facts here, which may possibly be more systematically and fully pointed out hereafter, for the purpose of showing that such a work as the "Penny Magazine" could not exist in its present state—and its present state is dependant upon its large sale—except in a country where civilization is carried forward to very high degrees of perfection. The vast number of the existing race of readers, to which we have already alluded, might be supposed sufficient to warrant this assertion; but let us examine it a little more in detail.

The Number of the "Penny Magazine" which the reader is now perusing will be left ready to be printed off—to "go to press" as it is technically termed—on the 19th of December. Its previous preparation will have employed writers and artists, and that class of printers called compositors, for several weeks. The paper for 160,000 copies, (the quantity required for the consumption during the first month after publication,) consisting of 160 double reams (each sheet printing two copies), will have been previously delivered from the mill, and will have been charged with the excise duty of 3*d.* in the lb. upon 5,600 lbs.—the tax upon that quantity amounting to 70*l.* Up to this point a great deal of technical knowledge and mechanical skill will have been employed. Chemical knowledge and machinery are indispensable in the manufacture of the paper; and without the very ingenious invention of Stereotype Founding, in which practical improvements have been made within a few years, the "Penny Magazine" could not be printed in duplicate, which diminishes the expense, nor could the supply be proportioned to the demand. As we have already explained, the printing *machine* begins its work when every preparation is complete. In ten days one machine produces 160,000 copies from two sets of plates. If the printing machine had not been invented it would have taken a single press, producing a thousand perfect copies each day, one hundred and sixty days, or more than five calendar months, to complete the same number. We see, therefore, that up to this point there are many conditions for the production of a Penny Magazine which could not exist except in a high state of civilization, where there were large accumulations of knowledge.

This Number of our periodical work, which thus goes to press on the 19th of December, will be sold in every part of the United Kingdom, generally on the 1st of January,—in remote districts, on the 3d or 4th at latest. No one who wishes for a copy of this Magazine, whether in England, Scotland, or Ireland, can have any difficulty in getting it, if he can find a bookseller. The communication between the capital and the country, and between large towns in the country and villages, is now so perfect, that wherever there is a sufficient demand of any commodity there will be a supply. But the "Penny Magazine" is still a Penny Magazine all over the country. No one charges three-halfpence or twopence for it. The wholesale dealer and the retailer derive their profit from the publisher; and the carriage is covered by that profit. But that could not be if there were no *cheap* as well as *ready* communication through all parts of the United Kingdom. The steam-boat upon the seas—the canal—the railway—the quick van—these as well as the stage-coach and mail—place the "Penny Magazine" within every one's reach in the farthest part of the kingdom, as certainly as if he lived in London, and without any additional cost. This is a striking illustration of the civilization of our country; and when unthinking people therefore ask, what is the benefit of steam-engines, and canals, and fine roads to the poor man, they may be answered by this example alone. In this, as in all other cases, ready and cheap communication breaks down the obstacles of time and space,—and thus, bringing all ends of a great kingdom as it were together, greatly reduces the inequalities of fortune and situation, by equalizing the price of commodities, and to that extent making them accessible to all.

Some people have foolishly said that the "Penny Magazine" is a monopoly. There were formerly a great many monopolies of literature in this country;—that is, certain privileges were granted by the government to particular individuals, with the intent of *diminishing* the circulation of books by keeping up the price. Then the government was afraid that the people would learn to think. The object of those concerned in the "Penny Magazine" is, contrary to the spirit of a monopoly, to circulate as many copies as they can, as cheaply as they can. This Work has no exclusive privileges, and can have no exclusive privileges. *It stands upon the commercial principle alone*; and if its sale did not pay its expenses, with a profit to all concerned in it (except to the individual members of the Society who give it the benefit of their superintendence), it would not stand at all. The Society has no funds to assist the "Penny Magazine;" for its subscriptions are scarcely sufficient to defray the rent of the chambers in which it holds its meetings. But the "Penny Magazine" contributes materially to the funds of the Society, which funds are ready to be devoted to new undertakings, where success may not be so assured. The public, who buy the "Penny Magazine" to the extent of two hundred thousand, are its only pecuniary supporters. It is the duty of those who receive this large encouragement to carry forward their work to as high a point of excellence as they may attain by liberal and judicious arrangements.

### THE BRITISH MUSEUM*

"The characteristic of the English populace,—perhaps we ought to say people, for it extends to the middle classes,—is their propensity to mischief. The people of most other countries may safely be admitted into parks, gardens, public buildings, and galleries of pictures and statues; but in England it is necessary to exclude them, as much as possible, from all such places."

This is a sentence from the last published number of the "Quarterly Review." Severe as it is, there is much truth in it. The fault is not entirely on the side of the people (we will not use the offensive term populace); but still they are in fault. The writer adds, speaking of this love of mischief, which he calls "a disgraceful part of the English character," that "anything tends to correct it that contributes to give the people a taste for intellectual pleasures,—anything that contributes to their innocent enjoyment,—anything that excites them to wholesome and pleasurable activity of body and mind." This is quite true. We hope to do something, speaking generally, to excite and gratify a taste for intellectual pleasure; but we wish to do more in this particular case. We wish to point out many unexpensive pleasures, of the very highest order, which all those who reside in London have within their reach; and how the education of themselves and of their children may be advanced by using their opportunities of enjoying some of the purest gratifications which an instructed mind is capable of receiving. Having learnt to enjoy them, they will naturally feel an honest pride in the possession, by the Nation, of many of the most valuable treasures of Art and of Science; and they will hold that person a baby in mind—a spoilt, wilful, mischievous baby—who dares to attempt the slightest injury to the public property, which has been collected together, at an immense expense, for the public advantage.

Well, then, that we may waste no time in general discussion, let us begin with the BRITISH MUSEUM. We will suppose ourselves addressing an artisan or tradesman, who can sometimes afford to take

* From *The Penny Magazine*, I (April 7, 1832), 3–4.

a holiday, and who knows there are better modes of spending a working day, which he some half-dozen times a year devotes to pleasure, than amidst the smoke of a tap-room, or the din of a skittle-ground. He is a family man; he enjoys a pleasure doubly if it is shared by his wife and children. Well, then, in Great Russell-street, Bloomsbury, is the British Museum; and here, from ten o'clock till four, on Mondays, Wednesdays, and Fridays, he may see many of the choicest productions of ancient art—Egyptian, Grecian, and Roman monuments; and what will probably please the young people most, in the first instance, a splendid collection of natural history—quadrupeds, birds, insects, shells—all classed and beautifully disposed in an immense gallery, lately built by the Government, for the more convenient exhibition of these curiosities. "But hold," says the working man, "I have passed by the British Museum: there are two sentinels at the gate-way, and the large gates are always closed. Will they let me in? Is there nothing to pay?" That is a very natural question about the payment; for there is too much of paying in England by the people for admission to what they ought to see for nothing. But here there is nothing to pay. Knock boldly at the gate; the porter will open it. You are in a large square courtyard, with an old-fashioned house occupying three sides. A flight of steps leads up to the principal entrance. Go on. Do not fear any surly looks or impertinent glances from any person in attendance. You are upon safe ground here. You are·come to see your own property. You have as much right to see it, and you are as welcome therefore to see it, as the highest in the land. There is no favour in showing it you. You assist in paying for the purchase, and the maintenance of it; and one of the very best effects that could result from that expense would be to teach every Englishman to set a proper value upon the enjoyments which such public property is capable of affording. Go boldly forward, then. The officers of the Museum, who are obliging to all strangers, will be glad to see you. Your garb is homely, you think, as you see gaily-dressed persons going in and out. No matter; you and your wife, and your children, are clean, if not smart. By the way, it will be well to mention, that very young children (those under eight years old) are not admitted; and that for a very sufficient reason: in most cases they would disturb the other visitors.

You are now in the Great Hall—a lofty room, with a fine staircase. In an adjoining room a book is presented to you, in which one of a party has to write his name and address, with the number of persons accompanying him. That is the only form you have to go through; and it is a necessary form, if it were only to preserve a record of the number of persons admitted. In each year this number amounts to about seventy thousand: so you see that the British Museum has afforded pleasure and improvement to a great many people. We hope the number of visitors will be doubled and trebled; for exhibitions such as these do a very great deal for the advance of a people in knowledge and virtue. What reasonable man would abandon himself to low gratifications—to drinking or gambling—when he may, whenever he pleases, and as often as he pleases, at no cost but that of his time, enjoy the sight of some of the most curious and valuable things in the world, with as much ease as a Prince walking about in his own private gallery. But that he may enjoy these treasures—and that every body else may enjoy them at the same time it will be necessary to observe a few simple rules.

1st. *Touch nothing.* The statues, and other curious things, which are in the Museum, are to be seen, not to be handled. If visitors were to be allowed to touch them, to try whether they were hard or soft, to scratch them, to write upon them with their pencils, they would be soon worth very little. You will see some mutilated remains of two or three of the finest figures that ever were executed in the world; they form part of the collection called the Elgin Marbles, and were brought from the Temple of Minerva, at Athens, which city at the time of the sculpture of these statues, about two thousand three hundred years ago, was one of the cities of Greece most renowned for art and learning. Time has, of course, greatly worn these statues: but it is said that the Turkish soldiers, who kept the modern Greeks under subjection, used to take a brutal pleasure in the injury of these remains of ancient art; as if they were glad to destroy what their ignorance made them incapable of valuing. Is it not as great ignorance for a stupid fellow of our own day slily to write his own paltry name upon one of these glorious monuments? Is not such an act the most severe reproach upon the writer? Is it not, as if the scribbler should say, "Here am I, in the presence of some of the great masterpieces of art, whose antiquity ought to produce reverence, if I cannot comprehend their beauty; and I derive a pleasure from putting my own obscure perishable name upon works whose fame will endure for ever." What a satire upon such vanity. Doubtless, these fellows, who are so pleased with their own weak selves as to poke their names into every face, are nothing but grown babies, and want a fool's cap most exceedingly.

2dly. *Do not talk loud.* Talk, of course, you must; or you would lose much of the enjoyment we wish you to have—for pleasure is only half pleasure, unless it be shared with those we love. But do not disturb others with your talk. Do not call loudly from one end of a long gallery to the other, or you will distract the attention of those who derive great enjoyment from an undisturbed contemplation of the wonders in these rooms. You will excuse this hint.

3dly. *Be not obtrusive.* You will see many things in the Museum that you do not understand. It will be well to make a memorandum of these, to be inquired into at your leisure; and in these inquiries we shall endeavour to assist you from time to time. But do not trouble other visitors with your questions; and, above all, do not trouble the young artists, some of whom you will see making drawings for their improvement. Their time is precious to them; and it is a real inconvenience to be obliged to give their attention to anything but their work, or to have their attention disturbed by an over-curious person peeping at what they are doing. If you want to make any inquiry, go to one of the attendants, who walks about in each room. He will answer you as far as he knows. You must not expect to understand what you see all at once: you must go again and again if you wish to obtain real knowledge, beyond the gratification of passing curiosity.

In future numbers we shall briefly mention what is most worthy your attention in this National Collection.

HENRY PETER BROUGHAM

# Practical Observations upon the Education of the People*

ADDRESSED TO THE
WORKING CLASSES
AND THEIR EMPLOYERS

HENRY PETER BROUGHAM, LATER BARON
Brougham and Vaux (1778–1868), was one of the most energetic
and important of the great Whigs of the early century. He helped
set up the *Edinburgh Review* in 1802 and remained for decades one
of its most voluminous contributors. He campaigned tirelessly for
the abolition of slavery, in defense of progressive causes and in

* From pamphlet, First Edition (London: 1825), printed by Richard
Taylor and sold by Longman, Hurst, Rees, Orme, Brown, and Green, for
The Benefit of the London Mechanics Institution.

opposition to reactionary ones, like the Six Acts of 1819. He was also, however, strongly opposed to the radicals, and, because of his great egotism and desire to lead, he made enemies of many Whigs, including Macaulay, who agreed with almost all of his policies. The *Encyclopaedia Brittanica* characterizes his position in this way: "Brougham's was the unhappy role of the political liberal, unable to subordinate either himself or his principles to the demand of party."

It would be difficult in less than a volume to recount briefly even the major political battles of his life. One of his favorite causes, popular education, is the subject of the pamphlet reproduced here, which was extraordinarily popular and influential. He also helped to establish Mechanics' Institutes and the University of London.

It is possible from the present essay to see why he antagonized so many people who joined him in voting for reforms, and to recognize that it was something other than brilliance and literary style which gained him his fame. But it is difficult, nonetheless, to withhold admiration from a man who worked so tirelessly and effectively on the right side of so many issues: abolition of slavery, law reform, Catholic Emancipation, repeal of the Test and Corporation Acts, parliamentary reform, popular education. If the pamphlet here reproduced seems rather less than sensational, one ought not to forget that, one hundred and fifty years ago, it was a very valuable instrument in the spread of popular education in England.

I begin by assuming that there is no class of the community so entirely occupied with labour as not to have an hour or two every other day at least, to bestow upon the pleasure and improvement to be derived from reading—or so poor as not to have the means of contributing something towards purchasing this gratification, the enjoyment of which, besides the present amusement, is the surest way both to raise our character and better our condition.—Let us consider how the attainment of this inestimable advantage may be most successfully promoted.

It is no doubt manifest, that the people themselves must be the great agents in accomplishing the work of their own instruction. Unless they deeply feel the usefulness of knowledge, and resolve to make some sacrifices for the acquisition of it, there can be no reasonable prospect of this grand object being attained. But it is equally clear, that to wait until the whole people with one accord take the determination to labour in this good work, would be endless. A portion of the community may be sensible of its advantages, and willing at any fair price to seek them, long before the same laudable feeling becomes universal; and their successful efforts to better their intellectual condition cannot fail to spread more widely the love of learning, and the disrelish for sensual and vulgar gratifications.

But although the people must be the source and the instruments of their own improvement, they may be essentially aided in their efforts to instruct themselves. Impediments which might be sufficient to retard or wholly to obstruct their progress, may be removed; and efforts which, unassisted, might prove fruitless, arising perhaps from a transient, or only a partial enthusiasm for the attainment of knowledge, may, through judicious encouragement, become effectual, and settle into a lasting and an universal habit. A little attention to the difficulties that principally beset the working classes in their search after information, will lead us to the knowledge both of the direction in which their more affluent neighbours can lend them most valuable assistance, and of the part which must be borne by themselves.

Their difficulties may all be classed under one or other of two heads—want of money, and want of time. To the first belongs the difficulty of obtaining those books and instructors which persons in easier circumstances can command; and to the second it is owing that the same books and instructors are not adapted to them, which suffice to teach persons who have leisure to go through the whole course of any given branch of science. In some lines of employment, there is a peculiar difficulty in finding time for acquiring knowledge; as in those which require severe labour, or, though less severe, yet in the open air; for here the tendency to sleep immediately after it ceases, and the greater portion of sleep required, oppose very serious obstacles to instruction: on the other hand those occupations are less unfavourable to reflection, and have a considerable tendency to enlarge the mind.

The first method, then, which suggests itself for promoting knowledge among the poor, is the encouragement of cheap publications; and in no country is this more wanted than in Great Britain, where, with all our expertness in manufactures, we have never succeeded in printing books at so little as double the price required by our neighbours on the continent. A gown, which any where else would cost half a guinea, may be made in this country for half a crown; but a volume, fully as well or better printed, and on paper which, if not as fine, is quite fine enough, and far more agreeable to the eyes, than could be bought in London for half a guinea, costs only six francs, or less than five shillings, at Paris. The high price of labour in a trade where so little can be done, or at least has been done by machinery, is one of the causes of this difference. But the direct tax upon paper is another; and the determination to print upon paper of a certain price is a third; and the aversion to crowd the page is a fourth. Now all of these, except the first, may be got over. The duty on paper is threepence a pound, which must increase the price of an octavo volume eighteenpence or ninepence; and this upon paper of every kind, and printing of every kind; so that if by whatever means the price of a book were reduced to the lowest, say to three or four shillings, about a fourth or a fifth must be added for the tax; and this book, brought as low as possible to accommodate the poor man, with the coarsest paper and most ordinary type, must pay exactly as much to government as the finest hot-pressed work of the same size. This tax ought, therefore, by all means, to be given up; but though, from its being the same upon all paper used in printing, no part of it can be saved by using coarse paper, much of it may be saved by crowding the letterpress, and having a very narrow margin. This experiment has been tried of late in London upon a considerable scale; but it may easily be carried a great deal further. . . .

The method of publishing in Numbers is admirably suited to the circumstances of the classes whose income is derived from wages. Twopence is easily saved in a week by almost any labourer; and by a mechanic sixpence in a week may without difficulty be laid by. Those who have not attended to such matters, would be astonished to find how substantial a meal of information may be had by twopennyworths. Seven numbers, for fourteen pence, comprise Franklin's Life and Essays; four for eightpence, Bacon's Essays; and 36 for six shillings, the whole of the Arabian Nights. Cook's Voyages, in threepenny numbers, with many good engravings, may be had complete for seven shillings; and Plutarch's Lives, for ten shillings, will soon be finished. The Mirror, a weekly publication, containing much matter of harmless and even improving amusement, selected with very considerable taste, has besides, in almost every number, information of a most instructive kind. Its great circulation must prove highly beneficial to the bulk of the people. I understand, that of some parts upwards of 80,000 were printed, and there can be no doubt that the entertainment which is derived from reading the lighter essays, may be made the means of conveying knowledge of a more solid and useful description—a consideration which I trust the conductor will always bear in mind. . . . It is a weekly paper, . . . and although, being principally intended for the use of the workmen, it bestows peculiar attention on whatever concerns that order, yet the occurrences which it communicates, and the discussions which it contains, are also those most interesting to philosophers themselves. The day, indeed, seems now to break, when we may hope to see no marked line of separation between the two classes. I trust another distinction will also soon be known no more. The circulation of cheap works of a merely amusing kind, as well as of those connected with the arts, is at present very great in England; those of an aspect somewhat more forbidding, though at once moral, interesting, and most useful, is very limited; while in Scotland there is a considerable demand for them. Habits of reading longer formed in that country, have taught the inhabitants, that nothing in reality can be more attractive than the profound wisdom of every day's application, sustained by unbounded learning, and embellished with the most brilliant fancy, which so richly furnishes every page of the Essays of Bacon.

It is undoubtedly from the circumstance just mentioned, that in looking over the list of those cheap publications, which are unconnected with the arts, we certainly do not find many that are of a very instructive cast; and here it is that something may be done by way of encouragement. That the demand for books, cheap as well as dear, must tend to produce them, no one denies; but then it is equally certain, that the publication of cheap books increases the number of readers among the poor; and one can hardly conceive a greater benefit than those would confer, who should make a judicious selection from our best authors upon ethics, politics and history, and promote cheap editions of them in Numbers, without waiting until the demand was such as to make the sale a matter of perfect certainty. Lord John Russell,[1] in his excellent and instructive speech upon Parliamentary Reform, delivered in 1822, stated, that "an establishment was commenced a few years ago, by a number of individuals, with a capital of

1. Lord John Russell (1792–1878) was a member of one of the great Whig families. He introduced the Reform Bill which finally passed Parliament in 1832. He espoused most of the Whig causes and was leader of the Whigs in the House of Commons despite the fact that King William hated him. He later became Prime Minister (1846–52; 1865–66).

not less than a million, for the purpose of printing standard works at a cheap rate;" and he added, that it had been "very much checked in its operation by one of those Acts for the suppression of knowledge which were passed in the year 1819, although one of its rules was not to allow the venders of its works to sell any book on the political controversies of the day." The only part of this plan which appears at all objectionable, is the restriction upon politics. Why should not political, as well as all other works, be published in a cheap form, and in Numbers? That history, the nature of the constitution, the doctrines of political economy, may safely be disseminated in this shape, no man now-a-days will be hardy enough to deny. Popular tracts, indeed, on the latter subject, ought to be much more extensively circulated for the good of the working classes, as well as of their superiors. The interests of both are deeply concerned in sounder views being taught them; I can hardly imagine, for example, a greater service being rendered to the men, than expounding to them the true principles and mutual relations of population and wages; and both they and their masters will assuredly experience the effects of the prevailing ignorance upon such questions, as soon as any interruption shall happen in the commercial prosperity of the country, if indeed the present course of things, daily tending to lower wages as well as profits, and set the two classes in opposition to each other, shall not of itself bring on a crisis. To allow, or rather to induce the people to take part in those discussions, is therefore not merely safe, but most wholesome for the community, and yet some points connected with them are matter of pretty warm contention in the present times; but these may be freely handled, it seems, with safety; indeed, unless they are so handled, such subjects cannot be discussed at all. Why then may not every topic of politics, party as well as general, be treated of in cheap publications? It is highly useful to the community that the true principles of the constitution, ecclesiastical and civil, should be well understood by every man who lives under it. The great interests of civil and religious liberty are mightily promoted by such wholesome instruction; but the good order of society gains to the full as much by it. The peace of the country, and the stability of the government, could not be more effectually secured than by the universal diffusion of this kind of knowledge. The abuses which through time have crept into the practice of the constitution, the errors committed in its administration, and the improvements which a change of circumstances require even in its principles, may most fitly be expounded in the same manner. And if any man or set of men deny the existence of such abuses, see no error in the conduct of those who administer the government, and regard all innovation upon its principles as pernicious, they may propagate their doctrines through the like channels. Cheap works being furnished, the choice of them may be left to the readers. Assuredly, a country which tolerates every kind, even the most unmeasured, of daily and weekly discussion in the newspapers, can have nothing to dread from the diffusion of political doctrines in a form less desultory, and more likely to make them be both well weighed at the time, and preserved for repeated perusal. It cannot be denied, that the habit of cursory reading, engendered by finding all subjects discussed in publications, which, how great soever their merits may be, no one looks at a second time, is unfavourable to the acquisition of solid and permanent information.

Although the publication of cheap works is the most effectual method of bringing knowledge within the reach of a poor man's income, there are other modes deserving our attention, whereby a similar assistance may be rendered, and his resources economized. Circulating libraries may in some circumstances be of use; but, generally speaking, they are little suited to those who have only an hour or two every day, or every other day, to bestow upon reading. *Book Clubs*, or *Reading Societies*, are far more suited to the labouring classes, may be established by very small numbers of contributors, and require an inconsiderable fund. If the associates live near one another, arrangements may be easily made for circulating the books, so that they may be in use every moment that any one can spare from his work. Here, too, the rich have an opportunity presented to them of promoting instruction without constant interference; the gift of a few books, as a beginning, will generally prove a sufficient encouragement to carry on the plan by weekly or monthly contributions; and with the gift a scheme may be communicated, to assist the contributors in arranging the plan of their association. I would here remark the great effect of combination upon such plans, in making the money of individuals go far. Three-halfpence a week laid by in a whole family, will enable it to purchase in a year one of the cheap volumes of which I have spoken above, and a penny a week would be sufficient, were the publications made as cheap as possible. Now, let only a few neighbours join, say ten or twelve, and lend each other the books bought; and it is evident, that for a price so small as to be within the reach of the poorest labourer, all may have full as many books in the course of the year as it is possible for them to read, even supposing that the books bought by every one are not such as all the others desire to have. The publication of books in Numbers greatly helps this plan; for it enables those who choose to begin it at any time, without waiting until they have laid by enough to purchase a volume in each family; and where books not so published are wanted, booksellers would do well to aid such associations by giving them a year's credit; whatever propagates a taste for reading must secure their interest in the end. . . .

An excellent plan was about ten years ago adopted by Mr. S. Brown, of Haddington, for instructing the towns and villages of the county of East-Lothian, in succession, by means of the same books. It began with only a few volumes; but he now has 19 *Itinerant Libraries* of 50 volumes each, which are sent round the different stations, remaining a certain time at each. For these there are 19 divisions, and 15 stations, 4 divisions being always in use at the chief town, and 2 at another town of some note. An individual at each station acts as librarian. There are 700 or 800 readers, and the expenses, under 60L. a year, are defrayed by the produce of a sermon, the sale of some tracts, and subscriptions, in small sums averaging 5s. . . .

It is, however, not only necessary that the money of the working classes, but their time also, should be economized; and this consideration leads to various suggestions.

In the first place, there are many occupations in which a number of persons work in the same room; and unless there be something noisy in the work, one may always read while the others are employed. If there are twenty-four men together, this arrangement would only require each man to work one extra day in four weeks, supposing the reading to go on the whole day, which it would not; but a boy or a girl might be engaged to perform the task, at an expense so trifling as not to be felt. This expedient, too, it may be observed, would save money as well as time; one copy of a book, and that borrowed for the purpose, or obtained from a reading society or circulating library, would suffice for a number of persons. I may add, that great help would be given by the better informed and more apt learners, to such as are slower of apprehension and more ignorant; and discussion (under proper regulations) would be of singular use to all, even the most forward proficients; which leads me to observe,

Secondly, That societies for the express purpose of promoting conversation are a most useful adjunct to any private or other education received by the working classes. Those who do not work together in numbers, or whose occupation is of a noisy kind, may thus, one or two evenings in the week, meet and obtain all the advantages of mutual instruction and discussion. An association of this kind will naturally combine with its plan the advantages of a book club. The members will most probably be such as are engaged in similar pursuits, and whose train of reading and thinking may be nearly the same. The only considerable evils which they will have to avoid, are, being too numerous, and falling too much into debate. From twenty to thirty seems a convenient number; and nearer the former than the latter. The tone ought to be given from the beginning, in ridicule of speech-making, both as to length and wordiness. A subject of discussion may be given out at one meeting for the next; or the chairman may read a portion of some work, allowing each member to stop him at any moment, for the purpose of controverting, supporting, or illustrating by his remarks the passage just read. To societies of this kind master workmen have the power of affording great facilities. They may allow an hour on the days when the meetings are holden; or if that is too much; they may allow the men to begin an hour earlier on those days; or if even that cannot be managed, they may let them have an hour and a half, on condition of working half an hour extra on three other days. But a more essential help will be the giving them a place to meet. There are hardly twenty or thirty workmen in any branch of business, some of whose masters have not a room, workshop, ware-house, or other place sufficient to accommodate such a society: and it is quite necessary that the place of rendezvous should on no account be the alehouse. Whoever lent his premises for this purpose, might satisfy himself that no improper persons should be admitted, by taking the names of the whole club from two or three steady men, who could be answerable for the demeanour of the rest. Any interference beyond this would be unwise: unless in so far as the men might voluntarily consult their masters from time to time; and their disposi-tion to do so must depend wholly upon the relations of kindness and mutual confidence subsisting between the parties. . . .

In the third place, it is evident that as want of time prevents the operative classes from pursuing a systematic course of education in all its details, a more summary and compendious method of in-struction must be adopted by them. The majority must be content with never going beyond a certain point, and with reaching that point by the most expeditious route. A few, thus initiated in the truths of science, will no doubt push their attainments much further; and for these the works in common use will suffice; but for the multitude it will be most essential that works should be prepared adapted to their circumstances. Thus, in teaching them geometry, it is not necessary to go through the whole steps of that beautiful system, by which the most general and remote truths are connected with the few simple definitions and axioms; enough will be accomplished, if they are made to perceive the nature of geometrical investigation, and learn the lead-ing properties of figure. In like manner, they may be taught the doctrines of mechanics with a much more slender previous knowledge both of geometry and algebra, than the common elementary works on dynamicks pre-suppose in the reader. Hence, a most essential service will be rendered to the cause of knowledge by him who shall devote his time to the composition of elementary treatises on the Mathematics, sufficiently clear, and yet sufficiently compendious, to exemplify the method of reasoning employed in that science, and to impart an accurate knowledge of the most useful fundamental propositions, with their application to practical purposes; and treatises upon Natural Philosophy, which may teach the great principles of physics, and their practical application, to readers who have but a general knowledge of mathematics, or who are even wholly ignorant of the science beyond the common rules of arithmetic. Nor let it be supposed, that the time thus bestowed is given merely to instruct the people in the rudiments of philosophy, though this would of itself be an object sufficiently brilliant to allure the noblest ambition; for what higher achievement did the most sublime philosophy ever aspire after, than to elevate the views and refine the character of the great mass of mankind—at least in later times, when science no longer looks down as of old upon the multitude, supercilious, and deeming that great spirits alone perish not with the body? But if extending the bounds of science itself be the grand aim of all philosophers in all ages, they indirectly, but surely, accomplish this object, who enable thousands to speculate and experiment for one to whom the path of investigation is now open. It is not necessary that all who are taught, or even any large proportion, should go beyond the rudiments; but whoever feels within himself a desire and an aptitude to proceed further, will press forward; and the chances of discovery, both in the arts and in science itself, will be thus indefinitely multiplied. Indeed, those discoveries immediately connected with experiment and observation, are most likely to be made by men, whose lives being spent in the midst of mechanical operations, are at the same time instructed in the general principles upon which these depend, and trained betimes to habits of speculation. . . .

Although much may be done by the exertions of individuals, it is manifest that a great deal more may be effected by the labours of a body, in furthering this important measure. The subject has for some time past been under consideration, and I am not without hopes of seeing formed a Society for promoting the composition, publication, and distribution of cheap and useful works.[2] To qualify persons for

2. This society was, of course, formed as The Society for the Diffusion of Useful Knowledge, in 1826.

becoming efficient members of this association, or co-operating with it all over the country, neither splendid talents, nor profound learning, nor great wealth are required. Though such gifts, in their amplest measure, would not be thrown away upon so important a design, they are by no means indispensable to its success. A well-informed man of good sense, filled with the resolution to obtain for the great body of his fellow-creatures, that high improvement which both their under-standings and their morals are by nature fitted to receive, may labour in this good work, either in the central institution or in some remote district, with the certainty of success, if he have only that blessing of leisure for the sake of which riches are chiefly to be coveted. Such a one, however averse by taste or habit to the turmoil of public affairs, or the more ordinary strifes of the world, may in all quiet and in-nocence enjoy the noblest gratification of which the most aspiring nature is susceptible; he may influence by his single exertions the character and the fortunes of a whole generation, and thus wield a power to be envied even by vulgar ambition for the extent of its dominion—to be cherished by virtue itself for the unalloyed blessings it bestows.

*Fourthly,* The preparation of elementary works is not the only, nor, at first, is it the most valuable service that can be rendered towards economizing the time of the labouring classes. The institution of Lectures is, of all the helps that can be given, the most valuable, where circumstances permit; that is, in towns of a certain size. Much may thus be taught, even without any other instruction; but, combined with reading, and subservient to it, the effects of public lectures are great indeed, especially in the present deficiency of proper elementary works. The students are enabled to read with advantage; things are explained to them which no books sufficiently illustrate; access is afforded to teachers, who can remove the difficulties which occur perpetually in the reading of uneducated persons; a word may often suffice to get rid of some obstacle which would have impeded the unassisted student's progress for days; and then, whatever requires the performance of experiments to become intelligible, can only be learnt by the bulk of mankind at a lecture, inasmuch as the wealthy alone can have such lessons in private, and none but men highly gifted can hope to master those branches of science without seeing the experi-mental illustrations.

The branches of knowledge to which these observations chiefly apply, are Mechanical Philosophy and Chemistry, both as being more intimately connected with the arts, and as requiring more explanation and illustration by experiment. But the Mathematics, Astronomy, and

Geology, the two former especially, are well fitted for being taught publicly, and are of great practical use. Nor is there any reason why Moral and Political Philosophy should not be explained in public lectures, though they may be learnt by reading far more easily than the physical sciences.

In all plans of this description, it is absolutely necessary that the expenses should mainly be defrayed by those for whose benefit they are contrived. It is the province of the rich to lay the foundation, by making certain advances which are required in the first instance, and enabling the poor to come forward, both as learners and contributors. But no such scheme can either take a deep root, or spread over the country so as to produce its full measure of good, unless its support is derived from those who are chiefly to reap the benefits. Those benefits are well worth paying for; they are not only of great value in the improvement and gratification which they afford to the mind, but in the direct addition which they make to the pecuniary resources of the labouring classes. Instruction in the principles upon which the arts depend, will repay in actual profit to those who live by the arts, far more than the cost of learning. An artisan, a dyer, an engine-maker, will gain the more in money or money's worth for being an expert chemist or mechanician; and a farm-servant, or bailiff, for knowing the economy and diseases of cattle. I have before me the extract of a letter from one of the greatest engine-makers in the country, stating, that a young man in humble life had been selected from among many applicants, to fill a considerable place in the manufactory, on account of his proficiency in science. The profit directly accruing from the knowledge of those sciences provides an immediate fund, out of which the cost of acquiring it may be easily defrayed; but a fund is as certainly though somewhat more remotely secured for repaying, with large interest, the expense of acquiring knowledge of a more general description—those branches of learning which improve the morals, expand the understanding, and refine the taste. That invaluable fund is composed of the savings made by substituting pure and harmless and cheap gratifications, in the stead of luxuries which are both grosser and more costly—hurtful to the health, and wasteful of time.

The yearly cost of a lecture in the larger cities, where enlightened and public-spirited men may be found willing to give instruction for nothing, is indeed considerably less than in smaller places, where a compensation must be made for the lecturer's time and work. But it seems advisable, that, even where gratuitous assistance could be obtained, something like an adequate remuneration should be afforded, both to preserve the principle of independence among the working classes, and to secure the more accurate and regular discharge of the duty. We shall therefore suppose, that the lectures, as well as the current expenses of the room, and where there are experiments, of the apparatus, are to be paid for; and still it appears by no means an undertaking beyond the reach of those classes. . . .

. . . To make a beginning, the parties must make a shift with any public room or other place that may be vacant; the great point is to begin: the numbers are certain to increase, and the income with the numbers, as the plan becomes known and its manifold attractions operate upon the people. For the same reason I reckon a small sum for apparatus. Great progress may be made in teaching with very cheap and simple experiments. Indeed some of the most important, if not the most showy, are the least costly and complicated. By far the grandest discoveries in natural science were made with hardly any apparatus. . . .

The difficulty of obtaining a fit lecturer is one likely for some time to be much felt, especially in small towns. One method of removing it is by sending an experienced teacher from place to place; and the man qualified for the task, who should fastidiously reject so useful and so honourable an occupation, might be a man of science, but would little deserve to be called a philosopher. No talents and no acquirements are too great to be thus applied; and no use to which parts and learning can be put is more dignified. But another supply of instructors will soon be ready. Each Institution now established must in a short time form teachers. Among a great number of students, some must be found to make such progress as will qualify them for the office. In the Edinburgh School of Arts a joiner has for some time past been teaching mathematics, which he learnt there. At Glasgow, a person of the same trade, who had been taught at the school established by Dr. Birkbeck,[3] has lectured on geography, chemistry, and mechanics. These instances prove that the men will be able to teach; it is equally clear that the wages of a lecturer will make them turn their attention to this business in places where one is wanted.

3. Dr. George Birkbeck (1776–1841), a friend of Brougham's, was for a while Professor of Natural Philosophy at Andersonian University, Glasgow. He began efforts there toward popular education, and by 1800 had established courses of lectures for workingmen at low fees. In 1823, the organization he founded became the Glasgow Mechanics Institute. Birkbeck lived in London as a medical doctor after 1804. In 1824, following the suggestion of the *Mechanics Magazine*, he began to develop an institution in London similar to the one he had founded in Glasgow. This was known as the London Mechanics Institute (and has since become Birkbeck College). He was also one of the founders of University College, London, in 1827.

After all, it may often happen that a lecture cannot be undertaken on however moderate a plan; in that case it will be advisable to begin with a library, to which a lecture may afterwards be added.—This was the course pursued at Kendal, where a *"Mechanics and Apprentices Library"* was begun last spring, and in autumn a course of lectures was delivered upon the Philosophy of Natural History. At Carlisle, and I believe at Hawick, the same method has been adopted.

I have remarked, that in forming these Institutions, it is a fundamental principle to make the expenses be mainly defrayed by the mechanics themselves; it is another principle, in my opinion equally essential, that they should have the principal share in the management. This seems necessary for securing both the success and the independence of the system. Nor is there the least reason to apprehend mismanagement. If benefit societies are, upon the whole, well managed, we may rely upon institutions being still better conducted, where the improvement of the mind being the object, those only will ever take an active part, who are desirous of their own advancement in knowledge, and of the general instruction of the class to which they belong. Indeed there seems no better means of securing the continued attention of the Directors, than placing the direction in the hands of those who are alone interested in the prosperity of the concern. Neither is there any fear that the suggestions of persons in a higher station, and of more ample information, may not be duly attended to. Gratitude for the assistance received, and the advice offered, together with a conviction that the only motive for interfering is the good of the establishment, will give at least their just weight to the recommendations of patrons; and if it were not always so, far better would it be to see such influence fail entirely, than to run the risk of the apathy which might be occasioned among the men, and the abuse of the Institutions themselves, which might frequently be produced by excluding from the control of their affairs those whose interests are the only object in view. The opinions of patrons are always sure to have influence as long as their object plainly is to promote the good of those for whom the Institution was founded; and as soon as they are actuated by any other views, it is very fit that their influence should cease. . . .

I have said that the *independence* of these undertakings, as well as their success, is to be considered. I really should be disposed to view any advantage in point of knowledge gained by the body of the people, as somewhat equivocal, or at least as much alloyed with evil, if purchased by the increase of their dependence upon their superiors. They will always be abundantly thankful for the help afforded them in beginning such institutions, and quite ready to receive advice from those who render them assistance. But if the latter keep the management entirely in their own hands, they enforce the appeal to gratitude by something very like control; and they hurt the character of those whom they would serve. For this reason, as well as for promoting more effectually and generally the establishment of these institutions, it is of the last importance that the yearly expense should be reduced to such a sum as can be wholly raised by the students. What they receive in money from their superiors will then be given once for all at the outset; what they receive from time to time in good counsel, and in teaching, either by lectures or publications, shows much real kindness, confers a great benefit, and ensures a grateful return, without bringing into action any of those feelings alike painful and injurious, which arise from the assumption of authority grounded on the mere differences of rank and wealth.

It is now fit that we advert to the progress that has already been made in establishing this system of instruction. Its commencement was the work of Dr. Birkbeck, to whom the people of this island owe a debt of gratitude, the extent of which it would not be easy, perhaps in the present age not possible, to describe; for as, in most cases, the effective demand precedes the supply, it would have been more in the ordinary course of things, that a teacher should spring up at the call of the mechanics for instruction: but long before any symptoms appeared of such an appetite on their part, and with the avowed purpose of implanting the desire in them, or at least of unfolding and directing it, by presenting the means of gratification, the most learned and excellent person formed the design, as enlightened as it was benevolent, of admitting the working classes of his fellow-countrymen to the knowledge of sciences, till then almost deemed the exclusive property of the higher ranks in society, and only acquired accidentally and irregularly in a few rare instances of extraordinary natural talents, by any of the working classes. Dr. Birkbeck, before he settled in London, where he has since reached the highest station in the medical profession, resided for some time in Glasgow as Professor in the Anderson College; and about the year 1800, he announced a Course of Lectures on Natural Philosophy, and its application to the Arts, for the instruction of mechanics. But a few at the first availed themselves of this advantage; by degrees, however, the extraordinary perspicuity of the teacher's method, the judicious selection of his experiments, and the natural attractions of the subject, to men whose lives were spent in directing or witnessing operations, of which the principles were now first unfolded to them, proved successful in diffusing a general taste for the study; and when he left Glasgow two or three years afterwards, about seven hundred eagerly and constantly attended the class.

For some time after Dr. Birkbeck's departure, the lectures of his able and worthy successor Dr. Ure[4] were well frequented; and when the number of the students began to decline, probably from the circumstance of their having no direct share in the management of the Institution, the Professor happily thought of adding to it a library for the use of the mechanics, and entrusting the direction of it entirely to a committee chosen by themselves. This gave new life to the enterprise, and the Gas Light Company having in return for some services rendered them by the Professor, agreed to light the book-room two evenings in the week, a custom arose among the men who came to change their books, of remaining to converse upon the subjects of their reading, and an extraordinary impulse was thus given to their spirit of inquiry. The Library Committee, too, being chosen by the whole body, became in some sort its representative, and claimed to interfere in the management of the Institution. It soon happened that some of their suggestions were not attended to; and a difference, at first to be regretted, led to consequences highly beneficial; for a great number seceded from the lectures and formed an Institution entirely under the management of the mechanics themselves. It has been successful beyond all expectation; a thousand working men attended it last winter, while the numbers of the parent establishment were scarcely diminished. . . .

The complete success of Dr. Birkbeck's plan both at Glasgow originally, and afterwards in a place abounding far less with artisans, very naturally suggested the idea of giving its principles a more general diffusion by the only means which seem in this country calculated for universally recommending any scheme—its adoption in London. An Address was published by Messers. Robertson and Hodgkin, in the Mechanics Magazine, October 1823; and the call was answered promptly by Dr. Birkbeck himself, and other friends of education, as well as by the master mechanics and workmen of the metropolis. A meeting was held in November; the Mechanics Institution was formed; a subscription opened; and a set of regulations adopted. Of these by far the most important and one which in common, I believe, with all my colleagues, I consider to be altogether essential, provides that the committee of management shall be chosen by the whole students, and consist of at least two-thirds working men. The plan was so speedily carried into execution, that in January Dr. Birkbeck, our president, most appropriately opened the Institution with an introductory ad-

4. Andrew Ure (1778–1857) was a chemist and scientific writer who took Birkbeck's Professorship when Birkbeck moved to London. He inaugurated popular scientific lectures and wrote books on the philosophy of manufacture and on geology.

dress to many hundred workmen, crowding from great distances in the worst season and after the toils of the day were over, to slake that thirst of knowledge which forms the most glorious characteristic of the age; nor was the voluntary offer of a course of lectures upon Mechanics less appropriate on the part of Professor Millington, who with an honest pride declared to his audience, that he had originally belonged to the same class with themselves. In the course of the year, lectures were delivered by Mr. Phillips on Chemistry, Mr. Dotchin on Geometry, Dr. Birkbeck on Hydrostatics, Mr. Cooper on the application of Chemistry to the Arts, Mr. Newton on Astronomy, and Mr. Black on the French language, to great and increasing numbers of workmen. About a thousand now belong to the Institution, and pay 20s. a year. . . .

[What follows is a description of similar institutions established at Newcastle, Kendal, Carlisle, Manchester, Leeds, Liverpool, Sheffield, and Aberdeen-ed.]

To encourage good men in these exertions—to rouse the indifferent and cheer the desponding by setting plain facts before them—has been the object of these details. The subject is of such inestimable importance that no apology is required for anxiously addressing in favour of it all men of enlightened views, who value the real improvement of their fellow-creatures, and the best interests of their country. We are bound upon this weighty matter to be instant, in season and out of season. I now speak not merely of seminaries for teaching mechanics the principles of natural and mathematical sciences, but of schools where the working classes generally may learn those branches of knowledge which they cannot master by private reading. It must be a small town indeed, where some useful lecture may not, with a little exertion and a little encouragement, be so established that the quarterly contributions of the students may afterwards suffice to continue it. Moral and political philosophy may be acceptable even where there is no field for teachers of chemistry and mechanics; and where no lecture at all can be supported, a library may be set on foot, and the habit of useful reading encouraged. We constantly hear of public-spirited individuals; of men who are friendly to the poor and the working classes; of liberal-minded persons, anxious for the diffusion of knowledge and the cultivation of intellectual pursuits. But no one has a right to assume such titles—to take credit for both zeal and knowledge—if he has done nothing in his own neighbourhood to found a popular lecture, or, should the circle be too narrow for that, to establish a reading club, which, in many cases, will end in a lecture. For such a club, there is hardly a village in the country too small; and

I have shown that towns of a very moderate size may support a lecture. After the success of the experiments already made, indeed, it seems little less than shameful that there should be any considerable town without establishments for popular education. I speak from the actual history of some of the instances which I have cited, when I say that one man only is wanted in each place to ensure the success of the plan. Where there is such a man, and workmen in sufficient numbers, —there are all the materials that can be required. He has but to converse with a few master-workmen; to circulate, in concert with them, a notice for a meeting; or if it be deemed better to have no meeting, let them ascertain how many will attend a class; and the room may be hired and the lecturer engaged in a month. The first cost will be easily defrayed by a subscription among the rich; or, if that fail, the collection of a library will be made by degrees out of the money raised by the students. The expense of providing apparatus ought not to deter any one from making the attempt. I have shown how much may be done with but little machinery, and a skilful lecturer can give most useful help to private study, by drawings and explanations, with hardly any experiments at all. The facilities too will increase; the wish for scientific education will beget an effectual demand, and teachers will present themselves to supply the want. Already it would be a safe adventure for a lecturer to engage in, where there are great bodies of artisans. In any of the large manufacturing towns of Lancashire and Yorkshire, a person duly qualified to teach the principles of mechanics and chemistry, and their application to the arts, would now find it easy to collect a large class, willing and able to remunerate him for his trouble; and it is highly probable, that, before long, there will be established, in each of those places, permanent teachers upon private speculation.

But, great as the disposition to learn already is among the working classes, and certain as a lecture would be of attendants wherever it was once set on foot, there is still a necessity for the upper classes coming forward to assist in making the first step. Those seminaries are still too new; they are too little known among the artisans generally to be thought of and demanded by themselves; still more difficult would it be for them to set about forming the plans for themselves. Even in the largest towns, it is hardly to be expected that the workmen should yet concert measures for their own instruction, although sufficiently numerous to require no pecuniary assistance in procuring the necessary teachers. The present then is the moment for making an effort to propagate the system; and for giving that encouragement which may at once spread those Institutions and render universally habitual the desire of knowledge that already prevails. Nor can the means be wanting among the upper, or even the middle ranks of society. There exist ample funds at present applied to charitable purposes, which at best are wasted, and more frequently employed in doing harm. I speak not now of the large revenue, a million and a half or more from endowments, which is almost altogether expended in a manner injurious to the community; not above a third part belonging to charities connected with education, and of that third by far the greatest portion going to maintain poor children, which is nearly the worst employment of such funds;[5] while of the remaining two thirds, only a very small proportion is spent on perhaps the only harmless objects of common charity, hospitals for the sick poor, or provision for persons ruined by grievous and sudden calamities. But I allude to the large sums yearly collected in every part of the country to support charitable institutions; and, though given from the best of motives, yet applied to increase the number of the poor almost as certainly as the parish rates themselves. These funds are entirely under the control of the contributors; and to them I would fain address most respectfully a few words.

Every person who has been accustomed to subscribe for the support of what are commonly called charities, should ask himself this question. "However humane the motive, am I doing any real good by so expending my money? or am I not doing more harm than good?" In either case, indeed, harm is done; because, even if the money so applied should do no mischief, yet, if it did no good, harm would be done by the waste. But in order to enable him to answer the question, he must reflect, that no proposition is more undeniably true than this, that the existence of a known and regular provision for the poor, whether in the ordinary form of pensions, doles, gratuities, clothing, firing, &c., or in the shape of maintenance for poor children, in whole, or only in part, as clothing, has the inevitable tendency to bring forward not only as many objects as the provision will maintain, but a far greater number. The immediate consequence of such provisions is, to promote idleness and poverty beyond what the funds can relieve: the continued and known existence of the provisions trains up a race of paupers; and a provision for children, especially, promotes improvident marriages, and increases the population by the addition of paupers. It is therefore a sacred duty which every one owes to the community, to refrain from giving contributions to begin such funds; and if he has already become a yearly contributor,

5. It is possible to perceive here one of the extraordinary consequences of the theories of Malthus and political economists: maintaining poor children is evil because it encourages them to be dependent, to continue in their poverty, and because it contributes to the increase of the poor population.

it is equally his duty to withdraw his assistance, unless one condition is complied with,—namely, that no new objects shall be taken into the establishment, but that those only who at present belong to it shall be maintained; so that the mischief may be terminated within a limited time, and nothing unfair or harsh done towards those who had previously depended on its funds. I remember the time when money given to beggars was supposed to be well bestowed—a notion now exploded; yet even this exercise of benevolence is less mischievous than the support of regular establishments for the increase of paupers.

The wise and considerate manner of proceeding which I venture to recommend, would speedily place at the disposal of charitable and enlightened individuals ample funds for supporting works of real, because of most useful charity. Let any one cast his eye over the Reports of the Education Committee and Charity Commissioners, and he may form some idea of the large funds now profusely squandered under the influence of mistaken benevolence. Of the many examples that might be given, let one suffice; its history is in the Report of 1816. The income was above 2000*l.*, of which 1500*l.* arose from yearly subscriptions and donations. This large fund clothed 101 boys, and maintained 65 girls; but the expense of boarding and clothing the girls was of course by far the greatest part of it, perhaps 1200*l.* Much abuse appeared to have crept into the management, in consequence of tradesmen acting as trustees, and voting on the orders to themselves, and on the payment of their own accounts. It was deemed right to check this; and a rule was adopted, at a meeting of trustees, to prevent so scandalous a practice for the future. It was, however, rejected at a meeting of the subscribers, for which, in all probability, the tradesmen had made a canvass, and obtained the attendance of friends. Nay, a most learned and humane Judge, who was one of the trustees, having afterwards proposed a resolution merely to forbid any trustee or subscriber voting on matters in which he was personally interested, it "was rejected instantly, and therefore not recorded on the minutes;" whereupon his lordship abstained from attending any future meeting, and, I trust, from ever contributing to the fund. This is one instance only of thousands, where the money collected from well-disposed persons, who take no further charge of a charity than to pay their subscriptions, is wasted by the jobbing of too active and interested managers. But suppose there had been no direct abuse, and all the income had been honestly and carefully employed in promoting the objects of the establishment, by far the greater part of it would have been hurtfully bestowed. Instead of clothing 101 boys, and maintaining 65 girls, at the rate of 2000*l.* a year, the fixed income alone of 500*l*. might have educated a thousand children, and left 1500*l*. a year free for establishing other schools, if wanted: and as two others of the same size would in all probability have more than sufficed to supply the defect of education which appears by the report of the West London Lancaster Association to exist in that district, a fund would have remained sufficient to support an institution for the instruction of 700 or 800 mechanics. Thus, the same money which is now uselessly, but perniciously bestowed, might, by a little care, and a due portion of steadiness in resisting the interested clamours of persons who subscribe for the purpose of turning it to their own profit, be made the means of at once educating all the children in the worst district of London, and of planting there the light of science among the most useful and industrious class of the community. Now, within the same district, or applicable to it, there are probably other charitable funds, arising from voluntary contribution, to five or six times the amount of this single charity, and it is most likely that there is hardly one of the benevolent individuals who support it but contributes to one or more charities besides. How important, then, does it become for each man carefully to reconsider the use he is making, or suffering others to make, of that money which his humanity has set apart for the relief of his fellow-creatures, and the improvement of their condition; and how serious a duty is it to take care that what originates in the most praiseworthy motives should also end in results really beneficial to the objects of his bounty!

I rejoice to think that it is not necessary to close these observations by combating objections to the diffusion of science among the working classes, arising from considerations of a political nature. Happily the time is past and gone when bigots could persuade mankind that the lights of philosophy were to be extinguished as dangerous to religion; and when tyrants could proscribe the instructors of the people as enemies to their power. It is preposterous to imagine that the enlargement of our acquaintance with the laws which regulate the universe, can dispose to unbelief. It may be a care for superstition— for intolerance it will be the most certain cure; but a pure and true religion has nothing to fear from the greatest expansion which the understanding can receive by the study either of matter or of mind. The more widely science is diffused, the better will the Author of all things be known, and the less will the people be "tossed to and fro by the sleight of men, and cunning craftiness, whereby they lie in wait to deceive." To tyrants, indeed, and bad rulers, the progress of knowledge among the mass of mankind is a just object of terror: it is fatal to them and their designs; they know this by unerring instinct, and unceasingly they dread the light. But they will find it more easy to curse than to extinguish. It is spreading in spite of them, even in those countries where arbitrary power deems itself most secure; and in England, any attempt to check its progress would only bring about the sudden destruction of him who should be insane enough to make it.

To the Upper Classes of society, then, I would say, that the question no longer is whether or not the people shall be instructed—for that has been determined long ago, and the decision is irreversible —but whether they shall be well or ill taught—half informed or as thoroughly as their circumstances permit and their wants require. Let no one be afraid of the bulk of the community becoming too accomplished for their superiors. Well educated, and even well versed in the most elevated sciences, they assuredly may become; and the worst consequence that can follow to their superiors will be, that to deserve being called their *betters*, they too must devote themselves more to the pursuit of solid and refined learning; the present public seminaries must be enlarged; and some of the greater cities of the kingdom, especially the metropolis, must not be left destitute of the regular means within themselves of scientific education.

To the Working Classes I would say, that this is the time when by a great effort they may secure for ever the inestimable blessing of knowledge. Never was the disposition more universal among the rich to lend the requisite assistance for setting in motion the great engines of instruction; but the people must come forward to profit by the opportunity thus afforded, and they must themselves continue the movement once begun. Those who have already started in the pursuit of science, and tasted its sweets, require no exhortation to persevere; but if these pages should fall into the hands of any one at an hour for the first time stolen from his needful rest after his day's work is done, I ask of him to reward me (who have written them for his benefit at the like hours) by saving threepence during the next fortnight, buying with it Franklin's Life, and reading the first page. I am quite sure he will read the rest; I am almost quite sure he will resolve to spend his spare time and money, in gaining those kinds of knowledge which from a printer's boy made that great man the first philosopher, and one of the first statesmen of his age. Few are fitted by nature to go as far as he did, and it is not necessary to lead so perfectly abstemious a life, and to be so rigidly saving of every instant of time. But all may go a good way after him, both in temperance, industry and knowledge, and no one can tell before he tries how near he may be able to approach him.

E. W. GRINFIELD

# A Reply to Mr. Brougham's "Practical Observations upon the Education of the People"*

EDWARD WILLIAM GRINFIELD (1785–1864) IS
not a particularly important writer or clergyman, but he is representative of one type of orthodox opinion, and in this light, his
reply to Brougham's pamphlet is significant. Grinfield was a biblical scholar, a writer on relations between Church and State, and
most particularly a propagandist for orthodoxy in all respects.

* From pamphlet, First Edition (London: C. & J. Rivington, 1825).

This pamphlet on education provides the point of view of the High Church and conservative elements of English society, and makes comprehensible his dislike and distrust of Brougham, as well as his apparent fear of the lower classes becoming, as W. B. Adams remarked, "wiser than their rulers." The whole essay is written with a clarity and apparent moderation that disguises what radicals of the time would probably have called bigotry, and what we can recognize as a fear of the social revolution taking place around him. But it is interesting that Grinfield concedes the inevitability of change and of the extension of education, although he wants to be sure that this education will lead the masses to acquiescence in the status quo.

The extraordinary anxiety which has been manifested by Mr. Brougham and his friends, to give circulation and publicity to his late Pamphlet on the scientific Education of the People, is of itself a sufficient evidence of the importance which he attaches to the subject on which it treats. Having first made its appearance as an article in the Edinburgh Review, it has since been republished with his name, and has already, I believe, realized the most ardent wishes of his Reviewer, "by having circulated an hundred times more widely," than the brief notice of it in the last number of the same Journal. The copy which I possess, is designated as the "thirteenth edition." It is printed "for the benefit of the London Mechanics Institution," and the work is evidently intended as a manifesto to all the mechanics and artizans of Great Britain and Ireland.

That Mr. Brougham is a man of great genius, and of still greater energy and ambition, is well known to men of all parties and opinions; but whether his genius is sufficiently controlled by his judgment to render him a safe legislator on the delicate subject of National Education, or whether his ambition is sufficiently chastised by prudence and moderation to give him the possession of public confidence, are questions on which his friends and admirers, perhaps, think very differently from the great body of the English nation.

On the one hand we are told, by his eulogists, that "of the many titles to distinction we meet with in the person of Mr. Brougham, there is none we should so much envy as that which rests on his services in the cause of education. The good he has done *there* is the most unquestioned and extensive; and the honours he has gained, the least alloyed with faction, the least troubled even by eager contention or dispute, whilst the efforts he has lately made in behalf of the Mechanics' Institutions, appear to us the most important and meritorious of all," etc. But by others, much of this praise is thought entirely misplaced; that Mr. B., by his constitutional violence and impetuosity, is altogether unfitted for plans and objects which demand the exercise of a calm and dispassionate judgment; that the habits of a pleader and an advocate have destroyed the equilibrium of his talents; and that he has so identified himself with those who are habitually opposed to the measures of government, that a spirit of faction and violence is mingled with all his projects.

Without pretending to decide which of these estimates of Mr. Brougham's public character is the more judicious and correct, if we make the appeal to what he has already accomplished or attempted on the subject of National Education, we shall discover but little to justify such exalted encomiums on his merits. . . .

Still his ambition remains undaunted; and though, if we believe his friends, "he has no other excitement than that general philanthropy, and that high-minded anticipation of the love and gratitude of posterity, by which patriots are supported, when they silently confer lasting blessings on their countrymen, without raising their passions, or making any demand on their applause;" yet, he pursues this object amidst victory and defeat, with all his characteristic earnestness and avidity. It appears, that he has been for some time engaged on a large and extensive work on Popular Education "in its three branches,— Infant Schools,—Elementary Schools (for reading and writing),— and Adult Schools;" and that the present Pamphlet is only a synopsis of his sentiments on the last: however, he seems to claim the whole ground as exclusively belonging to himself and his friends.—"Any meddling on the part of government with the first (*Infant Schools!*), would be inexpedient; and with the last (*Adult Schools*), perilous to civil and religious liberty." "It is only with the second (*Elementary Schools*,) that the Legislature can safely interfere:" or, as the version runs in the Edinburgh Review, "the interference of government may not only be safe but advantageous, and even necessary in providing the means of Elementary Education for Children; but that no interference can be tolerated, in the smallest extent, with the subsequent instruction of the people."

Now since Mr. Brougham, "in concert with those friends who hold the same doctrines, has endeavoured to establish *Infant* Schools, it seems to follow," he adds, "from the same view of the subject, that I should lend any little help in my power towards fixing the public attention on the Education of *Adults*:" but, as the "Elementary Schools" "have been repeatedly brought before Parliament" by the same authority, it also follows, that he looks upon *them* with all the fondness and affection of a patron; and thus *Popular Education*, in all its branches, belongs to Mr. Brougham and his friends; and "from tail to snout the pig is eaten."

It has been necessary to premise these observations, to put my reader in possession of the large and extensive views which Mr. B., and "his fellow-labourers in the North," entertain on this subject. Already he speaks with the authority of a legislator;—the empire of "the Education of the People," he considers as peculiarly his own;— he invests himself with the importance of a dictator, both to the Senate and to the People, nor does he over-rate his dignity and importance, *if* this empire should be conceded to his hands.

It is in vain to deny that literature, as it is well or ill conducted, is the great engine by which all civilized governments must stand or fall; and that the influence of literature is becoming daily of greater magnitude and importance in this country. But the attempt to gain the chief if not the sole direction of this engine, as it is worked by *the people*, is no other than an attempt to gain the supreme direction of public sentiment. This it is the object of "Mr. Brougham and his friends," to achieve, by becoming the real or apparent patrons of "the Education of the People;" whether pursued under the form of Infant, Elementary, or Adult Schools, the object is still the same. A more grand, sublime, and noble object it never entered into the heart of man to conceive; it is the που στω[1] by which the nation itself may be lifted up or depressed: but whether Mr. Brougham should be allowed to act as the Archimedes on this occasion is happily a question, not "for his friends," but for the *public* to determine.

· · · · ·

According to Mr. Brougham's representation we are to suppose that "the Elementary Schools," being confined to the mere instruction in reading and writing, have no connection nor influence on the future character and conduct of the individual, who, upon quitting such

1. "where do I stand"

schools, must begin his own education by entering upon what he very ambiguously denominates *an Adult School.* But there are few persons who can rightly conjecture what is meant by these words in Mr. Brougham's vocabulary. Hitherto it has been usual to signify by an *Adult* School, those charitable institutions at which *adults* whose education has been neglected in their youth, may compensate for such defects by attaining the knowledge of reading and writing. But we are introduced by Mr. Brougham's pamphlet to another, and to us a very strange application of these expressions. Be it known, then, to all who are equally ignorant and uninformed, that by an adult school is henceforward to be understood, a philosophical institute for the labouring orders, including a library and apparatus, at which lectures are delivered on Mathematics and Astronomy and Geology, on Chemistry and Hydrostatics, on Electricity, and what surprises us most of all, *"on the French language;"* at least such, gentle reader, was the course pursued by Professor Millington and by Dr. Birkbeck and by Messrs. Phillips, Dotchin, Cooper, Newton and Tatum, during last winter in our metropolis. It is proper to observe that the peculiar and original merit of lecturing *English* workmen and mechanics on the *French* language belongs exclusively to Mr. Black. Now we say, that as Mr. Brougham supposes nothing more to be taught in the Elementary Schools than the mere faculty of reading and writing, it is plain the pupils must come to these Adult Schools very indifferently prepared to enter on such scientific investigations. It may be humbly suggested, that before this audience can take the full benefit of Dr. Lindsay's Chapel in Monkwell Street, or of Mr. Brougham's omens, "and surely," as he observes, "a scheme for the improvement of mankind could not be commenced under happier auspices than in the place which so virtuous and enlightened a friend to his country had once filled the spirit of genuine philanthropy and universal toleration;" that the instructions which are furnished by Mr. Brougham's Elementary Schools should be somewhat enlarged; for I fear that if he should hereafter carry his Education Bill it will be found beyond the omnipotence of parliament, though assisted by all the justices in the kingdom, to render such lectures intelligible to those who have learnt only to read and to write.

But the subject is grave, and it demands the most grave investigation. If Mr. Brougham is serious in his wishes to give the labouring classes a *scientific* education, nothing can be more absurd than to confine the Elementary Schools, at which they must be previously educated, to the mere objects of reading and writing. It is plain that such schools ought then to be brought into harmony with such an object, and that the previous culture and improvement of the mind should correspond to his ulterior designs. But in the present want of all proportion we can regard his scheme as nothing better "than the baseless fabric of a vision," as happily quite beyond his or any man's power to accomplish on a large and permanent scale; but calculated, so far as it can be accomplished, to alarm all sober and prudent persons amongst the middle and upper orders of society, and to render the labouring classes uneasy, unhappy, and dissatisfied.

To what extent the education of the people should be carried is a question on which a variety of opinions will be entertained, but no prudent man can doubt that in exact proportion to its extent ought to be the pains and care bestowed on their elementary instruction. To take a man who can only just read and spell and to invite him to lectures on Chemistry or Mathematics, is one of the most absurd and foolish projects that was ever brought forward. It is exactly on minds like these, "that a little learning is a dangerous thing;" all the previous habits and discipline are wanted which might turn it to a good and beneficial account, the man becomes conceited and inflated by his supposed acquirements, and thus popular education would fall into disrepute from the mistakes and blunders of those who seem the most desirous to advance it.

It is on these grounds that I strongly object to the whole system which Mr. Brougham proposes, as calculated, in my opinion, to defeat the very object which he designs to attain. Let the Elementary Schools for the common people first produce their effects in raising the standard of their minds to their proper pitch, before any attempts are made to give them a philosophical and scientific education. Let them become conversant with Morals and History and Biography before we introduce them to Chemistry, Hydrostatics, or Astronomy. Instead of encouraging restless or self-interested individuals to rove about the country, distracting the minds of our mechanics by lecturing on civil or political economy, or by giving them a smattering in the higher branches of abstract science, let cheap collections of books be formed in our towns and cities, consisting of the popular literature of our country, containing voyages and travels, the lives of eminent individuals, and the history of the most distinguished nations. What Johnson said of education in general, is still more strictly applicable to the education of the common people—"Whether we provide for action or conversation, whether we wish to be useful or pleasing, the first requisite is the religious knowledge of right and wrong; the next an acquaintance with the history of mankind, and with those examples which embody truth, and which prove by events the reasonableness of opinions. Prudence and justice are virtues of all times and of all places. We are perpetually moralists, we are geometricians only by chance." And the force of these remarks may be still further demonstrated from the consideration that the highest improvements of abstract science have a very remote connection with any improvement of the heart, and that a man whose hours are chiefly devoted to handicraft labour or mechanical operations is likely to derive far greater benefit from reading on moral and miscellaneous subjects than from any researches into the philosophy of trade and commerce. He is like a plant which requires a change of soil, and to accomplish this change you must take him off, if possible, from his daily and constant avocations. Hence it will be found that an instructive tale or history will be much more calculated to enlarge and improve his mind, than if he were to pore over the mysteries of steam and gas, or to confound himself with all the theories of Malthus or Ricardo.[2]

Another very strong reason for giving the labouring orders a moral and literary rather than a scientific education, arises from its superior effect on their economical and domestic habits. Lectures and institutions which tempt the labourer or mechanic to leave his home and family are at best of very dubious advantage; I should prefer the simplest improvement gained by his fire-side, and in company with his wife and family, to the most ostentatious meetings of the London Institution. When seven or eight hundred mechanics meet together in the evening after their daily occupations, it may be feared, that not all the allurements of science could always prevent them adjourning afterwards to the tavern or the alehouse; to say the least of it, it is a

2. Thomas Robert Malthus (1766–1834) was the author of the enormously influential *Essay on the Principles of Population as it Affects the Future Improvement of Society, with Remarks on the Speculations of Mr. Godwin, M. Condorcet, and Other Writers* (1798). The essay was written as an answer to Godwin's views that society was perfectible. Malthus argued that perfectibility is impossible because population necessarily increases faster than subsistence—population moving in a geometrical, subsistence in an arithmetical, progression—and always increases to the limits of subsistence. It can be checked only by wars, famines, and natural catastrophes. Thus, Malthus believed that systematic assistance to the poor is evil because it encourages population to increase beyond the limits of subsistence, although in the second edition of his *Essay* he moderated this argument somewhat. He was also a theoretician of economics, and greatly influenced political economy. David Ricardo (1772–1823), perhaps the most important organizer of the new "science" of political economy, wrote the highly important *Principles of Political Economy and Taxation* (1817). He was a friend of Malthus and later of James Mill and Bentham. His views were central to the position of the "classical political economists," and he gave renewed strength to arguments for free trade.

selfish indulgence from which their wives and children can gain no benefit. They return home quite unfitted to join in the domestic circle, and it is well if self-conceit and self-importance do not tempt them to look down upon others with disdain.

I am far from imputing any bad motives to those who have patronized such meetings. I am inclined to think that Mr. Brougham has been led away by his ardent genius, and by his well-known predilection for abstract science, to imagine that great benefits may thus be derived to artizans and mechanics from what he calls "the scientific education of the people." But not all his threatening that "any attempt to check its progress would only bring about the sudden destruction of him who should be insane enough to make it," shall deter me from giving my free opinions respecting the plan which he proposes, and from recommending a far more safe, sound, and judicious method of spreading light and knowledge amongst the labouring part of the community.

To his suggestion for the encouragement of cheap publications for the use of this part of society, consisting of our most admired and popular authors, there can be no reasonable objection. I have long wished to see collections of this kind universally established in our large towns and cities, and have laboured to the utmost of my power to recommend the plan to public notice. But surely it is desirable that the choice of such books should be left to those whose superior knowledge may enable them to direct the reading of others. I would suggest then that cheap circulating libraries should be generally established for this purpose, that the books should consist of tales and voyages, of history and biography, of elementary books on trade and arts and manufactures, in fact of all the plain and miscellaneous literature of the country. Something of this kind, though upon a very small scale, has already been undertaken by the Society for Promoting Christian Knowledge, which has added a supplemental list of books on miscellaneous subjects to its regular catalogue of religious works; but it is plain that far greater variety is requisite to give success to this plan, and that the minds of the working orders are now arriving at such a degree of strength and maturity that they will no longer be satisfied with the simple food which contented their forefathers.

The case is this, we must either undertake to meet this demand for popular information by furnishing them with cheap editions of our most popular writers, or we must leave them to chance and accident to make their own selection; or, what appears to be the worst of all, we must leave them to the tricks of wandering lecturers who shall harangue them on subjects little fitted to their rank and condition in society, and still less fitted to promote their private and domestic happiness.

In this dilemma the duty of all who wish well to the safety and security of our present establishments in Church and State is plain and incontrovertible. The day has gone by for arguing the previous question whether the poor shall be educated or not, the period is rapidly approaching when the fruits and effects of this education will become visible to all. Already restless and artful men are attempting to pervert it to their own mischievous purposes; some under the mask of diffusing science are teaching them a species of knowledge which may give them power but will not furnish them with the means or desire of self-government; others under the pretence of the love of liberty, are inviting them to discuss questions of politics, and to attend lectures on moral and political science; but every friend to our present establishments in Church and State is bound now to lend his influence to keep things in their proper channels, by making the knowledge and education of the poor subservient to their advancement in piety and morals, and by encreasing their attachment to the laws and institutions of our country.

But though it is desirable that cheap editions of our most popular writers should be printed for the labouring orders, I cannot agree with Mr. Brougham, "that the method of publishing in *numbers* is admirrably suited to the circumstances of the class whose income is derived from wages." On the contrary, I believe that the pockets of the poor are almost invariably pillaged by the hawkers who vend such periodical publications. When it is considered how liable a poor man is to such imposition, how easily single numbers may be lost or torn. the difficulty and expense of the binding, and perhaps the uncertainty of the work being ever finished, it appears far better for him to lay by a few shillings till he can purchase the book entire, than thus to run the risk of loss and imposition.

Nor can I agree with Mr. Brougham in thinking, that any great benefit will accrue to the working classes from studying the crabbed doctrines of "political economy," nor "from expounding to them the true principles and mutual relation of population and wages." Whatever abstract truth may be contained in such speculations, I would, with all deference, submit that they are likely to produce very little practical benefit. It is not likely any poor man could be deterred from a premature or imprudent marriage from making himself acquainted with the theory of Mr. Malthus, though a lively and animated story which displayed the evils of such an imprudent connection, might *possibly* produce a salutary effect. Still less am I inclined to admit with

Mr. Brougham that "every topic of politics, party as well as general," should be forced on the attention of this part of society; or "that the abuses which through time have crept into the practice of the constitution, the errors committed in its administration, and the *improvements which a change of circumstances require even in its principles,* may most fitly be expounded in the same manner." I am as much a friend, I trust, to the civil and religious liberties of my country as Mr. Brougham or any of his Northern allies, but there is a time and place for all things, and it is very clear that no moral or political benefit could arise to the community from bringing such topics under the *especial* notice of our mechanics or artizans.

With respect to "book clubs and reading societies" amongst the poor, they appear to be far too formal and expensive to be generally adopted. A poor man can give at most but the odds and ends of his time to reading, it is much better then that he should pay a small annual subscription, say a shilling a year, for the use of such books as he may wish to look into, than to burden himself by their purchase. In a library of this kind at Bath, the books have been found to last good for several years, though they have been read by many hundred individuals, and during the whole time not an instance has occurred of any book being stolen or purloined. Mr. Brougham need not have travelled into Scotland for "parish or cottage libraries," as the plan has been very generally adopted in many parts of this kingdom, and has thence extended to several of the colonies and dependencies of Great Britain.

But the advantages of reading at home by the cottager's fire-side, and in the midst of his own family, is so very apparent if compared with any sort of "association" or "club," that I am surprised to find Mr. Brougham giving any sanction to such tumultuous assemblies. It is scarcely possible to think that any prudent or sensible master would encourage or countenance such meetings of his workmen, but if any could be so foolish or absurd, I doubt not that a "strike" would soon awake him from his reveries. It is easy to observe that there is a strange ignorance of human nature discoverable in many of Mr. Brougham's speculations.

Several of his suggestions, however, as to the best mode of communicating scientific instruction to artizans and mechanics are both ingenious and solid, *if* I could bring myself to believe that this kind of instruction would really benefit those classes of the people. But, feeling persuaded, that, with a few rare and splendid exceptions, the knowledge of "Geometry" and "Algebra" and "Dynamics" is not necessary to carpenters, and that the study of "Mathematics" and

"Natural Philosophy" is little adapted to those who must earn their bread with their daily labour, it is not in my power to admire this Utopian scheme of popular education. Nothing should be denied to the poor that is calculated to render them more virtuous and happy; but it seems to be a gross delusion, if not absolute quackery, to call their attention to lectures on "mechanical philosophy and chemistry, astronomy and geology," nor can I see any reason why "moral and political philosophy should be explained to them in public lectures, though they may be learnt by reading far more easily than the physical sciences."

Such strange projects appear to argue much more of a restless ambition, bent on trying rash novelties, than they indicate of that "good sense which though no science is fairly worth the seven." Doubtless it is possible, by continued and repeated efforts, to force a kind of unnatural enquiry amongst the common people. Men who love popularity and display may easily collect large assemblages of workmen to listen to things which they do not and cannot understand; they may fire them with the hope of becoming "a working Chemyst, like Scheele," or "a working Printer, like Franklin," and whilst they are thus disturbing and agitating society they may imagine themselves actuated "by no other excitement than that of general philanthropy." But I confess that I behold all such spectacles with some diffidence and distrust, and that a less noisy and less ostentatious mode of doing good would have greater attractions, even though "fit lecturers" should be obtained for every town and village in the United Kingdom.

The most suspicious feature of this system remains still to be mentioned. It consists in the total independence of all such undertakings on the assistance or co-operation of the upper orders, just as if the man who had been originally taught to read and write by others should spurn at any aid or encouragement which might be afforded to him in the subsequent stages of his improvement. Friends as we are to civil and religious liberty, we really cannot perceive what injury could possibly arise to the poor from a continuance of this interchange of kindness; and circumstanced as society is in this country, in which the various ranks insensibly fall into each other, it does not appear either practicable or expedient that the knowledge and improvement of the labouring classes should not, in a great measure, be derived from the aid and munificence and encouragement of their employers.

To attempt to prevent such influence is neither just nor practicable; a man must gain his knowledge and opinions from some quarter, and if not obliged to his employer, he must be influenced by the hireling lecturer to whom he listens. If the education of the labouring orders is not to produce confusion and jealousy, it ought to harmonize with that of the upper classes of society; to attempt to keep them distinct is to set them at variance with each other; I am quite at a loss, threrefore, to understand the morbid jealousy of Mr. B. on this subject. "I really should be disposed to view," says he, "any advantage in point of knowledge gained by the body of the people, as somewhat equivocal, or at least as much alloyed with evil, if purchased by the increase of their dependence on their superiors." I shall only add, that, without wishing for any servility from the poor, it is fervently to be hoped that the moral influence which God and nature meant to be possessed by the richer and more educated classes of society should ever be retained, and that it should exert itself exactly in proportion to the extent to which the education of the labouring orders is carried.

. . . . .

I am far from asserting that any branch of useful and practical knowledge may not very properly engage the leisure of those who have time and talents to cultivate an acquaintance with art or science, but here, as in every other pursuit, good sense and sobriety should prevail over mere declamation and vague enthusiasm. A labouring man can devote only a very small portion of his time to such enquiries; it is folly therefore to throw open the whole field of science to his view, or to attempt to force him on pursuits which are calculated neither to improve his station in society, nor to render him more happy in that station to which Providence has called him.

Individuals there are, in every rank of society, who by their native superiority of talent may find their way to eminence and distinction, and it is the pride and boast of our country, that no man, whatever be his origin, is necessarily excluded from such advancement. But it is neither wise nor expedient to speak as if "the day were now to break in which we may hope to see no marked line of separation between the workman and the philosopher." The leading distinctions of society will always remain the same, and to attempt to confound them, is to do no real service to any rank of the community: and if it would be illiberal and unjust to place any *definite* limit to the acquirements of our mechanics, it is, on the other hand, both dangerous and absurd to attempt to push such acquirements beyond their just and natural level, instead of leaving them to their ordinary progress and natural development.

Upon a calm review of these combined efforts to give a *scientific* turn to the education of the common people, I think that there is sufficient ground to put all prudent men upon their guard, though I am by no means prepared to assert that it ought to be regarded with unfriendly or hostile feelings. That such a project may be easily perverted by artful and designing men to the most mischievous purposes is not a sufficient reason for offering it any opposition, but it furnishes good ground for endeavouring to prevent such dangers; and having laid the case fully before my reader, I shall now conclude by shortly stating what appears to be the best and wisest course to pursue.

First, then, as Mr. Brougham and his friends are using all their efforts to give the common people a scientific and philosophical education, it should be the earnest endeavour of those who do not place an *implicit* trust in science or philosophy, to furnish them with the far more powerful restraints of religion and morals. To whatever height the pyramid is carried, we ought to proportion our care and zeal respecting its foundation.

To this end nothing will so much conduce as a steady and judicious support of the national system of education, as it is developed and exhibited in the National Schools. These are schools at which something better and more important than the arts of "reading and writing" are communicated to the children of the poor. It is here they learn their duties towards God and man, a strong attachment to the laws and institutions of their country is early engrafted on their minds. It is here they are taught that knowledge and science are of very secondary value when compared with piety and virtue, "that godliness with contentment is great riches," and that "the fear of the Lord is the beginning of wisdom."

It is the peculiar recommendation of these schools that something fixed and definite is taught, and that their system accords with the order of society existing amongst us. Mr. Brougham and his friends may hint "at the abuses which have crept into the constitution, the errors committed in its administration, and the improvement which a change of circumstances require in its principles," but these are discoveries which we do not seek to impress on our pupils. We inculcate a strong attachment to the constitution, *such as it now is*; we teach them to love and revere our establishments in Church and State, even with all their real or supposed imperfections; and we are far more anxious to make them good and contented citizens, than to fit them for noisy patriots, who would perhaps destroy the constitution whilst pretending to correct it.

In this respect the schools which are connected with the Established Church, present a far more safe and practical system of national education, than any which pretend to lead the individual to the search of future and unknown improvements. And hence it is that the schools of the National Society for the education of the Poor in the principles of the established Church are so very different in their aims and objects from those "Elementary Schools" which aspire to teach nothing beyond the abstract powers of reading and writing, and then to remit their pupils to those "Adult Schools" at which they are to become smatterers in science. But to render these schools of the National Society still more powerful and effective in their influence, they should be connected, as far as possible, with the ancient and endowed charities of the country. By such an union they may be rendered far more alluring to the parents, who may be thus led to prefer them on this account, and be willing to keep their children at them for a longer period, from the hope of seeing them afterwards apprenticed by an endowed institution.

Another method of rendering them far more useful and popular is by conjoining them to some establishment of manual industry, such as the cultivation of a garden or the employment of a factory. These plans have been tried with the happiest effect at the Bath National School, and if similar trials were made in other parts of the country they would be attended with the most beneficial result.

A small library of useful and elementary books of a religious and moral description, together with the most popular travels and voyages, should always be connected with these schools, to which the children should be invited to subscribe, and from which they should be at liberty to take books to their homes, and to purchase them at reduced prices.

But, as I have already hinted, circulating libraries of a much larger description should be opened for the general use of working classes in all our large towns and cities; and which should comprise the most plain and popular works in all branches of general knowledge, and also embrace elementary books on trade and arts. Let the wealthier orders encourage such libraries by becoming honorary members, and by taking an active interest in their formation; and let the books be named by the subscribers, or be chosen by a committee. These are schemes for the improvement of the minds of the labouring orders which I have long wished to see generally adopted, and which are far more safe and practicable than inviting them to listen to discourses from travelling lecturers upon sciences that are beyond their habits of attention, and which, if acquired, could prove of little or no service to their happiness. Whatever tends to draw a working man from his home and from the company of his wife and family is most strongly to be deprecated; whatever be his occupations, he should find them, if possible, by his own fire-side. It is on this account that I strongly protest against clubs and reading rooms, against lectures and public institutes, as hostile to those quiet and domestic habits which are of far more real value than any advancement which they can hope to make in abstract science.

To conclude—it is evident that Mr. Brougham and his friends are intent on carrying forward the education of the people on certain principles peculiar to those "who hold the same doctrines" in politics and theology; and it therefore becomes those who do *not* hold the same doctrines to put themselves into the posture of self-defence. The National Schools for the instruction of the labouring orders in the principles of the Established Church, are the natural bulwarks to which we must look for the permanence of our present institutions, whether civil or ecclesiastical; and it is more than ever requisite that these schools should be encouraged and supported by those who do not desire any great and fundamental alteration in our present system of government. If my observations are correct, these schools may now be said to be *in a state of siege*; they are encompassed on every side by those who are attempting to introduce a different course of popular education. The project of *infant* schools has been chiefly brought forward by men who have always shewn themselves hostile to the National Society; and that Mr. Brougham's "*adult schools*" are altogether supported by the same party is matter of public notoriety. Under these circumstances nothing but a most effective support of the "National System of Education" will enable it eventually to make head against such a powerful opposition; an opposition which is founded on the most plausible and fascinating theory, but which, if successful, must turn the whole tide of popular education against our present national establishments.

To shew the force and reality of this assertion it is necessary only to turn to the concluding paragraphs of Mr. Brougham's pamphlet, which are devoted to an attempt to subvert the present charitable institutions existing "in every part of the country" for the sake of "making an effort at the present moment to propagate this system." I know not whether he is addressing the working classes or their employers on this occasion, but I feel certain that this endeavour to withdraw the benevolence of the public from its customary channels to the formation of such dubious and new-fangled institutions, will only create universal indignation. Though "happily, the time is past and gone when bigots could persuade mankind that the lights of philosophy were to be extinguished as dangerous to religion, and when tyrants could proscribe the instructors of the people as enemies to their power," yet happily the day is *not* arrived when we can be scared by the sneers at "superstition" or "intolerance" from warning the public of its dangers; nor when all the pretences about "genuine philanthropy" and "universal toleration" can prevent our developing the real views and objects of "those who lie in wait to deceive."

To the upper classes of society *I* would say—do every thing in your power to give the labouring orders a religious, virtuous, and *useful* education, by founding this education on the love and the fear of God, and by associating it with a strong attachment to the *existing* institutions of our country. To the working classes *I* would say—be upon your guard against quacks and impostors of all kinds; remember that knowledge is valuable only as it is connected with an advancement in piety and religion; that sobriety and contentment are far more valuable qualifications than any attainments in mere art or science; and that those who would confine your education *exclusively* to the purposes of the present life are no real friends to your happiness and welfare.

EDWARD GEORGE EARLE BULWER-LYTTON

# England
# and the English*

BULWER-LYTTON (1803–73) WAS A NOVELIST
and politician whose career might serve to summarize a very large
part of the history of nineteenth-century England. He was a voluminous writer who apparently knew how to produce at any moment what the public wanted. In his early years, he was known as
a dandy and wrote "silver fork" novels of high society that were
very popular, one of which, a study of dandyism entitled *Pelham*
(1828), insured his fame. In 1831, he entered Parliament espousing Bentham's utilitarian views and, continuing his usual success,
became a baronet in 1838. He did not turn from the liberal cause
until 1852.

In the course of his long career, he also wrote plays and works

* From Edward Bulwer-Lytton, *England and the English*, 2 vols., First
Edition (London: Bentley, 1833), II, Chapter III.

of nonfiction like the one included here, and edited several journals. His *England and the English* is a fascinating and sometimes acute analysis of contemporary English society and literature. Bulwer's political sympathies led him to side with the March of Mind, but his analysis of the phenomenon suggests with some acuity what the dangers of the "March" might be. Many of Bulwer's remarks obviously parallel those of J. S. Mill in his essay *Civilization.*

I think, sir,[1] that when our ingenious countryman, Joshua Barnes,[2] gave us so notable an account of the Pigmies, he must, in the spirit of prophecy, have intended to allegorize the empire of the Penny Periodicals. For, in the first place, these little strangers seem, Pigmy-like, of a marvellous ferocity and valour; they make great head against their foes—they spread themselves incontinently—they possess the land —they live but a short time, yet are plenteously prolific; they owe much to what the learned Joshua terms "the royal Lescha," viz. a certain society (evidently the foretype of that lately established under the patronage of my Lord Brougham)—set up as he sheweth "for the increase and propagation of experimental knowledge;" above all, and a most blissful peculiarity it is, *"for taxes, they are wholly unacquainted with them!"* they make vigilant war against the cranes, whom I take it are palpably designed for tax-gatherers in general, *quocunque gaudentes nomine*[3]—a fact rendered clear to the plainest understanding by the following description of these predatory birds: "The cranes being the only causers of famine in the land, by reason they are so numerous that they can devour the most plentiful harvest, both by eating the seeds beforehand, and then picking the ears that remain."

Certes, however, these little gentry seem of a more general ambi-

1. Isaac D'Israeli (1766–1848), the father of the famous Benjamin Disraeli, was himself a well-known man of letters. He began his career with pretensions to poetry, but eventually abandoned verse for research and criticism. This section of Bulwer's book is dedicated and addressed to D'Israeli.

2. Joshua Barnes (1654–1712) wrote a book entitled *Gerania, or the Discovery of a Little Sort of People Anciently Discoursed of, Called Pygmies* (1675). It described an imaginary voyage that might have influenced Swift's voyage to Lilliput.

3. "rejoicing in whatever name."

tion than their Pigmæan types; for the latter confined themselves to a limited territory "from Gadazalia to Elysiana;" but these, the pigmies of our time, overrun us altogether, and push, with the rude insolence of innovation, our most venerable folios from their stools. The rage for cheap publications is not limited to Penny Periodicals; family libraries of all sorts have been instituted, with the captivating profession of teaching all things useful—bound in cloth, for the sum of five shillings a month! Excellent inventions, which, after showing us the illimitable ingenuity of compilation, have at length fallen the prey of their own numbers, and buried themselves amongst the corpses of the native quartos which they so successfully invaded.

Cheap publications are excellent things in themselves. Whatever increases the reading public, tends necessarily to equalize the knowledge already in the world; but the process by which knowledge is equalized is not altogether that by which the degree of knowledge is heightened. Cheap publications of themselves are sufficient for the *diffusion* of knowledge, but not for its *advancement*. The schoolmaster equalizes information, by giving that which he possesses to others, and for that very reason can devote but little time to increasing his own stock.

Let me make this more familiar by telling you an anecdote of our friend Dr. _____. You know that he is a man of the very highest scientific attainments? You know also that he is not overburdened with those same precious metals on the history of which he can so learnedly descant? He took a book some months ago to a publisher of enterprise and capital: it was full of the profoundest research; the bookseller shook his head, and—

"Pray, sir," said he, musingly, "how many persons in England are acquainted with the ultimate principles by which you come to your result?"

"Not fifty, sir," cried the doctor, with all the enthusiasm of a discoverer.

"And how many can understand the elementary principles which occupy your first chapter?"

"Oh!" said the doctor, with indifference, "those principles are merely plain truths in mechanics, which most manufacturers ought to know, and which many literary dandies think it shows learning to allude to; perhaps, therefore, several thousands may be familiar with the contents of the first chapter; but, I assure you, sir, you don't get far before"—

"Pardon me, doctor," interrupted the bookseller, shortly—"if you address the fifty persons, you must publish this work on your own account; if you address the thousands, why it is quite another matter. Here is your MS.; burn all but the first chapter: as a commercial speculation, the rest is mere rubbish; if you will then spin out the first chapter into a volume, and call it *The Elements of* _____ *Familiarly Explained*—why, I think, sir, with your name, I could afford you three hundred pounds for it."

Necessity knows no law. *The Elements* are published to teach new thousands what other thousands knew before, and the *Discoveries* lie in the doctor's desk, where they will only become lucrative, when some richer man shall invent and propagate them, and the public will call on the poor doctor "to make them familiar."

Now observe a very curious consequence from this story: Suppose a certain science is *only* cultivated by five hundred men, and that they have all cultivated the science to a certain height. A book that should tell them what they knew already, they would naturally not purchase, and a book that told them more than they knew they would eagerly buy; in such a case, the doctor's position would have been reversed, and his *Discoveries* would have been much more lucrative to him than his *Elements.*—Thus we may observe, that the tone of knowledge is usually more scholastic in proportion as the circle of readers is confined. When scholars are your audience, you address them after the fashion of a scholar. Hence, formerly, every man thought it necessary, when he wrote a book, to bestow upon its composition the most scrupulous care; to fill its pages with the product of a studious life; to polish its style with the classic file, and to ornament its periods with the academical allusion. He knew that the majority of those who read his work would be able to appreciate labour or to detect neglect; but, as the circle of readers increased, the mind of the writer became less fastidious; the superficial readers had outnumbered the profounder critics. He still addressed the majority, but the taste of the majority was no longer so scrupulous as to the fashion of the address. Since the Revival of Letters itself, the more confined the public, the more laborious the student. Ascham is more scholastic than Raleigh; Raleigh than Addison; and Addison than Scott.

The spirit of a popular assembly can enter into the crowd you write for, as well as the crowd you address; and a familiar frankness, or a superficial eloquence, charm the assembly when full, which a measured wisdom, and a copious knowledge were necessary to win, when its numbers were scattered and select.

It is natural that writers should be ambitious of creating a sensation: a sensation is produced by gaining the ear, not of the few, but the many; it is natural, therefore, that they should address the many;

the style pleasing to the many becomes, of course, the style most frequently aimed at: hence the profusion of amusing, familiar, and superficial writings. People complain of it, as if it were a proof of degeneracy in the knowledge of authors—it is a proof of the increased number of readers. The time is come when nobody will fit out a ship for the intellectual Columbus to discover new worlds, but when everybody will subscribe for his setting up a steam-boat between Calais and Dover. You observe then, sir, (consequences which the fine talkers of the day have wholly overlooked) that the immense superficies of the public operates two ways in deteriorating from the profundity of writers: in the first place, it renders it no longer necessary for an author to make himself profound before he writes; and in the next place, it encourages those authors who are profound, by every inducement, not of lucre alone, but of fame, to exchange deep writing for agreeable writing: the voice which animates the man ambitious of wide fame, does not, according to the beautiful line in Rogers,[4] whisper to him "ASPIRE," but "DESCEND." "He stoops to conquer." Thus, if we look abroad, in France, where the reading public is less numerous than in England, a more elevated and refining tone is more fashionable in literature; and in America, where it is infinitely larger, the tone of literature is infinitely more superficial. It is possible, that the high-souled among literary men, desirous rather of truth than fame, or willing to traverse their trial to posterity, are actuated, unconsciously, by the spirit of the times; but actuated they necessarily are, just (to return to my former comparison) as the wisest orator, who uttered only philosophy to a thin audience of sages, mechanically abandons his refinements and his reasonings, and expands into a louder tone and more familiar manner as the assembly increases;—the temper of the popular meeting is unavoidably caught by the mind that addresses it.

4. Samuel Rogers (1763–1855) was a poet highly praised by Hazlitt in *The Spirit of the Age*. Although he produced relatively little poetry, he was something of a literary dictator for a long time, and he refused the position of poet laureate on Wordsworth's death in 1850. (Tennyson then became the laureate.)

# III

# SOCIETY AND REFORM

There can be no doubt that the middle rank,
which gives to science, to art, and legislation
itself, their most distinguished ornaments, and
is the chief source of all that has exalted and
refined human nature, is that portion of the
community of which, if the basis of Representation was ever so far extended, the opinion would ultimately decide. Of the people
beneath them, a vast majority would be sure
to be guided by their advice and example.

JAMES MILL
*Essay on Government*

WILLIAM COBBETT

# A Third Lecture
# on the French
# Revolution and
# English
# Boroughmongering*

WILLIAM COBBETT (1762–1835), OF ALL THE
extraordinary and productive men of the period with which this
book is concerned, was probably the most extraordinary and the
most productive. It was impossible for anyone—Tory, Whig,
radical, socialist—if he were concerned with the society in which

* From pamphlet, First Edition (London: Strange, 21 Paternoster Row,
1830).

he lived, to ignore Cobbett. Although not perhaps a great writer (and the point is debatable), there were few people in the history of the language who wrote more clearly, forcefully, and influentially than he. Hazlitt, who found much about him inimical, argued that he "might be said to have the clearness of Swift, the naturalness of Defoe, and the picturesque satirical description of Mandeville; if all such comparisons were not impertinent. A really great and original writer is like nobody but himself." Cobbett was, indeed, like nobody but himself. The son of a farmer and innkeeper, he was altogether self-taught. He was for eight years (1783–91) a soldier, and, fearing the consequences of a court-martial he instigated against what he felt to be a corrupt group of officers, he fled to America after his discharge. He was a Tory by inclination and, taking the federal side in American politics, steadily defended England. Because of his outspoken nature he was always in trouble, and having set up newspapers in Philadelphia, he returned to England in 1800, where he set up other papers (antigallican in policy). In 1802 he established the *Political Register*, which was published regularly throughout the rest of his life. In 1809, however, he switched allegiances from the Tory to the Radical party, not because he lost his loyalty to the land (he never did), but partly because he needed always to be in opposition, and partly because his allegiance to the lower classes drove him away from Tory policies. An article on military flogging landed him in prison, but the *Register* kept appearing, and in 1802 he reduced its price of twopence, thus producing what was perhaps the first important working-class newspaper.

Cobbett became in the years following the most powerful spokesman to and for the lower classes in England, despite his second flight to America after suspension of the Habeas Corpus Act. He toured the agricultural areas to discover the condition of the rural poor (what he discovered appeared in *Rural Rides* [1831], his most famous book). He wrote and lectured endlessly, relishing the confrontation with audiences whose rapt attention he commanded. Curiously, he was radical without being liberal, and he managed to offend almost everyone at one time or other excepting those audiences that he addressed directly. To the end of his life he maintained the prejudices of a man who looks back on a golden rural age that was unsullied by industrialism, minority groups, urban filth, or paper money. He always involved himself in the crisis of the moment, fought furiously, won or lost, and went on to the next crisis. Having won a battle, he tended to forget the victors in his zeal to start another. Only in his writing on rural conditions is it possible to find a genuine consistency in Cobbett's thought.

But it is impossible to overestimate his importance in arousing and publicizing popular sentiment. In the lecture included here, delivered as part of a series in the Rotunda at Blackfriars Bridge, Cobbett is urging reform of Parliament and removal of abuses imposed by the same Tory government he turned against two decades before. Although it is not the best of Cobbett's lectures, it indicates the power of his demagoguery, the magnificent clarity and concreteness of his language, and his strength in the service of popular causes.

GENTLEMEN,

When I last had the honour of addressing you, I promised that I would produce this evening that which I thought would be a proper petition for us, the working classes, to present to the King; but I have not been able to find time to do the thing to my own mind: however, I will be prepared with such a petition by next Monday evening, when I hope again to have the honour to address you here. (Applause.) I will have it printed on a sheet of paper, and any person who desires may procure it as he passes in or out, at what it will cost printing, which I should think will be about one penny. (Cheers.) The subject is of the greatest possible importance to all. We have been talking about a reform in parliament for many years; we are all pretty well satisfied that there is no remedy for the disorders of the country and the sufferings of the people without it; and it now depends, I verily believe, on yourselves, whether you shall have it or not. (Immense cheering.) It is a matter, therefore, which requires the greatest deliberation; a thing that ought to be done well, and with all the consideration that we are able to bestow on the subject. A statement of our grievances—or at least part of them, for God knows that to state them all would fill a book as large as the Bible—but a statement of the more prominent of them ought to be clearly made, and in such a manner as is likely to produce an effect on the mind of his Majesty; and I have not the smallest doubt of its being received by the King, and also of its being properly attended to. (Applause.) Gentlemen, we have another encouragement, I am of opinion, to pursue this course, and it is this; there is every reason to think that the prime minister himself is inclined to give us parliamentary reform. (Immense applause.) I know well enough that the state of parties is not what we ought in general to amuse ourselves about; but now they are somewhat interesting. There is a general combination against the minister; divers parties have combined to turn him out. Gentlemen, it is not likely that the Duke of Wellington would like to be turned out. (Laughter.) Not, gentlemen, that he cares a fig about the profit of the thing—that must be beneath his consideration—but it is matter of great importance to him as concerns his fame. If he were turned out now, especially by a vote of the House of Commons, he must be sensible that he would sink down, not only in the eyes of his own country, but also in the eyes of all Europe—for all eyes are upon him. Therefore, it appears that he will be placed in this predicament—either to give the people parliamentary reform, or to be driven from his post. (Cheers.) If he come forward with a proposition for reform, all of a sudden, as he did for Catholic emancipation, he will do now what he did then, and much more effectually; and he will silence all his opponents at once. Gentlemen, the Whigs are talking about parliamentary reform; they want reform—a very indefinite one, certainly,—in fact, they want none, or the least possible; but if the Duke come forward, and in the king's speech propose a real reform, they will be struck dead, as if they had been shot through the head with a bullet. (Laughter.) The Duke, on the other hand, will see that he will have the people at his back. Why, gentlemen, the Duke has got a head nearly as white as mine; he cannot have a great number of years to live; and it must, therefore, be a matter of concern to end his days well; to be sure it must. He cannot want his fame to be tarnished—in his last days, to be beaten by the Whigs, or by any-body else. He has plenty of wealth, and he knows this, that by giving the people parliamentary reform he would not only secure his property for himself, but for his descendants. He would not only have all the people to protect his immense estates; but instead of grudging him, or saying he had too much, they would say he had not half enough—for the generosity of the people always exceeds the benefits they receive. (Applause.)

The times, then, I say, are propitious—most propitious for obtaining reform. Then, on the other hand, the example of the French people[1] is not very consoling to the boroughmongers. They have shown that soldiers are not omnipotent—that the working classes, when they choose to muster, can assert their own rights, and can succeed in asserting them. The subject which has drawn us together, gentlemen, and which has procured for me the greatest honour of addressing you, that very subject is a subject of serious contemplation with the boroughmongers. They know that men are men, in all countries; they know that the people of England hear of what is done in France, and they know this also, that there is not a working man in England who does not say to his fellow workman, in the field or the shop, while suffering under grinding taxation, "What! shan't we do as well as the French!" (Immense and long-continued cheering.) "Shall we be afraid? Shall Englishmen, at last, be afraid to do that which the French have so well done?" They are aware of this feeling in the minds of Englishmen, gentlemen, depend upon it, and therefore they will not be in a temper to offer very great resistance. (Cheers.) Under these circumstances, then, it becomes us to petition the king. That is our constitutional right. We may petition the houses of parliament and the king. The houses of parliament we have petitioned long enough, God knows; we will do it again if you like; indeed, I think I shall be for plying them again with petitions when they meet; but the first and the most important thing for us is to petition the king. (Cheers.)

In the mean while, permit me to state some of the grievances which we shall respectfully and dutifully lay before his Majesty. One thing, above all others, we ought to observe at this time—all Europe appears to be in commotion. Even Hamburgh, that little commercial republic, is in a state of half rebellion. The newspapers say, it is strange there should be riots at Hamburgh. Oh! it is a servile imitation of the French, says a correspondent of the *Morning Herald*. The people at Hamburgh have nothing to complain of—they are so happy —so well off—they have such a nice little commercial republic. Upon these occasions, however, I always inquire what is the matter; what

1. The "French Revolution" Cobbett alludes to in the title is that of 1830. Following the defeat of Napoleon in 1815, the aristocracy once again gained control of France. In three days of fighting ("les trois glorieuses"), July 27–29, a revolution was accomplished against the repressive measures of Charles X and the aristocracy. A "citizen king" was placed upon the throne, to be called, rather than Philippe VII, Louis Philippe. Many liberal Englishmen hailed the Revolution as a great triumph for the cause of the people, and the threat it represented was used to argue for the passage of the Reform Bill of 1832.

have the people done these things for? "Oh, for nothing," say they,
Well, but surely there is *some* reason for doing them. "No, none at
all." Well, but what reason do they say they have? "Oh, none—no,
they have no reason; they have done it all for nothing." Well, but
surely they say they have some reason; what do they say is the reason
for their rioting? Come, what do they say is the reason? "Oh, the
reasons they give are all false; they are very well off; they have no
reason in the world." Well, but let us hear what they do say, whether
it be false or true. (Laughter.) Why, then, after three or four days
it came out, that all the working people had to complain of was this,—
A little while ago, some pretty heavy taxes were taken off from imported goods; that is, the great merchants were relieved from some
heavy taxes; but at the same time, these were transferred to the working people, and a tax was put upon the bread, and the meat, and even
an excise upon the milk. We ought not to be surprised, therefore, that
Hamburgh is in a state of revolt. Belgium complains of oppressive
taxes. Some of the Belgium states of Prussia—even at dear Hanover
—the common people, doubtless without any cause, cry out, "Down
with the nobility!" Why, gentlemen, the Duke of Wellington knows,
if the boroughmongers do not; the Duke of Wellington knows something about the nations of Europe; he knows the people of most of
them; he knows what kind of persons they are; he knows that the
people of England are in a somewhat similar condition; that the poor
man has to pay a tax of fourpence-half-penny upon every sixpenny-
worth of beer he purchases; and therefore he must perceive that something MUST be done. (Cheers.) This, as I said before, I believe to
be one of the reasons why the Duke will propose, in the speech from
the throne, that there should be a real and effectual reform in the
parliament. I may be mistaken; if I am I shall be very sorry. Now,
before I proceed to an enumeration of some of the grievances which
we shall we shall lay before the king, I shall make one observation.
Whenever we propose that any-thing should be effected for the benefit
of the people—to repeal any laws—to remove any oppressions;—in
fact, whenever we complain of any-thing, they cry out—"Oh, that's
an innovation," and the man who asks for it is accused of being an
innovator. "Oh, you are an innovator," they say; "you are given to
change; you are an innovator." Now, gentleman, I want a change,
it is true, but I am no innovator—I am against innovation. I complain
of no grievance that is not of modern date; it is of innovations that
I complain, and of nothing else;—because they have not adhered to
the ancient laws of the country. I will mention four or five instances,
by way of specimens; and I here say, that the reign of George IV. has

been marked with greater innovations—greater alterations in the laws affecting the common people, than in all the reigns that have occurred since the passing of Magna Charta. This is a bold assertion, but it has been formed after the most deliberate consideration and examination, and I state it here in the most deliberate amnner. I will mention a few of these.

In the year 1818, two bills—very little things we think these bills, generally,—in the year 1818 two bills were brought into the House of Commons, and passed into laws, which totally changed the situation of the labouring people. These bills attracted very little notice in London; we are here too thickly put together in one place, and too much engaged in getting money for the tax-gatherer, to pay attention even to those things which most materially affect us. Two bills, however, which, in the year I have named, passed into laws, have totally changed the situation of the labouring people. These bills were introduced and carried through the House of Commons by Mr. STURGES BOURNE, and they made the most material alteration in the poor-laws. Gentlemen, I had the honour to state to you the other night, that the poor-laws originated in consequence of the property originally appropriated to their support having been taken away from the people. The poor-laws did, however, in some measure, supply the place of these; more degradingly, not so honourably, not so much in the spirit of Christian charity; but still the poor-laws of the 43d year of the reign of Elizabeth, did, if faithfully adhered to, in some measure supply the place of the original estates. These laws said this; That no person in England should suffer from want of food, clothing, or shelter, whatever may have been his previous character, or whatever the causes which had produced his poverty. Now, these laws continued from the latter end of the reign of Elizabeth, with some trifling alterations, till the year 1818. In this year, the two bills of which I have spoken were brought in and passed. And what was their effect? I beg your attention to the alteration now made in the condition of the working classes. The first bill enacted, that in future, in the meetings of vestries, not every parishioner should have a vote—not, as it had been previously, that every rate-payer should have a vote, and no more; but in addition to this, that for every fifty pounds that a parishioner paid as a rental, he should have another vote. So that some had TEN votes, and others but ONE. Now, you see how this law was made in favour of the rich, and to the disadvantage of the poor, how it took away the power of that class of persons who were the nearest to the poor, and therefore had the greater sympathy with them. The poor laws originally provided, that there should be a common feeling between some of the rate-payers and those who needed relief; for some of those who paid and had the power to grant relief, were very near to those who required it. And so it should be. But this bill took away all that sympathy; it set aside all the small rate-payers; the rich necessarily overpowered them, and became lords of the vestry: they then became, gentlemen, what the House of Commons has so long been. The decided majority of the vestry were rich, and all know that they have less feeling for the poor than those nearer to them. But it did not stop there. Not satisfied with what he had here affected, Sturges Bourne brought in another bill, which, in fact, was to take the power out of the hands of the magistrates and overseers, and transfer it to the select vestries. The mode of relief was this,—If a man needed relief, he was to go to the overseer (who was elected by the vestry); if the overseer refused him relief, he went to the nearest magistrate, who gave an order for relief, and the overseer was obliged to comply. The protection to the poor man, then, was nearly as complete as it could have been. But this was all done away with by the select vestry bill, about which I am speaking. The select vestry was to decide as to the applications for relief, and the overseer was not to relieve—unless a man were just going to die—without the sanction of the select vestry, that is, a vestry chosen by persons voting as I have before described, the rich having the sole voice, because their votes necessarily constituted the majority. The magistrate was forbidden to order relief, and the overseer was not permitted to give relief, except with the permission of the select vestry. (Cries of shame, shame.) Thus are the poor stripped of the great protection afforded by the sympathies of those who are not far removed from them in their circumstances, and who know not how soon they may be placed in exactly the same situation.

. . . .

The next thing I will mention, is an innovation in the game laws. In the first place, it is a very odd thing to say to a man, You shall not meddle with a wild animal; if they were to extend this law to sparrows, and blackbirds, and linnets, we should see its strangeness at once; but there are only three things, partridges, pheasants, and hares, and these no man may touch, unless he possess freehold property to the amount of 100*l.* a year, or copyhold, or some other descriptions of property, amounting to 150*l.* These laws, as Blackstone said, are against the natural rights of mankind; because all wild animals remain in a state of nature, and can be claimed by no man. They are no man's property; they are given by God to all men; and how is it possible for a hare or a pheasant, who is here today, and twenty miles off tomorrow, to be called the property of this man or that? How can any man pretend to have a property in a thing like this? Blackstone[2] himself has remarked upon the unreasonableness and absurdity of the thing—but the game laws were made for the rich. (Cheers.) They were severe enough in the time of Blackstone, the punishment was great enough then, for unqualified persons killing game, or having it in their possession. But what have they made it now? What has it been made during the reign of George IV.—the reign of innovations? The utmost penalty before, was this, That if a man were seen in pursuit of game, or with game in his possession, there was a penalty of five pounds to pay, which might be taken by a distress on his goods. That was the utmost punishment they could inflict. But what have they done since? Why, now they have done this; and judge you of the heart-burnings that must exist in every village in consequence: you hear of fights between poachers and game-keepers, but they soon pass from your minds, and you know not how the country jails are crammed full of poachers and felons, whom the game laws have made such. The law now is:— that if a man in the pursuit of game, or out in the night, as if he were in the pursuit of game, that is, armed with a club or a gun, or any other instrument calculated to kill game, he is liable to be taken by force—it is not done as it was before, by information—no; a man may be taken by force, be taken before a magistrate, be committed to prison, be tried at the quarter sessions;—and for this act, being out at night in quest of a hare, a pheasant, or a partridge,—these justices, who are themselves the game preservers, mind, have the power of transporting a man for seven years. (Loud murmurs.) Now, this is an innovation, if they talk of innovations. . . .

Another new law, gentlemen, brought in by that softener of the laws—Mr. Peel—for they call what he has done, an amelioration of the criminal code;—but it is a very strange thing that while they have softened it by repealing some acts for the burning of witches and wizards—for this they certainly have done; Sir James Mackintosh,[3] you know, has been a great mover in the concern—they should have

2. Sir William Blackstone (1723–80) was an eminent English jurist who tried to create a general view of English law as a coherent and logical system. He was attacked consistently by Bentham, and later by all who felt that English law was anything but logical and coherent.
3. Sir James Mackintosh (1765–1832) was the author of the famous *Vindiciae gallicae*, the only effective answer to Burke's attack on the French Revolution of 1789. Mackintosh, a leading Whig, fought for Catholic Emancipation, the Reform Bill, and reform of the criminal code.

*Society and Reform*

passed others much more severe in their practical effects on the working man. However, Mr. Peel,[4] the great ameliorator of the criminal code, brought in a bill, which passed into a law, making it felony for any man to take an apple from a tree. That law is now in force, and all the consequences of felony will fall upon a man's head who gets over a hedge—no matter whether he break a lock or not—and plucks an apple from a tree. (Murmurs.) I would say, that if it be necessary to pass such a law as this in any country, one of two things must be, either they must be the most complete set of tyrants in the world, or the people the wretchedest thieves that ever lived. The consequences of felony are, the forfeiture of a man's estates, all rights he possessed, every-thing, in fact, but the mere protection of his life from destruction. These are the consequences of felony, unless a man receive a pardon; and I insist that it is monstrous to talk of having softened the criminal code while an act exists to visit a man with such a punishment for taking an apple from a tree. (Applause.) I do not know that the law has ever been carried into effect more than once, and that was by a parson in Dorsetshire. But this makes no difference, the act is in force, and may be carried into effect at any time.

Another law brought in by Peel—here are the innovations!—is what is called the new Trespass law. This is most important, as it characterises the reign of George IV. They talk of the mildness of his reign; of the mild and generous character of his majesty; and Peel said we were too near the period of the beneficent occurrences which marked it, to be able to estimate in their full force all the benefits we have derived from them! Gentlemen, I am not imputing to the king any ferocity of disposition—for it is very possible that he knew nothing about what was doing, but still we must look at these things to estimate his "mild and beneficent government." Well, then, let us look at this new trespass law. The law of trespass was this. If a man went on another man's land, or property of any description, he might bring an action against him, but if he did not get a verdict of 40s.,

4. Sir Robert Peel (1788–1850) was one of the great statesmen and politicians of the Victorian age. By origin a Tory, he nevertheless did as much toward reform of the worst aspects of English law and government as any liberal or Whig. Cobbett was not at all satisfied with his work (although Peel had already gained reputation as "the great ameliorator of the criminal code"), but then, Cobbett was hardly satisfied with anyone. The history of Peel's major political work is not altogether relevant here, although he was extremely important in Catholic Emancipation and in the repeal of the Test and Corporation Acts. His greatest achievements were accomplished during his tenure as Prime Minister between 1841 and 1846.

each party to pay their own costs. The consequence of this salutary law was, that no man was likely to harass another with a vexatious suit. But the law went farther than this. The original law was made more severe when the Whigs came to reign. Yes, it has been the Whigs who have made all the hard laws. As soon as the Whigs came into power, a law was passed to enable the judge to certify that it was a malicious trespass of which the defendant had been guilty. That consisted in this. If a man came frequently into my garden or field, after having been cautioned against it, then the judge was required to certify, and he had to pay the whole costs. Certainly this might be a very provoking kind of a trespass, a man might say, "Oh, yes, I'll not do you forty shillings' worth of harm, but I'll annoy you pretty well; I'll come pretty often into your grounds, and do you frequent petty mischiefs." And no man should be permitted to do this with impunity. But the operation of this law was most partial: it was very well for the rich, but very oppressive for the poor. But what have they done now? Mr. Peel, the ameliorator of the criminal code, brought in a bill, which has become a law, and is now in force, that if a man be seen trespassing on the land of another—though he has had no warning;—for instance, if you were going across a field having a path in it, in a dark night, and were accidentally to get out of the path—this law authorizes either the proprietor of the field himself, or any deputy for him, to go out and seize the man on the spot—not to bring an action at law—but to seize the man at once; or if he cannot seize him, to get a warrant for his apprehension—a warrant, mind ye—to get a warrant for his apprehension, and to take him before a magistrate, who is authorised to assess what damages he pleases under 5*l.*; and if the man charged with the trespass cannot pay them on the nail, he may be sent off to jail and to hard labour. Well, but this is not all; for if a trespass be to the amount of more than 5*l.*—and, gentlemen, it is not likely to be to a greater amount than 5*l.* unless done with dogs and horses—then the justice of the peace is to take no notice of it; then he is to leave the sufferer to his action at law against the rich man. Oh, yes, the rich man is not to be seized by the poor man, and taken before the justice; oh, no. But this is not all, for any man who has a game certificate, and is qualified to kill game, is not to be prosecuted at all; he is not to have his horses, or his dogs, or his followers seized, on any account. So that a rich man may come into my barleyfield, trample down the grain, and do me immense mischief; yet I dare not take hold of his horse's bridle to stop him, or in any other way interrupt him; but I may bring my action at law. Why, gentlemen, the rich man has plenty of money, the poor man has none, and therefore he cannot bring his action at law. (Murmurs, and cries of shame.) Is not this one law for the rich, and another for the poor? Thus are all things. They tell us we have nothing to complain of; we shall muster up something, however, in our petition to the king, I warrant ye. (Cheers.) We shall make out that we have just grounds of complaint; that we are not factious people, but that we understand we have grievances, and know how to represent them. And yet, gentlemen, we will complain of nothing but innovations. (Cheers.)

Another thing exists, the effects of which have lately been illustrated in Oxfordshire. Gentlemen, there can be neither nature, nor reason, nor did the law of the land ever contemplate that there should not be an inch of land on which the poor man should set his foot, or have a cow, or a pig, or a goose. But according to their construction of the law, the commons, or waste lands, as they call them, belong to certain lords of manors and other properties. Whenever they can agree, therefore, they go to that famous thing that does all the fine deeds (laughter),—the House of Commons, and begin with a law to authorise them to enclose the commons; that is, to take away the last blade of grass from those who live on the skirts of the common. I know, that in strictness of law, they may take it—and I know, too, if they come to strictness of law, that there are many things which might be taken from themselves—I know that in strictness of law they may take the commons from the poor people, but according to the usages of the country—and our ancestors always included usages in their estimate of public and private rights—they can do no such thing. (Cheers.) Well, from one end of England to the other, they have been at work for forty years enclosing the commons, and thus stripping the labouring poor of the last inch of ground on which they could feed a cow or a pig, or keep a bee. Nothing has done more mischief in England than this; nothing has more altered the state of the labouring people. I know one common on which a thousand families had settled; in 1827 a bill was passed in the Commons to enclose it, but a number of petitions, among which was one from myself, went up to the Lords, praying them to stop it, and the Lords did stop it, and saved that part of the country from the cruel intentions of these rich men. (Applause.) Gentlemen, this is not the only instance in which the lords have prevented the intolerable oppressions consented to by the House of Commons. . . .

The altered state of the labourers in this country is not unknown by any means to the parliament; and judge you what sympathy they have with them, how acutely they feel for the people, when they suffer such a state of things to continue. In 1821, during the reign, the "mild and beneficent reign of George IV." (laughter), a committee was appointed by the House of Commons, to inquire into the causes of the agricultural distress; that means, the causes why the land-holders do not get their rents (laughter); and also into the causes of the vast increase in the poor-rates. The committee met. Well, "how comes this vast increase in the poor-rates?" they inquire. "Oh, it is quite monstrous!" Why, the people are poorer than they used to be, was the answer. "Well, but what is the cause of that? Why do they make them paupers?" Nobody told them it was the taxes. However, a Mr. Ellman, a very respectable farmer in Sussex, was called as a witness, and was asked what was the state of the poor in his parish. "Very badly off, indeed," was his answer. "How many are there on the poor-rates?" They were rather angry with the man for saying they were very badly off. This Mr. Ellman, who was a sensible man, gave them this illustration, in a very sensible manner: "Forty-five years ago, when I began farming, there was not a man in the parish who did not brew his own beer, and enjoy it at his own fire-side; now there is not one in the whole parish who does so." The committee did not stop to inquire whether this arose from the malt-tax or the hop-tax; or whether it arose from a deficiency of wages, which stripped the labourer of his little utensils, one by one; oh no; this was of no con-sequence to the committee. Well, by and by they had a witness from Wiltshire—the high sheriff of the county—they asked him, "Well, how are the people off?" "Very badly; their common food is potatoes; they have scarcely any-thing else to eat; neither meat nor bread." They then asked him how they lived formerly! About forty years ago, he said, they had plenty of meat, bread, and beer. "What do they drink now?" was asked by some one on the committee, "Water." Somebody, however, remarked, that when a ploughman went out into the field, he must take something with him to eat besides potatoes. "No, they have only cold potatoes in the field"! Here is a state of things! These facts are notorious, and they are as disgraceful as they are notorious; and they should awaken indignation in the breast of every man, particularly if he have a belly-full of victuals. However, the committee made a report to the house; to that report they subjoined, of course, the evidence, and among the rest that to which I have referred. And what did the house do? What did they do? Why, to be sure, they went to work to inquire into the causes of this change in the condition of the working people. To be sure they did! I'll be bound that they fasted themselves till they found out the reason why the people fasted, or were living upon potatoes. I'll be bound they never quenched their thirst till they found out why the people did not now brew their beer. Not at all! They did nothing at all! If there had been one man in that house worthy of being called a representative of the people— if there had been only one such man in the house; with this evidence before him, would he not have made a motion that the house never should separate till they had inquired into the causes of this suffering? You are quite satisfied of this (cheers), gentlemen, there has not been one word said about it from that day to this. (Loud cries of shame, shame.) Can any-thing characterise the house more than this? If it were chosen by the people at large; if they felt themselves to be the representatives of the whole of the people, would they have acted in this manner? (No, no.) No, gentlemen, they did not inquire into the causes of the privations and sufferings of the working people—but they immediately set about inquiring how it came to pass that corn was so cheap, and how they could make it dearer! (It is impossible to describe the effect this statement produced on the audience with which the theatre was crammed.) Yes, gentlemen, they proceeded to inquire how they could ensure the agriculturists a higher price for corn; that is, how they could ensure themselves higher rents. . . .

In the year 1828—still in the mild and beneficent reign of George IV.—another committee was sitting to inquire into that part of the poor-laws relating to the employment of able-bodied persons from the poor-rates—not into the causes of the sufferings of the people, but into the increase of the poor-rates—this being in fact the thing—for they said, "If they continue to increase as they have hitherto done, all the land in the kingdom will be eaten up—it will pay no rents." Well, among other witnesses that came before the committee was a Mr. BOYCE, a great farmer of Waldershare, in the county of Kent. He told them that the poor were very badly off, for though he gave his people higher wages than any-body else in the parish, even they were very badly off. He further stated that he had seen thirty or forty young men in the prime of life, and who ought to have been at work in the fields, degraded in their own estimation as well as in the estimation of be-holders, hooked on to carts and wheelbarrows, dragging stones, because they could not get other employment! (Shame, shame.) To chairman of the committee, lawyer SLANEY, said "But why do you not employ them in the fields? Is there too great a population?" "No; there is not too many men," said Mr. Boyce, "for we could employ more than the whole of them if we had the means to pay them." And why not the means? Because, gentlemen, the taxes take away so much, as not to leave them the means. (Cheers.) In all manner of ways you can imagine, this Mr. lawyer Slaney tried to carry Mr. Boyce round, and catch him some how or another. They cross-questioned him like they do a witness at the Old Bailey. They did not like his answers, and they wanted to get rid of them. "Mr. Boyce," they said, "you have leave to amend your evidence, if you will." "No," said Mr. Boyce, "I do not want to amend my evidence." Over and over again he said, "We cannot employ the men, because we have not the means to pay them." That is, the taxes take away so large a part of the produce of our labour, that we have not sufficient left to procure the cultivation of the land.

. . . .

Upon the same occasion, a farmer from Pelham, in Hertfordshire, who gave his evidence, mentioned something upon which Mr. lawyer Slaney wanted to establish the belief, that the distress of the labouring people arose from premature marriages. Why, gentlemen, what a pretty race we should soon become, if none but old people married! (Laughter.) Mr. Slaney examined this farmer in a smock frock. *Slaney* —"Farmer, at what age do your labourers marry?" *Farmer*—"Not very early, Zur; they marry when they get about eighteen or nineteen." Oh, no wonder there is such a state of misery, then; no wonder at the weight of the poor-rates. By the bye, I believe this Slaney has eight or nine children himself—I dare say he wants some rates, or relief. (Laughter.) However, Slaney proceeded—"But why do you suffer them to marry so early?" "Why, Zur, we be glad to get 'em to marry." (Renewed laughter.) Gentlemen, I am not giving you a ludicrous description of the thing, but the very words of the parties.—"Glad to get them to marry! Why, man, what do you mean?" *Farmer*—"Why, Zur, if not, who's to feyther the child?" (Much laughter.) Gentlemen, we may not be able to restrain our laughter at the narration of this, but I assure you it is a very serious affair. "Father the child!" said Slaney, who, I dare say, is a very moral man, "Father the child! why you do not mean to say that the young women are with child before they are married?"—"Ez—always." "Eh? what always?" "Ez; always." (Great laughter.) By and by there came before the committee a parson from Little Horwood, in Buckinghamshire. They asked him if this was the case there? "Yes." Oh, what monstrous immorality! However, the farmer explained to them what ought to have produced an impression on them, and what would have produced an impression on any other body of men;—they asked him the cause of this state of things. "Why d'ye see, this is merely a manœuvre to make the parish pay the expenses of the wedding," Now, gentlemen, mark the progress of taxation and oppression. Forty or fifty years ago, circumstances like these would have been deemed a disgrace among these very people. The girl would have been pointed at, marked with disgrace, and not readily forgiven by her parents; now it is all cast away, and the reason the farmer gives is, that they are too poor to pay the expenses of the wedding. They therefore manœuvre to make the parish pay them. These expenses cannot be paid without the select vestry; but the young woman being in this state, something must be done, and therefore they lay hold of the man, and make him marry her—but the parish is obliged to pay the expenses. Such, gentlemen, is one specimen of the progress of taxation; such one specimen of the progress of morality, during "the mild and beneficent reign of George IV."

.    .    .    .

The other great thing I shall mention, and which touches everybody, is the Corn Bill. What is the state of the country, as they describe it? Why, there are too many people; that is, they have not the means of subsistence, and therefore they come on the poor-rates; and yet they are afraid of too much food coming into the country! They have a project before them to mortgage the poor-rates to send the people out of the country for want of food, and at the same time they pass a law to prevent food coming in! At once, there are too many mouths, and too much food. (Laughter.) But this is the complaint of all complaints, because it reaches the manufacturers, and prevents them competing with foreigners. I say that nothing but the superior skill and industry of the English manufacturers would enable them to maintain any part of the foreign trade. And this arises chiefly from the corn laws, which are designed to put high rents into the pockets of the landlords. They say to the farmer, "Oh, you could not carry on your concerns without these laws; you must have a protecting price." Gentlemen, it is not the farmer they protect; it is themselves; and the law is to give them a monopoly of the sale of corn and bread. That is what it is; and though the exciseman does not come into the shop to impose a tax on the loaf, they do the same thing in a much better manner for themselves. And this tax is made for themselves only, and purely, and against the rest of the community. Every man of us is taxed in his bread, in order that the riches may go into the pockets of the owners of the land. Is not this a subject of complaint? Is not this an innovation? The law passed first in 1815, and I believe I was the only person who petitioned parliament against it. I was then a farmer, but I saw so clearly that it would give no relief to the farmers, that I sent up a petition to the House of Lords, in which I affirmed, that it was against the whole community, for the benefit of the aristocracy. And, gentlemen, it is a law against which every man should set his face, and on which he should make his voice heard. By these means, and various others, to what a condition have they brought the working classes! The Scripture says, "He who will not work, shall not eat;" but they have studied how they can act in opposition to the precepts of the Gospel. If they had said, "Whereas it is right and expedient that those who work should not eat, and they who do not work should have all the victuals," they could not have acted differently to what they have done. . . .

But the miserable state into which they have brought us, what does it present? Gentlemen, we ought to be ashamed of the present state of things, unless we are resolved to get rid of it. (Cheers.) We ought to be ashamed to talk of liberty, of constitutional law; to own ourselves to be the sons of those men who made those laws which are now so abused; we ought to blush deeply when we think on these things, and above all we ought to be ashamed to talk about them, unless we are fully resolved to effect a change. If this be not our determination, we ought to blush to call ourselves Englishmen. (Cheers.) What do we behold! Within my recollection, throughout the country, the people were well fed, well clothed, and well housed; England was famed throughout the world for a well-clad, decent, moral, and honest people. What is our state now? Why, in innumerable instances, and for many years during "the mild and beneficent reign of George IV.," in various parts of England, people have been drawing wagons, chained or harnessed together like beasts of burden. In Nottinghamshire I met twenty men harnessed in this way, and in Sussex, in Hertfordshire, and in Hampshire, it has been common. Gentlemen, we ought to blush to speak about such things, unless we call upon the people to make an effort to get rid of them. They talk about the hardships of negro slaves, why, it is enough to fill us with indignation to hear them whine over the sorrows of a fat and greasy negro in Jamaica—by the way, they moan over his fate while they are sipping the sugar and the coffee produced by his labour—but it fills us with indignation to see their sympathies called forth in behalf of the well-fed negroes, while their own countrymen are found in such a condition under their very eyes. (Applause.) Oh, yes, while talking about the poor dear negroes they can look out of the window, and say, "Oh, it's only some men drawing a wagon." Gentlemen, it is very curious that last winter the Lords were all at once struck with the impropriety of this state of things. The Duke of Richmond called their Lordships' attention to the circumstance of men drawing loaded wagons, about which he talked very pathetically, and insisted that it ought not to continue. Why, Gentlemen, the Duke of Richmond might have learned the fact from me sixteen years ago. But can you wonder that the poor people are vindictive? When they come to the select vestry, they say to them, "Oh, yes, we'll give you relief; yes, you shall draw loaded wagons, like horses, and have a driver; you shall do that or starve." This I say, has been the case for many years—I believe they will not attempt it again. (Cheers.) . . .

But this drawing of wagons is not the most provoking and humiliating part of the inflictions on the people in the country; though we know little of them. In many parts, when a man who has a wife and family becomes chargeable on the parish, they will take good care that he shall not increase it. They shut his wife up in the poorhouse, and place the man somewhere else; and never suffer them even to speak to each other but in the presence of the master of the workhouse. This alone would afford a criterion for judging of the degradation of the country. Can you blame such a man for resorting to violence? Is it not in nature? Let any man consider if he were to happen to fall into misfortune, and should thus be separated from his wife; not be able even to speak to her in private,—not permitted to speak to her but in the presence of the master of the workhouse; and all this without his having committed any crime. Yet, gentlemen, this is the state of England, and we ought not to disguise it from ourselves. We who know how extensively it exists, should communicate it to others, and they should talk of it wherever they come, and resolve to make use of all means in their power to alter such a state of things.

Another thing the labourers have to suffer—and they may try this again, but if they do, I am sure it will lead to a convulsion in the country—but another thing is what they have the impudence to tell us cannot be done. They say, "Oh they cannot sell you like they do negroes; you may not be quite so well fed, to be sure; but then, you are free-born Englishmen, and they cannot sell you like they do the negroes." Now, gentlemen, the fact is, that Englishmen can be bought and sold, and are bought and sold, from one end of the country to the other. It [is] as common in various parts of the country, to sell the labouring men for the week and the month, as it is to sell a sheep or a pig, or any other description of article. In Norfolk, last winter, (see what it leads to!) it was the practice to bring the poor men every month into the church porch, and in that very place, erected for the purposes of charity, for if you look into the foundation, you will find

that it was erected for God and the poor—that is the grant always—
in the very church porch, then, the poor were brought once a month,
and sold by the hammer to the highest bidder. (Shame, shame.) At
least, in one parish the consequences were these: the farmers who
were the most active in sanctioning this monstrous proceeding, found,
upon getting up in the morning, the spokes of all their wheels sawed
through, the beams of their ploughs quietly cut across, the shafts of
their carts severed—so that nothing could be done in the morning.
Wheelwrights and others were wanted to repair the damage done, and
thus labour was created. (Cheers.) All this while the poor men were
laughing, to be sure; such things cannot go on for ever. They have
been going on during the ten last years of the "mild and beneficent
reign of George IV.," but be you assured that they will not go on for
five years more (applause), under the really mild reign of William IV.
(Renewed applause.) Gentlemen, how could they go further than
this? How could they exceed the selling of men's carcases?—for, as I
said last week, it is not the blood and bones of the negroes that they
sell; it is their labour; and it is the same that they sell the whites for.
So that it seems impossible to go farther than this; it seems impossible
that they should be able, by any ingenuity, to find out how to inflict
a greater degradation than this. But, gentlemen, it is possible, for, as
far as the House of Commons is concerned, they have gone farther
than this, for they actually passed a bill to sell our dead bodies.
(Shame, shame, monstrous.) Gentlemen, though at the time I was
greatly enraged at this monstrous attempt, I do almost wish they had
passed the bill in the Lords, for then there must have been an end
to the thing altogether; for though in London, where poor creatures
find their way and die, without any one knowing them, the sale of a
dead body might not attract much notice, it is not so in the country.
There every man is known to his neighbours; and rest you assured,
that had they attempted the thing, there would not have been a
gentleman's house unburnt. The very first man's body that had been
sold in any county in England, the sellers, and buyers, and all in any
way connected with the transaction, immediately or remotely, would
have been destroyed by the people. . . . Gentlemen, the Lords threw
out the bill, but the passing of it in the House of Commons shows
what that assembly is made of. There it passed without any division;
almost unanimously; and one time it was read with only sixteen or
seventeen members in the house. Oh, to be sure, it was nothing to
sell the dead bodies of the poor. Gentlemen, would any man among
you sanction the selling of the dead body of a poor man, even though
the price it fetched were applied to the support of other poor people?

(Cries of, No, no.) Or the selling of it all? (No, no.) And, gentlemen, let us not, because we may not now be in that situation ourselves, let us not imagine that the poor, who were the objects of this
bill, have not their feelings, as well as we have. (Cheers.) Think of
the feelings of the father of a family, or any other man, knowing that
he was going to die, and contemplating at the same time that his
body was to be taken, and chopped up, and his body thus to be put
upon a level with that of the murderer; for they did not dare, as the
Lord Chief Justice told them, they did not dare to remove that stigma
from the character of a murderer, or there would have been no difference made between him and another man. I say then, that to pass
this bill, was to pass a law that every poor man, who died on the
parish-books, should be punished after death as a murderer. But they
tell us it was necessary for the purposes of science. Science! Why, who
is science for? Not for poor people. Then if it be necessary for the
purposes of science, let them have the bodies of the rich, for whose
benefit science is cultivated. (Cheers.) Or, gentlemen, let them take
the placemen and pensioners, if they must have subjects. as they call
them, for the benefit of science. (Laughter.) What so reasonable, as
to have the bodies of men who have been subsisting at the public
expense, and done nothing in exchange for their sustenance? If these
men would give up their bodies, there would be some little reason in
pensions. (Renewed laughter.) They might then say, "Why, true, we
have done you no service while we have been living, but you shall have
our carcases when we are dead." (Great laughter.) On the contrary,
those who had laboured, and who, very likely, had been brought to
death's door by excessive labour, the bodies of these men were to be
taken, and that for the benefit of those who had brought them into
this condition. They had another argument. "Why," they said, "if we
don't do this—if we don't sell the dead bodies of the poor, they will
be taken out of the graves, and sold by other people. There will be
smuggling; there will be an illicit and contraband trade. If we don't
establish a regular trade in dead bodies, we shall have a contraband
one. They will have them!" So then those men who could pass a
law for authorising the bank to refuse to pay its creditors—who could
pass a law to shut up Englishmen in prison whenever ministers pleased,
and keep them in prison as long as they pleased, and let them out
when they pleased, without ever bringing them to trial, or letting
them know the nature of their offence—those men who made these
laws, could not make a law to prevent men stealing dead bodies.
(Cheers.) What! our omnipotent parliament could not do this? A
parliament which could pass laws like these, had not skill enough to

pass a law to prevent men taking dead bodies from the tomb! They who passed a law to protect the bodies of pheasants, hares, and partridges—wild animals, which are here one hour and twenty miles off the next—could not they pass a law to prevent fellows violating the sacredness of the grave! I say there was nothing more easy than to pass such a law; to make it felony to have possession of a dead body without it had been delivered by a due course of law. Gentlemen, a reformed parliament would have a due feeling for the whole people, poor as well as rich. They talk about the sacredness of the tomb. Yes, it is the TOMB they mean—those they bury in the church or the vault; but those who are laid in the ground can have no law passed to prevent their being taken up.

Gentlemen, these are a few of the grievances of which we have to complain, as having emanated from our law-makers during "the mild and beneficent reign of George the Fourth." There are others innumerable, but I fear I have this evening exhausted your patience. (Loud and general cries of "No, no; go on, go on.") Gentlemen, on Monday evening I shall, as I said before, bring before you such a petition as I think we should present to his Majesty. Perhaps we may be able to devise some method of taking the signatures of those present at the time, and thus get it into a forward state. (Loud cheers.) After stating that he should himself be happy at least to make one of a deputation to present the petition to the King, Mr. Cobbett sat down amidst the most enthusiastic applause.

ALBANY FONBLANQUE

# The Year One[*]

ALBANY FONBLANQUE (1793–1872) BECAME
the principal writer for the *Examiner* after Leigh Hunt left in
1826. The *Examiner*, under Hunt and Fonblanque, was the chief
organ of intellectual radicalism in England, and Fonblanque in
particular was a highly influential writer with a reputation for
great wit. He was also intimate with the utilitarians. In retrospect,
his essays do not seem as pungent as they apparently did to his contemporaries, but collected as they are in his *England Under Seven
Administrations* (1837), they nevertheless give a rich view of the
history of the time through the eyes of a highly intelligent and
committed journalist.

The essay presented here affords a sense of the enormous
confidence in the coming new age that Victorian radicals tended
to share, and suggests how important the French Revolution of
1830 was to English reformers. A brief portion of the essay (dealing in some detail with the Revolution itself) has been omitted

[*] From *Examiner* (January 2, 1831), 1–2.

here, even as it was when collected in *England Under Seven Administrations*. "The year One," of course, is the first year after the Revolution.

We have closed the year ONE of the People's Cause. We have closed a year that has teemed with events of a grandeur and importance to mankind, unparalleled in the history of the world. We have closed a year in which Justice has wielded the sword of Victory, and Fortune lent her wheel to Truth. We have closed a year which has carried the mind of Europe forward an interval of ages beyond its antiquated trammels and thraldoms. We have closed a year which has dated the decrepitude of despotism, and the Herculean infancy of the democratic power; and must not our recollections swell with pride, and our expectations be full of confidence? The past indicates the future. Abroad we have the example of France, both for imitation and for warning. Her people have set before us the great lesson of virtue—her Government of error. The Representative Government, which rests on a narrow constituency, is like the Logan stones, which the finger of a child may move. Reverse the position—place the cone on its broad basis, and a giant cannot stir it. The existing error our neighbours will redress; but the process is one that we wish could have been spared to their temper and virtue. If we draw too much, even on the wisdom of men, we are sure to come to the lees. France has not done enough for herself, but she has done enough for the world, and her after-troubles will not affect the force of her example. The fault is as palpably marked as the passage of glory. The tyranny of one went down, and a hydra wriggled into usurpation. An oligarchy settled into power. The French Chamber of Deputies is now not much better than the British House of Commons.

It cannot be denied, that for the last ten years, step after step has been won by the liberal party, and not one inch of ground any where lost. We have experienced no defeats—we have been stayed, indeed, but never thrust back; and, despite of obstinate opposition, object after object has been obtained. The Liberals struggled long for Catholic Emancipation. Catholic Emancipation was declared the destruction of Religion, the deliverance of society to all the powers of evil, the unloosing of Anti-Christ and Satan. It was carried: and all the world perceived the Liberals had been right. Nearly the same history applies to the Test Laws. The alteration of the Commercial System was demanded: the Economists were forthwith declared visionaries, and their doctrines were condemned, under the all-convincing description of "new-fangled,"—one of the most potent phrases in the English language. With the success of the experiments came the late acknowledgment, that the economists were not such fools as the ignoramuses had thought them.

Reformers complained of the abuses, defects, and vices of the laws. The law is perfection, was the first defence; and the objectors were denounced as false preachers of discontent, the inveterate enemies of all the excellencies in our unrivalled institutions; and yet Law Reform is now the great business of the day; and judges claim, and merit praise, for their application to the purifying of the Augean stable. Thus again, after all, the Reformers were right. Lastly, we come to the grand question.

Who were they who have for years past denounced the corruption of the Lower House, called for its re-constitution, and insisted on the people's right to representation as the only security against the abuse of power? Radicals, clamourers without cause, it was said; men void of truth and justice, who slandered an institution as perfect as the wit of man could make it, and which, whatever theoretical flaws might be objected by visionaries, worked excellently well in practice. Two years ago the Honourable House declared, upon a division, that there was no rotten representation. Less than two months ago, a Minister fell because he offered the same impudent outrage to truth. Now, the vast majority of society, Whig, Tory, and Moderates, acknowledge the necessity of Parliamentary Reform. So again the Reformers, after all, were right. Two years back, when Sir Robert Peel invented a clap-trap sentiment against the suggestion of the Ballot (by Mr. WARBURTON we believe), the collective wisdom received it with shouts of applause. Six months ago, Mr. BROUGHAM spouted fallacies and nonsenses of all sorts against it at popular meetings, without provoking signs of displeasure or retort; now the conviction of the country is for the Ballot. Men of all classes and denominations, not interested in the foul influences, are converts to the necessity. So here again, it will soon be seen, that the Reformers were right, after all. Where are they yet said to be wrong? Only, we reply, upon the ground where the battles are not yet fought out. They are said to be wrong, or wicked, or mischievous, for demanding the principle of universal suffrage; or that the franchise shall be co-extensive with the education and property of the country, and descending to the people as information is spreading among them. They are said to be wrong for objecting to an expensive Church Establishment, and for thinking that the wealth of the Priesthood is not apostolic or conducive to religion. They are said to be wrong, or wicked, or mischievous, because they think it hard, unjust, and impolitic, to maintain an aristocracy in luxury, or affluent idleness, out of the taxes wrung from the toil-worn hands of the people. They are said to be wrong, or disloyal, and seditious, for supposing that the dignity of the Crown can be maintained without extravagant ostentation, and that the conduct of the chief magistrate is a better security for it than his cost.

They are said to be wrong, or to betray an ignorant impatience of taxation, for contending that it is the duty of a Government to raise the moral character of the people by knowledge, and that it is barbarous impolicy to place out of their reach, by stamp duties, the information which would teach them prudence and conduct. They are said to be wrong for arguing that it is cheaper and better to direct men with books, than to controul them with bayonets, and that letters are more explanatory missives than bullets.

Under these, and a very few other imputations of error, the Reformers may be cheered by reflecting that such opposition has resisted, for a season, every measure (without any single exception) they have carried; and in relation to those positions we have recited, as well as to those already won, it will be confessed, at no distant day, that, after all, the Radicals were right.

We ask of our opponents to reflect on the many questions which the voice of society, and the acts of the State, have determined in our favour; and to consider whether it is not probable that we are as right, in the doctrines which remain unsettled, as in those now sanctioned and established? Have they not as much cause for self-distrust as the Reformers have for confidence?

Against what combined forces of sinister interest, custom and prejudice, have the Liberals made their impressions, and achieved their victories, by a vast power of truth alone! To the conviction of society, and to nothing else, do we owe our proud successes.

WILLIAM MAGINN

# The Desperate System. Poverty, Crime, and Emigration*

WILLIAM MAGINN (1793–1842) WAS A FASCI-
nating if rather dissolute scholar, poet, and journalist, most famous
for establishing *Fraser's Magazine* in 1830. He was connected with
*Blackwood's Magazine* as a parodist and writer of humorous verse,
and he did some of the best writing in the famous *Noctes ambrosianae* series. Maginn was always a heavy drinker, and when John
Murray gave him a job on his journal, *The Representative*, Maginn
hurried the magazine to its early death. In 1830 he arranged,

* From *Fraser's Magazine*, I (July, 1830), 635–42.

almost spontaneously, for the establishment of *Fraser's*, for which he wrote most of the copy in the first few numbers, despite the fact that he was not editor. *Fraser's*, which prided itself on its idiosyncratic style, also recruited writers like Carlyle and Thackeray, and rapidly became the best of the English monthlies.

Despite his dissipation and irresponsibility, Maginn was a fine and intelligent writer. His essay, *The Desperate System*, is full of the usual *Fraser's* dash, but suggests an underlying humanity that redeems it from mere idiosyncrasy. It deals with the problem of the increased number of people on relief, that, in the public mind, was becoming increasingly serious; and it shows with some clarity that the proposed solution of emigration (espoused as it was by a large portion of the intelligent community) was essentially inhumane.

The rapid and alarming increase of crime in this country, within the last few years, seems very much to astonish the present race of philosophers and political economists. Mr. Potter Macqueen, in his last pamphlet, partly attributes it to the laxity of morals and the principles of infidelity "introduced into this country by the French revolution." Dr. Blomfield, the Bishop of London, ascribes it to the profanation of the Sabbath. Mr. Fowell Buxton,[1] and Mr. Nathan Drab, of Exeter, ascribe it to the morbid sympathy which exists between the law and

---

I have not been able to identify all the figures Maginn alludes to in this essay, and have decided, therefore, to confine footnotes of identification to the more obviously important people mentioned.—ed.

1. Sir Thomas Fowell Buxton (1786–1845) was one of England's first philanthropists, and was active in the development of the Bible Society, in education reform, and particularly in the antislavery campaign in Parliament, which, at Wilberforce's request, he took over in 1822. In 1818 he published a work relevant to Maginn's concerns here: *Whether Crime and Misery are Produced or Prevented by our Present System of Prison Discipline.*

the gallows. Lord Wharncliffe[2] is of opinion that it is caused by the game-laws. "Why should peasants be hung," he asks, "that pheasants may *not* be stolen?" Mr. Barclay, the brewer, thinks that it has its origin in the enormous increase in the consumption of gin and British spirits. A Mr. Dunlop endeavours to prove that it is the natural effect of the malt and beer monopolies. The philanthropic society of Bristol attribute it to the unprecedented importation of "the *low* Irish," by which we suppose they mean hodmen, pigs, ribbonmen, and "gentlemen of the press." Mr. Robert Owen ascribes it to the universal ignorance that prevails of the "science of circumstances." Mr. Hume[3] alleges that it is produced by the taxes and the tithes. Boatswain Smith imputes it to the neglect of the "pure word," of which he, the said Smith, is the only unadulterated spring; while Lord Bexley,[4] on the other hand, attributes it to the decline of the Bible Society. The Duke of Wellington, borrowing his notion from Lord Goderich[5]—for his grace never hazards any idea of his own—assigns the cause to "overproduction;" while the Reverend Mr. Malthus and Mr. Wilmot Horton[6] ascribe it to a "redundancy of population." Mr.

2. James Archibald Stuart-Wortley-Mackenzie, first Baron Wharncliffe (1776–1845), was a Tory politician who nevertheless backed a good many radical reforms, including an inquiry into the Peterloo Massacre of 1819, the relief of the poor from taxation, and Catholic Emancipation. Although he entered Parliament in opposition to reform, he led the general discussion of it in the House of Lords and ultimately backed it.

3. Joseph Hume (1777–1855) was a Tory politician who, after a study of the condition of the working classes, converted to the liberal cause. He remained an outspoken and extremely diligent leader of the Radical party in Parliament for thirty years.

4. Nicholas Vansittart, first Baron Bexley (1766–1851), was chancellor of the exchequer from 1812 to 1823 and, despite his apparent mediocrity, was an extremely important figure in the Tory government. Very unpopular because of his refusal to cut expenses or taxes, he was also a Tory evangelical opposed to Catholic Emancipation and reform.

5. John Frederick Robinson, Viscount Goderich (1782–1859), sometimes called "Prosperity Robinson" because of his refusal to admit the existence of poverty and distress, was an extremely important figure in Tory government. After he introduced the Corn Laws in 1815, his house was destroyed by mobs. He did a good deal toward financial reform, and saw to it that large appropriations were made for museums, galleries, and restorations of old buildings.

6. Sir Robert John Wilmot-Horton (1784–1841) was a politician and writer on political matters who gained some importance in the Tory government as undersecretary of war in 1821 and a member of the Privy Council in 1827. He also lectured frequently at Mechanics' Institutes on political economy. From 1831 to 1837, he served as governor of Ceylon.

Projector Gudgeon, of the Transportation Society, charges the evil upon the superfecundity of "young couples;" while Mr. Henry Wilson says (with some reason we admit) that it is caused by the higher rate of profits obtained in the trade of larceny than in the trade of honesty.

Heaven preserve us! here are reasons sufficient to overturn a world. Pandora's box was a mere jest to this. If crime have its origin in so many sources—if it flow with the stream and against the stream —if it be caused by overproduction as well as by bad harvests—if it be caused by the French revolution and the Irish invasion—by cheapness as well as dearness—by excessive industry as well as excessive indolence —if men increase the faster that men are hanged—if boys steal with greater alacrity the more severely they are punished—and if poaching increase in a geometrical ratio with the committals of poachers to gaol, then, sure enough, the last days are come—the march of crime is irresistible, and burglars and thieves, like his Majesty's ministers, will speedily be in a triumphant majority.

We, however, who are extremely humble persons, entertain a very different opinion from any one of those promulgated by the philosophers.—That crime has increased, is increasing, and will continue to increase for some time, we are most willing to concede. Its increase since 1823, is rapid and unexampled in the history of any country. The returns laid before parliament present a picture, which, with the profane, is calculated to bring religion and human laws into contempt. It is enough to make the minister of justice lay violent hands upon himself. Its horrid details are sufficient to convert the priest into a hermit; and send him who ministers at the altar into a cavern; in order to propitiate heaven by a life of seclusion, abstinence, and severe penance. . . .

. . . During seven years the mass of guilt has augmented at the rate of from five to seven per cent. per annum. If it proceed at the same rate it will double itself in twelve years; or, in other words, in 1835 we shall have just twice as many criminals as we had in 1823. It is true that murders have not increased in the ratio of other crimes. In 1823 we had twelve, and in 1829 only thirteen. This certainly is consoling; but as to shooting, stabbing, wounding, and poisoning, the increase is shocking. In 1823 the number of persons convicted of these crimes was only fourteen; in 1829 their number amounted to sixty-five. If we advance at this rate long, Ireland, and even Naples, will be outdistanced in these sanguinary and mortal feats by England. Embezzlement *by servants* is progressing with similar strides. In 1823 we had only sixty-four such persons; but in 1829 we had one hundred and thirty. In 1823 there were one hundred and twenty-four persons convicted of breaking into dwelling houses; but in 1829 no less than five hundred and sixty-one were convicted of this crime. Gentlemen who usurp the king's prerogative, and make sovereigns as they need them, numbered one hundred and seventy-five in the year 1823; but, in 1829, they numbered two hundred and fifty-six. Larcenies have increased from 6,000 to 10,000. Assaults have increased about fifty per cent., and sheep-stealing is doubled.

.   .   .   .

There are some people, philosophers of course, who do us the favour to propound remedies, without deigning to enquire into the origin of this criminal prolificness. The leaders of these political Sangrados have but one specific. They propose banishment, under the milder term, *removal.* They generously recommend the deportation of "young couples." They perceive that the nation is struggling with a mortal consumption; and they prescribe bleeding. They see that we are infirm and helpless, and they recommend the removal of what constitutes our powers of vitality and strength. They find the head giddy, and the feet weak; and they suggest the expediency of cutting out the heart. We shall not argue with these learned persons. The tread-mill and the water-gruel diet ought to be the only answer to their impertinence, and the certain punishment of their ignorance and presumption.

But, THE CAUSE! Need we conceal it? Need we shelter cant and oppression at the expense of justice? The source of crime, the fountain-head of pauperism and its consequences—is POVERTY! Since 1823, this unhappy country has been cursed by the visionary measures of a set of men, than whom, greater fools or more mischievous empirics never existed in any land. In 1823, the Liberals commenced their experiments, and from that period we have been doomed to undergo all the alternations of increasing embarrassment and pauperism. The ministers then committed a fatal mistake. They had not sufficient penetration to perceive that the reduction of wages, prices, and profits, which they aimed at, and which they have unfortunately accomplished, was a certain approach towards poverty. Cheapness in all countries, is only another word for indigence. Cheapness that affects the cultivator, the manufacturer, and the labourer, without affecting the placeman, the pensioner, the fundholder, the soldier, the sailor, or the mortgagee, is a term, the proper definition of which, is—robbery. It is as much an offence against the person and the property of the poor, as is the act of entering a man's house, assaulting him in the presence of his servants, and carrying off his plate and ready money. Had there been, since the death of Lord Londonderry,[7] any man of talent, of honour, or even of ordinary information combined with integrity in the cabinet, the acts of spoliation which have been perpetrated, the loss of property which has been incurred, the ruin of millions which has followed, could not have taken place, and England would have been saved, even in defiance of its corrupt and subservient parliaments. Lord Londonderry fell a victim to his own apprehensions. He had twice saved his country from the scourge of the currency bill; but he saw that public opinion was in its favour; that his colleagues approved it; that the age of empiricism had commenced, and that the nation would sink under the numberless theories, and insane experiments, which were soon to be carried into practice. He foresaw the ruin which he could not prevent; his mind fell a prey to its own anxieties; and he anticipated death rather than witness the calamities which were to befall his country.

Since 1823, our progress towards the minimum of endurable privation, has been as rapid as the most inveterate enemy of England could desire. The industry of the country has gradually become less remunerative. Not that we have toiled less—not that the farmer has relaxed in his exertions—not that the velocity of the shuttle has decreased—not that those who earn their bread by the sweat of their brows, have been sleeping in the sunshine and giving a holiday to the earth, and the things under the earth; no such thing; they have toiled more unintermittently than they ever did before; and yet the meal has disappeared from their garner, the oil of the cruise has dried up, their fare has become more scanty, their children more hungry, their clothes more ragged; till at last the feast of the soup kitchen, and the pittance of the overseer, have accomplished the climax of their moral and physical degradation.

We trust that none of our readers belong to that class of sceptics, who would here call upon us to produce satisfactory proof upon oath of the distress and misery we have attempted to describe. Every man who has his eyes open—who can read, or hear, or see—or is capable of comprehending what he reads, hears, or sees, must assent to the

7. Robert Stewart, Viscount Castlereagh and Marquis of Londonderry (1769–1822), was one of the most important members of the Tory government that reigned after the Napoleonic wars. He attempted to establish a balance of power (Russia, Prussia, Austria, and England) against France, but he was, nevertheless, generous to France after its defeat. He was generally despised by reformers and found himself in a difficult position as defender of the policies of the repressive and reactionary government at home. Finally, under enormous strain and harassed by the difficulties of his office as foreign secretary, he committed suicide.

accuracy of the picture. The common people are steeped in wretched-ness to the very lips. England may have been, as Napoleon averred, a nation of shopkeepers; now it is a land of beggars. Nearly 10 millions of poor rates are levied annually to support, at the rate of from two shillings to five shillings per week, the infirm, the unemployed, and the destitute. And yet there is more real benevolence, more active philanthropy, and more charitable institutions in England, than in any three nations of Europe, if united. The great mass of the people are unable, by their utmost exertions, to earn wages sufficient to render them more comfortable, or more than one or two degrees more respect-able or independent, than the actual pauper. Hence the prolific and increasing crop of criminals. Crime is not so much the offspring of poverty, as it is of reduced circumstances. For instance, a Scotch high-lander, accustomed to a scanty fare, is far from being demoralized in the ratio of his sustenance or his poverty. The *lord* of an Irish cabin, who lives solely upon potatoes, sometimes with, and sometimes with-out salt, is not naturally a thief. It is only when the circumstances of a people are declining towards poverty—when increased industry has to contend with decreasing remuneration—when disappointment preys upon hope deferred—when the peasant considers himself oppressed, and the artisan robbed—then it is that crime marches hand in hand with privation, and an increase of suffering produces an increase of guilt.

And yet it is but justice to say that, at the outset, the latter rarely increases with the hasty strides of the former. There is much long-suffering, many painful struggles, many a countervailing qualm of remorse, and as many delays in the court of Conscience as in the court of Chancery, before the victim of penury becomes an adventurer on the highway, or a shoplifter in the streets. A farm labourer without employment, and without bread, on the first night after his discharge, as he lays his head upon his pillow, if he have a pillow, puts the follow-ing questions to himself: "Shall I apply to the overseer, or live upon Squire Stubbs's preserve?—Shall I be a pensioner on the parish, or merely a private pensioner of my Lord Rump, Sir John Goose, or Parson Ratwell, who is a distant relation of my Lord Chancellor Turncoat?" Pride, or perhaps the Devil, whispers the hind, that it will be more *honourable* to poach, than be degraded as a pauper. He com-mences poaching accordingly. He is caught in "my Lord's" preserve, and the justices send him to gaol to do penance, but, in fact, to finish his education. He is liberated at length—his wife, meanwhile, has died of poverty and grief, or perhaps she has eloped with a neighbouring journeyman tailor, who earns excellent wages, by working to a buyer and seller of stolen goods. What, then, is the convicted poacher to do? If he should be seen within a mile of any preserve, he is liable to be shot. He accordingly joins a new confederacy, composed of those companions whose *friendship* he acquired in prison. He consults them in the emergency; and, under their advice, he steals a sheep, or perhaps a horse;—is discovered, tried, convicted, and either hanged or transported.

Such is, in innumerable instances, the cause, the rise, and progress of crime in the agricultural districts. The same cause produces the same effect in large towns, where the population is more dense and more mechanical. There is a boy, we are told, at this moment confined in Newgate on a charge of larceny, who, before he had transgressed the law, when he sought relief from the overseer, was told gruffly to "go and steal!" In short, if we were disposed to illustrate our hypothesis—that crime is caused by poverty—by examples we could fill the whole of this number of Regina, together with an appendix—twice the size of the *Quarterly Review*, advertisements included.

It is perhaps more desirable that we take a glance at the living authors of this demoralization, and these calamities. The representatives of the country are irresponsible agents. Those of them who buy seats, represent no interest but their own. They have nothing at stake, but the money paid to the seat-vender; therefore *they* are independent! Those who have constituents cannot be called to account until that interesting period arrives, when they venture to solicit from their electors a renewal of their patronage. If they have jobbed with public money, trafficked with the minister for places and appointments, neglected the interests of the people and injured their country, their only punishment is the preference given to a new candidate, who, in all probability, may prove more venal than the former.

Be this as it may—however responsible these men are morally, they are not legally nor constitutionally responsible for the evils they inflict on the nation. But the ministers are responsible, even though they should plead the sanction of the houses of legislature. The ministers who have been in office since 1823, are responsible for all the pauperism and demoralization which have increased since that period. *Their* measures—not the measures of parliament—but the measures they have devised, recommended, and carried by majorities composed of their own retainers—have caused this increase in pauperism and crime. They are the guilty parties. Ignorance in a minister is as much a crime, as felony is in a mender of copper kettles. If he have done the state wrong, it is no defence to say he meant well. If by his policy he has reduced thousands of families to beggary, thence to poaching, thence to criminal acts generally, he is the author of both the suffering and the crime, and is more culpable than the sheep-stealer whom he transports, or the house-breaker whom he hangs.

For these reasons, we charge upon the ministers of the King, not only the distress that prevails, but the crime that degrades England in the eyes of the whole world—which places her lowest in the scale of morality, and paralyzes the example of her boasted benevolence, her apostolic missions, her public schools of instruction, her bible distributors, her cheap libraries, the purity of her reformed doctrines, and the excellence of her laws. We charge the increase of 23,841 criminals, since the year 1823, upon his Majesty's government. We affirm that they are answerable, at some bar of judgment, for the deep and incurable wounds they have inflicted upon the nation. Sympathy is not atonement. A hypocritical minister may shed an artificial tear over the sorrows of an orphan, whose father, driven to despair, outraged the laws of nature and paternal love, as well as the duties of religion, by an act of self-destruction. His sorrow, even if unfeigned, would not sanctify his guilt. . . .

But here we pause to inquire, if the amount of national suffering, of which we complain, and of crime, which we lament, has reached its maximum. Is it true that the fury of the storm is spent—that the winter of penury is warming into spring—that we have reached the extreme ebb of the tide, and that the waters of hope and life and proisperity have commenced their much desired and salutary reflux? . . .

. . . .

The struggling land-owners, and those merchants and manufacturers who are at the present moment contending with severe losses and inevitable bankruptcy, are easily flattered by any delusion which acts like a narcotic upon the paroxysms of despair. They cling to every floating straw, as if it were a cable spun by Hope under the superintendence of a special providence. They imagine that a good harvest, a full crop, and perseverance, even in bad measures, provided it be a *steady* perseverance, will make evil good, and yield a fair return to patience, even at the expense of justice and sound policy. They trust to chance, as the culprit trusts to the chances of a muddled jury, an oblivious judge, and a bad law. In short, they think that the very blunders of the state physician will operate as beneficially for them as Nature did *in extremis* for Roderick Random.

Alas! alas! They are only sowing the wind to reap the whirlwind. They, perhaps, forget that so long as we continue measuring our wealth, by a standard that is gradually increasing in value, the fixed annuitant may be benefitted, but every other class—all producers, land-owners, manufacturers, and labourers—must be injured. Gold is our standard; and its quantity is daily becoming less. There is more of it consumed in manufactures than is supplied by the mines. It is daily disappearing from our English circulation. Even at this hour, after thirty millions of sovereigns have been issued from the Bank, the mint is busily employed in supplying the wants of 1830. Most of the pieces which one receives in exchange for a ten pound note bear the impression of the present year. Where those already coined have gone, Heaven knows; but certain it is they have vanished from the current of our circulating medium. While this continues, prices must fall lower—wages must fall in proportion—the value of every kind of property in land or houses, in shipping or farm-stock, in iron or cotton goods, must proportionally decline. If we have a good harvest, and more than an average crop, Mr. Goulburn[8] will lose more than a million sterling of corn duties, and in October next the farmer will be obliged to sell *two* bushels of wheat for the price which *one* realized last year. If we have a deficient crop, the exchequer will be replenished; but the sufferings of the labouring population will be seriously increased. With these prospects before us, and they are the natural and inevitable effects of the avowed policy of the ministers, it would evince both weakness and ignorance to expect relief from time, or a steady perseverance in that which is radically pernicious. If distress continue, crime, therefore, must increase. Its prevention, or its cure is not a matter of police. No gendarmerie can stay the "superfecundity" of crime. They may detect, but they cannot restrain. They may fill the prisons, and load the hulks, and give an impetus to the increase of population in New South Wales; but they cannot eradicate the parent root of crime. Peel's soldiers, even though drilled on Sunday, are nothing more than clodpoles, armed with hangers, traversing a field of furze, and cutting down the green shoots and the withered stumps which they consider to be dead. With respect to this last indication they are mistaken. The roots are sound; the police may apparently clear the soil; but as they cannot, or rather dare not penetrate the surface, the shoots of next year will be more abundant than they were the year before.

To what then, it will probably be asked, must this state of things lead? The question may be pertinent, but we decline answering it. . . .

8. Henry Goulburn (1784–1856) had a series of high positions in government from 1810 until the fall of the Tories. He was particularly involved with Ireland, where he was for a while chief secretary to the Lord Lieutenant, and regularly opposed to Irish claims and Catholic Emancipation.

We would, therefore, advise the curious reader to propound his question to his Majesty's ministers. We stand upon our prerogative, satisfied that we do enough when we point out the evil. Others are paid to devise remedies—we are not. On them devolves the duty of relieving us; if they neglect this duty, it must be at the peril of a certain conspicuous adjunct of the human form, which is generally considered the guardian of the lower extremities. The head, says somebody, is to the feet, what a watchbox on a tower is to the sentinels who snore in the hall.

One word, however, before we conclude, with respect to the many-headed monster whose multifarious plans are offered as cures for the existing distress. The lesser quacks assume the character of legal reformers; the greater are transmigrant philosophers. The latter propose to relieve us of our pauper dead-weight, by transporting the consumers of poor rates—by removing an English cottager, in order to make room for an itinerant corn-cutter from the Sister Island. These gentlemen monopolize but one idea, and this, they conceive, embraces the cause as well as the cure of penury. The cause is—a redundancy of population; the cure is—emigration. The present crisis, therefore, is quite a harvest for these persons. If by any chance or mistake the ministry were to adopt any salutary or corrective measure, their beautiful hobby would break down, and their system be blown up. If the Duke of Wellington should, by some happy blunder, commit violence on Peel's bill, and Huskisson's[9] theories, these gentlemen would be unable to lay their hands upon a single beggar. The *materiel* of emigration would disappear; the "young couples" would marry at home; and the philosophers would be deprived even of the consolation of a full workhouse. For these reasons they are, at the present moment, equally clamorous and industrious. And they are encouraged in their schemes by the government. They attract attention; and they entice the thoughts of the multitude from the real cause of their embarrassments. When the juggler wishes to deceive the sense, he diverts the eye. We are induced to look at the only thing we should not see; and as we gaze, the trick is accomplished, and we are imposed upon. Just so with the emigrationists. We find ourselves meandering in New South Wales, when we ought to be in England. . . .

To show the folly of all this, on the part of the sincere encouragers

9. William Huskisson (1770–1830) was for several years (1800–1805, 1807–09) secretary of the treasury and president of the board of trade and treasurer of the navy. He was a leading advocate of free trade. Ironically, he was killed by the railroad, great symbol of the advance of commerce and technology—a locomotive ran over him at a ceremony opening the Liverpool and Manchester Railway.

of emigration, and the criminality of it on the part of the mere pre-
tenders and the tools of the government, we have only to compare
the condition of this country, at the present juncture, with that of
France, antecedent to the revolution. Before that tremendous volcano
burst forth, which poured its human lava upon France, the middle
and lower classes in that country had long endured the most extreme
privation. Famine had visited the poor. The queen had actually sold
her plate to furnish food for the wretches who were dying in the
streets of Paris. The finances of the nation were in a state of fearful
derangement. Credit was paralyzed—confidence had fled. Had
Neckar's currency plans been adopted, the nation might have been
saved. But the philosophers of that day, like the philosophers of
England in the present day, clung to a metallic medium, and poverty
increased, wages fell, prices declined, profits diminished, just as the
amount of available currency was hoarded from fear, or circumscribed
by law. France, then was in a precisely similar state to that with which
we are now contending. She had more labourers than she could
employ—more artisans than she could support—more paupers than
she could maintain. But did she then complain of a redundant population? Was there to be found a man so heartless or so depraved as to
propose the deportation of her unemployed labourers? If such a
philosopher had appeared, he would have been the *maiden* martyr of
the guillotine. No man was so senseless or so wicked as to ascribe the
sufferings of France to providence, to improvident marriages, or to
superfecundity. Events have proved that these were not the causes of
either her calamities or her excesses. It was a long series of bad laws—
of arbitrary measures—of oppressive monopolies—of despotic exactions
—of insufferable favouritism—and of grinding taxes; which led to an
event from which we fear the rulers of Europe have not learned those
lessons which were intended for their instruction.

So much the worse for us under similar circumstances. Emigration is considered the sovereign and the only cure in England. Crime
is to be diminished by banishing the virtuous. The arts are to be
improved by expatriating the most useful and ingenious of our
mechanics. The soil is to be rendered more productive by exiling the
active farmer, and the industrious cultivator with his remnant of
capital. The sinews of the country are to be strengthened by exporting
its young blood and its "young couples." God forgive the heartless
men who prescribe these remedies! The credulous only are their
victims; and if the folly be chargeable on the nation, they alone are
answerable for the guilt.

J. W. CROKER

# Stages of the
# Revolution*

JOHN WILSON CROKER (1780–1857) WAS A
Tory politician and writer so rigid in his views that he refused to
sit in Parliament after reform. He was a severe, almost brutal,
critic who from 1831 to 1854 was the chief political writer for the
Quarterly, which he helped found, along with Southey, Gifford,
and Scott, in 1809. Because of the unrestrained presentation of
his views, he was constantly under attack from his opponents, and
between 1809 and 1854 he had sufficient time to make a good
many enemies in the 270 or so essays he wrote for the Quarterly.
Perhaps his most famous public battle was waged with Macaulay,
who savagely, brilliantly, and unfairly attacked his edition of
Boswell's *Life of Johnson*. When Macaulay's history began to
appear almost two decades later, Croker was ready to repay in
full measure.

* From Quarterly Review, XLVII (July, 1832), 559–89.

There are redeeming features in Croker's life and work (he was active in the encouragement of the arts and in the purchase of the Elgin Marbles, although even at that juncture he aroused antagonism among radicals and the poor, who felt that so much money would be better spent on feeding starving people). But Croker's blind fidelity to the Tory ideal, his brutal attacks on anything that seemed to vary from that ideal, his intolerance, and his narrowness, make him an unattractive figure. The present essay is the culmination of a series that appeared in the *Quarterly* from the moment agitation for reform began. The vision of the future Croker presents is altogether a party vision. None of the great writers, however appalled by the activities of the time, managed to take so dim a view of a reform that, after all, did little more than enfranchise a few more wealthy men and stumble toward a more equitable distribution of representation.

If it were possible for us to indulge any personal feelings in the calamitous situation of the country, it might be some consolation to reflect how wonderfully the events of the last two months have corroborated our reasonings and accomplished our predictions. The march of events has been in the exact line that we traced, though its rapidity towards the revolutionary goal has been rather greater than we had anticipated. *Three weeks* have done what, we thought, might have required *three months,* and which others hoped it might take *three years* to accomplish. The fictitious popularity of the King has vanished; he has been menaced, insulted, assaulted—all respect for monarchical government is gone—the independence of the House of Lords[1] has been annihilated, and that power which calls itself *the People,*—but which is really the combination of illegal clubs and a licentious press— has arrogated and exercises, uncontrolled, all the real authority of the

1. In the long struggle for reform, the House of Lords persistently resisted change and voted against reform measures passed in the House of Commons. Under severe pressures from reformers like Brougham, from newspapers, and from popular demand, William IV was pressured into threatening to create enough new peers to carry the Reform Bill through the Lords. After much bitterness and resistance, Lords finally passed the Bill on June 4, 1832.

state. There is not one man in the country of any party, or shade of party, (save only the narrow circle of their immediate dependents,) with whom the king's Ministers are not objects of detestation or contempt, or both. And if we are not greatly misinformed, they are themselves "perplexed in the extreme,"—terrified at what they see,—appalled at what they foresee,—devoured by remorse for what they have done,—and distracted by the most painful doubts as to what they ought to do. They are in the state of the wretched man, of whose misfortune the newspapers have lately been full, who having incautiously or criminally lighted a fire in the lower parts of his house, saw it spread among the combustible materials with such sudden and ungovernable fury, that his first impulse was to make his own personal escape, leaving his family, his lodgers, and his neighbours to perish in protracted agony and successive torments, the victims of his rashness or his guilt!

In our number for July, 1831, we endeavoured to "show his Majesty how different was that *semblance of popularity* with which the radical enemies of the crown *mocked* the Patron of the Reform Bill, from that sober, but steady, that moderated because rational, affection and reverence with which the people of England regard the *Sovereign Guardian* of their Constitution in church and state." We took the liberty of expressing our more than suspicions of the sincerity or the permanence of that *new-born* loyalty and affection towards his Majesty which had so suddenly seized all those who had been, during their whole lives, the enemies and the libellers of royalty in every shape and under every name; and we intimated, that popularity of that nature was an object unworthy the solicitude of the first magistrate of the state, because, in general, it was to be purchased only by an abandonment of his duties, and to be maintained only by compliances, to which no man of feeling or of sense could long submit his judgment or his conscience. "When"—we took the liberty of saying—"when the orator of old found himself applauded by the giddy multitude, he exclaimed, "What folly have I said?" When a king finds himself extravagantly popular, he may well inquire whether he has not committed some folly; and if he finds that the popularity is like all new-born zeal, most violent amongst those who had hitherto been the bitterest opponents and revilers of everything *royal*, he may not unwisely suspect that he has unintentionally done something derogatory or injurious to the royal authority."

Of the truth of these observations we have had recent and lamentable experience. The fatal elections of May, 1831, were perpetrated, as we then showed, under an abuse of the King's name, and under, as is now supposed, a misrepresentation of his personal sentiments. The *royal standard* was displayed by the same hands which had shortly before carried the tricoloured flag—*brick-bat* and *bludgeon* protectors of the freedom of election mobbed it to the tune of *God save the King;* and there was not one contest in the whole country in which Ministers did not ostentatiously produce the KING as the auxiliary of the most violent of the democratic candidates.

By such arts those elections were carried in favour of the Reformers,—by such arts a flame was excited which survived the elections, and which,—on the first attempt of the King to express his own real opinion,—on his first pause in his downward course of compliance— suddenly, as if by a change of the wind, turned all its violence against both the office and the person of the sovereign, and bids fair to consume every symbol and vestige of the British monarchy.

It is now stated, by those who are supposed to have access to the King, that all this was an abuse of his name, and a misrepresentation of his sentiments, to which His Majesty was—not only no party, but —ignorant of the extent to which they were carried, and far from friendly to the purposes for which they were employed. It was always presumed by those who considered the nature and duties of the kingly office, that in his heart the King must have been, from the first, a *very moderate Reformer;* and we ourselves endeavoured to show that it was contrary to the essence of the monarchical institution itself, that the highest constituted authority should take the lead in the race of innovation. From the nature of individual man, and from the principles of social order, it seemed a moral impossibility that a *king could* be a Radical Reformer; but, against all such reasonings, the ministers of His Majesty alleged the *fact!*—and, as the King,—carrying to its extreme the constitutional doctrine of hearing only by the ear of his ministers, and speaking only with their voice,—had no means of controverting their assertion,—it passed with the judicious as a mysterious and inexplicable anomaly, and, with the public at large, as a certain though extraordinary truth. The *fact,* however, is now confidently denied; and the day will perhaps come, when the ministers must answer at the bar of the public for the statements which they have made, and for the measures which those statements enabled them to carry. That time is not yet arrived,—and certainly *this* is not the place, —nor is it our province to enter into so momentous an inquiry. Thus much only will we venture to say, that when the ministers persuaded or deluded the King into a consent to their proceedings, they were, in our opinion, guilty of giving to His Majesty the most unconstitutional and fatal advice that ever was suggested to a sovereign, except, perhaps, that advice by which Charles I, was induced to send Lord Strafford to the block, or that which prevailed on Louis XVI. to double the number of the representatives of the *Tiers Etat;* but *if* it shall appear, that—having failed so to persuade the conscience or delude the judgment of the monarch,—they *falsely* attributed to him sentiments that he did not entertain, and instituted, in his name, proceedings which he did not approve, the guilt would assume a still deeper colour, and its authors would be deservedly liable to the most extreme responsibility with which an indignant sovereign and people can visit their prevaricating servants.

But we leave this part of the subject, which, although of the first interest and importance, is, with our present means of information, only matter of conjecture and argument, to proceed to notice the disastrous facts on which there is neither doubt nor dispute, and to lay before our readers a continuation of the history of the events which, like the successive and increasing billows of a storm, have swelled around the vessel of the state, till the boldest heart and the most experienced heads have abandoned the unhappy ship to a destruction which seems inevitable.

In our last Number we endeavoured to show the fatal impolicy of the House of Lords concurring in the principles of the Reform Bill by allowing it to be read a second time. We chiefly addressed ourselves to that class of the Peers, (now commonly called the Waverers,) who, after having been among the most violent as well as able of the opponents of the former bill, were induced, by motives which we never could clearly understand, to advocate a different course as to the present measure. They professed indeed a hope, that by reading the Bill a second time they might obtain such an accession of public opinion in their favour as would enable them to extract in the committee the more deadly venom of the Bill,—to correct its most outrageous injustice, and to remove or mitigate its most fatal violences; and they alleged that certain communications, which, during the recess, they had had with Lord Grey, authorised them to expect his concurrence in some of the most important of these amendments. We endeavoured to persuade them that they were wholly mistaken—that the Bill, and every part of it, would receive such additional sanction, and be endowed with such uncontrollable strength, by the *adoption of its principle*, that, not only would they fail to make any substantial amendment, but that the minstry would not dare to concede one jot, and that the attempt to alter would be attended with fully as much difficulty and danger, as they could anticipate from the more manly, more straightforward, and consistent course of rejecting it on the second reading.

We asked,

What hope can any rational man entertain that the ministry, if they accomplish the second reading, will admit *any* modification of the bill? *Could* they if they would? For instance, we believe the Waverers are most anxious to save the country from the Metropolitan boroughs; but can they expect that the ministers will abandon that clause?—that clause is, with a vast body of the supporters of the bill, the keystone of the whole structure—remove it, and a fiercer outcry will follow, than the most violent predict, or the most timid fear, from the refusal of the second reading.

And again,

Is there more of dissatisfaction to be apprehended from the rejection of the bill, than from any important alterations in its most objectionable details?

These, and many other similar considerations, were urged upon those noble Lords—but in vain. The Reform Bill was read a second time by a majority of 184 to 175—and by that vote the fate of the constitution was sealed!

We should, we think, be pardoned, if we were unable to abstain from some reproaches against the inconsistency and folly of those who brought about so fatal an event; but in truth, we have towards them no feeling but of sorrow for our common misfortune, not unmixed with pity for what *they* must individually suffer, at finding themselves the dupes of the ministers, and the unintentional instruments of their deplorable success. The Waverers meant well, though they judged ill; and in this crisis, it would little become us to aggravate, by contentious observations, the mischief of their error. But there are other considerations, also, which tend to mitigate our resentment and even our grief, and as these considerations may probably, when fairly stated, have a similar effect on the country at large, we shall proceed to develop them with uncompromising sincerity.

It is, in our opinion, but justice to the Waverers to confess, that their conduct deprived us only of the *chance* of salvation—we believe, that, at worst, they have only to reproach themselves with having accelerated and made certain, that which those who had most closely observed the whole course of the affair, considered as eventually hardly to be avoided. From the day in which Lord John Russell, *as the official organ of the* KING *and the* GOVERNMENT, propounded a measure of Reform so reckless of all private, personal, and corporate rights —so insulting to every existing institution and authority—so subversive of all the bases, moral and political, on which our constitution was founded—and so utterly destructive of the great principle of *prescription* by which alone human society is held together; from THAT HOUR we anticipated, as nearly inevitable, the consummation at which we are now about to arrive.

Up to that day, the wildest reformers had only proposed partial alterations—mere repairs, as they called them—of the ancient edifice, some more and others less extensive, but none avowedly destructive of the main body of the temple, and all professing a religious respect for its sacred foundations. Moreover, even those who had hitherto proposed the most extensive changes were in no condition to excite any grave alarm; they were mere *individuals*, more or less respectable, but still only individuals, and obviously actuated by party or personal motives, or indulging in theoretical fancies:—few of them had any wish, and none of them had any power, to make serious alterations in our system, or to establish such broad and general principles of innovation, as should survive the particular object which they respectively proposed. And these reformers, personally so little formidable, were still less so when opposed, as they constantly and firmly were, by all the constituted authorities of the empire, and by the pride, the respect, and reverence with which (whatever might be felt as to minute flaws and local imperfections) the great body of mankind, at home and abroad, in early and in recent times, acknowledged and admired the practical excellence of the British constitution. But the case was frightfully altered when it was no longer some factious demagogue— some political partizan—some flighty vision-monger, who proposed, for the gratification of his own vanity or the advancement of his party, some modicum of Reform; but when THE KING'S MINISTERS,—by their stations the official conservators of the existing system, and by their rank, property, and opinions, supposed to be indissolubly attached to the institutions from which they were enjoying such eminent advantages—when THESE, we say, the head and the hands of the existing system, proclaimed the whole to be "a scandalous and intolerable abuse"—"a flagitious usurpation"—"the cause of all the private misery of millions and all the public calamities of ages," it was evident to our minds that a wound,—a poisoned wound,—was inflicted on the Constitution, from which it was hardly possible it should recover.

.    .    .    .

On reviewing, then, the course of this struggle, we console ourselves with thinking, that, however the conduct of the conservative party may be criticised on individual points, and as to particular occasions, the ultimate issue of the contest must have been nearly the same. To a revolution, the dissolution of April, 1831, irrevocably doomed us.[2] It might, by a bolder opposition, have been, perhaps, delayed; but, on the other hand, it might also, by a rash step or a false move, have been *accelerated* and, on the whole, (with the single exception of the *extent* to which Lord Ellenborough[3] was induced by the Waverers to carry his concessions,) we do not know that there is any part of the battle, since the first reading of the first bill, which, if it were to be fought over again, we should much care to see differently managed.

And now, what is to be the result of all? We must answer—as we did in the very outset—Revolution! And we have made great progress towards that goal even since the bill has been passed;—the quieting medicine, the anodyne potion, has been mixed and swallowed, but the disease is so much more urgent than ever, that even the quacks themselves, who compounded it, begin to think that they have by mistake poisoned their patient. How has the celebrated promise of the King's speech on the 21st June, 1831, been fulfilled? Where is now "the security for the prerogatives of the Crown, and the authority of both houses of Parliament?" Gone—vanished—and the words remain on the journals, a solemn mockery—a sarcastic antithesis—which belie themselves and deride the unhappy dupes whom they have deceived, insulted, and undone. We spare ourselves and our readers the pain of recapitulating all the atrocious insults offered, not merely to the royal authority, but to the very persons of their Majesties. We say nothing of the attempts to incite a cowardly mob to inflict the fate of *De Witte*[4] upon the glory of England, the saviour of Europe. We will not dwell on the bewildered incapacity of the ministry, nor taunt them with the *failure* of their proclamations against the Unions, or the

2. On March 23, 1831, Lord Russell's Reform Bill passed its second reading by one vote in the House of Commons after one of the most dramatic moments in the history of Parliament. But in April, the king agreed to dissolve Parliament after the Tories defeated the Whig government in committee. There followed a general election concerned almost exclusively with reform, and the Whigs returned with a large majority. Croker is right in thinking that the dissolution and subsequent election made passage of the Bill inevitable.

3. Edward Law, Earl of Ellenborough (1790–1871), who became governor general of India, was at once a moderate Tory and a strong opponent of reform.

4. Johann De Witt (1625–72), a Dutch statesman, was an opponent of the House of Orange. As Grand Pensionary (rather like Prime Minister) he was long successful in keeping the House of Orange from power, but after the French invasion of the Netherlands, he resigned from this position. His brother was convicted of conspiracy and, while visiting him in prison, De Witt was killed by a mob of Orange partisans.

success of their denunciations against order and property—their strength to do mischief and their impotence to do anything else; the fatal catalogue of their follies and faults is, we fear, incomplete; the awful account is still current, and we, as yet, see only the first items of the series of misfortune and crime with which they are chargeable. We know not whether the day of retribution will come, but the day of reckoning assuredly will, and a repentant people, looking back with horror and remorse at the maniacal follies and atrocities which they may have committed, will, like the Santon in the story, curse the tempter who administered the intoxicating draught which produced at once their frenzy and their crimes.

And yet—is there no hope? Far be it from us to venture to say so: —hope from mere human efforts we have little, but we cannot believe that Providence, to whom we owe so long a series of happiness and glory, can have doomed this great country to entire and irretrievable desolation. We are disposed, even now . . . to cling still to the hope of better things. That we have merited a severe chastisement, no one, who has observed our moral and religious condition, with Christian eyes, can doubt; and though the extent to which that just chastisement may be carried be inscrutable to human eyes, we cannot but feel so much confidence in the mercy of the great Disposer of events, as to believe that redemption is yet possible, if it be sought with that spirit of contrition and humiliation towards heaven, and that moral firmness and Christian courage towards men, which the instincts of religion and nature alike suggest as the last refuge and best auxiliaries, *"in all our troubles and adversities, whensoever they oppress us."* In the midst of our deep apprehensions, we hail some auspicious appearances. We would fain persuade ourselves, that we see "some spots of azure in the cloudy sky." The King is undeceived—the House of Lords has been saved from utter contamination and degradation—those classes of society, on whose good sense all society must be founded, seem to be resuming their authority over public opinion—the demagogues are not quite satisfied with their prospects, and begin to suspect that fraud and frenzy will be found, in the long run, no match for common honesty and common sense. France, so long our salutary lesson, and so lately our delusive guide, is resuming her *monitory* aspect; and the *despotic* revolution of June, 1832, has already weakened the dangerous precedent of the *democratic* revolution of July, 1830. The sceptre of the citizen king is become the sword of an autocrat. By employing more than ten times the force which defended the legitimate throne, and by a slaughter twice greater than that of the *Three Great Days*, Louis Philippe still painfully and perilously balances himself on the tight rope, from which Charles X., with less nerve and more humanity, was willing to fall. The license of the press, which the legitimate monarch endeavoured to restrain by *ordonnances*, the republican king has silenced by cannon and scaffolds. Paris—the glorious example of revolutionary moderation and good order—is in a *state of siege*: the prisons are fuller from one day of *liberty*, than they had been for fifteen years of what was called *oppression*: and the tribunals—the legal guardians of persons and property—vanished, at the *word of command* from Marshal Soult, before the liberal and constitutional authority of *courts martial!* The example of *July* had but too much effect upon us—let us hope that the lesson of *June* may not be thrown away.

Desperate as our condition may seem, there are these and many other consolatory considerations; and it is the duty of every honest man—of all who have hearts to feel, heads to understand, and hands to execute the duties of brave and highminded Britons—to do all that may belong to each man in his individual station to endeavour to arrest the progress of the enemy, and by courage and, if necessary, self-devotion, to retrieve the day, or at least to secure such a position as may enable them to resume the contest with better hope to-morrow. The Romans after a great calamity did not waste their energies in complaints nor bury them in gloomy torpor; and they surrounded with public honours the man who, whatever were his errors, had the redeeming quality of not despairing, even in the last emergency, of the fortunes of his country. That heroic spirit saved the state in many emergencies, which a faint-hearted people would have considered as desperate. Rome recovered herself after Italy had been overrun by Hannibal—after the Gothic invaders had profaned the curule chairs of her Senate and burned the Capitol—after plebeian seditions and even a servile war had devasted the very heart of the empire and extinguished all but the undying courage of patriot hope. Our posterity will honour those brave and illustrious men who have hitherto so nobly fought an unequal battle; but it will still more, and more deservedly, honour the bolder and still more illustrious men, who, after our Constitution has passed through the Caudine forks of the Reform Bill, shall be still found not to have despaired of the salvation of England.

Let us recollect, as an incentive to hope, though it has been disregarded as a lesson of prudence, that we have *once before* had a revolution—a reformed parliament—suppression of close boroughs—a subjugation of the House of Lords—and a substitution of cheap republican forms for the costly trappings of the monarchy. We have had all that; and we shall have it again; and again, we trust, with the same result. Those theories of government, which captivate and delude for the moment, cannot stand the test of time. They neither possess the reverence which antiquity gives, nor gratify the hope which their novelty inspired: all parties—the adherents of the old system and the aspirants of the new—are equally dissatisfied: turbulence, tumults, anarchies ensue: and all mankind, even those who were foremost in the first commotions, are, by and bye, glad to revert, for the security of persons and stability of property, to the sober experience of better days. The Regicide Reform of 1649 ended in a royal triumph, and Charles II. rode, crowned with the garlands of popular joy, over the very spot on which had stood, ten years before, his father's scaffold. As certainly, shall we, or our *children*, see the Revolution of 1832, with all its consequences, however fatal or extensive they may be, terminate its execrated career in another more joyful and triumphant *Restoration*. Let us watch then with courageous hope and pious confidence for that day; and let us husband our strength and nourish our spirit, to enable us to take advantage of such means as Heaven may employ to bring about, in due season, that happy consummation!

WILLIAM THOMPSON

# Labor Rewarded.
# The Claims of Labor
# and Capital
# Conciliated*

## OR, HOW TO SECURE LABOR
## THE WHOLE PRODUCT OF ITS
## EXERTIONS

WILLIAM THOMPSON (1775–1833) WAS PROB-
ably the most important theoretician among early English social-
ists. (For a study of his life and work, see R. K. P. Pankhurst,
*William Thompson* [1954], from which all the information used
here is drawn.) Thompson came from a wealthy, class-proud
family in Ireland, where he owned an estate of 1,400 not very

* From William Thompson, *Labor Rewarded.*, First Edition (London:
Longman's, 1827), pp. 111–19.

fruitful acres. He turned away from the traditional views of his
family and against capitalism itself to decry the injustices perpetrated by the idle rich. Although he was greatly influenced by
Bentham, he rejected the views of the orthodox political economists and tried reforms on his own estate not very different from
those tried by Robert Owen at New Lanark. He continued, however, to feel guilty about his own position as landlord and spent
the rest of his life, apparently in an attempt to atone for this guilt,
by devoting himself to the welfare of others.

He was attracted to the rationalist, scientistic views of Bentham but, through his growing belief in cooperation, he turned
from Bentham to Owen. His great work was *An Inquiry into the
Principles of Wealth Most Conducive to Human Happiness,
applied to the newly proposed system of voluntary equality of
wealth* (1824). He became Owen's equal in importance and provided an alternative to Owen's paternalistic, perhaps tyrannical,
cooperation. Moreover, unlike Owen, he was not averse to political
action. With William Lovett and others, he launched the British
Association for the Spread of Cooperative Knowledge, which later
became the National Union of the Working Classes. This organization was extremely important in the history of the English
working classes, especially as it anticipated and prepared the way
for Chartism.

. . . Thus, my friends, it having been already demonstrated to you
that capital is the mere creature of labor and materials, instead of being
in any way their creator; that capital may be accumulated by the Industrious Classes, the creators of it, much more advantageously than by
the Idle Classes who are a burthen to themselves (those few excepted
who create for themselves a voluntary sphere of activity) as well as to
the industrious. I have endeavoured further to show you that it would
tend wonderfully to increase the mass of human happiness that "labor
should possess the whole products of its exertions." I have endeavoured
to show you that the abettors of the existing system of force, fraud,
and competition, differently modified on every spot of the globe, *do*

not wish that labor should possess the whole products of its exertions; that they themselves, whether under the name of capitalists, privileged classes, economists, poets, players, or public instructors, are the most insatiable candidates for the prizes of unequal distribution; that it is idle and impracticable to talk of excluding capitalists alone from the chances of exchanges or the "higgling of the market," while every juggler and buffoon are permitted (and ought to be permitted) to exchange their imaginary values for whatever voluntary equivalents they can command; nay more, that you cannot interdict freedom of exchanges to capitalists without at the same time interdicting freedom of exchanges for voluntary equivalent to the industrious themselves.

It has been shown that the common notion of merit, as implying the utility of factitious rewards, is not only groundless but pernicious; that inequality of the means of enjoyment, tends to great preponderant evil; that equality of remuneration (incompatible with the system of labor by individual competition) tends to the greatest production, improvement, virtue and happiness.

I have endeavoured fairly to lay before you the exact effects of all the expedients worth the trouble of examination, which the advocates of the existing systems of force, fraud, or competition, have proposed as calculated to ameliorate your situation, if not to put you in possession of the whole products of your labor. We have seen how utterly inefficient these expedients are, not only to the only object worthy of your exertions, the possession of the whole products of your labors, but even to the attainment of the inferior benefits which they promise you.

It has been shown to you that the fatal disseverance of capital from labor and skill, and the consequent ignorance of the industrious, have led to the monstrous systems of force, fraud, and competition, (when free, the worst species of free exertion,) engendering enormous inequalities of wealth, the parents of almost all the crimes and vices that desolate society; and that it is necessary for human welfare to reunite capital and labor, to render all the industrious *capitalist laborers*, laborers possessing all the materials and implements necessary to render their labor productive.

It has also, I hope, been demonstrated to you, that it is impossible, in the present state of improved machinery and complicated processes of industry, to award to any *individual* laborer the whole products of his labor, inasmuch as (amongst other obstacles) it would be impracticable to ascertain what those products are. It would also be impracticable, or very difficult, so to arrange, that every *individual* laborer should have even a fair chance of possessing the materials and implements, neither more nor less than are, necessary to render his isolated labor productive. Hence the imperative necessity of the Union of the Industrious, *in large numbers;* as well to enable them to ascertain what the products of their labor really are, as to enable them to acquire the materials and implements necessary to make that labor productive, and no more.

It has been shown, that even the unions of large numbers of the industrious possessing all the materials and implements requisite to make their labor productive, would not, if directed to the manufacture of any one article, or of various articles for sale in the common market of competition, secure to such industrious the whole products of their labor in any other articles consumed by them and acquired in exchange for such article or articles so by them fabricated. Variations of demand aside, they would acquire no more in addition to their former wages than the profits of their former employer the capitalist, on the articles of their manufacture, with the saving of the charges of carriage and distribution on such articles made by themselves as they consumed. For all other articles of their consumption they must pay the advanced cost of competition: if bought by wholesale for the use of the whole union, they would save the distributors' profit merely. The profits of the grower, landlord, manufacturer, carrier and wholesale dealer they would still be compelled to pay on all articles not fabricated, and about half of these charges on those not also raised, by themselves.

Therefore, unions, of even large numbers of the industrious must follow more than one trade, must produce more than one article of consumption, if they wish to possess the whole products of their labor. Particularly they must purchase, or at first rent, *land,* the basis of all the materials of industry, and produce and supply themselves, at the cost of labor, with their own food. The evils arising from rival improvements in machinery, from variations in demand, etc., would thus be obviated or rendered comparatively harmless. *In proportion to the number of articles consumed by them, which they produce and supply to each other, will be the advance which they make towards the possession of the whole products of their labor.* Hence, as well as for various other important reasons, the necessity of the co-operation of large numbers of the industrious. Hence, while competition exists around them and is the moving spring of society, the necessity of limiting their exchanges to such articles, of home or foreign growth, as cannot without great waste of labor though aided by machinery be produced by themselves from the raw material. One or more manufactories, therefore, whether of agricultural or other articles, *which might be employed in any the minutest subdivision of industry,* must be

carried on by every union for the purpose of wholesale *exchanges* with
society at large: or, some of their domestic manufactures of woollen,
linen or cotton clothing, or of furniture, must be increased for this
purpose.

Were numbers of these self-supplying unions of the industrious
established in the neighbourhood of each other, and were their exchanges made at the cost of production, labor for labor; it is true that,
in such case, these particular advantages (the cost of carriage excepted)
would not be reaped from fabricating almost all articles of consumption at home. Other considerations of a physical and moral nature,
would then come to be weighed against the facilities of local production. The system of mutual supply within each union, would be modified, but not essentially changed.

It has been, I hope, proved to you that FREEDOM OF EXERTION
is a paramount good; but that *competition*, were it possible to suppose
it (which it never has been, nor from its very nature ever can be,)
*perfectly free*, is the worst mode of the exercise of that freedom, while
*voluntary co-operation* is the best and the only yet devised mode of
free exertion affording you any chance of enjoying the products of your
labor.

Over and above the paramount advantage in the way of wealth, of
securing to yourselves the whole products of your labor, by unions of
*large numbers* of the industrious, I have endeavoured to give you a
glimpse of the vast multitude of collateral benefits, physical, intellectual, and social, which would proceed from the same fruitful source
of good; such as the means of knowledge to the adult, of education to
the young, of health to all, of elegancies and pleasures of the fine arts
procured of the best quality and at the cost of your own labor, (or, if
by exchange, at the *first cost* of competition,) such also as the benefits
of universal insurance against all casualties without any sort of apparatus, trouble, risk or anxiety in effecting such insurances, the common fund, the result of the spontaneous beneficence of all towards
all, being directed where and to whom wanting, without noise, effort,
or pretensions to merit of any sort. Add to these advantages, the ceasing, from absence of motive, to inflict on each other the persecutions
and punishments of the cruel and partial laws of society at large, the
annihilation of almost all the motives to vice by the substitution of
joint for individual possessions and pursuits, and by the ample gratification of every natural or acquired desire not attended with preponderant evil.

Where force is altogether excluded, where all are equal as to
wealth, each possessing all, where every operation of mind, thought

and expression of thought, are as free as the unappropriated elements, reason and kindness *must be cultivated* by all as the sole means of persuasion, of acquiring that sympathy which is one of the greatest wants, one of the greatest pleasures of life. Personal qualities, physical, intellectual and social, will rise into estimation and importance, and supersede the wretched distinctions of the baubles of the inequality of wealth. The anxieties of life will not be thrown away on chicane and over-reaching; the art of creating and increasing happiness, will spring up into existence. The science of mutual-tormenting and rising on each other's degradation, will be forgotten. The utmost gentleness of manners will be united with the utmost firmness of endurance. Fortitude will succeed the misnamed virtue, called courage, or an inclination to attack and destroy our fellow-creatures at the risk of evil to ourselves. The earth will be laid out by the hands of wisdom and taste for the greatest common happiness of all. The Industrious—and all in the end will become industrious—will indeed live in "gardens, pleasure-grounds, and palaces:" but the possession of these unconscious materials of happiness, will not be the end of life; they will serve but as a theatre on which the new course of human existence, the development of the physical and intellectual powers of the human race, will proceed unrestrained. Physical, intellectual, and social pleasures will be so united, and so varied, will throw such lustre and relief on each other; labor will proceed with such sweet accompaniments, so healthful, so cheerful, will so dispel the vacuum of unemployed and heavy hours, that every moment will be attended with its appropriate enjoyments. The miscalled pleasures of antipathy will exist no more, the circumstances which called them into existence being removed. How far, and in what directions this new science and art of creating bliss, this genuine Social Science will unfold itself, we know no more than we do what will be the future course of Mechanics or Chemistry. The road to these great results is pointed out to you. The means of entering on that road are before you, and in your power. Therefore, my friends of the Industrious Classes, become, as you may be, the fabricators of your own destiny.

Choose between isolated individual exertion, want, and antipathy, and collective exertion, abundance, and mutual happiness. Thus will your "Labor be rewarded;"—or will be eternally bereft, as it has hitherto been, of the products of its exertions.

Were it in the power of those few of the Idle, constituting the hereditary privileged classes and their men-of-business, who make the laws by which they levy whatever portion they think proper of the products of your labor, and dispose of those products as they please, to sympathize with you; they would afford you, at least on loan, such portions of the products of your labor (of which the money raised by taxation is the representative) as would enable you to possess and enjoy the future products of that labor. Were they wise to their own real interests, they would invite you into the paths of Co-operative Industry, as the only means of enabling you to pay with facility those numerous exactions which now degrade you in comfort beneath the domesticated animals which you support.

Were the laws, which controul and regulate your opinions, your words, your actions, which dispose of the products of your labor, which bring you up, by their direct or indirect operation, in ignorance and vice, and then reward you with bloody punishments,—were those laws made by yourselves and your own men-of-business; those men-of-business, esteeming themselves your equals and no more than your equals, and sympathizing entirely with your misery and your happiness, would immediately investigate the proposed system of Co-operative Industry, would institute at once experiments to establish or set to rest its pretensions; and if successful, would afford you every where the means of commanding, in a few years, for your own enjoyments, and not as auxiliary to any other purpose whatever, the whole products of your labor.

To attain such objects, to be enabled to work for yourselves, to supply each other's wants, there would be *some sense* in demanding political reform, or the making of all laws by none others but your men-of-business, instead of merely changing your masters, substituting a new edition of Competition, varied with fraud and force, for the old edition of Force, varied with fraud and competition. Such representatives, removable at your pleasure, would not only lend you, for such purposes, on adequate security, small loans out of the taxes produced by your labor; but would also remove all restraints on the transfer of lands to be conveyed to you by sale for settlements on which to exercise your industry. That industry would, in a very few years, pay off these loans, as well as the purchase-money of the land.

ADDRESS TO THE WORKING MEN OF THE UNITED
KINGDOM BY THE WORKING MEN'S ASSOCIATION

# Rotten House
of Commons*

BEING AN EXPOSITION OF THE
PRESENT STATE OF THE FRANCHISE
AND AN APPEAL TO THE NATION ON
THE COURSE TO BE PURSUED IN THE
APPROACHING CRISIS

IN 1836, A SERIOUS FINANCIAL CRISIS BEGAN
in England that led to general distress, and to a renewal of the
attempts of working men to organize and alleviate their common
suffering. The Grand National Confederation of Trades Unions,
established in 1834 under the leadership of Robert Owen, had
collapsed, partly as a result of Owen's aversion to political action.

* From pamphlet (London: H. Hetherington, 1836 [?]), published after
the Address was given.

In June 1836, William Lovett (1800–1877), one of the most important figures in the working class movement, led the formation of the London Working Men's Association. Lovett recognized the inadequacy of Owen's method for improving the conditions of the working man, and determined to apply to Parliament the same kinds of pressure that had originally succeeded in instituting reform.

This organization was the parent of Chartism. In an interesting pamphlet, most of which is reproduced here, it enunciated the demands that were, with one minor difference, to make up the Charter of 1838. The Charter demanded annual parliaments, universal male suffrage, equal electoral districts, secret ballot, payment of members, and the removal of the property qualification for membership in Parliament. The pamphlet demands annual parliaments, universal suffrage, equal representation, the protection of the ballot, no property qualification for members, and a free press.

The Charter marked the beginning of the working man's greatest political involvement to that time; it posed, to the classes in power, a terrifying threat. Some saw in it the shadow of the French Revolution and even liberals resisted it. For various reasons, including the demagoguery of some of its leaders, the Chartist Movement finally collapsed in 1848; but, in time, every one of its demands has been met.

Fellow Countrymen,

The Members of the Working Men's Association believing that a great and doubtful crisis is at hand, and that its result for evil or for good will principally depend on the mutual understanding among our own class, deem it to be their duty to address you on this important occasion. And in addressing you they are desirous of honestly and fearlessly avowing their sentiments regarding the great principle of right and justice, however in practice it may affect the selfish projects of any party in the state. We would willingly cast the mantle of oblivion over our past history—we would even endeavour to erase from our memories the atrocities, the persecutions, and the injustice, that for ages have been perpetrated against our class, if a disposition was even now evinced, on the part of our rulers, to commence the reign of JUSTICE and HUMANITY. And in expressing these our own feelings, we believe we express the feelings of every well-constituted and intelligent mind.

But, fellow countrymen, judging from the marshalling of forces and threats of defiance, we fear a similar disposition is not found among the various factions, whose continual strife for power and plunder is the curse of our country; their aim is to perpetuate the reign of wrong, and to consolidate their power at the expense of justice.

The strength, however, of any one of those parties will depend, fellow workmen, on us, on our united exertions to prevent the supremacy of any party, and to contend for the annihilation of all. Under a just system of government there would be but one party, *that of the people;* whose representatives would be actuated by one great motive, *that of making all the resources of our country tend to promote the happiness of all its inhabitants.*

Far different, however, are the views of those who now govern England, nay, (with few exceptions) of those of their constituents who give them the power to govern. Each seems actuated by an exclusive interest; and exclusive privileges seem, in their estimation, the wisest legislative measures.

Will it, think you, fellow countrymen, promote our happiness— will it give us more comforts, more leisure, less toil, and less of the wretchedness to which we are subjected, if *the power and empire of the wealthy be established on the wreck of title and privilege?*

Yet to this end we believe, is the tendency of the present contest now waging between the two great parties both in and out of parliament—between the agricultural and privileged classes on the one hand, and the monied and commercial classes on the other. If the past struggles and contentions we have had with the latter to keep up our wages—our paltry means of subsistence;—if the infamous acts they have passed since they have obtained a portion of political power form any criterion of their disposition to do us justice, little have we to expect from any accession to that power, any more than from the former tyrants we have had to contend against.

There are persons among the monied class, who, to deceive their fellow men, have put on the cloak of reform; but they mean not that reform shall so extend as to deprive them or their party of their corrupt advantages. Many boast of freedom, while they help to enslave us; and preach *justice,* while they assist the oppressor to practice wrongs and to perpetuate the greatest injustice towards the working millions. Others among them are fertile in devising endless plans for strengthening their own interests, or for hoodwinking their constituents for the time being into a belief of their sincerity for the public weal. Many are for step-by-step improvement; they are characterized by their earnest solicitude gradually to enlighten us, lest we should see our political degradation too soon, and make any advance towards depriving them of their exclusive prerogative of leading us from year to year through the political quagmire, where we are daily beset by plunderers, befooled by knaves, and misled by hypocritical impostors.

These persons, under various pretences, and with a show of liberality, daily enlist in their ranks some portion of our deluded countrymen; and by opposing them to each other, accomplish their objects of deceiving and fleecing the whole. So long as we continue to be duped by some new political chimera, which they have ever at hand to amuse us,—so long as we continue to seek political salvation through the instrumentality of others, instead of our own exertions, so long will party be triumphant, will corrupt legislation prevail, will private peculators and public plunderers flourish, and so long must we continue to be the mere supplicating cringing vassals of a proud, arrogant, speech-making few; whose interest it is to keep us the mere toiling charity-ridden set we are, the unhappy dupes of the idle and the designing.

Fellow countrymen, have you ever enquired how far a just and economical system of government, a code of wise and just laws, and the abolition of all the useless appendages of state would affect the interests of the present 658 members of the House of Commons? If you have not, begin now to enquire, and you will soon lose any vain hopes you may entertain from that house as at present constituted. Nay, if you pursue your enquiries in like manner respecting the present constituents of that house, to see how far their interests are identified with yours, how far just legislation and efficient reform would deprive them of their power to grind and oppress you, you would be equally hopeless of benefits from that quarter. To satisfy yourselves in this respect, propose for your own judgment and reflection the following questions:—

Is the FUNDHOLDER, whose interest it is to preserve the debt and burthens of the country, and who revels in extravagance on the cheap productions of labour, a fit representative for us?

Is the LANDHOLDER, whose interest leads him to keep up his rents by unjust and exclusive laws, a fit representative for working men?

Are the whole host of MONEYMAKERS, SPECULATORS, and USURERS, who live on the corruption of the system, fit representatives for the sons of labour?

Are the immense numbers of LORDS, EARLS, MARQUESSES,

KNIGHTS, BARONETS, HONORABLES, and RIGHT HONORABLES, who have
seats in that house, fit to represent our interests? many of whom have
the prospect before them of being the *hereditary legislators* of the
other house, or are the craving expectants of place or emolument, who
shine in the gilded circle of a court, or flutter among the gaieties of
the ball room, who court the passing smile of royalty, whine at the
ministers of the day, and when the interests of the people are at stake,
are found the revelling debauchees of fashion, or the duelling wranglers
of a gambling house.

Are the multitude of MILITARY and NAVAL OFFICERS in the
present House of Commons, whose interest it is to support that system
which secures them their pay, and whose only utility is to direct one
portion of our brethren to keep the other in subjection, fit to represent our grievances?*

Have we fit representatives in the multitude of BARRISTERS, AT-
TORNEYS, SOLICITORS, and all those whose interests depend on the dis-
sensions and corruptions of the people; persons whose prosperity, depending on the obscurity and intricacy of the laws, seek to perpetuate
the interests of "*their order*" by rendering them so unmeaning and
voluminous that none but *law conjurers* like themselves shall understand them, and therefore their *legal* knowledge (that is, of *fraud* and
*deception*) generally procure them seats in the legislature, and the
highest offices knavery and corruption can confer.

Is the MANUFACTURER or CAPITALIST, whose exclusive monopoly
of the combined powers of wood, iron, and steam, enables him to
cause the destitution of thousands, and who has an interest in forcing
labour down to the *minimum* reward, fit to represent the interests of
working men?

Is the MASTER, whose interest it is to purchase labour at the
cheapest rate, a fit representative for the WORKMAN, whose interest it
is to get the most he can for his labour?

Yet such is the description of persons composing that house, and
such the interests represented, to whom we, session after session, address our *humble petitions*, and whom we in our ignorant simplicity
imagine will generously sacrifice their hopes and interests, by beginning
the great work of political and social reformation.

Working men, enquire if this be not true, and then if you feel
with us, stand apart from all projects, and refuse to be the tools of any
party, who will not, as a *first and essential measure*, give to the work-

* There are a few honourable exceptions in this class (and it may be in
others) of persons whose benevolence prompts them to seek justice in opposition to their interests.

ing classes EQUAL POLITICAL AND SOCIAL RIGHTS; so that they may
send their own representatives from the ranks of labour into that house
to deliberate and determine among *all those other interests*, that the
interests of the labouring classes, of those who are the foundation of
the social edifice, shall not be daily sacrificed to glut the extravagances
and luxuries of the few. If you feel with us, then you will proclaim it in
the workshop, preach it in your societies, publish it from town to village, from county to county, and from nation to nation, that there is
no hope for the sons of toil, till those who feel with them, who sym-
pathise with them, and whose interests are identified with theirs,
have an *equal right* to determine what laws shall be enacted or plans
adopted for justly governing this country.

To this end, fellow workmen, are wanted, a FREE PRESS, UNI-
VERSAL SUFFRAGE, the Protection of the BALLOT, ANNUAL PARLIA-
MENTS, EQUAL REPRESENTATION, and no PROPERTY QUALIFICATION
for members.

To the attainment of these essentials, embracing one great object
—EQUAL POLITICAL RIGHTS—you must direct the sole attention of
those representatives who call themselves RADICAL REFORMERS. Suffer
them not, as far as your influence extends, to divert attention away to
other projects of minor importance; test their sincerity by their dropping all paltry questions of policy or expediency, and contending with
all their energies and talents for the attainment of this our only hope.
Let no specious, eloquent, or delusive sophistries divert you from your
purpose. Spurn the hypocritical pretensions of those who presume to
sympathize with your wretchedness, but who would deny you, or delay,
the only means of improving it by wise and just legislation. Equally
despise the man who would refuse you the franchise on the plea of
your ignorance, when your corrupt legislators seek to perpetuate that
ignorance by the most infamous of laws, and whose interest it is to
do so as long as they can gratify their plundering propensities with
impunity. If knowledge is to be the qualification for political right, it
is questionable whether you are not equally eligible with the paltry
number of electors who have virtually the power of determining what
laws shall be imposed on twenty-four millions of people. That you may
have some standard by which to judge of the present rotten, unequal,
and unjust state of the franchise of the United Kingdom, our Association have taken considerable pains to compile the following document,
by which you will see that, notwithstanding there are 6,023,752 males
above the age of twenty-one, that there are only 839,519 persons who
have any portion of political right; and that owing to the unequal state
of the representation, about one-fifth of that number have the power of

returning the majority of the House of Commons. Nay, further, that owing to the present mode of registration, coupled with the ignorance or blunderings of the tools employed in an object so important, the real numbers, if they could be correctly estimated, would be considerably less even than this fifth. And these being the constituents of the smaller boroughs, must be regarded as persons more likely to be influenced or corrupted by their lords and masters than if they belonged to larger constituencies. Thus this miserable fraction of the people, whose interest may be opposed to the millions, have the power of forcing on them what laws, what despotic ordonnances they may think proper. Can we wonder then at the injustice and gross profligacy that pervade every department of the state, when the real power of the country is so limited? Read, therefore; think, fellow countrymen; and enquire if it be not high time to arouse from your political apathy, and trusting to your own honest exertions, to firmly resolve, that as your power and energies forced the Whig Reform Bill, so by similar or still more powerful exertions you will force a real Radical Reform, by which all may be benefited.

No doubt there are persons of great political power and high standing in public opinion, who, while despising these sentiments (supported as they are by facts) will endeavour to persuade you that we are violent theorists, destructives, and levellers of the constitutional order of things; that our aim is revolution, that our object is plunder, and thereby they will seek to frighten the timid among you out of the propriety of their reason and better judgment. Fellow men, do not be deceived; we are working men like yourselves; we seek not any privilege or benefit that cannot be shared with the poorest amongst you. We seek just legislation as a means of adding to the happiness of every human being. While we feel intensely we may express ourselves warmly; but our knowledge of human nature can make allowances even for the feelings of our oppressors towards us; we, therefore, wish, with all the anxiety of fathers, husbands, and brothers, that all classes and all creeds would see the necessity of uniting for the attainment of our objects peaceably—and not by delay and by oppression, risk the sullying of our beloved country by violence or revolutions. But that each benevolent heart and head would seek to forward our truly benevolent end, that of obtaining a legislature equally representing all interests, chosen by a free people, composed of the wise and the good of every class, and actuated by an enthusiastic desire to promote the happiness of every human being.

# IV

# RELIGION

Perversion of the term unity, from a practicable and useful sense to one at once impracticable and unimportant, has been the great mischief both of the Christian church in general, and of the Church of England in particular, and has brought about in the latter that monstrous state of things in which a total Reform can alone save it from total destruction.

THOMAS ARNOLD,
*Principles of Church Reform*

JOHN HENRY NEWMAN

# Thoughts on
# the Ministerial
# Commission*

TRACT ONE.

JOHN HENRY NEWMAN (1801–90) BECAME,
at thirty-two, one of the leaders of a movement to reshape the
Anglican Church. Newman was possibly the finest prose writer of
the century, and he certainly possessed one of the subtlest intellects
as well. As a youth, he was influenced by evangelical (Low
Church) religion, but after his years as an undergraduate and
then fellow at Oxford, he began his efforts to find in the Anglican
Church the inheritor of the apostolic succession—the true Catholic Church.

Newman was a profoundly religious man whose intensity of
faith, however well elaborated intellectually, led him into what

* From John Henry Newman, Tract One (London: John Rivington,
publisher, 1833).

many of his contemporaries regarded as mere superstition. Aware of the weakness of the Anglican Church as it existed in 1833, and concerned with the encroachment of the new liberalism on religion and on the Church itself, he—with Keble and Pusey—established what has been known as Tractarianism, or the Oxford Movement. In a series of tracts, which became increasingly elaborate through the years, Newman and others worked out their views of the Church until, in Tract Ninety, Newman attempted to prove that the thirty-nine Articles of Anglican faith were compatible with a Catholic interpretation. Newman was censured by his Oxford college and in 1845, after years of deliberation, he converted to Roman Catholicism. The story of this conversion is told powerfully in the *Apologia pro vita sua* (1864).

Newman's conversion confirmed the suspicions of many who, finding it difficult to follow the subtleties of his thought, had previously disliked and distrusted him. Newman's unquestionably genuine religion and faith in miracles, in an age in which all mysticism and irrationality were being challenged by "positive" knowledge, seemed to many of his contemporaries to be either superstition or charlatanism. He antagonized, therefore, not only the traditional High-Church parties that saw the Oxford Movement as a threat to their own position, but sceptics, evangelicals, and liberal Christians as well.

The first tract in the series is more manifesto than tract, and is somewhat atypical of Newman. It reveals, however, the sense of urgency and the intensity of commitment that lay behind all the theological and political wranglings that followed. Tract Seventy-three is, on the other hand, a very interesting foreshadowing of Newman's fully developed theory of the relation between faith and reason as it appears in his *Grammar of Assent* (1870). The rationalist attack on religion destroyed the faith of an important segment of the educated community. Others, like F. D. Maurice, tried to work out a more liberal and socially relevant faith. Still others retreated into an anti-intellectual evangelical narrowness. Newman's activities within the Angelican Church and his ultimate conversion from it can be interpreted as a retreat also. But his retreat was, as he understood it, to the ultimate truth of a faith that could not be disturbed by secular activity or secular knowledge. Against the arguments of reason (which, he believed, could be employed to prove anything) he found that only the dogmatic and hierarchical Roman Catholic Church could remain stable.

There is, of course, much in Newman's writing that remains even today rather more like superstition than rational thought. But the beauty of his language is paralleled by a precision of thought that still presents a formidable front against the easy scepticism of rationalism.

I am but one of yourselves,—a Presbyter; and therefore I conceal my name, lest I should take too much on myself by speaking in my own person. Yet speak I must; for the times are very evil, yet no one speaks against them.

Is not this so? Do not we "look one upon another," yet perform nothing? Do we not all confess the peril into which the Church is come, yet sit still each in his own retirement, as if mountains and seas cut off brother from brother? Therefore suffer me, while I try to draw you forth from those pleasant retreats, which it has been our blessedness hitherto to enjoy, to contemplate the condition and prospects of our Holy Mother in a practical way; so that one and all may unlearn that idle habit, which has grown upon us, of owning the state of things to be bad, yet doing nothing to remedy it.

Consider a moment. Is it fair, is it dutiful, to suffer our Bishops to stand the brunt of the battle without doing our part to support them? Upon them comes "the care of all the Churches." This cannot be helped; indeed it is their glory. Not one of us would wish in the least to deprive them of the duties, the toils, the responsibilities of their high office. And, black event as it would be for the country, yet, (as far as they are concerned,) we could not wish them a more blessed termination of their course, than the spoiling of their goods, and martyrdom.

To them then we willingly and affectionately relinquish their high privileges and honors; we encroach not upon the rights of the SUCCESSORS OF THE APOSTLES; we touch not their sword and crosier. Yet surely we may be their shield-bearers in the battle without offence; and by our voice and deeds be to them what Luke and Timothy were to St. Paul.

Now then let me come at once to the subject which leads me to address you. Should the Government and Country so far forget their GOD as to cast off the Church, to deprive it of its temporal honors and substance, *on what* will you rest the claim of respect and attention which you make upon your flocks? Hitherto you have been upheld by your birth, your education, your wealth, your connexions; should these secular advantages cease, on what must CHRIST's Ministers depend? Is not this a serious practical question? We know how miserable is the state of religious bodies not supported by the State. Look at the Dissenters on all sides of you, and you will see at once that their Ministers, depending simply upon the people, become the *creatures* of the people. Are you content that this should be your case? Alas! can a greater evil befal Christians, than for their teachers to be guided by them, instead of guiding? How can we "hold fast the form of sound words," and "keep that which is committed to our trust," if our influence is to depend simply on our popularity? Is it not our very office to *oppose* the world, can we then allow ourselves to *court* it? to preach smooth things and prophesy deceits? to make the way of life easy to the rich and indolent, and to bribe the humbler classes by excitements and strong intoxicating doctrine? Surely it must not be so;—and the question recurs, on *what* are we to rest our authority, when the State deserts us?

CHRIST has not left His Church without claim of its own upon the attention of men. Surely not. Hard Master He cannot be, to bid us oppose the world, yet give us no credentials for so doing. There are some who rest their divine mission on their own unsupported assertion; others, who rest it upon their popularity; others, on their success; and others, who rest it upon their temporal distinctions. This last case has, perhaps, been too much our own; I fear we have neglected the real ground on which our authority is built,—OUR APOSTOLICAL DESCENT.

We have been born, not of blood, nor of the will of the flesh, nor of the will of man, but of GOD. The Lord JESUS CHRIST gave His Spirit to His Apostles; they in turn laid their hands on those who should succeed them; and these again on others; and so the sacred gift has been handed down to our present Bishops, who have appointed us as their assistants, and in some sense representatives.

Now every one of us believes this. I know that some will at first deny they do; still they do believe it. Only, it is not sufficiently, practically impressed on their minds. They *do* believe it; for it is the doctrine of the Ordination Service, which they have recognised as truth in the most solemn season of their lives. In order, then, not to prove, but to remind and impress, I entreat your attention to the words used when you were made Ministers of CHRIST's Church.

The office of Deacon was thus committed to you: "Take thou authority to execute the office of a Deacon in the Church of GOD committed unto thee: In the name," etc.

And the Priesthood thus:

"Receive the HOLY GHOST, for the office and work of a Priest, in the Church of GOD, now committed unto thee by the imposition of our hands. Whose sins thou dost forgive, they are forgiven; and whose sins thou dost retain, they are retained. And be thou a faithful dispenser of the Word of GOD, and of His Holy Sacraments: In the name," etc.

These, I say, were words spoken to us, and received by us, when we were brought nearer to GOD than at any other time of our lives. I know the grace of ordination is contained in the laying on of hands, not in any form of words;—yet in our own case, (as has ever been usual in the Church,) words of blessing have accompanied the act. Thus we have confessed before GOD our belief, that through the Bishop who ordained us, we received the HOLY GHOST, the power to bind and to loose, to administer the Sacraments, and to preach. Now *how* is he able to give these great gifts? *Whence* is his right? Are these words idle, (which would be taking GOD's name in vain,) or do they express merely a wish, (which surely is very far below their meaning,) or do they not rather indicate that the Speaker is conveying a gift? Surely they can mean nothing short of this. But whence, *I* ask, his right to do so? Has he any right, except as having received the power from those who consecrated him to be a Bishop? He could not give what he had never received. It is plain then that he but *transmits*; and that the Christian Ministry is a *succession*. And if we trace back the power of ordination from hand to hand, of course we shall come to the Apostles at last. We know we do, as a plain historical fact; and therefore all we, who have been ordained Clergy, in the very form of our ordination acknowledged the doctrine of the APOSTOLICAL SUCCESSION.

And for the same reason, we must necessarily consider none to be *really* ordained who have not *thus* been ordained. For if ordination is a divine ordinance, it must be necessary; and if it is not a divine ordinance, how dare we use it? Therefore all who use it, all of us, must consider it necessary. As well might we pretend the Sacraments are not necessary to Salvation, while we make use of the offices of the Liturgy; for when GOD appoints means of grace, they are *the* means.

I do not see how any one can escape from this plain view of the subject, except, (as I have already hinted,) by declaring, that the words do not mean all that they say. But only reflect what a most unseemly time for random words is that, in which Ministers are set apart for their office. Do we not adopt a Liturgy, in order to hinder inconsiderate idle language, and shall we, in the most sacred of all services, write down, subscribe, and use again and again forms of speech which have not been weighed, and cannot be taken strictly?

Therefore, my dear Brethren, act up to your professions. Let it not be said that you have neglected a gift; for if you have the Spirit of the Apostles on you, surely this is a great gift. "Stir up the gift of GOD which is in you." Make much of it. Show your value of it. Keep it before your minds as an honorable badge, far higher than that secular respectability, or cultivation, or polish, or learning, or rank, which gives you a hearing with the many. Tell them of your gift. The times will soon drive you to do this, if you mean to be still any thing. But wait not for the times. Do not be compelled, by the world's forsaking you, to recur as if unwillingly to the high source of your authority. Speak out now, before you are forced, both as glorying in your privilege, and to ensure your rightful honor from your people. A notion has gone abroad, that they can take away your power. They think they have given and can take it away. They think it lies in the Church property, and they know that they have politically the power to confiscate that property. They have been deluded into a notion that present palpable usefulness, produceable results, acceptableness to your flocks, that these and such like are the tests of your Divine commission. Enlighten them in this matter. Exalt our Holy Fathers the Bishops, as the Representatives of the Apostles, and the Angels of the Churches; and magnify your office, as being ordained by them to take part in their Ministry.

But, if you will not adopt my view of the subject, which I offer to you, not doubtingly, yet (I hope) respectfully, at all events, CHOOSE YOUR SIDE. To remain neuter much longer will be itself to take a part. Choose your side; since side you shortly must, with one or other party, even though you do nothing. Fear to be of those, whose line is decided for them by chance circumstances, and who may perchance find themselves with the enemies of CHRIST, while they think but to remove themselves from worldly politics. Such abstinence is impossible in troublous times. HE THAT IS NOT WITH ME, IS AGAINST ME, AND HE THAT GATHERETH NOT WITH ME SCATTERETH ABROAD.

JOHN HENRY NEWMAN

# On the Introduction of Rationalistic Principles Into Religion*

TRACT SEVENTY-THREE
THE RATIONALISTIC AND THE
CATHOLIC SPIRIT COMPARED
TOGETHER

To rationalize is to ask for reasons out of place; to ask improperly how we are to account for certain things, to be unwilling to believe them unless they can be accounted for, i.e., referred to something else as a cause, to some existing system as harmonizing with them or taking them up into itself. Again, since whatever is assigned as the reason for the original fact canvassed, admits in turn of a like question being raised about itself, unless it be ascertainable by the senses, and be the subject of personal experience, Rationalism is bound properly to pursue onward its course of investigation on this principle, and not

* From John Henry Newman, *Tract Seventy-Three* (London: John Rivington, 1836).

to stop till it can directly or ultimately refer to self as a witness, whatever is offered to its acceptance. Thus it is characterised by two
peculiarities; its love of systematizing. and its basing its system upon
personal experience, on the evidence of sense. In both respects it
stands opposed to what is commonly understood by the word Faith,
or belief in Testimony; for which it deliberately substitutes System,
(or what is popularly called Reason) and Sight.

I have said that to act the Rationalist is to be unduly set upon
*accounting* for what is offered for our acceptance; *unduly,* for to seek
reasons for what is told us, is natural and innocent in itself. When
we are informed that this or that event has happened, we are not
satisfied to take it as an isolated fact; we are inquisitive about it; we
are prompted to refer it, if possible, to something we already know,
to incorporate it into the connected family of truths or facts which
we have already received. We like to ascertain its position relatively
to other things, to view it in connexion with them, to reduce it to a
place in the series of what is called cause and effect. There is no harm
in all this, until we insist upon receiving this *satisfaction* as a necessary
condition of believing what is presented for our acceptance, until we
set up our existing system of knowledge as a legitimate test of the
credibility of testimony, until we claim to be told the mode of re-
conciling alleged truths to other truths already known, the *how* they
are, and *why* they are; and then we Rationalize.

· · · ·

Rationalism then in fact is a forgetfulness of God's power, dis-
belief of the existence of a First Cause sufficient to account for any
events or facts, however marvellous or extraordinary, and a consequent
measuring of the credibility of things, not by the power and other
attributes of God, but by our own knowledge; a limiting the possible
to the actual, and denying the indefinite range of God's operations
beyond our means of apprehending them. Mr. Hume openly avows
this principle, declaring it to be unphilosophical to suppose that
Almighty God can do any thing, but what we see He does. And,
though we may not profess it, we too often, it is to be feared, act
upon it at the present day. Instead of looking out of ourselves, and
trying to catch glimpses of God's workings, from any quarter,—
throwing ourselves forward upon Him and waiting on Him, we sit at
home bringing everything to ourselves, enthroning ourselves as the
centre of all things, and refusing to believe any thing that does not
force itself upon our minds as true. Our private judgment is made
every thing to us,—is contemplated, recognized, and referred to as
the arbiter of all questions, and as independent of every thing external

to us. Nothing is considered to have an existence except so far forth as our minds discern it. The notion of half views and partial knowledge, of guesses, surmises, hopes and fears, of truths faintly apprehended and not understood, of isolated facts in the great scheme of providence, in a word, of Mystery, is discarded. Hence a distinction is drawn between what is called Objective and Subjective Truth, and religion is said to consist in a reception of the latter. By Objective Truth is meant the Religious System considered as existing in itself, external to this or that particular mind: by Subjective, is meant that which each mind receives in particular, and considers to be such. To believe in Objective Truth is to throw ourselves forward upon that which we have but partially mastered or made Subjective, to embrace, maintain, and use general propositions which are greater than our own capacity, as if we were contemplating what is real and independent of human judgment. Such a belief seems to the Rationalist superstitious and unmeaning, and he consequently confines faith to the province of Subjective Truth, or to the reception of doctrine, as, and so far as it is met and apprehended by the mind, which will be differently in different persons, in the shape of orthodoxy in one, heterodoxy in another; that is, he professes to *believe* in that which he *opines*, and he avoids the apparent extravagance of such an avowal by maintaining that the moral trial involved in faith does not lie in the submission of the reason to external truths partially disclosed, but in that candid pursuit of truth which ensures the eventual adoption of that opinion on the subject, which is best for us, most natural according to the constitution of our minds, and so divinely intended. In short he owns that faith, viewed with reference to its objects, is never more than an opinion, and is pleasing to God, not as an active principle apprehending definite doctrines, but as a result and fruit, and therefore an evidence, of past diligence, independent inquiry, dispassionateness, and the like. Rationalism takes the words of Scripture as signs of Ideas; Faith, of Things or Realities.

For an illustration of Faith, considered as the reaching forth after and embracing what is beyond the mind or Objective, we may refer to St. Paul's description of it in the Ancient Saints; "These all died in faith, *not having received* the promises, but *having seen them afar off*, and were persuaded of them, and embraced them, and confessed that they were strangers and polgrims on the earth"; or to St. Peter's; "Of which salvation the Prophets have inquired and searched diligently, who *prophesied* of the grace that should come *unto you, searching what, or what manner of time* the Spirit of Christ, which was in them, did signify, when it testified beforehand the sufferings of

Christ, the glory that should follow; unto whom it was revealed, that *not unto themselves,* but unto us they did minister the things which are now reported unto you by them that have evangelized you." Here the faith of the ancient Saints is described as employed, not on truths so far as mastered by the mind, but truths beyond it, and even to the end withheld from its clear apprehension.

On the other hand, if we would know to what a temper of mind the Rationalistic Theory of Subjective Truth really tends, we may study the following passage from a popular review. It will be found to make use of the wonders of nature, not as "declaring the glory of God, and showing His handywork," but in order to exalt and deify the wisdom of man. Of the almost avowed infidelity contained in it, I do not speak.

"For the civil and political historian the past alone has existence, the present he rarely apprehends, the future never. To the historian of science it is permitted, however, to penetrate the depths of past and future with equal clearness and certainty; facts to come on to him as present, and not unfrequently more assured than facts which are past. Although this clear perception of causes and consequences characterizes the whole domain of physical science, and clothes the natural philosopher with powers denied to the political and moral inquirer, yet *foreknowledge is eminently the privilege of the astronomer.* Nature has raised the curtain of futurity, and displayed before him the succession of her decrees, so far as they affect the physical universe, for countless ages to come; and the *revelations* of which she has made him the instrument, are supported and verified by a never-ceasing train of predictions fulfilled. He [the astronomer] "shows us the things which will be hereafter;" not obscurely shadowed out in figures and in parables, as must necessarily be the case with other revelations, but attended with the most minute precision of time, place, and circumstance. He converts the hours as they roll into an ever-present miracle, *in attestation of those laws which his Creator through him has unfolded;* the sun cannot rise, the moon cannot wane, a star cannot twinkle in the firmament without bearing testimony to *the truth of his* [the astronomer's] *prophetic records.* It has pleased the "Lord and Governor" of the world, in his inscrutable wisdom, to baffle our inquiries into the nature and proximate cause of that wonderful faculty of intellect,—that image of his own essence which he has conferred upon us, etc. etc. . . . But how nobly is the darkness which envelopes metaphysical inquiries compensated by the flood of light which is shed upon the physical creation! *There* all is harmony, and order, and majesty, and beauty. From the chaos of social and political phenomena exhibited in human records, phenomena unconnected to our imperfect vision by any discoverable law, a war of passions and prejudices governed by no apparent purpose, tending to no apparent end, and setting all intelligible order at defiance,—*how soothing and yet how elevating* it is to turn to the splendid spectacle which offers itself to the habitual contemplation of the astronomer! How favourable to the development of all the *best and highest feelings* of the soul are such objects! The only passion they inspire being the *love of truth*, and the chiefest pleasure of their votaries arising from excursions through the imposing scenery of the universe, scenery on a scale of grandeur and magnificence compared with which whatever we are accustomed to call sublimity on our planet, dwindles into ridiculous insignificancy. Most justly has it been said, that nature has implanted in our bosoms *a craving after the discovery of truth*, and assuredly that glorious instinct is never more irresistibly awakened than when our notice is directed to what is going on in the heavens, etc.

Here desire after Truth is considered as irreconcileable with acquiescence in doubt. Now if we do not believe in a First Cause, then indeed we know nothing except so far as we know it clearly, consistency and harmony being the necessary evidence of reality; and so we may reasonably regard doubt as an obstacle in the pursuit of Truth. But, on the other hand, if we *assume the existence of* an unseen Object of Faith, then we already possess the main truth, and may well be content even with half views as to His operations, for whatever we have is so much gain, and what we do not know does not in that case tend at all to invalidate what we do know.

A few words may be necessary to bring together what has been said. Rationalism then, viewed in its essential character, is a refusal to take for granted the existence of a First Cause, in religious inquiries, which it prosecutes as if commencing in utter ignorance on the subject. Hence it receives only so much as may be strictly drawn out to the satisfaction of the reason, advancing onwards in belief according to the range of the proof; it limits Truth to our comprehension of it, or *subjects* it to the mind, and admits it only so far as it is subjected. Hence again it considers faith to have reference to a *thing* or *system*, far more than to an *agent*, for an agent may be supposed as acting in unknown ways, whereas a system cannot be supposed to have existence beyond what is ascertained of it. Hence moreover it makes the credibility of any alleged truth to lie solely in its capability of coalescing and combining with what is already known.

Mr. Hume, as has been observed, avowed the principle of Rationalism in its extent of Atheism. The writers, I shall have to notice, have religious sensibilities, and are far less clear-sighted. Yet even Mr. Erskine[1] maintains or assumes that the main object of Christian faith is, not Almighty God, but a certain work or course of things which He has accomplished; as will be manifest to any reader either of His Essay on Internal Evidence, or on Faith. He says, for instance, in the latter of these works,

> I may understand many things which I do not believe: but I cannot believe any thing which I do not understand, unless it be something addressed merely to my senses, and not to my thinking faculty. A man may with great propriety say, I understand the Cartesian System of Vortices, though I do not believe in it. But it is absolutely impossible for him to believe in that system without knowing what it is. A man may believe in the ability of the maker of a system without understanding it; but he cannot believe in the system itself without understanding it. Now there is a meaning in the Gospel, and there is declared in it the system of God's dealings with men. This meaning, and this system, must be understood, before we can believe the Gospel. We are not called on to believe the Bible merely that we may give a proof of our willingness to submit in all things to God's authority, but that we may be influenced by the objects of our belief, etc.

Every word of this extract tells in illustration of what has been drawn out above. And it is cited here merely in illustration; what judgment is to be formed of it shall be determined in its place. To resume the thread of our discussion.

We shall now perhaps be prepared to understand a very characteristic word, familiarly used by Mr. Erskine among others to designate his view of the Gospel dispensation. It is said to be a Manifestation, as if the system presented to us were such as we could trace and connect into one whole, complete and definite. Let me use this word "Manifestation," as a token of the philosophy under review; and let me contrast it with the word "Mystery" which on the other hand may be regarded as the badge or emblem of orthodoxy. Revelation considered as a Manifestation, is a doctrine variously received by various

1. Thomas Erskine (1788–1870) defended J. MacLeod Campbell, who was deposed by the general assembly of the Church of Scotland for preaching the doctrine of "universal atonement and pardon through the death of Christ." Erskine carried his arguments beyond Campbell. In his Remarks on the Internal Evidence for the Truth of Revealed Religion (1820), he argued that belief in the Bible as an inspired text is founded upon the testimony of conscience.

minds, but nothing more to each than that which it appears to be. Considered as a Mystery, it is a doctrine enunciated by inspiration, in human language, as the only possible medium of it, and suitably according to the capacity of language; a doctrine *lying hid* in language, to be received in that language from the first by every mind, whatever be its separate power of understanding; entered into more or less by this or that mind, as it may be; and admitting of being apprehended more and more perfectly according to the diligence of the person receiving it. It is one and the same, independent and real, of depth unfathomable, and illimitable in its extent.

This is a fit place to make some remarks on the Scripture sense of the word Mystery. It may seem a contradiction in terms to call Revelation a Mystery; but is not the book of the Revelation of St. John as great a mystery from beginning to end as the most abstruse doctrine the mind ever imagined? yet it is even called a *revelation*. How is this? The answer is simple. No revelation can be complete and systematic, from the weakness of the human intellect; *so far as* it is not such, it is mysterious. When nothing is revealed, nothing is known, and there is nothing to contemplate or marvel at; but when something is revealed and only something, for all cannot be, there are forthwith difficulties and perplexities. A Revelation is religious doctrine viewed on its illuminated side; a Mystery is the self-same doctrine viewed on the side unilluminated. Thus Religious Truth is neither light nor darkness, but both together; it is like the dim view of a country seen in the twilight, with forms half extricated from the darkness, with broken lines, and isolated masses. Revelation, in this way of considering it, is not a revealed *system*, but consists of a number of detached and incomplete truths belonging to a vast system unrevealed, of doctrines and injunctions mysteriously connected together, that is, connected by unknown media, and bearing upon unknown portions of the system. And in this sense we see the propriety of calling St. John's prophecies, though highly mysterious, yet a revelation.

And such seems to be the meaning of the word Mystery in Scripture, a point which is sometimes disputed. Campbell[2] in his work on the Gospels, maintains that the word means a *secret*, and that, whatever be the subject of it in the New Testament, it is always, when mentioned, associated with the notion of its being now revealed. Thus it is, in his view, a word belonging solely to the Law, which was a system of types and shadows, and is utterly foreign to the Gospel which has brought light instead of darkness. This sense might

2. John MacLeod Campbell (1800–1872), the man to whose defense Erskine came. Even after being dismissed from the ministry, he remained a successful preacher in Glasgow.

seem to be supported by our Lord's announcement, for instance, to His disciples that to them was given to know the mysteries of His kingdom; by His command to them at another time to speak abroad what they had heard from Him in secret. And St. Paul in like manner glories in the revelation of mysteries hid from the foundation of the world.

But the sense of Scripture will more truly be represented as follows. What was hidden altogether before Christ came could not be a Mystery; it became a Mystery then, for the first time by being disclosed at all, at His coming. What had never been dreamed of by "righteous men," before Him, when revealed, as *being* unexpected, if for no other reason, would be strange and startling. And such unquestionably is the meaning of St. Paul, when he uses the word; for he applies it, not to what was passed and over, but what was the then state of the doctrine revealed. Thus in the 1 Cor. xv. 51, 52, "Behold I show you a Mystery; we shall not all sleep, but we shall all be changed in a moment, in the twinkling of an eye, at the last trump." The resurrection and consequent spiritualizing of the human body, was not dreamed of by the philosophy of the world till Christ came, and, when revealed, was "mocked," as then first becoming a Mystery. Reason was just where it was; and, as it could not discover it beforehand, so now it cannot account for it, or reconcile it to experience, or explain the manner of it: the utmost it does is by some faint analogies to show it is not inconceivable. . . . Now, is the revelation of these truths a Manifestation (as above explained) or a Mystery? Surely the great secret has, by being revealed, only got so far as to be a Mystery, nothing more; nor could become a Manifestation, (i.e. a system connected in its parts by the human mind,) without ceasing to be any thing great at all. It must ever be small and superficial, viewed only as received by man; and is vast only when considered as that external truth into which each Christian may grow continually, and ever find fresh food for his soul. . . .

.  .  .  .

The practical inference to be drawn from this view, is first, that we should be very reverent in dealing with revealed truth; next, that we should avoid all theorising and systematising as relates to it, which is pretty much what looking into the ark was under the Law; further, that we should be solicitous to hold it safely and entirely; moreover, that we should be zealous and pertinacious in guarding it; and lastly, which is implied in all these, that we should religiously adhere to the form of words and the ordinances under which it comes to us, through which it is revealed to us, and apart from which the revelation does not exist, there being nothing else given us by which to ascertain or enter into it.

Striking indeed is the contrast presented to this view of the Gospel, by the popular theology of the day! That theology is as follows;—that the Atonement is the chief doctrine of the Gospel;— again, that it is chiefly to be regarded, not as a wonder in heaven, and in its relation to the attributes of God and the unseen world, but in its experienced effects on our minds, in the change it effects where it is believed. On this, as on the horizontal line in a picture, all the portions of the Gospel system are placed and made to converge; as if it might fearlessly be used to regulate, adjust, correct, complete, every thing else. Thus, the doctrine of the Incarnation is viewed as necessary and important to the Gospel, *because* it gives sacredness to the Atonement; of the Trinity, *because* it includes the revelation, not only of the Redeemer, but also of the Sanctifier, by whose aid and influence the Gospel message is to be blessed to us. It follows that faith is nearly the whole of religion, for through it the message or Manifestation is *received*; on the other hand, the scientific language of Catholicism is disparaged, as having no tendency to enforce the operation of the revelation of the Atonement on our minds, and the Sacraments are limited to the office of representing, and promising, and impressing on us the promise of divine influences, in no measure of conveying them. Thus the Dispensation is practically identified with its Revelation or rather Manifestation. Not that the reality of the Atonement is formally denied, but it is cast in the back ground, except so far as it can be discovered to be influential, viz. to show GOD's hatred of sin, the love of CHRIST and the like; and there is an evident *tendency* to consider it as a *mere* Manifestation of the love of CHRIST, to the denial of all real virtue in it as an expiation for sin; as if His death took place, merely to show His love for us, as a sign of God's infinite mercy, to calm and assure us, without any *real* connexion existing between it and GOD's forgiveness of our sins. And the dispensation thus being hewn and chiselled into an intelligible human system, is represented, when thus mutilated, as affording a remarkable evidence of the truth of the Bible, an evidence level to the *reason*, and superseding the *testimony* of the Apostles. That is, according to the above observations, that Rationalism, or want of faith, which has first invented a spurious gospel, next looks complacently on its own offspring, and pronounces it to be the very image of that notion of the Divine Providence according to which it was originally modeled; a procedure, which, besides more serious objections, incurs the logical absurdity of arguing in a circle.

SAMUEL TAYLOR COLERIDGE

# On the Constitution
# of Church and State*

SAMUEL TAYLOR COLERIDGE (1772–1834) WAS
probably the most important intellectual influence—barring
Jeremy Bentham—on early- and mid-nineteenth-century thought.
John Stuart Mill, in his essays on Bentham (1836) and Coleridge
(1840), divides all educated people into Coleridgeans and Benthamites. For him, the two men are intellectual opposites, each possessing, as the basis of his system, a half-truth that needs the other
for completion. Coleridge's thought and career are far too complex
to go into here. Briefly, however, to use Mill's terms, Bentham
led people to ask themselves of any opinion, "Is it true?" while
Coleridge led them to ask, "What is the meaning of it?" Mill
regards Coleridge as a true and valuable conservative who found
in things established some buried truths in need of extrication and
reactivation.

* From S. T. Coleridge, On the Constitution of Church and State, First
Edition (London: Hurst, Chance and Co., 1830), pp. 63–71.

Near the end of his long and painful career, Coleridge turned his attention to the Church. He found it to be corrupt and practically useless, and he attempted to formulate a system that would allow it to fulfill its ideal functions. His solution, similar in many ways to that of Thomas Arnold, was—as Mill understood—a radical proposal entailing a revolution within the Church.

Some of the elements of the system are included in this excerpt from his book on the Church, a work that—like so much of Coleridge's writing—is rambling and digressive, but rich with insight and intelligence. More important, it is infused with a deep humanity that Coleridge never lost, despite his flight from the radical principles of his youth into Toryism and German mysticism.

. . . The National Church was deemed in the dark age of Queen Elizabeth, in the unenlightened times of Burleigh, Hooker, Spenser, Shakespeare, and Lord Bacon, A GREAT VENERABLE ESTATE OF THE REALM; but now by "all the intellect of the kingdom," it has been determined to be one of the many theological sects, churches or communities, established in the realm; but distinguished from the rest by having its priesthood endowed, durante bene placito,[1] by favour of the legislature—that is, of the majority for the time being, of the two Houses of Parliament. The Church being thus reduced to a religion, Religion in genere is consequently separated from the church, and made a subject of parliamentary determination, independent of this church. The poor withdrawn from the discipline of the church. The education of the people detached from the ministry of the church. Religion, a noun of multitude, or nomen collectivum, expressing the aggregate of all the different groups of notions and ceremonies connected with the invisible and supernatural. On the plausible (and in this sense of the word, unanswerable) pretext of the multitude and variety of Religions, and for the suppression of bigotry and negative persecution, National Education to be finally sundered from all religion, but speedily and decisively emancipated from the

1. "for as long as it pleased"

superintendence of the National Clergy. Education reformed. Defined
as synonimous with Instruction. *Axiom of Education so defined.*
Knowledge being power, those attainments, which give a man the
power of doing what he wishes to obtain what he desires, are alone
to be considered as knowledge, or to be admitted into the scheme
of National Education. Subjects to be taught in the National Schools.
Reading, writing, arithmetic, the mechanic arts, elements and results
of physical science, but to be taught, as much as possible, empirically.
For all knowledge being derived from the Senses, the closer men are
kept to the fountain head, the *knowinger* they must become.—
Popular Ethics, *i.e.* a Digest of the Criminal Laws, and the evidence
requisite for conviction under the same: Lectures on Diet, on Digestion, on Infection, and the nature and effects of a specific virus
incidental to and communicable by living bodies in the intercourse of
society. N. B. In order to balance the Interests of Individuals and the
Interests of the State, the Dietetic and Peptic Text Books, to be under
the censorship of the Board of Excise.

Shall I proceed with my chapter of hints? Game Laws, Corn
Laws, Cotton Factories, Spitalfields, the tillers of the land paid by
poor-rates, and the remainder of the population mechanized into
engines for the manufactory of new rich men—yea, the machinery
of the wealth of the nation made up of the wretchedness, disease and
depravity of those who should constitute the strength of the nation!
Disease, I say, and vice, while the wheels are in full motion; but at
the first stop the magic wealth-machine is converted into an intolerable weight of pauperism! But this partakes of History. The head and
neck of the huge Serpent are out of the den: the voluminous train is
to come. What next? May I not whisper as a fear, what Senators have
promised to demand as a right? Yes! the next in my filial bodings is
Spoliation. —Spoliation of the NATIONALTY, half thereof to be distributed among the landowners, and the other half among the stock-
brokers, and stock-owners, who are to receive it in lieu of the interest
formerly due to them. But enough! I will ask only one question. Has
the national welfare, have the wealth and happiness of the people,
advanced with the increase of its circumstantial prosperity? Is the increasing number of wealthy individuals that which ought to be understood by the wealth of the nation? In answer to this, permit me to
annex the following chapter of contents of the moral history of the
last 130 years.

A. Declarative act, respecting certain parts of the constitution,
with provisions against further violation of the same, erroneously
entitled, "THE REVOLUTION of 1688."

B. The Mechanico-corpuscular Theory raised to the title of the Mechanic Philosophy, and espoused as a revolution in philosophy, by the actors and partizans of the (so called) Revolution in the state.

C. Result illustrated, in the remarkable contrast between the acceptation of the word, Idea, *before* the Restoration, and the *present* use of the same word. *Before* 1660, the magnificent SON OF COSMO was wont to discourse with FICINO, POLITIAN and the princely MIRANDULA[2] on the IDEAS of Will, God, Freedom. SIR PHILIP SIDNEY, the star of serenest brilliance in the glorious constellation of Elizabeth's court, communed with SPENSER, on the IDEA of the beautiful; and the younger ALGERNON—Soldier, Patriot, and Statesman—with HARRINGTON, MILTON, and NEVIL,[3] on the IDEA of the STATE: and in what sense it may be more truly affirmed, that the people (*i.e.* the component particles of the body politic, at any moment existing as such) are in order to the state, than that the state exists for the sake of the people.

Dr. HOLOFERNES, in a lecture on metaphysics, delivered at one of the Mechanics' Institutions, explodes all *ideas* but those of sensation; and his friend, DEPUTY COSTARD, has no *idea* of a better flavored haunch of venison, than he dined off at the London Tavern last week. He admits (for the Deputy has travelled) that the French have an excellent *idea* of cooking in general; but holds that their most accomplished *Maitres du Cuisine* have no more *idea* of dressing a turtle, than the Parisian Gourmands themselves have any *real* idea of the true *taste* and *colour* of the fat.

D. Consequences exemplified. State of nature, or the Ouran Outang theory of the origin of the human race, substituted for the

2. Coleridge is referring here to a school of Italian Renaissance Platonists. Cosimo de Medici (1369–1464) was a great patron of the arts and had Ficino (1453–99) educated in Latin and Greek in order to translate Plato. Through Ficino, he founded a Platonic Academy. Politian (1454–94) was a brilliant scholar and poet in Greek, Latin, and Italian. Pico della Mirandola (1463–94) moved from Aristotelianism to Ficino's Platonism, and attempted to establish a compromise between the two.

3. James Harrington (1611–77) was a political theorist. Like Sir Henry Neville (1620–94), he was a republican opposed to Cromwell.

Book of Genesis, ch. I.—X. Rights of nature for the duties and privileges of citizens. Idealess facts, misnamed proofs from history, grounds of experience, etc., substituted for principles and the insight derived from them. State-policy, a Cyclops with one eye, and that in the back of the head! Our measures of policy, either a series of anachronisms, or a truckling to events substituted for the science, that should command them: for all true insight is foresight. (Documents. The measures of the British Cabinet from the Boston Port Bill, March 1774; but particularly from 1789, to the Union of Ireland, and the Peace of Amiens.) Mean time, the true historical feeling, the immortal life of an historical Nation, generation linked to generation by faith, freedom, heraldry, and ancestral fame, languishing, and giving place to the superstitions of wealth, and newspaper reputation.

E. Talents without genius: a swarm of clever, well-informed men: an anarchy of minds, a despotism of maxims. Despotism of finance in government and legislation—of vanity and sciolism in the intercourse of life—of presumption, temerity, and hardness of heart, in political economy.

F. The Guess-work of general consequences substituted for moral and political philosophy, adopted as a text book in one of the Universities, and cited, as authority, in the legislature: Plebs pro Senatu Populoque[4]; the wealth of the nation (i.e., of the wealthy individuals thereof, and the magnitude of the Revenue) for the well-being of the people.

G. Gin consumed by paupers to the value of about eighteen millions yearly. Government by journeymen clubs; by saint and sinner societies, committees, institutions; by reviews, magazines, and above all by newspapers. Lastly, crimes quadrupled for the whole country, and in some counties decupled.

Concluding address to the parliamentary leaders of the Liberalists and Utilitarians. I respect the talents of many, and the motives and character of some among you too sincerely to court the scorn, which I anticipate. But neither shall the fear of it prevent me from declaring aloud, and as a truth which I hold it the disgrace and calamity of a professed statesman not to know and acknowledge, that a permanent, nationalized, learned order, a national clerisy or church, is an essential element of a rightly constituted nation, without which it wants the best security alike for its permanence and its progression; and for which neither tract societies, nor conventicles, nor Lancastrian schools, nor mechanics' institutions, nor lecture-bazaars under the absurd

---

4. "the people for the legislature and the nation"

name of universities, nor all these collectively, can be a substitute. For they are all marked with the same asterisk of spuriousness, shew the same distemper-spot on the front, that they are empirical specifics for morbid *symptoms* that help to feed and continue the disease.

But you wish for *general* illumination: you would spur-arm the toes of society: you would enlighten the higher ranks per ascensum ab imis.[5] You begin, therefore, with the attempt to *popularize* science: but you will only effect its *plebification*. It is folly to think of making all, or the many, philosophers, or even men of science and systematic knowledge. But it is duty and wisdom to aim at making as many as possible soberly and steadily religious;—inasmuch as the morality which the state requires in its citizens for its own well-being and ideal immortality, and without reference to their spiritual interest as in-dividuals, can only exist for the people in the form of religion. But the existence of a true philosophy, or the power and habit of contem-plating particulars in the unity and fontal mirror of the idea—this in the rulers and teachers of a nation is indispensable to a sound state of religion in all classes. In fine, Religion, true or false, is and ever has been the centre of gravity in a realm, to which all other things must and will accommodate themselves. . . .

5. "by ascent from the depths"

THOMAS ARNOLD

# Principles of
# Church Reform*

THOMAS ARNOLD (1795–1842), FATHER OF
Matthew Arnold, was well-known for his educational reforms at
Rugby, where he became headmaster in 1827. Arnold was the
butt of some of the strongest satire in Lytton Strachey's *Eminent
Victorians*, but he was a man of stern integrity, piety, and intellectual vigor. His life was based on his belief in the union of the
divine and the human in Christ; thus, for him, Church and State
were one, and in his teaching he assumed that there could be no
distinction between the secular and the religious. Through him,
Rugby became the training ground for Christian gentlemen and
left its mark on large segments of English society.

He regarded the Church as a secular as well as a spiritual
instrument, and he would have approved Coleridge's suggestion
that the established church be run by a clerisy intent on moral

* From Thomas Arnold, *Principles of Church Reform*, First Edition
(London: B. Fellowes, 1833), pp. 82–8.

and intellectual as well as spiritual training. According to Arnold, the Church should become the home of the most intelligent and useful men. In the book from which material is included here, Arnold argues the need to put aside doctrinal differences, to welcome all varieties of Christianity within the Church, and to insist only on the points upon which all Christians can agree. His desire to liberalize the Church made him the enemy of the Oxford Movement, which he attacked in an essay in the *Edinburgh Review* (April, 1836), "The Oxford Malignants and Dr. Hampden." His theory, like that of Coleridge, grows out of a deep human sympathy and a need for justice. His combination of religious and social concern helped influence attempts in the next decade to bring the Church back into the mainstream of contemporary life.

. . . In venturing even to suggest so great a change in the constitution of our Church, I may probably expose myself to a variety of imputations. Above all, whoever pleads in favour of a wide extension of the terms of communion, is immediately apt to be accused of latitudinarianism, or, as it is now called, of liberalism. Such a charge in the mouths of men at once low principled and ignorant, is of no importance whatever; neither should I regard it if it proceeded from the violent fanatical party, to whom truth must ever remain unknown, as it is unsought after. But in the Church of England even bigotry often wears a softer and a nobler aspect; and there are men at once pious, high minded, intelligent, and full of all kindly feelings, whose intense love for the forms of the Church, fostered as it has been by all the best associations of their pure and holy lives, has absolutely engrossed their whole nature; they have neither eyes to see of themselves any defect in the Liturgy or Articles, nor ears to hear of such when alleged by others. It can be no ordinary church to have inspired such a devoted adoration in such men;—nor are they ordinary men over whom the sense of high moral beauty has obtained so complete a mastery. They will not, I fear, be willing to believe how deeply painful it is to my mind, to know that I am regarded by them as an adversary; still more to feel that I am associated in their judgments with principles and with a party which I abhor as deeply as they do. But while I know the devotedness of their admiration for the Church of England, as it is now constituted, I cannot but wish that they would regard those thousands and ten thousands of their countrymen, who are excluded from its benefit; that they would consider the wrong done to our common country by these unnatural divisions amongst her children. *The Church of Christ* is indeed far beyond all human ties; but of all human ties, that to our country is the highest and most sacred: and *England*, to a true Englishman, ought to be dearer than the peculiar forms of *the Church of England*.

For the sake, then, of our country, and to save her from the greatest possible evils,—from evils far worse than any loss of territory, or decline of trade,—from the sure moral and intellectual degradation which will accompany the unchristianizing of the nation, that is, the destroying of its national religious Establishment, is it too much to ask of good men, that they should consent to unite themselves with other good men, without requiring them to subscribe to their own opinions, or to conform to their own ceremonies? They are not asked to surrender or compromise the smallest portion of their own faith, but simply to forbear imposing it upon their neighbours. They are not called upon to give up their own forms of worship, but to allow the addition of others; not for themselves to join in, if they do not like to do so, but simply to be celebrated in the same church, and by ministers, whom they shall acknowledge to be their brethren, and members no less than themselves of the National Establishment. The alterations which should be made in their own Litnrgy should be such as, to use Bishop Burnet's[1] words, "are in themselves desirable, though there were not a Dissenter in the nation;" alterations not to change its character, but to perfect it.

"But it is latitudinarian not to lay a greater stress on the necessity of believing the truth, and to allow by public authority, and sanction by our own co-operation, the teaching of error." I will not yield to any man in the strength of my convictions of truth and error; nor in the wish that the propagation of error could be prevented. But how is it possible to effect this? How many of the sermons and other writings of our best divines contain more or less of error, of foolish

1. Gilbert Burnet (1643–1715), Bishop of Salisbury, was the author of *A Modest and Free Conference Between a Conformist and a Nonconformist* (1669). He was a well-loved and successful clergyman who favored a comprehensive scheme that would leave room for nonconformists within the Church.

arguments, of false premises, of countervailing truths unknown or neglected, so that even the truth on the other side, being stated alone, becomes virtually no better than falsehood! How many passages of Scripture are misinterpreted in every translation, and in every commentary! But are we to refuse to co-operate with our neighbour because of these errors; or shall our own love of truth be impeached because of our union with him? Every one knows, that it is a question of degree and detail; but with a discipline watching over a man's practice, and with a sincere acknowledgment of the authority of the New Testament, although much and serious error may yet be maintained and propagated, yet it is better even to suffer this, than by insisting on too great an agreement, necessarily to reduce our numbers, and bring upon our country the fearful risk of losing the establishment of Christianity altogether.

Men are alarmed by the examples of Germany and Geneva. But what do they prove? The latter proves admirably the mischiefs of an over-strict creed; and ultra-Calvinism was likely to lead to ultra-Socinianism, with the change of times in other respects. But at this moment the mischief in Geneva consists in the enforcement of the exclusive principle, not in its abandonment: the Church is now exclusively Arian or Socinian, as it was once exclusively Calvinistic; and Trinitarian ministers are not allowed to teach to their congregations the great and peculiar doctrines of Christianity. And with regard to the Germans; had the Protestant Churches there retained ever so exclusive a body of articles, yet the strong tendency of the national character would probably have led to the same result: with no other difference than the addition of the evil of hypocrisy to that of ultra-rationalism. For let any man observe the German literature in other branches besides theology; and he will see the same spirit of restless inquiry every where pervading it. Nor is it confined in theology to the German Protestants; the Catholics are not exempt from it; only there, from the nature of their Church, it is displayed less sincerely, and therefore, I think, much more painfully. As an instance of this covert rationalism, I should name a book which has been translated into English, and has had some circulation in this country, "Hug's Introduction to the Study of the New Testament."

For us, on the other hand, critical and metaphysical questions have but small attractions; we have little to fear from the evil of indulging in them to excess. Unbelief, with us, is mostly the result of moral and political causes; to check which nothing would be so efficient as a well-organized and comprehensive National Church, acting unitedly and popularly, and with adequate means, upon the whole mass of our population. The widest conceivable difference of opinion between the ministers of such a Church would be a trifling evil compared with the good of their systematic union of action.

Lastly, if it be said that the changes proposed are too great,— that the scheme is visionary and impracticable; I answer, that the changes proposed are great, because the danger threatening us is enormous; and that although the scheme very probably will be impracticable, because men will persist in believing it to be so without trial, yet that it remains to be shown that it is impracticable in itself. But if the Reform of the Church be impracticable, its destruction unhappily is not so, and *that* its enemies know full well. It may be that a patchwork reform will be deemed safer, as assuredly it is easier; it may be, too, that after such a reform has been effected, and has left the great evils of the Church just where it found them, so that its final destruction shall be no less sure, the blame of its destruction will be laid by some on the principle of reform, and we shall be told that had no pretended improvements been attempted in it, it would have stood for ever. So it is, that no man is ever allowed to have died from the violence of his disease; but from the presumption of his physician, whose remedies, tried at the eleventh hour, he was too weak to bear. If I have seemed to speak confidently, it is not that I forget the usual course of human affairs; abuses and inefficient institutions obstinately retained, and then at last, blindly and furiously destroyed. Yet, when interests of such surpassing value are at stake, it may be allowable to hope even against hope; to suppress no plan which we conscientiously believe essential to our country's welfare, even though no other result should follow than that we should be ridiculed as theoretical, or condemned as presumptuous.

TIMOTHY EAST

# On Amusements[*]

NOBODY WHO HAS NOT BEEN THE VICTIM OF
a good deal of insipid evangelical moralizing and didacticism can
claim to be adequately acquainted with the nineteenth century.
Out of a staggering mass of tracts, journals, pamphlets, and books,
the single item included here will have to suffice. It represents a
fairly typical method by which the lessons of morality were inculcated, and will, perhaps, recall to readers some of the worst
passages in their favorite Victorian novels. The moralizing was
blatant, rigid, narrow-minded, but in wholesale quantities it was
effective: it changed the manners of a whole society.

This passage should suggest as well how closely connected
evangelical morality was to the growth of the middle class. This
is not to imply that evangelicalism (especially in its dissenting
forms) did not reach to the lower classes. But the religion of
Wesley, the reformism of Wilberforce, were not at all the products
of radicals intent on changing the social structure. Too often,

[*] From *The Evangelical Rambler*, 72 (1824), 1–12.

evangelicalism operated simply to reinforce the status quo with quotations from the Bible.

On the other hand, one ought not to underestimate the good effects of evangelicalism. *The Evangelical Rambler*, for example, like almost all other evangelical publications, made very loud and moral noises about slavery, and—in combination with liberals and radicals—the evangelicals were the power behind the abolition of slavery.

Thus life rolls away, with too many, in a course of "shapeless indolence." Its recreations constitute its chief business. Watering places—the sports of the field—cards! never-failing cards!—the assembly—the theatre,—all contribute their aid,—amusements are multiplied, and combined, and varied, "to fill up the void of a listless and languid life," and by the judicious use of these different resources, there is often a kind of sober, settled plan of domestic dissipation, in which, with all imaginable decency, year after year wears away in unprofitable vacancy.    *Wilberforce.*

"INDEED," said Miss Emma, "I think WE have been kept too much out of the world: and though I certainly respect the motive which has induced our parents to act as they have done, yet I may express my disapprobation of it. We are like so many state-prisoners, who have every indulgence except unfettered liberty, which I regard as

'Heaven's best gift to man.' "

Miss Orme.    "I have no doubt, my dear, but your parents act conscientiously in prohibiting the novel, and the cards; but you must know that religious people in general do so: though I have known some who have made a very splendid profession, who have not objected to play a game at whist after family prayer in the evening."

"Yes, and so have I. I was on a visit at Mr. R———'s some few months since, when the bagatelle-table and backgammon-board were brought out for our amusement; and I don't know when I have spent a more pleasant evening."

"And who is Mr. R———, my dear? Is he a pious man? or does he belong to the world?"

"He professes to be a pious man; and I should suppose he is one, for he has prayer in his family morning and evening."

"Had he family prayer, the evening you refer to, *before* or *after* these innocent games were introduced?"

"Oh, it was omitted that evening."

*Miss Holmes.* "And why, my dear, was it omitted? Was it not because he was ashamed to place the Bible on the same table with the bagatelle and gammonboard?—and because, after *enticing* others to a conformity to the customs of the world, he could not, in their presence, go and pray, that they might be *renewed in the spirit of their mind?* Do you recollect the remarks which you made on your return home?"

"They have escaped my recollection."

*Miss Holmes.* "After paying a compliment to his politeness, and extreme courteousness, you observed, that he only wanted one quality to finish his character."

"And did I say what that quality was?"

*Miss Holmes.* "Yes; you said, and said very justly, it was *consistency.*

"Oh! I recollect, that was the opinion I THEN entertained."

*Miss Holmes.* "And have you changed your opinion? Do you not think that religious people ought to abstain from the *appearance of evil,* instead of conforming to its customs?"

"Yes, most certainly. I remember a young satirical friend came and whispered in my ear, just as we began a fresh game,—'Make haste, as Mr. R——— has just rung the bell for family prayer.' This remark was heard by all our party; and I must confess that I was hurt by some of the observations which were made."

*Miss Orme.* "I don't know why the most religious people may not indulge themselves in all these amusements; but certainly our prejudices receive a violent shock when we know that they do."

*Miss Emma.* "I love consistency. If a family have prayer, they ought not, in my opinion, to spend the evenings in games which certainly have not a *religious* tendency; and if they have these games, they had better leave off prayer, as they cannot be prepared for it. I *knew* a young friend, the daughter of pious parents, who once had her mind very deeply impressed by a sense of the vanity of the world, and the importance of religion; but in consequence of paying a visit to the house of a very flaming professor, who in the temple was grave, and in the parlour gay—who alternately played and prayed—sang songs or psalms, as fancy dictated,—lost all her pious impressions, and from that time she became averse to religion; nor can she conquer her aversion."

*Miss Holmes.* "Example has a powerful influence, especially in doing moral injury: but the most pernicious and dangerous, is the example of a professor who acts in opposition to the obligations of his profession—of the man, who, while he professes to be a disciple of Jesus Christ, displays a spirit that is unconsonant with the sacredness of that character—and retains his religious habits, even while he conforms himself to the world."

*Miss Orme.* "Well, my dear, no one will impeach your consistency; for you are, without exception, one of the most decidedly religious I ever knew."

*Miss Emma.* "Yes; my sister goes rather too far; and I tell her sometimes, that she is in danger of becoming a Pharisee. She sees, or thinks she sees, a dangerous moral tendency in almost every amusement: and such is the influence she possesses over the fears of our parents, that they are kept in a state of constant terror, lest I should read a novel, or dance a minuet."

"And is it possible, my dear Miss Holmes, that either you, or your parents can object to dancing? An exercise so conducive to health —so calculated to give elegance to the form, to the walk, and to the action—an accomplishment of so much importance, that no female can be fit to move in genteel society who has not attained it. I believe you learnt at school, my dear Emma; did you not?"

"Yes; but now I am not permitted to go into a party, which I consider very mortifying. My parents gave their consent for me to learn; and now I have learnt, and am fond of the amusement, they will not suffer me to practise."

*Miss Holmes.* "They permitted you to learn, that you might derive from it those personal accomplishments which your friend Miss Orme has so well described; but as they are aware of its dangerous moral tendency, they very properly object to your going into parties."

"Then, ought they not to have refused letting me learn to dance, if they intended to deny me the pleasure of it?* This is like a father

---

* The author knows a lady, who, when young, requested her pious father to permit her to learn to dance. "No, my child," he replied, "I cannot consent to comply with a request which may subject me to your censures at some future period." "No, father, I will never censure you for complying with my request." "Nor can I consent to give you an opportunity. If you learn, I have no doubt but you will excel; and when you leave school, you may then want to go into company to exhibit your skill. If I then object to let you, as I most likely should, you would very naturally reply,—Why, father, did you permit me to learn, if I am not permitted to practise?" This reply con-

teaching his son the art of engraving, and then taking away his tools lest he should be hung for coining."

*Miss Holmes.* "You may dance for the purposes for which you were permitted to learn; but I appeal to your good sense, if it be not an act of kindness on the part of your parents, in withholding their consent from your visiting the ball-room, when they apprehend you will sustain some moral injury."

*Miss Orme.* "But you know, Miss Holmes, that the chief gratification which we derive from any attainment or accomplishment, is the opportunity of displaying it. What pleasure would there be in learning to paint, unless we had the liberty of exhibiting our drawings?—or who would submit to the labour of learning the notes of the gamut, if, after she has succeeded, she is to be prohibited from playing?"

*Miss Holmes.* "But are you not aware, that the love of display is one of those passions which ought to be suppressed rather than cherished, especially in a female? Are we not often censured by the other sex for our vanity? and shall we continue to sanction the correctness of such charges by fostering the passion? I admit, that we ought to attain those accomplishments which the present improved state of society demands; but to attain them for the mere sake of display, is no less destructive of our influence over the other sex, than injurious to the moral tone of our mind."

*Miss Orme.* "I am sure the gentlemen admire a lady who can sing well—and play well—and dance well—and move with grace as she enters, or leaves a room."

*Miss Holmes.* "Yes, my dear; but if she have no higher accomplishments, though she may be admired, she will not be respected —she may have her name mentioned with eclât in the circles of fashion, but she will not be held in esteem among the wise and the good—and she may do as a companion for the evening dance, but no man of sense will think of her as a companion for life."

*Miss Orme.* "But do you wish the assembly-rooms deserted? If

---

vinced her that her father acted wisely, though he opposed her inclination: and though she did learn, yet, not having his consent, she never presumed to expose herself to the dangers of the assembly-room; as she well knew, that she could not do it without inflicting a wound on that paternal breast which glowed with the most pure and tender affection for her. She is now become a parent—has often mentioned this occurrence as having had a powerful moral influence over her mind in the days of her juvenile vanity—and has incorporated this maxim in her system of domestic economy,—Never to comply with a request which may subject her to any future reflections from her children.

so, I fear you will never have your wishes realized. But to come to the point,—What are the evils which you think result from such scenes of amusement?"

*Miss Holmes.* "I do not expect to see such places deserted, as there are too many temptations presented to each sex within the assembly-room to make them unpopular in this age of degeneracy; but they are productive of so many evils, that I consider them essentially injurious to the morals of society. There is the expence which they incur, and the long train of evils which often follow. What costly dresses! what a profusion of useless ornaments must be purchased! beside the incidental items of expence, in going, and returning, and paying for the admission ticket. If the whole expence of one evening's gratification were accurately calculated, it would astonish us. And what is the consequence of this? The bills of tradesmen are often left undischarged—the claims of benevolence are rejected—and a habit of useless extravagance is formed, which extends its destructive influence to other branches of domestic expenditure. But I have a still more serious objection to urge against such scenes of amusement;—the perilous risk which a female often runs. She goes, clad in a light attire— moves about in a warm room—and then suddenly exposes herself, without any adequate increase of cloathing, to a cold and damp atmosphere; by which she often sacrifices her health, and sometimes her life."*

*Miss Orme.* "But you know that this objection will apply with equal force against our attending a crowded place of worship."

*Miss Holmes.* "Not with equal force; my dear; because in a place of worship we remain *still* during the time of service, and usually go in *warmer*, not to say *more decent attire.*

"The moral influence which such public amusements have over the mind, is another very powerful objection against them. By your permission I will read a paragraph from a good writer, who expresses himself in very correct and forcible language.

" 'The objects which, during the season of youth, most easily excite vanity and envy in the female breast, are those which are presented in the ball-room. This is deemed the stage for displaying the attractions by the possession of which a young woman is apt to be most elated; and they are here displayed under circumstances most calculated to call forth the triumph and the animosities of personal com-

---

* The author refers the attention of his readers to No. 42 of this series, which records one of the several instances which have fallen under his notice within the last few years, and which have been owing to the cause which is here stated.

petition. This triumph, and these animosities betray themselves occasionally to the least discerning eye. But were the recesses of the heart laid open, how often would the sight of a stranger, of an acquaintance, even of a friend, superior for the evening in the attractions of dress, or enjoying the supposed advantage of having secured a wealthier, a more lively, a more graceful, or a more fashionable partner, be found to excite feelings of disgust, and of aversion, not always stopping short of malevolence! How often would the passions be seen inflamed, and every nerve agitated, by a thirst for precedence! and invention be observed, labouring to mortify a rival by the affectation of indifference or of contempt!' "

*Miss Orme.* "But do you not think it possible for a female to attend a ball without having her breast inflated with vanity, or surcharged with envy?"

*Miss Holmes.* "I certainly admit that it is possible, but not probable. If she excel others in the richness or the elegance of her dress, or if she receive any peculiar marks of attention from the leading fashionables of the scene, will she not feel the flush of vain glory?—And if others excel her, or receive higher honours, will she not retire from the company stung with envy?—And can either of these passions be excited without producing some demoralizing effect? If she become vain of the ornaments which decorate her person, she will be under a strong temptation to neglect the improvement of her mind; and while this passion enslaves and governs her, the more amiable and lovely tempers will be neglected.—And if she becomes envious of the superior attainments or honours of others, she will be restless—mortified—consume her time, and expend her money, in making useless efforts to equal or surpass them, and may be induced to invent or to circulate tales of calumny to their injury."

*Miss Orme.* "But you do not mean to say that these effects are invariably produced?"

*Miss Holmes.* "Not invariably; because there are some females who visit these places as a passing compliment to the fashion of the age, who look down with comparative contempt on such exhibitions of human folly. They attend as spectators* of the scene, rather than

---

* The author has known some professors of evangelical religion who have occasionally frequented these scenes of amusement; and though he would not condemn them as insincere in their religious profession, yet he cannot conceive how they can approve of their own conduct. If they go occasionally, others feel at liberty to go habitually: and though they may go, and retire without sustaining any material injury to their principles, yet they know not how much injury their example may do to others, and especially their own children.

as actors—to oblige a friend, rather than gratify themselves; and when the curtain drops, having answered the design of their visit, they retire uninjured, because they felt no desire to be seen or heard—alike indifferent to the charm of superior or inferior appearances."

*Miss Orme.* "You have stated the evils which you think generally result from such public amusements, but you have made no allusion to the advantages which attend them; amongst which I reckon, the introduction which they give to the best of society. You know that we are confined within the precincts of home—our duties and pursuits are of the more retired order; and though we may take our evening walks, and occasionally go to Margate, or Cheltenham, or some other fashionable resort, yet, if it were not for these public amusements, we should have no opportunity of being introduced to the company of the other sex. Here we are brought together; and you know, my dear, that the most important consequences often follow."

*Miss Holmes.* "Very true; but these important consequences are not always the most interesting. The writer to whom I have previously referred has made some good remarks on this subject, which, by your permission, I will read to you.

" 'An evil of great moment, which is too frequently known to occur at the places of amusement now under notice, is, the introducduction of women to undesirable and improper acquaintance among the other sex; undesirable and improper, as I would now be understood to mean, in a moral point of view. Men of this description commonly abound at all scenes of public resort and entertainment; and are not seldom distinguished by fortune and birth—gay and conciliating manners—and every qualification which is needful to procure a favourable reception in polite company. Hence, when they propose themselves as partners in an assembly-room, a lady does not always find it easy, according to the rules of decorum, to decline the offer; and is sometimes enticed, by their external appearance, and by having seen other ladies ambitious of dancing with them, into a reprehensible inclination not to decline it.

" 'Women, in various occurrences of life, are betrayed, by a dread of appearing ungenteelly bashful, and by a desire of rendering themselves agreeable, into an indiscreet freedom of manners and conversation with men of whom they know perhaps but little; and still more frequently, into a greater degree of freedom with those of whom they have more knowledge, than can fitly be indulged, except towards persons with whom they are connected by particular ties. The temptation is in no place more powerful than in a ball-room. Let not indiscriminate familiarity be shewn towards all partners, nor injudicious familiarity towards any. To reject every boisterous and unbecoming mode of dancing, and to observe, in every point, the strictest modesty in attire, are cautions on which, in addressing women of delicacy, it is surely needless to insist.' "

*Miss Orme.* "Well, I assure you, my dear Miss Holmes, I think both you, and the gentleman whose sentiments you have just quoted, overrate the dangers which we are exposed to by attending such scenes of amusement; for I have never known one friend injured by them, nor have I ever heard of such a thing."

*Miss Holmes.* "You forget Miss M———."*

*Miss Orme.* "I beg pardon, I do. Ah! that was a tragical event."

*Miss Holmes.* "And how many tragical events have risen out of these scenes of amusement! You have read, I have no doubt, the following account of one which befel a very holy man. *When Herod's birthday was kept, the daughter of Herodias danced before them, and pleased Herod. Whereupon he promised with an oath to give her whatsoever she would ask. And she, being before instructed of her mother, said, Give me here John Baptist's head in a charger. And the king was sorry: nevertheless, for the oath's sake, and them which sat with him at meat, he commanded it to be given her. And he sent,*

---

* Miss M——— was a young lady of rare accomplishments—the only child of a pious and affectionate mother. When she left school she enlarged the circle of her acquaintance—began to dress in the highest style of fashion—and after many intreaties, she obtained the consent of her Mamma to go once to the assembly-room, just to see the parties. She was dressed most elegantly; and having a graceful form, and a fine open countenance, glowing with health, she excited considerable attention, which was no less gratifying than it was unexpected. One gentleman, who had been very polite during the evening, and who was her superior in rank, solicited the honour of conducting her home, which was granted. Having ascertained the usual time and place of her evening walk, he met her—made her an offer, which she accepted; when, having secured her affections, he accomplished her ruin, and left her. This broke her mother's heart, and eventually broke her own; and the parent and the daughter were buried in the same grave at the distance of about six months from each other's funeral, both deploring, when too late, the danger resulting from the assembly-room. Nor is this an uncommon instance. At these places the spirits of evil resort,—availing themselves of the freedom of intercourse which is tolerated;—and having marked their victim, they proceed, with all the cunning and duplicity of the *author of all evil*, to accomplish their destructive purpose: and if parents wish to preserve the honour of their children uncontaminated, or females who are grown to years of discretion wish to avoid the snares in which others have been taken, they ought to shun the resorts of the licentious and impure; for in this age of degeneracy no one can be safe in their society.

and beheaded John in the prison. And his head was brought in a charger, and given to the damsel: and she brought it to her mother. How this damsel could so far subdue the common feelings of human nature, and still more the natural tenderness of her own sex, as not only to endure so disgusting a spectacle, but even to carry the bleeding trophy in triumph to her mother, is not easy to imagine; but it shews that a life of fashionable gaiety and dissipation not only prevents the growth of the more amiable and useful virtues, but sometimes calls into action those feelings and passions which lead to rapine and murder."

The late excellent Bishop Horne closes his life of St. John in such a forcible and beautiful manner, that the author does not conceive it necessary to offer any apology to his readers for its insertion on the present occasion.

"The Baptist's fate being determined, immediately the king sent an executioner, and commanded his head to be brought: and he went, and beheaded him in the prison. This deed of darkness must have been done in the season proper for it,—the middle of the night; and St. John was probably awakened, to receive his sentence, out of that sleep which truth and innocence can secure to their possessor in any situation. The generality of mankind have reason enough to deprecate a sudden death, lest it should surprize them in one of their many unguarded hours. But to St. John no hour could be such. He had finished the work which God had given him to do. He had kept the faith, and preserved a conscience void of offence. He had done his duty, and waited daily and hourly, we may be sure, for his departure. He was now, therefore, called off from his station with honour, to quit the well-fought field for the palace of the Great King—to refresh himself, after the dust, and toil, and heat of the day, by bathing in the fountain of life and immortality—to exchange his blood-stained armour for a robe of glory—and to have his temporary labours rewarded with eternal rest—to sit down with Abraham, and Isaac, and Jacob, in the kingdom of God—and as the friend of the Bridegroom, to enter into the joy of his Lord. From the darkness and confinement of a prison, he passed to the liberty and light of heaven; and while malice was gratified with a sight of his head, and his body was carried by a few friends in silence to the grave, his immortal spirit repaired to a court, where no Herod desires to have his brother's wife—where no Herodias thirsts after the blood of a prophet—where he who hath laboured with sincerity and diligence in the work of reformation is sure to be well received—where holiness, zeal, and constancy are crowned, and receive palms from the Son of God, whom they confessed in the world.

> So sinks the day-star in the ocean bed,
> And yet anon uprears his drooping head,
> And tricks his beams, and with new spangled ore,
> Flames in the forehead of the morning sky—
> He hears the unexpressive nuptial song
> In the blest kingdoms meek of joy and love.
> There entertain him all the saints above,
> In solemn troops, and sweet societies;
> That sing, and singing in their glory move,
> And wipe the tears for ever from his eyes.    MILTON.

CHARLES CHRISTIAN HENNELL

# An Inquiry
# Concerning the
# Origins of
# Christianity*

CHARLES CHRISTIAN HENNELL (1809–50) WAS
a member of a deeply religious Unitarian family, given strongly to
independence of thought. One of his sisters married Charles Bray,
a businessman and rigorously materialistic metaphysician. On his
own, with no knowledge of German critics of the Bible, Hennell
began investigating the scriptures to find evidence to support his
sister and her family against Bray's views.

Painfully, with rigorous honesty, Hennell began to discover
that the Bible is full of self-contradictions; that the Gospels were

* From C. C. Hennell, An Inquiry Concerning the Origins of Christianity, First Edition (London: John Chapman, 1838), pp. 369–79.

written long after the event; that they elaborate fancifully on a few accepted facts; that, in fact, the Bible cannot be accepted as an authority against unbelievers and that Christ, though a great man, was only a man. Hennell fought his own discoveries, but was forced to yield to them. In 1835 in Germany, David Friedrich Strauss, utilizing the research of many scriptural critics, produced his *Das Leben Jesu*, a monumental study of the New Testament that reached many of the conclusions Hennell was to draw later. Strauss, who achieved a worldwide reputation, was deeply impressed by Hennell's work when he saw it. Both men believed that, despite their discoveries, the "essence" of Christianity remained valid.

For Hennell, this belief was a necessity. The section of his work reproduced here demonstrates the honesty and clarity of the style, and the deepness of the devotion that produced so disrupting a work. Many Victorians, including George Eliot (who knew Hennell and translated Strauss), were to follow him into this essence of Christianity—a religion that has everything of Christianity but the God.

## CONCLUDING REFLECTIONS

Whatever be the spirit with which the four Gospels be approached, it is impossible to rise from the attentive perusal of them without a strong reverence for Jesus Christ. Even the disposition to cavil and ridicule is forced to retire before the majestic simplicity of the prophet of Nazareth. Unlike Moses or Mahomet, he owes no part of the lustre which surrounds him to his acquisition of temporal power; his is the ascendancy which mankind, in proportion to their mental advancement, are least disposed to resist—that of moral and intellectual greatness. Besides, his cruel fate engages men's affections on his behalf, and gives him an additional hold upon their allegiance. A noble-minded reformer and sage, martyred by crafty priests and brutal soldiers, is a spectacle which forces men to gaze in pity and admiration. The precepts from such a source come with an authority which no human laws could give; and Jesus is more powerful on the cross of Calvary than he would have been on the throne of Israel.

The virtue, wisdom, and sufferings of Jesus, then, will secure to him a powerful influence over men so long as they continue to be moral, intellectual, and sympathizing beings. And as the tendency of human improvement is towards the progressive increase of these qualities, it may be presumed that the empire of Christianity, considered simply as the influence of the life, character, and doctrine of Christ over the human mind, will never cease.

The most fastidious scepticism is forced to admit the truth of the facts, which such a view of Christianity requires. For no one who regards historical evidence will deny that such a person was put to death in Judea, and that he gave rise to a new system of religion. The four Gospels on these points are strengthened by many other testimonies, agree with each other, and contain relations conformable to the order of nature. Moreover, the excellence of the preceptive parts of the Gospels carries with it its own evidence in all ages.

But when a higher office is claimed for Christ, that of a messenger accredited from God by a supernatural birth, miraculous works, a resurrection, and an ascension, we may reasonably expect equal strength of evidence. But how stands the case? The four Gospels on these points are not confirmed by testimony out of the church, disagree with each other, and contain relations contrary to the order of things. The evidence on these points is reduced to the authority of these narratives themselves. In them, at least, the most candid mind may require strong proofs of authenticity and veracity; but again, what is the case? They are anonymous productions; their authorship is far from certain; they were written from forty to seventy years after the events which they profess to record; the writers do not explain how they came by their information; two of them appear to have copied from the first; all the four contain notable discrepancies and manifest contradictions; they contain statements at variance with histories of acknowledged authority; some of them relate wonders which even many Christians are obliged to reject as fabulous; and in general they present no character by which we can distinguish their tales of miracles from the fictions which every church has found some supporters ready to vouch for on its behalf.

In these books, and by the propagators of Christianity, the miraculous part of Christ's history is presented to us not as an indifferent fact, but as one which is to influence our whole life and conduct: the belief or non-belief of it is even to decide our condition in another world: we are called upon to count all things as loss for the sake of Christ: "He that believeth in his heart that God hath raised him from the dead shall be saved;" "He that believeth not shall be damned." One would have expected that the clearness of the evidence would have been in proportion to the necessity for belief, and that a fact of which the recognition was requisite to the salvation or improvement of mankind in after ages, would have been attested in such a manner as to leave no doubt of it in any reasonable mind. Mark, or the person who has finished his Gospel for him, would have done more to promote belief, if, instead of threatening damnation on the want of it, he had explained the apparent contradictions between his account and Matthew's;—how it was that the latter sends the eleven disciples into Galilee, whilst the others seem to represent them as remaining at Jerusalem; why Matthew omitted all notice of the ascension; where and when Jesus was seen by the five hundred brethren mentioned by Paul; and especially how he and his fellow evangelists obtained their information. But the fact is, that the accounts of Christ's resurrection are in so imperfect and slovenly a state, that the evidence afforded by them would be hardly deemed sufficient to establish an ordinary fact of any importance in a court of judicature. The accounts of the crucifixion are very circumstantial, and agree in the main so well, that we should have no difficulty in admitting this as a fact, even if it were not confirmed by Tacitus, Suetonius, and the Jews. But when the writers come to the account of the resurrection, on which, from its not being confirmed by heathen or Jewish testimonies, from its deviation from the laws of nature, and from the great importance attached to the belief of it, we should have looked, from their hands at least, for the fullest clearest, and most accordant evidence,—here we find the story replete with confusion, contradiction, and chasms, and even to be made up apparently of fragments of different dates.

If the resurrection of Christ were necessary, as is pretended, to account for the rest of his history, and the origin of Christianity, the attempts made to strain out a consistent account of it from the materials before us, by inventing supplementary facts *ad libitum*, might deserve some attention. But there is in reality no such necessity. The order of nature, the combination of human feelings and motives at the particular juncture in question, have been shown to be enough to account for the life and death of Jesus, and the proceedings of his followers. And whatever be our disposition to show deference towards Matthew, Mark, Luke, and John, or the persons writing under their names, the inquirers for truth are obliged to ask, Who are these that we should believe them in contradiction to the known order of nature, and receive from them, as indubitable truth, stories which, coming from other mouths, we should reject at once as palpable fiction? Where are the proofs of their caution, judgment, and veracity? How are we assured that they could neither be misled, nor attempt to mislead? They vouch for the resurrection of Christ; but who shall vouch for them, and certify that they were so far different from the rest of men as to be void of credulity, and incapable of mistake or falsehood? What witness is there to prove that they were so insensible to common human motives, as to be incapable of gratifying their love of the marvellous, and of serving their own cause, and that of their church, by either adopting or inventing "idle tales?"

That the resurrection of Jesus was intended as a pledge to mankind of a general resurrection, is a delightful idea. But the only safe basis for such a belief is historical evidence. If this fail to establish the fact, the agreeable nature of the belief is so far from proving it, that it rather furnishes an explanation of the general prevalence of the belief in the face of insufficient evidence.

It is not pretended that the foregoing pages prove the absolute impossibility of Christ's miracles and resurrection. If we be so determined, we may still indulge in the belief of them, by overlooking difficulties, inventing hypotheses, and concluding that the whole is a trial of our faith. But if the reasoner will still hold the reality of these miracles, to what scheme must he have recourse? That God has caused a deviation from the course of nature for the instruction of mankind, and has left the account of it to be conveyed to them by means which, on the closest examination, occasion it to bear a strong resemblance to human fictions; a supposition so monstrous and perplexing, that, notwithstanding the value of the supposed lesson, our minds turn at last from this mode of teaching in weariness, and resolve to be contented to learn where we are sure, at least, that the lessons proceed from God himself—and that is in nature.

The miraculous birth, works, resurrection, and ascension of Christ, being thus successively surrendered, to be classed amongst the fables of an obscure age, what remains of Christianity? and what is there in the life and doctrine of Jesus that they should still claim the attention and respect of mankind in remote ages? This: Christianity forms a striking passage in the history of human nature, and appears as one of the most prominent of the means employed in its improvement. It no longer boasts of a special divine origin, but shares in that which the Theist attributes to the world and the whole order of its events. It has presented to the world a system of moral excellence; it has led forth the principles of humanity and benevolence from the recesses of the schools and groves, and compelled them to take an active part in the affairs of life. It has consolidated the moral and religious sentiments into a more definite and influential form than had before existed, and thereby constituted an engine which has worked powerfully towards humanizing and civilizing the world.

Moreover, Christianity has given currency to the sublime doctrines of man's relationship to the Deity, and of a future state. The former was a leading feature of Judaism, and the latter of Platonism. Christianity has invested them with the authority of established principles, and thereby contributed much to the moral elevation of mankind.

It is impossible to disguise the momentous consequence of the rejection of the divine origin of Christianity—that a future state is thereby rendered a matter of speculation, instead of certainty. If Jesus was not seen after he was risen, we no longer see immortality brought to light; the veil which nature has left before this mysterious subject, still remains undrawn; and, like the Jews, and all heathen nations, we are compelled to rest satisfied with the conjectures to which reason alone can attain. With respect to one of the subjects most interesting to man, we return into the position in which the whole race stood for four thousand years, and in which a great part has remained ever since.

The withdrawal of a proof on which we had relied is not, however, equivalent to a disproof. The arguments of natural reason, on behalf of a future state, still remain; and when it is recognized that these are all which the order of things allows of, the mind which feels the want of this doctrine may learn to dwell upon them with increased interest, and to be content with that degree of evidence on this point which has been compatible with the happy existence of many generations of men, and with the tranquility of many virtuous and reflecting minds in all ages. Christianity has added, at least, so much light to the subject, that it has shown, on a large scale, the effect which the belief of this doctrine has upon the character; and if it be allowed that this effect is the strengthening and refinement of virtue, there arises an additional and strong presumption of the truth of the doctrine.

Yet if all the efforts of reason should end in demonstrating the mere probability of a future state, what must be our conclusion? That certainty on this point is not at present necessary, nor even desirable for men; and that the objects of their existence in this world are best answered by their having an obscure rather than a clear view of another. Whilst it was thought that Jesus had brought the guarantee of heaven for man's immortality, we persuaded ourselves that this was necessary to men's improvement and happiness. We were mistaken; no such guarantee has been given; it is wise still to acquiesce, and to conclude that happiness and improvement are best promoted by our present ignorance.

It is undeniable that, to reflecting and religious minds, the removal of the authority of revelation does at first seem to leave a blank on the subjects of the human condition and destiny which no reasoning can fill up. Those who had been accustomed to look to the New Testament as their only light, see nothing but confusion when it is taken away, and are tempted to look at human existence as a waste, of which both the beginning and the end are lost in darkness. It was natural, however, that in their anxiety to appreciate the supposed revelation, men should do injustice to the world and nature. When they are compelled to part with the former, these gradually resume their claims, and remind them that their position here, regarded for itself alone, is replete with interest and enjoyment. The return of first one object of pleasing thought and then another, forces upon them the conviction of the high privilege of existence; and the withdrawal into obscure remoteness of the future eternal life, may even leave them the more free to appreciate the advantages of their present more limited but more accessible sphere. The eye which fails to distinguish heaven falls contentedly into the more easy contemplation of the beauties of earth. A thicker veil being thrown before the incomprehensible joys of a future state, the mind returns to count over more earnestly the blessings within its immediate reach, and is surprised at the extent of its almost unheeded riches. It perceives that to *live* is gain. In accustomed occupations, or favourite pursuits; in its relationships and intercourse with mankind; in the perpetual novelty arising from the vicissitudes of national or individual life; in the free admission either to behold or take part in the great drama of the world; or in the tranquil cultivation of its powers, or exercise of its affections —it recognizes abundant and evervarying stores of enjoyment, requiring only its own energy to be immediately worked out. The voice of mankind, as well as of books, still captivates the attention; the hill and the river still delight the eye; solitude soothes, and society interests; and the mind, acquiring a keener perception of happiness from its review, is startled into the admission, that the heaven which it looked forward to in the remote distance is already close at hand.

But this is the language of prosperity. Christianity is preeminently the religion of adversity; and what can compensate the afflicted for the loss of the assurance of those mansions where Jesus is preparing a place for them? Even here it may, perhaps, be recognized, that the compensation supplied by nature and the mind's own resources had not been sufficiently estimated. The list of the pleasures arising out of adversity, and of which this alone can awaken the perception, is large enough to induce us to suspend the wish that there should be no gloomy side to the human condition. The consciousness of fortitude developed by emergencies, and of refinement of character produced by reverses; increased opportunities for the interchange of the kindly sympathies; and the enlargement of views proceeding from an acquaintance with the most diversified aspects of life;—afford pleasures felt to be so substantial, that few men probably, on calm consideration, would consent to have the dark pages of their history replaced by the most brilliant ones.

Yet it must be owned that there are states in which all such reasonings are felt to be insipid, and in which the human mind feels a deeper want,—that of Christianity, or of something equivalent to it. And why may not such a state itself bring with it the consoling convictions which itself requires, and be regarded as nature's silent but powerful argument, which she has framed in such a manner that its force shall only be understood in proportion as the want of it is felt? The extreme evils to which individuals are exposed, during the slow progress of the race towards perfection, form too conspicuous a feature in the history of man to be overlooked in our review of the final causes of his condition. Why should we not regard these evils, not as unavoidable or permitted imperfections, but as ordained for a direct and adequate object, to convey a solemn lesson, and to complete the evidence—imperfect if prosperity were the invariable human condition—for an existence beyond the grave? Prosperity is satisfied with the glaring surface of this world's picture, and neglects futurity: adversity leads aside to the contemplation of a more hidden scene, and discloses the necessity and value of a future state. Christianity itself proceeded from a nation in deep adversity; out of the distresses of Israel issued the cry of immortality. May we not regard all irremediable earthly afflictions as intended to suggest Christianity to each sufferer, and to whisper, that there must be a Father in heaven, and mansions of the blessed?

It has not unfrequently happened, that the untutored feelings of mankind have anticipated the results of philosophic investigation. Nature has spoken first; reasoning and science have followed slowly with a confirmation of her voice. Men had not been long upon the earth before the ideas of a great Father of the universe, and of a region of spirits, began to develop themselves. In this, as in every case which exhibits the progress of truth, rational doctrines have had to force their way through a primeval chaos of dark and mis-shapen notions; and Christianity exhibits the shape to which the workings of the human kind had brought these ideas at a certain stage of the world's progress. The extensive attainments of science in later ages have tended to confirm the former great doctrine; but hitherto philosophical research has not fallen upon the avenues which lead to the

development of the latter. Science and philosophy are, however, yet in
their infancy, and especially as regards their application to subjects
supposed to be connected with morality and religion. The belief that
Revelation has assumed these subjects as her own peculiar ground, has
hitherto impeded the growth of free inquiry upon them amongst
nations most competent to the task.* Released from this restraint, and
having unbounded scope to traverse the creation in search of evidence,
mankind may reach points in moral discovery which at present would
be at once pronounced visionary. The achievements of mechanical and
chemical science may be equalled or outdone by those of moral and
intellectual research; and a clearer confession be forced out of nature
concerning the character of the Creator, and the ultimate destination
of man. In the mean time may it not be, that the feelings of the human
heart have anticipated the laborious operations of the intellect, and
that Christianity has taken the advance of philosophy in ministering
to the deepest wants of man?

Let not, then, the mind which is compelled to renounce its belief
in miraculous revelations deem itself bound to throw aside, at the
same time, all its most cherished associations. Its generous emotions
and high contemplations may still find an occasion for exercise in the
review of the interesting incidents which have for ever consecrated the
plains of Palestine; but it may also find pleasure in the thought that,
for this exercise, no single spot of earth, and no one page of its

* Whenever any great revolutions in opinion have been in progress, it
has appeared to many that the ties of morality were being unloosed, and that
the mental world was falling into the darkest confusion. Such was the idea
of the heathens whilst Christianity was throwing down their venerable ancient
deities. Eunapius, a heathen sophist, who wrote in the time of the emperor
Theodosius I., giving an account of an Egyptian philosopher named Antoninus,
says, "He foretold to all his disciples that, after his death, there would be no
temples, but that the magnificent and sacred temple of Serapis would be laid
in ruinous heaps, and that fabulous confusion and unformed darkness would
tyrannize over the best parts of the earth. All which things time has brought
to pass."

We see at present the incipient upheavings of another of these revolutions—the subversion of the belief in miraculous revelations, and the gradual
advance of a system of natural religion, of which we cannot yet predict the
whole creed, but of which we may already perceive two essential features, the
recognition of a God, and that of an inherent moral nature in man. As the
clearing away of the antiquated piles of the old law made way for the simpler
structure of faith in Christ, so will the release from the exclusive authority
of written precept enable men to hear more distinctly the voice of the moral
nature within them. Reformed Judaism will be succeeded by reformed Christianity, and each change appear the transition to a more perfect law of
liberty.

history, furnishes the exclusive theme. Whatever dimness may gather from the lapse of time and the obscurity of records about the events of a distant age, these capabilities of the mind itself remain, and always will remain, in full freshness and beauty. Other Jersualems will excite the glow of patriotism, other Bethanies exhibit the affections of home, and other minds of benevolence and energy seek to hasten the approach of the kingdom of man's perfection. Nor can scriptures ever be wanting—the scriptures of the physical and of the moral world— the book of the universe. Here the page is open, and the language intelligible to all men; no transcribers have been able to interpolate or erase its texts; it stands before us in the same genuineness as when first written; the simplest understanding can enter with delight into criticism upon it; the volume does not close, leaving us to thirst for more, but another and another epistle still meets the inquisitive eye, each signed with the author's own hand, and bearing undoubted characters of divine inspiration. Unable at present to comprehend the whole, we can still feel the privilege of looking into it at pleasure, of knowing a part, and attempting the opening of further leaves. And if, after its highest efforts, the mind be compelled to sink down, acknowledging its inability, in some parts, to satisfy itself with any clear conclusion, it may remain serene at least, persuaded that God will not cause any soul to fare the worse for not knowing what he has given it no means to know. Enough is understood to enable us to see, in the Universe itself, a Son which tells us of a Father, and in all the natural beauty and moral excellence which meet us in the world an everpresent Logos, which reveals the grace and truth of its invisible source. Enough is understood to convince us that, to have a place on this beautiful planet, on almost any terms, is an unspeakable privilege; that virtue produces the highest happiness, whether for this or another world; and that there does exist an encircling mysterious Intelligence, which, as it appears to manifest its energy in arrangements for the general welfare of the creation, must ensure a provision for all the real interests of man. From all our occasional excursions into the abysses of the unseen world, and from all our efforts to reach upwards to the hidden things of God, both reason and piety bid us return tranquilly to our accustomed corner of earth, to use and enjoy fully our present lot, and to repose implicitly upon the higher wisdom in whose disposal we stand, whilst indulging the thought that a time is appointed when the cravings of the heart and of the intellect will be satisfied, and the enigma of our own and the world's existence be solved.

V

# ART AND LITERATURE

. . . as the sciences of morals and of mind advance towards perfection, as they become more enlarged and comprehensive in their views, as reason gains the ascendancy in them over imagination and feeling, poetry can no longer accompany them in their progress, but drops into the background, and leaves them to advance alone.

THOMAS LOVE PEACOCK,
*The Four Ages of Poetry*

# A. WELBY PUGIN

# Contrasts<sup>*</sup>

OR, A PARALLEL BETWEEN THE
NOBLE EDIFICES OF THE XIVTH
AND XVTH CENTURIES, AND
SIMILAR BUILDINGS OF THE
PRESENT DAY

A. W. N. PUGIN (1812–52) WAS ANOTHER EX-
traordinarily energetic and productive figure among those many
who seemed to have anticipated the Victorian Gospel of Work.
Pugin was the son of an architect and became fascinated with the
Gothic architecture of the late Middle Ages. This interest led
him to the religion which gave birth to the most magnificent
examples of Gothic structures, and in 1833 he became a member
of the Catholic Church. Pugin's actual work as an architect is not,
on the whole, as successful as his statements about it. *Contrasts*,
in particular, which became an extremely influential book, is mar-

* Printed for the Author and Published by Him at St. Marie's Grange,
near Salisbury, Wiltshire (1836).

velously readable. The first edition of 1836 is rather hotheaded, and sounds much like a manifesto, while the second edition (1841) is saner and more extensive. The central argument is the same in both editions. It is difficult not to be charmed by Pugin's enthusiasm and moved by the force of his some of his arguments (certainly those about the inadequacies of modern architecture).

The most delightful thing about both editions of *Contrasts* is the illustration. Supposedly objective illustrations of the difference between medieval buildings and their modern counterparts, the drawings are in fact powerful propaganda for the moral, spiritual, and aesthetic superiority of the medieval Catholic to the modern Protestant world.

Pugin is thus important as being among the first and the most influential to encourage renewed interest in things medieval. Victorian literature from Carlyle to Morris, as well as Victorian painting and architecture, demonstrates a fascination with the medieval, and this interest, as in Pugin's case, was rarely confined to the aesthetic. The Middle Ages—with its formal, hierarchical, ordered social structure; its concern for the spiritual condition of men; its close fusion of the spiritual with the secular—became a model against which to contrast the various defects of a world from which all stable values were, apparently, disappearing and in which order was giving place to the confusions of democracy.

Although Pugin is better with his pencil than with his pen, the following excerpt will give some idea of his moral and aesthetic energy, and of the dominant ideas which lay behind all of his work.

<br>

### ON THE FEELINGS WHICH
### PRODUCED THE GREAT EDIFICES
### OF THE MIDDLE AGES

On comparing the Architectural Works of the present Century with those of the Middle Ages, the wonderful superiority of the latter must strike every attentive observer; and the mind is naturally led to reflect on the causes which have wrought this mighty change, and to endeavour to trace the fall of Architectural taste, from the period of its first decline in this country to the present day; and this will form the subject of the following pages.

It will be readily admitted that the great test of Architectural beauty is the fitness of the design to the purpose for which it is intended, and that the style of a building should so correspond with its use that the spectator may at once perceive the purpose for which it was erected.

Acting on this principle, different nations have given birth to so many various styles of Architecture, each suited to their climate, customs, and religion; and as it is among edifices of this latter class that we look for the most splendid and lasting monuments, there can be but little doubt that the religious ideas and ceremonies of these different people had by far the greatest influence in the formation of their various styles of Architecture.

The more closely we compare the temples of the Pagan nations with their religious rites and mythologies, the more shall we be satisfied with the truth of this assertion.

But who can regard those stupendous Ecclesiastical Edifices of the Middle Ages (the more special objects of this work), without feeling this observation in its full force? Here every portion of the sacred fabric bespeaks its origin; the very plan of the edifice is the emblem of human redemption—each portion is destined for the performance of some solemn rite of the Christian church. Here is the brazen font where the waters of baptism wash away the stain of original sin; there stands the gigantic pulpit, from which the sacred truths and ordinances are from time to time proclaimed to the congregated people; behold yonder, resplendent with precious gems, is the high altar, the seat of the most holy mysteries, and the tabernacle of the Highest! It is, indeed, a sacred place; and well does the fabric bespeak its destined purpose: the eye is carried up and lost in the height of the vaulting and the intricacy of the ailes; the rich and varied hues of the stained windows, the modulated light, the gleam of the tapers, the richness of the altars, the venerable images of the departed just,—all alike conspire to fill the mind with veneration for the place, and to make it feel the sublimity of Christian worship. And when the deep intonations of the bells from the lofty campaniles, which summon the people to the house of prayer, have ceased, and the solemn chant of the choir swells through the vast edifice,—cold, indeed, must be the heart of that man who does not cry out with the Psalmist, Domine delixi [sic] decorum domus tuae, et locum habitationis gloriae tuae[1]

[1]. "God, I have cherished the splendor of your house and the place of your glorious habitation."

Such effects as these can only be produced on the mind by build-ings, the composition of which has emanated from men who were thoroughly embued with devotion for, and faith in, the religion for whose worship they were erected.

Their whole energies were directed towards attaining excellence; they were actuated by far nobler motives than the hopes of pecuniary reward, or even the applause and admiration of mankind. They felt they were engaged in the most glorious occupation that can fall to the lot of man, that of raising a temple to the worship of the true and living God.

It was this feeling that operated alike on the master mind that planned the edifice, and on the patient sculptor whose chisel wrought each varied and beautiful detail. It was this feeling that induced the ancient masons, in spite of labour, danger, and difficulties, to per-severe till they had raised their gigantic spires into the very regions of the clouds. It was this feeling that induced the ecclesiastics of old to devote their revenues to this pious purpose, and to labour with their own hands in the accomplishment of the work; and it is a feeling that may be traced throughout the whole of the numerous edifices of the middle ages, and which, amidst the great variety of genius which their varied styles display, still bespeak the unity of purpose which influenced their builders and artists.

They borrowed their ideas from no heathen rites, nor sought for decorations from the idolatrous emblems of a strange people. The foundation and progress of the Christian faith, and the sacraments and ceremonies of the church, formed an ample and noble field for the exercise of their talents; and it is an incontrovertible fact, that every class of artists who flourished during those glorious periods selected their subjects from this inexhaustible source, and devoted their greatest efforts towards the embellishment of ecclesiastical edifices.

Yes, it was, indeed, the faith, the zeal, and, above all, the unity, of our ancestors, that enabled them to conceive and raise those won-derful fabrics that still remain to excite our wonder and admiration. They were erected for the most solemn rites of Christian worship, when the term Christian had but one signification throughout the world; when the glory of the house of God formed an important con-sideration with mankind, when men were zealous for religion, liberal in their gifts, and devoted to her cause; they were erected ere heresy had destroyed faith, schism had put an end to unity, and avarice had instigated the plunder of that wealth that had been consecrated to the service of the church. When these feelings entered in, the spell was broken, the Architecture itself fell with the religion to which it owed its birth, and was succeeded by a mixed and base style devoid of science or elegance, which was rapidly followed by others, till at length, regulated by no system, devoid of unity, but made to suit the ideas and means of each sect as they sprung up, buildings for religious worship present as great incongruities, varieties, and extravagances, as the sects and ideas which have emanated from the new religion which first wrought this great change. In order to prove the truth of these assertions, I will proceed, first, to shew the state of Architecture in this country immediately before the great change of religion; secondly, the fatal effects produced by that change on Architecture; and, thirdly, the present degraded state of Architectural taste, and the utter want of those feelings which alone can restore Architecture to its ancient noble position.

## ON THE WRETCHED STATE OF ARCHITECTURE AT THE PRESENT DAY

Perhaps there is no theme which is more largely dilated on, in the present day, than the immense superiority of this Century over every other that has preceded it. This great age of improvement and increased intellect, as it is called, is asserted to have produced results which have never been equalled; and, puffed up by their supposed excellence, the generation of this day look back with pity and contempt on all that passed away before them.

In some respects, I am willing to grant, great and important inventions have been brought to perfection: but, it must be remembered, that these are purely of a mechanical nature; and I do not hesitate to say, that as works of this description progressed, works of art and productions of mental vigour have declined in a far greater ratio.

Were I to dilate on this subject, I feel confident I could extend this principle throughout all the branches of what are termed the fine arts; but as my professed object is to treat on Architecture, I will confine my observations to that point, leaving to some more able hand the task of exposing false colour and superficial style, which has usurped nature of effect and severity of drawing, and of asserting the immense superiority of the etchings of the old schools over the dry mechanical productions of the steel engravers of our time, whose miserable productions, devoid of soul, sentiment, or feeling, are annually printed by the thousand, and widely circulated, to remain an ever-lasting disgrace on the era in which they were manufactured.

Let us now, therefore, examine the pretensions of the present Century to a superiority in architectural skill; let us examine the results—that is, the edifices that have been produced: and, I feel confident, we shall not be long in deciding that, so far from excelling past ages, the architectural works of our time are even below par in the scale of real excellence.

Let us look around, and see whether the Architecture of this country is not entirely ruled by whim and caprice. Does locality, destination, or character of a building, form the basis of a design? no; surely not. We have Swiss cottages in a flat country; Italian villas in the coldest situations; a Turkish kremlin for a royal residence; Greek temples in crowded lanes; Egyptian auction rooms; and all kinds of absurdities and incongruities: and not only are separate edifices erected in these inappropriate and unsuitable styles, but we have only to look into those nests of monstrosities, the Regent's Park and Regent Street, where all kind of styles are jumbled together to make up a mass.

It is hardly possible to conceive that persons, who had made the art of Architecture the least part of their study, could have committed such enormities as are existing in every portion of these buildings. Yet this is termed a great metropolitan improvement: why, it is a national disgrace, a stigma on the taste of the country; and so it will remain till the plaster and cement, of which it is composed, decay.

Of an equally abominable description are the masses of brick and composition which have been erected in what are termed watering-places, particularly at Brighton, the favoured residence of royalty, and the sojourn of all the titled triflers who wait upon the motions of the court. In this place the vile taste of each villa and terrace is only surpassed by the royal palace itself, on which enormous sums have been lavished, amply sufficient to have produced a fabric worthy of a kingly residence. It would be an endless task to point out and describe all the miserable edifices that have been erected, within the last Century, in every class of Architecture; suffice it to observe, that it would be extremely difficult, if not impossible, to find one amongst the immense mass which could be handed down to succeeding ages as an honourable specimen of the architectural talent of the time.

This is a serious consideration, for it is true. Where, I ask, are the really fine monuments of the country to be found, but in those edifices erected centuries ago, during the often railed at and despised period of the Middle Ages? What would be the interest of the cities, or even towns and villages, of this country, were they deprived of their

ancient gigantic structures, and the remains of their venerable buildings? Why, even in the metropolis itself, the abbey church and hall
of Westminster still stand pre-eminent over every other ecclesiastical
or regal structure that has since been raised.

No one can look on Buckingham Palace, the National Gallery,
Board of Trade, the new buildings at the British Museum, or any of
the principal buildings lately erected, but must feel the very existence
of such public monuments as a national disgrace.

And if we regard the new castle at Windsor, although the gilding
and the show may dazzle the vulgar and the ignorant, the man of
refined taste and knowledge must be disgusted with the paucity of
ideas and meagre taste which are shewn in the decoration; and he will
presently discover, that the elongated or extended quatrefoil and
never-ending set of six pateras, in the rooms called Gothic, and the
vile scroll-work intended for the flowing style of Louis Quatorze,
announce it as being the work of the plasterer and the putty presser,
instead of the sculptor and the artist.

Nor is there to be found among the residences of the nobility,
either in their town mansions or country seats, lately erected, any of
those imposing and characteristic features, or rich and sumptuous
ornaments, with which the residences of the Tudor period abounded.

Nor can any thing be more contemptible than the frittered appearance of the saloons and galleries, crowded with all sorts of paltry
objects, as if for sale, in every corner, which have replaced the massive
silver ornaments, splendid hangings, and furniture of the olden time.

Indeed, I fear that the present general feeling for ancient styles
is but the result of the fashion of the day, instead of being based on
the solid foundation of real love and feeling for art itself; for, I feel
confident, if this were not the case, purchasers could never be found
for the host of rubbish annually imported and sold: nor could persons,
really acquainted with the beauty of what they profess to admire,
mutilate fine things when they possess them, by altering their greatest
beauties to suit their own caprice and purposes—a barbarity continually practised in what is called fitting-up old carvings.

Yes, believe me, this gout for antiquities is of too sudden a nature
to have proceeded from any real conviction of the beauty of those two
styles, or to have been produced from other motives but those of
whim and fashion; and I do believe that, were some leading member
of the *haut ton* to set the fashion for some new style, the herd of
collectors would run as madly after their new plaything, as they do
after the one they have got at present.

The continual purchase of these things, at extravagant prices, may benefit the broker and the salesman, but does not advance a restoration of such art or style one iota.

Were these people of power and wealth really impressed with a feeling of admiration for the glorious works of ancient days, and anxious for the restoration of the skill and art which produced them, instead of filling their apartments with the stock of a broker's shop, they would establish a museum, where the finest specimens of each style might be found, and from which the sculptor and the artist might school themselves in their principles. They would send forth men to preserve faithful representations of the most interesting monuments of foreign lands, and extend a fostering care for the preservation and repair of those fine remains rapidly falling into decay; and, by encouraging talent where it is to be found, raise up by such means a race of artists, who, I hesitate not to say, could be found able to conceive and execute things equally fine and masterly as in more ancient days, but who, for want of such support, are compelled to leave the study of what they most admire, and in which they would excel, for some grovelling occupation by which to gain a bare subsistence.

I state this to wrest from these mere buyers of curiosities the title of patrons of art, which has so undeservedly been bestowed upon them. It was under the fostering care of the Catholic church, and its noble encouragement, the greatest efforts of art have been achieved; deprived of that, the arts in vain look for an equivalent: for its professors must either starve neglected, or sacrifice the noblest principles and beauties of their art to the caprice and ignorance of their employers.

I could not refrain from making this digression, as I feel that what I have just stated is one of the great causes of the present wretched state of art.

I trust I have now shewn satisfactorily that this country, however it may excel in mechanical contrivances, has so little to boast on the score of improvement in art, that, were it not for the remains of the edifices produced during the Middle Ages, the architectural monuments of this country would be contemptible in the extreme.

The truth of this assertion, coupled with the fact that there never was a period when there were so many lectures, academies, drawing schools, and publications on the subject, proves how little the noble arts of Architecture, Painting, and Sculpture, are suited to the trammels of a system; and nothing has tended more to produce the vile results we see, than the absurd idea that persons can be brought up as easily to practise in those exalted professions, as to fill the humble station of a trafficker in merchandise or a mechanical trade; when, in truth, few are there who ever have, or ever can, attain to great excellence in the arts, and the station they arrive at must depend entirely on their own souls and exertions—for small indeed is the instruction that can be imparted on the subject, beyond the mere mechanical use of the tools, and the general principles of drawing.

It is quite lamentable to behold the manner in which good commonplace tradesmen by the present system are spoiled, and made into idle, unemployed, nominal architects, who either lounge about exhibition rooms, form societies, and pass the most sweeping censures on the finest productions of antiquity, because they have not sense enough to see their beauties; or, if through the interest of their friends they gain something to do, make frightful caricatures of Greek and Roman temples, which they designate as classic taste, or even viler compositions in the pointed style, where all proportion and propriety is so outraged, that the most beautiful features of the old buildings become disgusting and offensive when thus distorted and misapplied.

The cause which led these men to be educated, as it is called, for the profession, was most probably nothing more originally than scribbling on a slate; this was interpreted to signify a precocious talent for design, and after a few quarters under the school drawing-master, the youth is placed with some architect in town, who has acquired a name, and who will allow him to waste a few years in daily attendance at his office, for the consideration of some hundreds he receives with him. Here, at the appointed hours, he lolls over his desk, draws the five orders, then pricks off plans, and, when his apprenticeship is nearly expired, he may, perhaps, be able to rule the lines of an elevation clearly, and do a tolerably neat plan.

We next behold him admitted student at the Royal Academy, on the strength of having drawn out a portico, with a wing on each side, termed an original design, and shaded up the representation of two casts, bought at the nearest plaster shop. Here he idles a little more time, copies a few more casts, makes another composition; and perhaps he gets a medal, perhaps not. At any rate, it is time he set forth on his travels to classic shores; and thither, at a vast expanse, is he sent, and three or four more years of the most precious period of life is spent in going over, for the thousandth time, the same set of measurements on the same set of cornices and columns. Here he obtains a smattering, and a vocabulary of names; and returns a conceited, bustling pretender. Three alternatives then offer; for either he gets business, makes vile designs, and, by the help of some practical man, builds them; or he remains a burden on his friends, and a mere coverer of exhibition walls with wretched compositions; or, if neither of these, he settles down into a common surveyor—a man who writes architect on his door and on his card, but who is, in reality, a measurer of land, a valuer of dilapidations, and a cutter-down of tradesmen's accounts.

Such are the results which are produced by the present system of architectural education; nor can great results ever be produced by such means. Architecture, that grandest of sciences, is fallen to a mere trade, and conducted not by artists, but by mere men of business.

All the mechanical contrivances and inventions of the day, such as plastering, composition, papier-maché, and a host of other deceptions, only serve to degrade design, by abolishing the variety of ornament and ideas, as well as the boldness of execution, so admirable and beautiful in ancient carved works.

What can be so ludicrous as to see one of these putty-stamping manufacturers, with a whole host of pieces, cutting, paring, brading on, and contriving an ornament? then covering over the whole with priming to hide the joints: and when done, it is a heavy, disjointed, ugly composition. Yet it is cheap—that is, it is cheaper than what an artist can design and produce; and, without regard to its wretched inferiority, it is stuck up—where? in the royal palaces, and in the mansions of the nobles. And this introduction of pressed putty ornaments, which the commonest labourers can squeeze, is called a distinguishing mark of increasing taste, and encouragement for, what is falsely termed, splendid decoration, but which is, in reality, only a love of cheap, gaudy, and vulgar show.

The just sense of all these various degradations, into which Architecture has fallen, together with the desire of representing the effect the pretended Reformation had on the Architecture of this country, induced me to undertake the publication of this volume.

I own the attempt is a bold one. Books have generally been written, and plates published, to suit private and party views and interests, in consequence of which the truth has generally been wofully disguised, and flattery and falsehood replaced sincerity and reality.

In this work I have been actuated by no other feelings but that of advancing the cause of truth over that of error.

I feel acutely the fallen condition of the arts, when each new invention, each new proceeding, seems only to plunge them deeper in degradation. I wish to pluck from the age the mask of superior attainments so falsely assumed, and I am anxious to direct the attention of all back to the real merit of past and better days. It is among their remains that excellence is only to be found; and it is by studying the zeal, talents, and feelings, of these wonderful but despised times, that art can be restored, or excellence regained. (*Laus Deo.*)

THOMAS BABINGTON MACAULAY

# Milton*

THE PUBLICATION OF MACAULAY'S ESSAY ON
Milton occasioned his first literary success, and overnight turned
him into the most valuable of the writers for the *Edinburgh
Review*.

The passage presented here offers in an extreme form an
argument that Hazlitt and Peacock had already made: that poetry
and the advance of science are at odds. Peacock's statement, in
his famous essay, *The Four Ages of Poetry*, was intended to be
ironical, although it evoked Shelley's *Defense of Poetry*. Macaulay,
however, seems to present the argument with total seriousness.
If, as a description of the history of poetry, it is grossly exaggerated,
it nevertheless represents a point of view that seemed to many
literary people to pose a real threat to poetry. Certainly, it was
long thought that science and poetry were at odds, and much of
twentieth-century criticism has been an elaborate defense of
poetry against science.

* From *Edinburgh Review*, XLII (August, 1825), 304–46.

It is only fair to Macaulay to note that, although the style is typical of all of Macaulay's work, this was not his mature, considered opinion about poetry. In the preface to his published volume of essays, he wrote that his essay on Milton "contains scarcely a paragraph such as his mature judgment approves." But the essay did formulate ideas that were in the air, and that theorists of poetry had to take into account.

. . . It is by his Poetry that Milton is best known; and it is of his poetry that we wish first to speak. By the general suffrage of the civilized world, his place has been assigned among the greatest masters of the art. His detractors, however, though outvoted, have not been silenced. There are many critics, and some of great name, who contrive in the same breath to extol the poems and to decry the poet. The works, they acknowledge, considered in themselves, may be classed among the noblest productions of the human mind. But they will not allow the author to rank with those great men who, born in the infancy of civilization, supplied, by their own powers, the want of instruction, and, though destitute of models themselves, bequeathed to posterity models which defy imitation. Milton, it is said, inherited what his predecessors created; he lived in an enlightened age; he received a finished education; and we must therefore, if we would form a just estimate of his powers, make large deductions for these advantages.

We venture to say, on the contrary, paradoxical as the remark may appear, that no poet has ever had to struggle with more unfavourable circumstances than Milton. He doubted, as he has himself owned, whether he had not been born "an age too late." For this notion Johnson has thought fit to make him the butt of his clumsy ridicule. The poet, we believe, understood the nature of his art better than the critic. He knew that his poetical genius derived no advantage from the civilization which surrounded him, or from the learning which he had acquired; and he looked back with something like regret to the ruder age of simple words and vivid impressions.

We think that, as civilization advances, poetry almost necessarily declines. Therefore, though we admire those great works of imagination which have appeared in dark ages, we do not admire them the more because they have appeared in dark ages. On the contrary, we hold that the most wonderful and splendid proof of genius is a great poem produced in a civilized age. We cannot understand why those who believe in that most orthodox article of literary faith, that the earliest poets are generally the best, should wonder at the rule as if it were the exception. Surely the uniformity of the phenomenon indicates a corresponding uniformity in the cause.

The fact is, that common observers reason from the progress of the experimental sciences to that of the imitative arts. The improvement of the former is gradual and slow. Ages are spent in collecting materials, ages more in separating and combining them. Even when a system has been formed, there is still something to add, to alter, or to reject. Every generation enjoys the use of a vast hoard bequeathed to it by antiquity, and transmits it, augmented, by fresh acquisitions, to future ages. In these pursuits, therefore, the first speculators lie under great disadvantages, and, even when they fail, are entitled to praise. Their pupils, with far inferior intellectual powers, speedily surpass them in actual attainments. Every girl who has read Mrs. Marcet's[1] little Dialogues on Political Economy, could teach Montague or Walpole[2] many lessons in finance. Any intelligent man may now, by resolutely applying himself for a few years to mathematics, learn more than the great Newton knew after half a century of study and meditation.

But it is not thus with music, with painting, or with sculpture. Still less is it thus with poetry. The progress of refinement rarely supplies these arts with better objects of imitation. It may indeed improve the instruments which are necessary to the mechanical operations of the musician, the sculptor, and the painter. But language, the machine of the poet, is best fitted for his purpose in its rudest state. Nations, like individuals, first perceive, and then abstract. They advance from particular images to general terms. Hence the vocabulary of an enlightened society is philosophical, that of a half-civilized people is poetical.

This change in the language of men is partly the cause and

1. Jane Marcet (1769–1858) was a writer and popularizer of technical subjects. Her *Conversations on Political Economy* (1816) was widely read.
2. Charles Montagu, Earl of Halifax (1661–1715), while Lord of the Treasury in 1692, and Chancellor of the Exchequer in 1694, instituted many fiscal reforms. Sir Robert Walpole, first Earl of Oxford (1676–1745), was the most powerful and controversial statesman in the first half of the eighteenth century. He was Prime Minister from 1723 to 1742. Prior to his full rise to power, he had proved himself a great financial minister.

partly the effect of a corresponding change in the nature of their intellectual operations, a change by which science gains and poetry loses. Generalization is necessary to the advancement of knowledge, but particularly in the creations of the imagination. In proportion as men know more and think more, they look less at individuals and more at classes. They therefore make better theories and worse poems. They give us vague phrases instead of images, and personified qualities instead of men. They may be better able to analyze human nature than their predecessors. But analysis is not the business of the poet. His office is to pourtray, not to dissect. He may believe in a moral sense, like Shaftesbury.[3] He may refer all human actions to self-interest, like Helvetius,[4] or he may never think about the matter at all. His creed on such subjects will no more influence his poetry, properly so called, than the notions which a painter may have conceived respecting the lacrymal glands, or the circulation of the blood will affect the tears of his Niobe, or the blushes of his Aurora. If Shakespeare had written a book on the motives of human actions, it is by no means certain that it would have been a good one. It is extremely improbable that it would have contained half so much able reasoning on the subject as is to be found in the Fable of the Bees. But could Mandeville have created an Iago? Well as he knew how to resolve characters into their elements, would he have been able to combine those elements in such a manner as to make up a man,—a real, living, individual man?

Perhaps no person can be a poet, or can even enjoy poetry, without a certain unsoundness of mind, if any thing which gives so much pleasure ought to be called unsoundness. By poetry we mean, not of course all writing in verse nor even all good writing in verse. Our definition excludes many metrical compositions which, on other grounds, deserve the highest praise. By poetry we mean, the art of employing words in such a manner as to produce an illusion on the imagination, the art of doing by means of words what the painter does

3. Anthony Ashley Cooper, third Earl of Shaftesbury (1671–1713), was a famous politician and philosophical writer who argued for the existence of an innate moral sense that allows man to distinguish between right and wrong. All of his chief works were gathered in *Characteristics of Men, Manners, Opinions and Times* (1711).

4. Charles Andrieu Helvetius (1715–71) was a philosopher who emphasized the importance of physical sensation. His main doctrines consist in the belief that all men's faculties may be reduced to physical sensation; that self-interest is the spring of judgment, action, and affection; that all intellects are equal; and that philosophical rulers may achieve artificial identification of interests by suitably contrived legislation. These views, of course, are very similar to those of the utilitarians.

by means of colours. Thus the greatest of poets has described it, in lines universally admired for the vigour and felicity of their diction, and still more valuable on account of the just notion which they convey of the art in which he excelled.

> As imagination bodies forth
> The forms of things unknown, the poet's pen
> Turns them to shapes, and gives to airy nothing
> A local habitation and a name.

These are the fruits of the "fine frenzy" which he ascribes to the poet, —a fine frenzy doubtless, but still a frenzy. Truth indeed, is essential to poetry; but it is the truth of madness. The reasonings are just; but the premises are false. After the first suppositions have been made, every thing ought to be consistent; but those first suppositions require a degree of credulity which almost amounts to a partial and temporary derangement of the intellect. Hence of all people children are the most imaginative. They abandon themselves without reserve to every illusion. Every image which is strongly presented to their mental eye produces on them the effect of reality. No man, whatever his sensibility may be, is ever affected by Hamlet or Lear, as a little girl is affected by the story of poor Red Riding-hood. She knows that it is all false, that wolves cannot speak, that there are no wolves in England. Yet in spite of her knowledge she believes; she weeps, she trembles; she dares not go into a dark room lest she should feel the teeth of the monster at her throat. Such is the despotism of the imagination over uncultivated minds.

In a rude state of society men are children with a greater variety of ideas. It is therefore in such a state of society that we may expect to find the poetical temperament in its highest perfection. In an enlightened age there will be much intelligence, much science, much philosophy, abundance of just classification and subtle analysis, abundance of wit and eloquence, abundance of verses, and even of good ones,—but little poetry. Men will judge and compare; but they will not create. They will talk about the old poets, and comment on them, and to a certain degree enjoy them. But they will scarcely be able to conceive the effect which poetry produced on their ruder ancestors, the agony, the ecstacy, the plenitude of belief. The Greek Rhapsodists, according to Plato, could not recite Homer without almost falling into convulsions. The Mohawk hardly feels the scalping-knife while he shouts his death-song. The power which the ancient bards of Wales and Germany exercised over their auditors seems to modern readers almost miraculous. Such feelings are very rare in a civilized community, and most rare among those who participate most in its improvements. They linger longest among the peasantry.

Poetry produces an illusion on the eye of the mind, as a magic lantern produces an illusion on the eye of the body. And, as the magic lantern acts best in a dark room, poetry effects its purpose most completely in a dark age. As the light of knowledge breaks in upon its exhibitions, as the outlines of certainty become more and more definite, and the shades of probability more and more distinct, the hues and lineaments of the phantoms which it calls up grow fainter and fainter. We cannot unite the incompatible advantages of reality and deception, the clear discernment of truth and the exquisite enjoyment of fiction.

He who, in an enlightened and literary society, aspires to be a great poet, must first become a little child. He must take to pieces the whole web of his mind. He must unlearn much of that knowledge which has perhaps constituted hitherto his chief title to superiority. His very talents will be a hinderance to him. His difficulties will be proportioned to his proficiency in the pursuits which are fashionable among his contemporaries; and that proficiency will in general be proportioned to the vigour and activity of his mind. And it is well if, after all his sacrifices and exertions, his works do not resemble a lisping man, or a modern ruin. We have seen in our own time great talents, intense labour, and long meditation, employed in this struggle against the spirit of the age, and employed, we will not say absolutely in vain, but with dubious success and feeble applause. . . .

LEIGH HUNT

# Fiction and
# Matter-of-Fact*

JAMES HENRY LEIGH HUNT (1784–1859) WAS
an intimate of many of the most famous Victorian writers, and a
poet in his own right. Generous, spontaneous, a little irresponsible,
he befriended Keats, Hazlitt, Lamb, and Shelley, and became the
model for Dickens' Harold Skimpole in Bleak House (1852). As
editor of the Examiner from 1808 until it was taken over by Albany
Fonblanque, he helped to make it one of the most important
weeklies in England and the outlet for spokesmen of intellectual
radicalism.

Although he spent a good deal of his life developing his own
powers of enjoyment, his commitment to radicalism and the outspoken nature of his writing for the Examiner caused him many
difficulties. In 1813, he was sentenced to two years in prison for

* From Examiner (January 2, 1825).

an article on military flogging and became, for his public, a martyr
of radicalism. Hunt was involved with several other weekly periodicals of a non-political nature, but most of his life he mixed
art and literary criticism with social criticism.

In the essay included here, Hunt argues the compatibility of
science with poetry, but the tone of the essay suggests how wide-
spread was the view that the two were incompatible.

"There are more things in heaven and earth, Horatio,
    Than are dreamt of in your philosophy."—Shakspeare.

A passion for these two things is supposed to be incompatible. It is
certainly not so; and the supposition is founded on an ignorance of
the nature of the human mind, and the very sympathies of the two
strangers. Mathematical truth is not the only truth in the world. An
unpoetical logician is not the only philosopher. Locke had no taste
for fiction: he thought Blackmore[1] as great a genius as Homer; but
this was a conclusion he would never have come to, if he had known
his premises. Newton considered poetry as upon a par with "ingenious
nonsense;" which was an error as great as if he had ranked himself
with Tom D'Urfey[2] or made the apex of a triangle equal to the base
of it. Newton has had good for evil returned him by "a greater
than himself:" for the eye of imagination sees farther than the glasses
of astronomy. I should say that the poets had praised their scorner
too much, illustrious as he is, if it were not delightful to see that there
is at least one faculty in the world which knows how to do justice to
all the rest. Of all the universal privileges of poetry, this is one of the
most peculiar, and marks her for what she is. The mathematician, the
schoolman, the wit, the statesman, and the soldier, may all be blind
to the merits of poetry and of one another; but the poet, by the privilege which he possesses of recognizing every species of truth, is

1. Sir Richard Blackmore (1654–1729), dubbed "Father of the Bathos"
by Alexander Pope, was a physician who wrote four bad epics and one bad
philosophical poem.
2. Thomas D'Urfey (1653–1723) was a lively dramatist, satirist, and
song-writer.

aware of the merits of mathematics, of learning, of wit, of politics, and of generalship. He is great in his own art, and he is great in the appreciation of that of others. And this is most remarkable, in proportion as he is a *poetical* poet,—a high lover of fiction. Milton brought the visible and the invisible together "on the top of Fiesole," to pay homage to Galileo; and the Tuscan deserved it, for he had an insight into the world of imagination. I cannot but fancy the shade of Newton blushing to reflect that among the many things which he professed to *know not*, poetry was omitted, of which he knew nothing. Great as he was, he indeed saw nothing in the face of Nature but it's lines and colours; not the lines and colours of passion and sentiment included, but only squares and their distances, and the anatomy of the rainbow. He thought the earth a glorious planet; he knew it better than any one else, in its connexion with other planets; and yet half the beauty of them all, that which sympathy bestows and imagination colours, was to him a blank. He took space to be the sensorium of the Deity (so noble a fancy could be struck out of the involuntary encounter between his intense sense of a mystery and the imagination he despised!) and yet this very fancy was but an escape from the horror of a vacuum, and a substitution of the mere consciousness of existence for the thoughts and images with which a poet would have accompanied it. He imagined the form of the houses, and the presence of the builder; but the life and the variety, the paintings, the imagery, and the music, the loves and the joys, the whole riches of the place, the whole riches in the distance, the creations *heaped* upon creation, and the particular as well as aggregate consciousness of all this in the great mind of whose presence he was conscious, to all this his want of imagination rendered him insensible. The *Fairy Queen* was to him a trifle; the dreams of Shakspeare "ingenious nonsense." But courts were something, and so were the fashions there. When the name of. the Deity was mentioned, he used to take off his hat!

There are two worlds; the world that we can measure with line and rule, and the world that we feel with our hearts and imaginations. To be sensible of the truth of only one of these, is to know truth but by halves. Milton said, that he dared be known to think Spenser a better teacher than Scotus or Aquinas. He did not say than Plato or Pythagoras, who understood the two spheres within our reach. Both of these, and Milton himself, were as great lovers of physical and political truth as any men; but they knew it was not all; they felt much beyond, and they made experiments upon more. It is doubtful with the critics, whether Chaucer's delight in the handling of fictions, or in the detection and scrutiny of a piece of truth, was the greater. Chaucer was a conscientious Reformer, which is a man who has a passion for truth; and so was Milton. So, in his way, was Ariosto himself, and indeed all the great poets, part of the very perfection of their art, which is veri-similitude, being closely connected with their sense of truth in all things. But it is not necessary to be great in order to possess a reasonable variety of perception. That nobody may despair of being able to indulge the two passions together, I can answer for them by my own experience. I can pass with as much pleasure as ever, from the reading of one of Hume's Essays to that of the Arabian Nights, and *vice versa*; and I think, the longer I live, the closer, if possible, will the union grow. The roads are found to approach nearer, in proportion as we advance upon either; and they both terminate in the same prospect.

I am far from meaning that there is nothing real in either road. The path of Matter-of-fact is as solid as ever; but they who do not see the reality of the other, keep but a blind and prone beating upon their own surface. To drop the metaphor, Matter-of-fact is our perception of the grosser and more external shapes of truth; fiction represents the residuum and the mystery. To love Matter-of-fact is to have a lively sense of the visible and immediate; to love fiction is to have as lively a sense of the possible and the remote. Now these two senses, if they exist at all, are of necessity as real, the one as the other. The only proof of either is in our perception. To a blind man, the most visible colours no more exist, than the hues of a fairy tale to a man destitute of fancy. To a man of fancy, who sheds tears over a tale, the chair in which he sits has no truer existence in its way, than the story that moves him. His being touched is his proof in both instances.

But, says the mechanical understanding, modern discoveries have acquainted us with the cause of lightning and thunder, of the nature of optical delusions, and fifty other apparent wonders; and therefore there is no more to be feigned about them. Fancy has done with them, at least with their causes; and witches and will-o'-the-wisps being abolished, poetry is at a stand. The strong glass of science has put an end to the charms of fiction.

This is a favourite remark with a pretty numerous set of writers; and it is a very desperate one. It looks like reasoning on the face of it; and by a singular exercise of the very faculty which it asserts the death of, many persons take the look of an argument for the proof of it. Certainly, no observation can militate more strongly against existing matter-of-fact; and this is the reason why it is made. The mechanical writers of verse find that it is no longer so easy to be taken for poets, because fancy and imagination are more than usually in request: so they would have their revenge, by asserting, that poetry is no longer to be written.

When an understanding of this description is told, that thunder is caused by a collision of clouds, and that lightning is a well known result of electricity, there may be an end, if he pleases, of his poetry with him. He may, if he thinks fit, or if he cannot help it, no longer see anything in the lightning, but the escape of a subtle fluid, nor hear anything more noble in the thunder than the crack of a bladder of water. Much good may his accomplished ignorance do him. But it is not so with understandings of a loftier or a more popular kind. The wonder of a child, and the lofty speculations of wisdom, meet alike on a point, higher than he can attain to, and look over the threshold of the world. Mechanical knowledge is a great and a glorious tool in the hands of man, and will change the globe. But it will still leave untouched the invisible sphere above and about us; still leave us all the great and all the gentle objects of poetry,—the heavens and the human heart, the regions of Genii and Fairies, the fanciful or passionate images that come to us from the seas, and the towers, and all that we behold.

It is, in fact, remarkable, that the growth of science, and the reappearance of a more poetical kind of poetry, have accompanied one another. Whatever may be the difference of opinion as to the extent to which our modern poets have carried their success, their inclinations cannot be doubted. How is it, that poetical impulse has taken this turn in a generation described to be so mechanical? Whence has arisen among us this exceeding fondness for the fictions of the East, for solitary and fanciful reveries, for the wild taste of the Germans (themselves more scientific and wild than ever), and even for a new and more primitive use of the old Pagan Mythology, so long and so mechanically abused by the Chloes and Venuses of the French? Politics may be thought a very unlikely cause of poetry, and it is so with Ministers and Gazetteers; yet politics, pushed farther than common, have been the cause of the new and greater impetus given to the sympathies of imagination; and the more we know of any other science, the farther we see into the dominions of intellect, if we are not mere slaves of the soil. A little philosophy, says Bacon, takes men away from religion; a greater brings them round to it. This is the case with the reasoning faculty and poetry. We reason to a certain point, and are content with the discovery of second causes. We reason farther, and find ourselves in the same airy depths as of old. The imagination recognizes its ancient field, and begins ranging again at

will, doubly bent upon liberty, because of the trammels with which
it has been threatened.

Take the following APOLOGUE:

——During a wonderful period of the world, the kings of the
earth leagued themselves together to destroy all opposition, to root
out, if they could, the very thoughts of mankind. Inquisition was
made for blood. The ears of the grovelling lay in wait for every murmur.
On a sudden, during this great hour of danger, there arose in a
hundred parts of the world, a cry, to which the cry of the Blatant
Beast was a whisper. It proceeded from the wonderful multiplication
of an extraordinary Creature, which had already turned the cheeks
of the tyrants pallid. It groaned and it grew loud: it spoke with a
hundred tongues: it grew fervidly on the ear, like the noise of a million
of wheels. And the sound of a million of wheels was in it, together
with other marvellous and awful voices. There was the sharpening
of swords, the braying of trumpets, the neighing of warhorses, the
laughter of solemn voices, the rushing by of lights, the movement of
impatient feet, a tread as if the world were coming. And ever and
anon there were pauses with "a still small voice," which made a
trembling in the night-time; but still the glowing sound of the wheels
renewed itself; gathering early towards the morning.—And when
you came up to one of these creatures, you saw, with fear and reverence, it's mighty conformation, being like wheels indeed, and a
great vapour. And ever and anon the vapour boiled, and the wheels
went rolling, and the creature threw out of its mouth visible words,
that fell into the air by millions, and spoke to the uttermost parts of the
earth. And the nations (for it was a loving though a fearful Creature)
fed upon its words like the air they breathed: and the Monarchs
paused, for they knew their masters.

This is PRINTING BY STEAM.—It will be said that this is an
allegory, and that all allegories are but poor fictions. I am far from
producing it as a specimen of the poetical power now in existence.
Allegory itself is out of fashion, though a favourite exercise of our old
poets, when the public were familiar with shows and spectacles. But
allegory is the readiest shape into which imagination can turn a
thing mechanical; and in the one before us is contained the mechanical truth and the spiritual truth of that very matter-of-fact thing, called
a Printing Press: each of them as true as the other, or neither could
take place. A business of screws and iron wheels is, or appears to be,
a very common-place matter; but not so the will of the hand that
sets them in motion, not so the operations of the mind that directs
them what to utter. We are satisfied respecting the one by science,

But what renders us sensible of the wonders of the other, and their connection with the great and hidden mysteries of nature? Thought— Fancy—*Imagination*. What signifies to her the talk about electricity, and suction, and gravitation, and alembics, and fifty other mechanical operations of the marvellous? This is but the bone and muscle of wonder. Soul, and not body, is her pursuit; the first cause, not the second; the whole effect, not a part of it; the will, the intention, the marvel itself. As long as this lies hidden, she still fancies what agents for it she pleases. The science of atmospherical phenomena hinders not her angels from "playing in the plighted clouds." The analysis of a bottle of salt water does not prevent her from "taking the wings of the Morning, and remaining in the uttermost parts of the sea." You must prove to her first, that you understand the simple elements, when decomposed; the reason that brings them together; the power that puts them in action; the relations which they have to a thousand things besides ourselves and our wants; the necessity of all this perpetual motion; the understanding that looks out of the eye; love, joy, sorrow, death and life, the future, the universe, the whole invisible abyss. Till you know all this, and can plant the dry sticks of your reason, as trophies of possession, in every quarter of space, how shall you oust her from her dominion?

JOHN STUART MILL

# What Is Poetry

## AND

# The Two Kinds
# of Poetry*

AFTER HIS MENTAL CRISIS—IN FACT, DURING
it—Mill became quite interested in contemporary poetry and the
theory of poetry. Finding that Wordsworth's poetry had the power
to soothe him and to evoke emotions he thought had been dried
up by the analytic training of his early years, he, quite character-
istically, undertook to analyze the nature of poetry.

His conclusions are at once curious and brilliant. The Saint
of Rationalism formulates an aesthetic theory which is the apothe-
osis of romantic thought. Poetry is essentially feeling, and thought

* From *The Monthly Repository*, VII (January, 1833), 60–70; (November, 1833), 714–24.

plays only an ancillary role. Mill's emphasis on feeling is readily explicable. Recognizing the power of poetry to communicate to the senses, he came to understand how important feeling is in the life of a man—particularly in his own life, which had heretofore been subjected to a deliberate repression of the senses through his father's educational experiments. However, even in his most emotional moments, Mill never lost his commitment to the empirical-rationalist ideas of his father. Feeling was important, but it must be kept separate from philosophy and science.

Thus Mill's arguments, at the same time that they attribute great value to it, deprive poetry of much of its importance. However much feeling is a part of poetry, feeling must be anchored to fact; otherwise it will become mere sentimentality. In the twentieth century, as critics argue for the "cognitive" aspect of poetry, for its existence as a form of knowledge, it is not at all clear that Mill has been refuted.

Equally important, Mill formulates the distinction between poetry and rhetoric in a way that fully anticipates much modern theory and practice. "Eloquence is heard," says Mill, "poetry is overheard." Poetry, that is, is the expression of personal feeling and never consciously aims at producing an effect on an audience. Mill thus leaves to poetry no directly moral or public function and suggests that whenever it aims at persuasion it is corrupt. Twentieth-century criticism testifies to the general acceptance of this view and Victorian poetry—torn between self-expression and moral exhortation—is frequently seen as a demonstration of how potentially great poetry might be ruined by forsaking its exclusively personal nature. To be sure, scholars have argued that much great poetry was—to use Mill's term—"eloquent." But for the modern poet, who cannot count on a public that holds widely shared values, poetry has become almost exclusively the expression in private symbols of private experience; and Mill's formulation now seems startlingly (if depressingly) accurate.

It has often been asked, What is Poetry? And many and various are the answers which have been returned. The vulgarest of all—one with which no person possessed of the faculties to which Poetry addresses itself can ever have been satisfied—is that which confounds poetry with metrical composition: yet to this wretched mockery of a definition, many have been led back, by the failure of all their attempts to find any other that would distinguish what they have been accustomed to call poetry, from much which they have known only under other names.

That, however, the word "poetry" *does* import something quite peculiar in its nature, something which may exist in what is called prose as well as in verse, something which does not even require the instrument of words, but can speak through those other audible symbols called musical sounds, and even through the visible ones, which are the language of sculpture, painting, and architecture; all this, as we believe, is and must be felt, though perhaps indistinctly, by all upon whom poetry in any of its shapes produces any impression beyond that of tickling the ear. To the mind, poetry is either nothing, or it is the better part of all art whatever, and of real life too; and the distinction between poetry and what is not poetry, whether explained or not, is felt to be fundamental.

Where every one feels a difference, a difference there must be. All other appearances may be fallacious, but the appearance of a difference is itself a real difference. Appearances too, like other things, must have a cause, and that which can cause anything, even an illusion, must be a reality. And hence, while a half-philosophy disdains the classifications and distinctions indicated by popular language, philosophy carried to its highest point may frame new ones, but never sets aside the old, content with correcting and regularizing them. It cuts fresh channels for thought, but it does not fill up such as it finds ready made, but traces, on the contrary, more deeply, broadly, and distinctly, those into which the current has spontaneously flowed.

Let us then attempt, in the way of modest inquiry, not to coerce and confine nature within the bounds of an arbitrary definition, but rather to find the boundaries which she herself has set, and erect a barrier round them; not calling mankind to account for having misapplied the word "poetry," but attempting to clear up to them the conception which they already attach to it, and to bring before their minds as a distinct *principle* that which, as a vague *feeling*, has really guided them in their actual employment of the term.

The object of poetry is confessedly to act upon the emotions; and therein is poetry sufficiently distinguished from what Wordsworth affirms to be its logical opposite, namely, not prose, but matter of fact or science. The one addresses itself to the belief, the other to the feelings. The one does its work by convincing or persuading, the other by moving. The one acts by presenting a proposition to the understanding, the other by offering interesting objects of contemplation to the sensibilities.

This, however, leaves us very far from a definition of poetry. We have distinguished it from one thing, but we are bound to distinguish it from everything. To present thoughts or images to the mind for the purpose of acting upon the emotions, does not belong to poetry alone. It is equally the province (for example) of the novelist: and yet the faculty of the poet and the faculty of the novelist are as distinct as any other two faculties; as the faculty of the novelist and of the orator, or of the poet and the metaphysician. The two characters may be united, as characters the most disparate may; but they have no natural connexion.

Many of the finest poems are in the form of novels, and in almost all good novels there is true poetry. But there is a radical distinction between the interest felt in a novel as such, and the interest excited by poetry; for the one is derived from *incident*, the other from the representation of *feeling*. In one, the source of the emotion excited is the exhibition of a state or states of human sensibility; in the other, of a series of states of mere outward circumstances. Now, all minds are capable of being affected more or less by representations of the latter kind, and all, or almost all, by those of the former; yet the two sources of interest correspond to two distinct and (as respects their greatest development) mutually exclusive characters of mind. So much is the nature of poetry dissimilar to the nature of fictitious narrative, that to have a really strong passion for either of the two, seems to presuppose or to superinduce a comparative indifference to the other.

At what age is the passion for a story, for almost any kind of story, merely as a story, the most intense?—in childhood. But that also is the age at which poetry, even of the simplest description, is least relished and least understood; because the feelings with which it is especially conversant are yet undeveloped, and not having been even in the slightest degree experienced, cannot be sympathised with. In what stage of the progress of society, again, is story-telling most valued, and the story-teller in greatest request and honour?—in a rude state; like that of the Tartars and Arabs at this day, and of almost all nations in the earliest ages. But in this state of society there is little poetry except ballads, which are mostly narrative, that is, essentially *stories*, and derive their principal interest from the *incidents*. Considered as poetry, they are of the lowest and most elementary kind: the feelings depicted, or rather indicated, are the simplest our nature has; such joys and griefs as the immediate pressure of some outward event excites in rude minds, which live wholly immersed in outward things, and have never, either from choice or a force they could not resist, turned themselves to the contemplation of the world within. Passing now from childhood, and from the childhood of society, to the grown-up men and women of this most grown-up and unchildlike age—the minds and hearts of greatest depth and elevation are commonly those which take greatest delight in poetry; the shallowest and emptiest, on the contrary, are, by universal remark, the most addicted to novel-reading. This accords, too, with all analogous experience of human nature. The sort of persons whom not merely in books but in their lives, we find perpetually engaged in hunting for excitement from without, are invariably those who do not possess, either in the vigour of their intellectual powers or in the depth of their sensibilities, that which would enable them to find ample excitement nearer at home. The same persons whose time is divided between sightseeing, gossip, and fashionable dissipation, take a natural delight in fictitious narrative; the excitement it affords is of the kind which comes from without. Such persons are rarely lovers of poetry, though they may fancy themselves so, because they relish novels in verse. But poetry, which is the delineation of the deeper and more secret workings of the human heart, is interesting only to those to whom it recalls what they have felt, or whose imagination it stirs up to conceive what they could feel, or what they might have been able to feel, had their outward circumstances been different.

Poetry, when it is really such, is truth; and fiction also, if it is good for anything, is truth: but they are different truths. The truth of poetry is to paint the human soul truly: the truth of fiction is to give a true picture of *life*. The two kinds of knowledge are different, and come by different ways, come mostly to different persons. Great poets are often proverbially ignorant of life. What they know has come by observation of themselves; they have found *there* one highly delicate, and sensitive, and refined specimen of human nature, on which the laws of human emotion are written in large characters, such as can be read off without much study: and other knowledge of mankind, such as comes to men of the world by outward experience, is not indispensable to them as poets: but to the novelist such knowledge is all in all; he has to describe outward things, not the inward man; actions and events, not feelings; and it will not do for him to be numbered among those who, as Madame Roland said of Brissot, know man but not men.

All this is no bar to the possibility of combining both elements, poetry and narrative or incident, in the same work, and calling it either a novel or a poem; but so may red and white combine on the same human features, or on the same canvass; and so may oil and vinegar, though opposite natures, blend together in the same composite taste. There is one order of composition which requires the union of poetry and incident, each in its highest kind—the dramatic. Even there the two elements are perfectly distinguishable, and may exist of unequal quality, and in the most various proportion. The incidents of a dramatic poem may be scanty and ineffective, though the delineation of passion and character may be of the highest order; as in Goethe's glorious "Torquato Tasso"; or again, the story as a mere story may be well got up for effect, as is the case with some of the most trashy productions of the Minerva press:[1] it may even be, what those are not, a coherent and probable series of events, though there be scarcely a feeling exhibited which is not exhibited falsely, or in a manner absolutely common-place. The combination of the two excellencies is what renders Shakspeare so generally acceptable, each sort of readers finding in him what is suitable to their faculties. To the many he is great as a story-teller, to the few as a poet.

In limiting poetry to the delineation of states of feeling, and denying the name where nothing is delineated but outward objects, we may be thought to have done what we promised to avoid—to have not found, but made a definition, in opposition to the usage of the English language, since it is established by common consent that there is a poetry called *descriptive*. We deny the charge. Description is not poetry because there is descriptive poetry, no more than science

1. The Minerva Press was established by William Lane (1745?–1814) and was perhaps the most notorious publishing house in operation during the late eighteenth and early nineteenth centuries. It produced a series of ultrasentimental novels which most literate people thought to be trash, but which earned Lane a sizable amount of money. Frequently he reprinted under new titles old volumes long justly forgotten and circulated them through public libraries. The name of the press, which Lane adopted in 1790, became synonymous with trashy novels. A fascinating history of the press is given in Dorothy Blakey, *The Minerva Press, 1790–1820* (1939).

is poetry because there is such a thing as a didactic poem; no more, we might almost say, than Greek or Latin poetry because there are Greek and Latin poems. But an object which admits of being described, or a truth which may fill a place in a scientific treatise, may *also* furnish an occasion for the generation of poetry, which we thereupon choose to call descriptive or didactic. The poetry is not in the object itself, nor in the scientific truth itself, but in the state of mind in which the one and the other may be contemplated. The mere delineation of the dimensions and colours of external objects is not poetry, no more than a geometrical ground-plan of St. Peter's or Westminster Abbey is painting. Descriptive poetry consists, no doubt, in description, but in description of things as they appear, not as they *are*; and it paints them not in their bare and natural lineaments, but arranged in the colours and seen through the medium of the imagination set in action by the feelings. If a poet is to describe a lion, he will not set about describing him as a naturalist would, nor even as a traveller would, who was intent upon stating the truth, the whole truth, and nothing but the truth. He will describe him by *imagery*, that is, by suggesting the most striking likenesses and contrasts which might occur to a mind contemplating the lion, in the state of awe, wonder, or terror, which the spectacle naturally excites, or is, on the occasion, supposed to excite. Now this is describing the lion professedly, but the state of excitement of the spectator really. The lion may be described falsely or in exaggerated colours, and the poetry be all the better; but if the human emotion be not painted with the most scrupulous truth, the poetry is bad poetry, i.e. is not poetry at all, but a failure.

.   .   .   .

The distinction between poetry and eloquence appears to us to be equally fundamental with the distinction between poetry and narrative, or between poetry and description. It is still farther from having been satisfactorily cleared up than either of the others, unless, which is highly probable, the German artists and critics have thrown some light upon it which has not yet reached us. Without a perfect knowledge of what they have written, it is something like presumption to write upon such subjects at all, and we shall be the foremost to urge that, whatever we may be about to submit, may be received, subject to correction from *them*.

Poetry and eloquence are both alike the expression or uttering forth of feeling. But if we may be excused the seeming affectation of the antithesis, we should say that eloquence is *heard*, poetry is *overheard*.

Eloquence supposes an audience; the peculiarity of poetry appears to us to lie in the poet's utter unconsciousness of a listener. Poetry is feeling confessing itself to itself, in moments of solitude, and bodying itself forth in symbols which are the nearest possible representations of the feeling in the exact shape in which it exists in the poet's mind. Eloquence is feeling pouring itself forth to other minds, courting their sympathy, or endeavouring to influence their belief, or move them to passion or to action.

All poetry is of the nature of soliloquy. It may be said that poetry, which is printed on hot-pressed paper, and sold at a bookseller's shop, is a soliloquy in full dress, and upon the stage. But there is nothing absurd in the idea of such a mode of soliloquizing. What we have said to ourselves, we may tell to others afterwards; what we have said or done in solitude, we may voluntarily reproduce when we know that other eyes are upon us. But no trace of consciousness that any eyes are upon us must be visible in the work itself. The actor knows that there is an audience present; but if he act as though he knew it, he acts ill. A poet may write poetry with the intention of publishing it; he may write it even for the express purpose of being paid for it; that it should *be* poetry, being written under any such influences, is far less probable; not, however, impossible; but no otherwise possible than if he can succeed in excluding from his work every vestige of such lookings-forth into the outward and every-day world, and can express his feelings exactly as he has felt them in solitude, or as he feels that he should feel them, though they were to remain for ever unuttered. But when he turns round and addresses himself to another person; when the act of utterance is not itself the end, but a means to an end,—viz., by the feelings he himself expresses to work upon the feelings, or upon the belief, or the will of another,—when the expression of his emotions, or of his thoughts, tinged by his emotions, is tinged also by that purpose, by that desire of making an impression upon another mind, then it ceases to be poetry, and becomes eloquence.

Poetry, accordingly, is the natural fruit of solitude and meditation; eloquence, of intercourse with the world. The persons who have most feeling of their own, if intellectual culture have given them a language in which to express it, have the highest faculty of poetry; those who best understand the feelings of others, are the most eloquent. The persons, and the nations, who commonly excel in poetry, are those whose character and tastes render them least dependent for their happiness upon the applause, or sympathy, or concurrence of the world in general. Those to whom that applause, that sympathy, that concurrence are most necessary, generally excel most in eloquence. . . .

## THE TWO KINDS OF POETRY

*Nascitur poëta* is a maxim of classical antiquity, which has passed to these latter days with less questioning than most of the doctrines of that early age. When it originated, the human faculties were occupied, fortunately for posterity, less in examining how the works of genius are created, than in creating them: and the adage, probably, had no higher source than the tendency, common among mankind, to consider all power which is not visibly the effect of practice, all skill which is not capable of being reduced to mechanical rules, as the result of a peculiar gift. Yet this aphorism, born in the infancy of psychology, will perhaps be found, now when that science is in its adolescence, to be as true as an epigram ever is, that is, to contain some truth: truth, however, which has been so compressed and bent out of shape, in order to tie up into so small a knot of only two words, that it requires an almost infinite amount of unrolling and laying straight, before it will resume its just proportions.

We are not now intending to remark upon the grosser misapplications of this ancient maxim, which have engendered so many races of poetasters. The days are gone by, when every raw youth whose borrowed phantasies have set themselves to a borrowed tune, mistaking as Coleridge says an ardent desire of poetic reputation for poetic genius, while unable to disguise from himself that he had taken no means whereby he might become a poet, could fancy himself a born one. Those who would reap without sowing, and gain the victory without fighting the battle, are ambitious now of another sort of distinction, and are born novelists, or public speakers, not poets. And the wiser thinkers begin to understand and acknowledge that poetic excellence is subject to the same necessary conditions with any other mental endowment; and that to no one of the spiritual benefactors of mankind is a higher or a more assiduous intellectual culture needful than to the poet. It is true, he possesses this advantage over others who use the "instrument of words," that of the truths which he utters, a larger portion are derived from personal consciousness, and a smaller from philosophic investigation. But the power itself of discriminating between what really is consciousness, and what is only a process of inference completed in a single instant; and the capacity of distinguishing whether that of which the mind is conscious, be an eternal truth, or but a dream—are among the last results of the most matured and perfected intellect. Not to mention that the poet, no more than any other person who writes, confines himself altogether to intuitive truths, nor has any means of communicating even these, but by words, every one of which derives all its power of conveying a meaning, from a whole host of acquired notions, and facts learnt by study and experience.

Nevertheless, it seems undeniable in point of fact, and consistent with the principles of a sound metaphysics, that there are poetic natures. There is a mental and physical constitution or temperament, particularly fitted for poetry. This temperament will not of itself make a poet, no more than the soil will the fruit; and as good fruit may be raised by culture from indifferent soils, so may good poetry from naturally unpoetical minds. But the poetry of one, who is a poet by nature, will be clearly and broadly distinguishable from the poetry of mere culture. It may not be truer; it may not be more useful; but it will be different: fewer will appreciate it, even though many should affect to do so; but in those few it will find a keener sympathy, and will yield them a deeper enjoyment.

One may write genuine poetry, and not be a poet; for whosoever writes out truly any one human feeling, writes poetry. All persons, even the most unimaginative, in moments of strong emotion, speak poetry; and hence the drama is poetry, which else were always prose, except when a poet is one of the characters. What *is* poetry, but the thoughts and words in which emotion spontaneously embodies itself? As there are few who are not, at least for *some* moments and in *some* situations, capable of *some* strong feeling, poetry is natural to most persons at some period of their lives. And any one whose feelings are genuine, though but of the average strength,—if he be not diverted by uncongenial thoughts or occupations from the indulgence of them, and if he acquire by culture, as all persons may, the faculty of delineating them correctly,—has it in his power to be a poet, so far as a life passed in writing unquestionable poetry may be considered to confer that title. But *ought* it to be so? yes, perhaps, in the table of contents of a collection of "British Poets." But "poet" is the name also of a variety of *man*, not solely of the author of a particular variety of *book*: now, to have written whole volumes of real poetry is possible to almost all kinds of characters, and implies no greater peculiarity of mental construction, than to be the author of a history, or a novel.

Whom, then, shall we call poets? Those who are so constituted, that emotions are the links of association by which their ideas, both sensuous and spiritual, are connected together. This constitution belongs (within certain limits) to all in whom poetry is a pervading principle. In all others, poetry is something extraneous and superinduced: something out of themselves, foreign to the habitual course of their every-day lives and characters; a quite other world, to which they may make occasional visits, but where they are sojourners, not dwellers, and which, when out of it, or even when in it, they think of, peradventure, but as a phantom-world, a place of *ignes fatui* and spectral illusions. Those only who have the peculiarity of association which we have mentioned, and which is one of the natural consequences of intense sensibility, instead of seeming not themselves when they are uttering poetry, scarcely seem themselves when uttering any thing to which poetry is foreign. Whatever be the thing which they are contemplating, the aspect under which it first and most naturally paints itself to them, is its poetic aspect. The poet of culture sees his object in prose, and describes it in poetry; the poet of nature actually sees it in poetry.

This point is perhaps worth some little illustration; the rather, as metaphysicians (the ultimate arbiters of all philosophical criticism) while they have busied themselves for two thousand years, more or less, about the few *universal* laws of human nature, have strangely neglected the analysis of its *diversities*. Of these, none lie deeper or reach further than the varieties which difference of nature and of education makes in what may be termed the habitual bond of association. In a mind entirely uncultivated, which is also without any strong feelings, objects whether of sense or of intellect arrange themselves in the mere casual order in which they have been seen, heard, or otherwise perceived. Persons of this sort may be said to think chronologically. If they remember a fact, it is by reason of a fortuitous coincidence with some trifling incident or circumstance which took place at the very time. If they have a story to tell, or testimony to deliver in a witness-box, their narrative must follow the exact order in which the events took place: *dodge* them, and the thread of association is broken; they cannot go on. Their associations, to use the language of philosophers, are chiefly of the successive, not the synchronous kind, and whether successive or synchronous, are mostly *casual*.

To the man of science, again, or of business, objects group themselves according to the artificial classifications which the understanding has voluntarily made for the convenience of thought or of practice. But where any of the impressions are vivid and intense, the associations into which these enter are the ruling ones: it being a well-known law of association, that the stronger a feeling is, the more rapidly and strongly it associates itself with any other object or feeling. Where, therefore, nature has given strong feelings, and education has not created factitious tendencies stronger than the natural ones, the prevailing associations will be those which connect objects and ideas with emotions, and with each other through the intervention of emotions. Thoughts and images will be linked together, according to the similarity of the feelings which cling to them. A thought will introduce a thought by first introducing a feeling which is allied with it. At the centre of each group of thoughts or images will be found a feeling; and the thoughts or images are only there because the feeling was there. All the combinations which the mind puts together, all the pictures which it paints, all the wholes which Imagination constructs out of the materials supplied by Fancy, will be indebted to some dominant *feeling*, not as in other natures to a dominant *thought*, for their unity and consistency of character, for what distinguishes them from incoherencies.

The difference, then, between the poetry of a poet, and the poetry of a cultivated but not naturally poetical mind, is that in the latter, with however bright a halo of feeling the thought may be surrounded and glorified, the thought itself is still the conspicuous object; while the poetry of a poet is Feeling itself, employing Thought only as the medium of its utterance. In the one feeling waits upon thought; in the other, thought upon feeling. The one writer has a distinct aim, common to him with any other didactic author; he desires to convey the thought, and he conveys it clothed in the feelings which it excites in himself, or which he deems most appropriate to it. The other merely pours forth the overflowing of his feelings; and all the thoughts which those feelings suggest are floated promiscuously along the stream.

. . . . .

If, then, the maxim *nascitur poëta*, mean, either that the power of producing poetical compositions is a peculiar faculty which the poet brings into the world with him, which grows with his growth like any of his bodily powers, and is as independent of culture as his height, and his complexion; or that *any* natural peculiarity whatever is implied in producing poetry, real poetry, and in any quantity— such poetry too, as, to the majority of educated and intelligent readers, shall appear quite as good as, or even better than, any other; in either sense the doctrine is false. And nevertheless, there *is* poetry which could not emanate but from a mental and physical constitution, peculiar not in the *kind* but in the *degree* of its susceptibility: a constitution which makes its possessor capable of greater happiness than mankind in general, and also of greater unhappiness; and because greater, so also more various. And such poetry, to all who know enough of nature to own it as being *in* nature, is much *more* poetry, is poetry in a far higher sense, than any other; since the common element of all poetry, that which constitutes poetry, human feeling, enters far more largely into this than into the poetry of culture. Not only because the natures which we have called poetical, really feel more, and consequently have more feeling to express; but because, the capacity of feeling being so great, feeling, when excited and not voluntarily resisted, seizes the helm of their thoughts, and the succession of ideas and images becomes the mere utterance of an emotion; not, as in other natures, the emotion a mere ornamental colouring of the thought.

Ordinary education and the ordinary course of life are constantly at work counteracting this quality of mind, and substituting habits more suitable to their own ends: if instead of *substituting* they were content to *superadd*, then there were nothing to complain of. But when will education consist, not in repressing any mental faculty or power, from the uncontrolled action of which danger is apprehended, but in training up to its proper strength the corrective and antagonist power?

In whomsoever the quality which we have described exists, and is not stifled, that person is a poet. Doubtless he is a *greater* poet in proportion as the fineness of his perceptions, whether of sense or of internal consciousness, furnishes him with an ampler supply of lovely images, the vigour and richness of his intellect with a greater abundance of moving thoughts. For it is through these thoughts and images that the feeling speaks, and through their impressiveness that it impresses itself, and finds response in other hearts; and from these media of transmitting it (contrary to the laws of physical nature) increase of intensity is reflected back upon the feeling itself. But all these it is possible to have, and not be a poet; they are mere materials, which the poet shares in common with other people. What constitutes the poet is not the imagery nor the thoughts, nor even the feelings, but the law according to which they are called up. He is a poet, not because he has ideas of any particular kind, but because the succession of his ideas is subordinate to the course of his emotions.

·   ·   ·   ·

Our judgments of authors who lay actual claim to the title of poets, follow the same principle. We believe that whenever, after a writer's meaning is fully understood, it is still matter of reasoning and discussion whether he is a poet or not, he will be found to be wanting in the characteristic peculiarity of association which we have so often adverted to. When, on the contrary, after reading or hearing one or two passages, the mind instinctively and without hesitation cries out, This is a poet, the probability is, that the passages are strongly marked with this peculiar quality. And we may add that in such case, a critic who, not having sufficient feeling to respond to the poetry, is also without sufficient philosophy to understand it though he feel it not, will be apt to pronounce, not "this is prose," but "this is exaggeration," "this is mysticism," or "this is nonsense."

Although a philosopher cannot, by culture, make himself, in the peculiar sense in which we now use the term, a poet, unless at least he have that peculiarity of nature which would probably have made poetry his earliest pursuit; a poet may always, by culture, make himself a philosopher. The poetic laws of association are by no means incompatible with the more ordinary laws; are by no means such as *must* have their course, even though a deliberate purpose require their suspension. If the peculiarities of the poetic temperament were uncontrollable in any poet, they might be supposed so in Shelley; yet how powerfully, in the Cenci, does he coerce and restrain all the characteristic qualities of his genius! what severe simplicity, in place of his usual barbaric splendour! how rigidly does he keep the feelings and the imagery in subordination to the thought!

The investigation of nature requires no habits or qualities of mind, but such as may always be acquired by industry and mental activity. Because in one state the mind may be so given up to a state of feeling, that the succession of its ideas is determined by the present enjoyment or suffering which pervades it, that is no reason but that in the calm retirement of study, when under no peculiar excitement either of the outward or of the inward sense, it may form any combinations, or pursue any trains of ideas, which are most conducive to the purposes of philosophic inquiry; and may, while in that state, form deliberate convictions, from which no excitement will afterwards make it swerve. Might we not go even further than this? We shall not pause to ask whether it be not a misunderstanding of the nature of passionate feeling to imagine that it is inconsistent with calmness, and whether they who so deem of it, do not confound the state of *desire* which unfortunately is possible to all, with the state of *fruition* which is granted only to the few. But without entering into this deeper investigation; that capacity of strong feeling, which is supposed necessarily to disturb the judgment, is also the material out of which all *motives* are made; the motives, consequently, which lead human beings to the pursuit of truth. The greater the individual's capability of happiness and of misery, the stronger interest has that individual in arriving at truth; and when once that interest is felt, an impassioned nature is sure to pursue this, as to pursue any other object, with greater ardour; for energy of character is always the offspring of strong feeling. If therefore the most impassioned natures do not ripen into the most powerful intellects, it is always from defect of culture, or something wrong in the circumstances by which the being has originally or successively been surrounded. Undoubtedly strong feelings *require* a strong intellect to carry them, as more sail requires more ballast: and when from neglect, or bad education, that strength is wanting, no wonder if the grandest and swiftest vessels make the most utter wreck.

Where, as in Milton, or, to descend to our own times, in Coleridge, a poetic nature has been united with logical and scientific culture, the peculiarity of association arising from the finer nature so perpetually alternates with the associations attainable by commoner natures trained to high perfection, that its own particular law is not so conspicuously characteristic of the result produced, as in a poet like Shelley, to whom systematic intellectual culture, in a measure proportioned to the intensity of his own nature, has been wanting. Whether the superiority will naturally be on the side of the logician-poet or of the mere poet—whether the writings of the one ought, as a whole, to be truer, and their influence more beneficent, than those of the other—is too obvious in principle to need statement: it would be absurd to doubt whether two endowments are better than one; whether truth is more certainly arrived at by two processes, verifying and correcting each other, than by one alone. Unfortunately, in practice the matter is not quite so simple; there the question often is, which is least prejudicial to the intellect, uncultivation or malcultivation. For, as long as so much of education is made up of artificialities and conventionalisms, and the so-called training of the intellect consists chiefly of the mere inculcation of traditional opinions, many of which, from the mere fact that the human intellect has not yet reached perfection, must necessarily be false; it is not always clear that the poet of acquired ideas has the advantage over him whose feeling has been his sole teacher. For, the depth and durability of wrong as well as of right impressions, is proportional to the fineness of the material; and they who have the greatest capacity of natural feeling are generally those whose artificial feelings are the strongest. Hence, doubtless, among other reasons, it is, that in an age of revolutions in opinion, the contemporary poets, those at least who deserve the

name, those who have any individuality of character, if they are not
before their age, are almost sure to be behind it. An observation
curiously verified all over Europe in the present century. Nor let it be
thought disparaging. However urgent may be the necessity for a
breaking up of old modes of belief, the most strong-minded and discerning, next to those who head the movement, are generally those
who bring up the rear of it. A text on which to dilate would lead us
too far from the present subject.

ARTHUR HENRY HALLAM

# On Some of the Characteristics of Modern Poetry and on the Lyrical Poems of Alfred Tennyson*

ARTHUR HENRY HALLAM, (1811–33) SON OF
the famous historian, was one of the most promising young men
of his day. At Cambridge he became the greatly loved and respected friend of Tennyson, and pursued varied interests in poetry,
languages, politics, and law. His sudden death in Vienna in 1833

* From *Englishman's Magazine*, I (August, 1831), 616–28.

was a terrible shock for his family and especially for Tennyson, whose thoughts and feelings about it produced In Memoriam, published in 1850. The essay included here justifies the respect in which Hallam was held by so many people. It is a literary man's complement to Mill's rationalist essays on poetry. Where Mill talks about poetry as feeling, Hallam talks about it as beauty. But Hallam demonstrates a much richer and more valid sense of the values of poetry and traces, quite accurately, the continuity between Keats and Tennyson. The later Tennyson, burdened with a Victorian conscience and without Hallam to support him, increasingly turned to a moralistic and philosophical poetry of the kind that Hallam criticizes.

So Mr. Montgomery's[1] "Oxford," by the help of some pretty illustrations, has contrived to prolong its miserable existence to a second edition! But this is slow work, compared to that triumphant progress of the "Omnipresence," which, we concede to the author's friends, was "truly astonishing." We understand, moreover, that a new light has broken upon this "desolator desolate;" and since the "columns" have begun to follow the example of "men and gods," by whom our poetaster has long been condemned, "it is the fate of genius," he begins to discover, "to be unpopular." Now, strongly as we protest against Mr. Montgomery's application of this maxim to his own case, we are much disposed to agree with him as to its abstract correctness. Indeed, the truth which it involves seems to afford the only solution of so curious a phenomenon as the success, partial and transient though it be, of himself, and others of his calibre. When Mr. Wordsworth, in his celebrated Preface to the "Lyrical Ballads," asserted that immedi-

1. Robert Montgomery (1807–55) was a poet who, for a while, was among the most popular in England, although he was savagely (and justly) attacked by almost all serious critics. Notoriously, he advertised and "puffed" his own work and frequently had the title pages of his books set to indicate later editions than were actually true in order to suggest to the public that his books were selling well. His most famous poem was the Omnipresence of the Deity (1828).

ate or rapid popularity was not the test of poetry, great was the consternation and clamour among those farmers of public favour, the established critics. Never had so audacious an attack been made upon their undoubted privileges and hereditary charter of oppression. "What! 'The Edinburgh Review' not infallible!" shrieked the amiable petulance of Mr. Jeffrey.[2] " 'The Gentleman's Magazine' incapable of decision!" faltered the feeble garrulity of Silvanus Urban. And straightway the whole sciolist herd, men of rank, men of letters, men of wealth, men of business, all the "mob of gentlemen who think with ease," and a terrible number of old ladies and boarding-school misses began to scream in chorus, and prolonged the notes of execration with which they overwhelmed the new doctrine, until their wits and their voices fairly gave in from exhaustion. Much, no doubt, they did, for much persons will do when they fight for their dear selves: but there was one thing they could not do, and unfortunately it was the only one of any importance. They could not put down Mr. Wordsworth by clamour, or prevent his doctrine, once uttered, and enforced by his example, from awakening the minds of men, and giving a fresh impulse to art. It was the truth, and it prevailed; not only against the exasperation of that hydra, the Reading Public, whose vanity was hurt, and the blustering of its keepers, whose delusion was exposed, but even against the false glosses and narrow apprehensions of the Wordsworthians themselves. It is the madness of all who loosen some great principle, long buried under a snow-heap of custom and superstition, to imagine that they can restrain its operation, or circumscribe it by their purposes. But the right of private judgment was stronger than the will of Luther; and even the genius of Wordsworth cannot expand itself to the full periphery of poetic art.

It is not true, as his exclusive admirers would have it, that the highest species of poetry is the reflective: it is a gross fallacy, that, because certain opinions are acute or profound, the expression of them by the imagination must be eminently beautiful. Whenever the mind of the artist suffers itself to be occupied, during its periods of creation, by any other predominant motive than the desire of beauty, the result is false in art. Now there is undoubtedly no reason, why he may not find beauty in those moods of emotion, which arise from the combinations of reflective thought, and it is possible that he may delineate these with fidelity, and not be led astray by any suggestions of an

2. Francis Jeffrey (1773–1850) was the founder (along with Sydney Smith and Brougham) of the *Edinburgh Review*, and its editor for twenty-seven years. He was a brilliant editor and generous person despite the frequent nastiness and arrogance of his journal.

unpoetical mood. But, though possible, it is hardly probable: for a man, whose reveries take a reasoning turn, and who is accustomed to measure his ideas by their logical relations rather than the congruity of the sentiments to which they refer, will be apt to mistake the pleasure he has in knowing a thing to be true, for the pleasure he would have in knowing it to be beautiful, and so will pile his thoughts in a rhetorical battery, that they may convince, instead of letting them glow in the natural course of contemplation, that they may enrapture. It would not be difficult to shew, by reference to the most admired poems of Wordsworth, that he is frequently chargeable with this error, and that much has been said by him which is good as philosophy, powerful as rhetoric, but false as poetry. Perhaps this very distortion of the truth did more in the peculiar juncture of our literary affairs to enlarge and liberalize the genius of our age, than could have been effected by a less sectarian temper. However this may be, a new school of reformers soon began to attract attention, who, professing the same independence of immediate favour, took their stand on a different region of Parnassus from that occupied by the Lakers, and one, in our opinion, much less liable to perturbing currents of air from ungenial climates. We shall not hesitate to express our conviction, that the Cockney school (as it was termed in derision, from a cursory view of its accidental circumstances) contained more genuine inspiration, and adhered more speedily to that portion of truth which it embraced, than any *form* of art that has existed in this country since the day of Milton. Their *caposetta* was Mr. Leigh Hunt, who did little more than point the way, and was diverted from his aim by a thousand personal predilections and political habits of thought. But he was followed by two men of a very superior make; men who were born poets, lived poets, and went poets to their untimely graves. Shelley and Keats were, indeed, of opposite genius; that of the one was vast, impetuous, and sublime: the other seemed to be "fed with honey-dew," and to have "drunk the milk of Paradise." Even the softness of Shelley comes out in bold, rapid, comprehensive strokes; he has no patience for minute beauties, unless they can be massed into a general effect of grandeur. On the other hand, the tenderness of Keats cannot sustain a lofty flight; he does not generalize or allegorize Nature; his imagination works with few symbols, and reposes willingly on what is given freely. Yet in this formal opposition of character there is, it seems to us, a ground-work of similarity sufficient for the purposes of classification, and constituting a remarkable point in the progress of literature. They are both poets of sensation rather than reflection. Susceptible of the slightest impulse from external nature, their fine organs trembled into emotion at colours, and sounds, and movements, unperceived or unregarded by duller temperaments. Rich and clear were their perceptions of visible forms; full and deep their feelings of music. So vivid was the delight attending the simple exertions of eye and ear, that it became mingled more and more with their trains of active thought, and tended to absorb their whole being into the energy of sense. Other poets seek for images to illustrate their conceptions; these men had no need to seek; they lived in a world of images; for the most important and extensive portion of their life consisted in those emotions, which are immediately conversant with sensation. Like the hero of Goethe's novel, they would hardly have been affected by what are called the pathetic parts of a book; but the merely beautiful passages, "those from which the spirit of the author looks clearly and mildly forth," would have melted them to tears. Hence they are not descriptive; they are picturesque. They are not smooth and negatively harmonious; they are full of deep and varied melodies. This powerful tendency of imagination to a life of immediate sympathy with the external universe is not nearly so liable to false views of art as the opposite disposition of purely intellectual contemplation. For where beauty is constantly passing before "that inward eye, which is the bliss of solitude;" where the soul seeks it as a perpetual and necessary refreshment to the sources of activity and intuition; where all the other sacred ideas of our nature, the idea of good, the idea of perfection, the idea of truth, are habitually contemplated through the medium of this predominant mood, so that they assume its colour, and are subject to its peculiar laws—there is little danger that the ruling passion of the whole mind will cease to direct its creative operations, or the energetic principle of love for the beautiful sink, even for a brief period, to the level of a mere notion in the understanding. We do not deny that it is, on other accounts, dangerous for frail humanity to linger with fond attachment in the vicinity of sense. Minds of this description are especially liable to moral temptations, and upon them, more than any, it is incumbent to remember that their mission as men, which they share with all their fellow-beings, is of infinitely higher interest than their mission as artists, which they possess by rare and exclusive privilege. But it is obvious that, critically speaking, such temptations are of slight moment. Not the gross and evident passions of nature, but the elevated and less separable desires are the dangerous enemies which misguide the poetic spirit in its attempts at self-cultivation. That delicate sense of fitness, which grows with the growth of artist feelings, and strengthens with their strength, until it acquires a celerity and weight of decision hardly inferior to the correspondent judgments of conscience, is weakened by every indulgence of heterogeneous aspirations, however pure they may be, however lofty, however suitable to human nature. We are therefore decidedly of opinion that the heights and depths of art are most within the reach of those who have received from Nature the "fearful and wonderful" constitution we have described, whose poetry is a sort of magic, producing a number of impressions too multiplied, too minute, and too diversified to allow of our tracing them to their causes, because just such was the effect, even so boundless, and so bewildering, produced on their imaginations by the real appearance of Nature. These things being so, our friends of the new school had evidently much reason to recur to the maxim laid down by Mr. Wordsworth, and to appeal from the immediate judgments of lettered or unlettered contemporaries to the decision of a more equitable posterity. How should they be popular, whose senses told them a richer and ampler tale than most men could understand, and who constantly expressed, because they constantly felt, sentiments of exquisite pleasure or pain, which most men were not permitted to experience? The public very naturally derided them as visionaries, and gibbeted *in terrorem* those inaccuracies of diction, occasioned sometimes by the speed of their conceptions, sometimes by the inadequacy of language to their peculiar conditions of thought. But, it may be asked, does not this line of argument prove too much? Does it not prove that there is a barrier between these poets and all other persons, so strong and immovable, that, as has been said of the Supreme Essence, we must be themselves before we can understand them in the least? Not only are they not liable to sudden and vulgar estimation, but the lapse of ages, it seems, will not consolidate their fame, nor the suffrages of the wise few produce any impression, however remote or slowly matured, on the judgments of the incapacitated many. We answer, this is not the import of our argument. Undoubtedly the true poet addresses himself, in all his conceptions, to the common nature of us all. Art is a lofty tree, and may shoot up far beyond our grasp, but its roots are in daily life and experience. Every bosom contains the elements of those complex emotions which the artist feels, and every head can, to a certain extent, go over in itself the process of their combination, so as to understand his expressions and sympathize with his state. But this requires exertion; more or less, indeed, according to the difference of occasion, but always some degree of exertion. For since the emotions of the poet, during composition, follow a regular law of association, it follows that to accompany their progress up to the harmonious prospect of the whole, and to perceive the proper dependence of every step on that which preceded, it is absolutely necessary to start from the same point, i.e., clearly to apprehend that leading sentiment in the poet's mind, by their conformity to which the host of suggestions are arranged. Now this requisite exertion is not willingly made by the large majority of readers. It is so easy to judge capriciously, and according to indolent impulse! For very many, therefore, it has become *morally* impossible to attain the author's point of vision, on account of their habits, or their prejudices, or their circumstances; but it is never *physically* impossible, because nature has placed in every man the simple elements, of which art is the sublimation. Since then this demand on the reader for activity, when he wants to peruse his author in a luxurious passiveness, is the very thing that moves his bile, it is obvious that those writers will be always most popular, who require the least degree of exertion. Hence, whatever is mixed up with art, and appears under its semblance, is always more favourably regarded than art free and unalloyed. Hence, half the fashionable poems in the world are mere rhetoric, and half the remainder are perhaps not liked by the generality for their substantial merits. Hence, likewise, of the really pure compositions those are most universally agreeable, which take for their primary subject the usual passions of the heart, and deal with them in a simple state, without applying the transforming powers of high imagination. Love, friendship, ambition, religion, etc., are matters of daily experience, even amongst imaginative tempers. The forces of association, therefore, are ready to work in these directions, and little effort of will is necessary to follow the artist. For the same reason such subjects often excite a partial power of composition, which is no sign of a truly poetic organization. We are very far from wishing to depreciate this class of poems, whose influence is so extensive, and communicates so refined a pleasure. We contend only that the facility with which its impressions are communicated, is no proof of its elevation as a form of art, but rather the contrary. What then, some may be ready to exclaim, is the pleasure derived by most men from Shakspeare, or Dante, or Homer, entirely false and factitious? If these are really masters of their art, must not the energy required of the ordinary intelligences, that come in contact with their mighty genius, be the greatest possible? How comes it then that they are popular? Shall we not say, after all, that the difference is in the power of the author, not in the tenor of his meditations? Those eminent spirits find no difficulty in conveying to common apprehension their lofty sense, and profound observation of Nature. They keep no aristocratic state, apart from the sentiments of society at large; they speak to the hearts of all, and by the magnetic force of their conceptions elevate inferior intellects into a higher and purer atmosphere. The truth contained in this objection is undoubtedly important; geniuses of the most universal order, and assigned by destiny to the most propitious eras of a nation's literary developement, have a clearer and larger access to the minds of their compatriots, than can ever be open to those who are circumscribed by less fortunate circumstances. In the youthful periods of any literature there is an expansive and communicative tendency in mind, which produces unreservedness of communion, and reciprocity of vigour between different orders of intelligence. Without abandoning the ground which has always been defended by the partizans of Mr. Wordsworth, who declare with perfect truth that the number of real admirers of what is really admirable in Shakspeare and Milton are much fewer than the number of apparent admirers might lead one to imagine, we may safely assert that the intense thoughts set in circulation by those "orbs of song," and their noble satellites, "in great Eliza's golden time," did not fail to awaken a proportionable intensity in the natures of numberless auditors. Some might feel feebly, some strongly; the effect would vary according to the character of the recipient; but upon none was the stirring influence entirely unimpressive. The knowledge and power thus imbibed, became a part of national existence; it was ours as Englishmen; and amid the flux of generations and customs we retain unimpaired this privilege of intercourse with greatness. But the age in which we live comes late in our national progress. That first raciness, and juvenile vigour of literature, when nature "wantoned as in her prime, and played at will her virgin fancies," is gone, never to return. Since that day we have undergone a period of degradation. "Every handicraftsman has worn the mark of Poesy." It would be tedious to repeat the tale, so often related, of French contagion, and the heresies of the Popian school. With the close of the last century came an era of reaction, an era of painful struggle, to bring our overcivilised condition of thought into union with the fresh productive spirit that brightened the morning of our literature. But repentance is unlike innocence: the laborious endeavour to restore has more complicated methods of action, than the freedom of untainted nature. Those different powers of poetic disposition, the energies of Sensitive, of Reflective, of Passionate Emotion, which in former times were intermingled, and derived from mutual support an extensive empire over the feelings of men, were now restrained within separate spheres of agency. The whole system no longer worked harmoniously, and by intrinsic harmony acquired external freedom; but there arose a violent and unusual action in the several component functions, each for itself, all striving to reproduce the regular power which the whole had once enjoyed. Hence the melancholy, which so evidently characterises the spirit of modern poetry; hence that return of the mind upon itself, and the habit of seeking relief in idiosyncracies rather than community of interest. In the old times the poetic impulse went along with the general impulse of the nation; in these, it is a reaction against it, a check acting for conservation against a propulsion towards change. We have indeed seen it urged in some of our fashionable publications, that the diffusion of poetry must necessarily be in the direct ratio of the diffusion of machinery, because a highly civilized people must have new objects of interest, and thus a new field will be opened to description. But this notable argument forgets that against this *objective* amelioration may be set the decrease of *subjective* power, arising from a prevalence of social activity, and a continual absorption of the higher feelings into the palpable interests of ordinary life. The French Revolution may be a finer theme than the war of Troy; but it does not so evidently follow that Homer is to find his superior. Our inference, therefore, from this change in the relative position of artists to the rest of the community is, that modern poetry, in proportion to its depth and truth, is likely to have little immediate authority over public opinion. Admirers it will have; sects consequently it will form; and these strong under-currents will in time sensibly affect the principal stream. Those writers, whose genius, though great, is not strictly and essentially poetic, become mediators between the votaries of art and the careless cravers for excitement. Art herself, less manifestly glorious than in her periods of undisputed supremacy, retains her essential prerogatives, and forgets not to raise up chosen spirits, who may minister to her state, and vindicate her title.

One of this faithful Islâm, a poet in the truest and highest sense, we are anxious to present to our readers. He has yet written little, and published less; but in these "preludes of a loftier strain," we recognise the inspiring god. Mr. Tennyson belongs decidedly to the class we have already described as Poets of Sensation. He sees all the forms of nature with the "*eruditus oculus*,"[3] and his ear has a fairy fineness. There is a strange earnestness in his worship of beauty, which throws a charm over his impassioned song, more easily felt than described, and not to be escaped by those who have once felt it. We think he has more definiteness, and soundness of general conception, than the late Mr. Keats, and is much more free from blemishes of diction, and hasty capriccios of fancy. He has also this advantage over that poet, and his friend Shelley, that he comes before the public, unconnected

3. "educated eye"

with any political party, or peculiar system of opinions. Nevertheless, true to the theory we have stated, we believe his participation in their characteristic excellencies is sufficient to secure him a share in their unpopularity. The volume of "Poems, chiefly Lyrical," does not contain above 154 pages; but it shews us much more of the character of its parent mind, than many books we have known of much larger compass, and more boastful pretensions. The features of original genius are clearly and strongly marked. The author imitates nobody; we recognise the spirit of his age, but not the individual form of this or that writer. His thoughts bear no more resemblance to Byron or Scott, Shelley or Coleridge, than to Homer or Calderon, Ferdusi or Calidas. We have remarked five distinctive excellencies of his own manner. First, his luxuriance of imagination, and at the same time his control over it. Secondly, his power of embodying himself in ideal characters, or rather moods of character, with such extreme accuracy of adjustment, that the circumstances of the narration seem to have a natural correspondence with the predominant feeling, and, as it were, to be evolved from it by assimilative force. Thirdly, his vivid, picturesque delineation of objects, and the peculiar skill with which he holds all of them fused, to borrow a metaphor from science, in a medium of strong emotion. Fourthly, the variety of his lyrical measures, and exquisite modulation of harmonious words and cadences to the swell and fall of the feelings expressed. Fifthly, the elevated habits of thought, implied in these compositions, and imparting a mellow soberness of tone, more impressive, to our minds, than if the author had drawn up a set of opinions in verse, and sought to instruct the understanding, rather than to communicate the love of beauty to the heart. . . .

HENRY TAYLOR

# Preface to
# Philip van Artevelde*

HENRY TAYLOR (1800–1886) WAS A FREE
lance literary man in his early years, writing for the *Quarterly
Review*. He soon tried his hand at poetic drama and, after the
appearance of his elaborate epic drama, *Philip van Artevelde*, he
won a good deal of respect from other literary men. He withdrew
from London society after a few years of success and his productions diminished as he grew older.

Although well respected as a poet in his own day, he was
clearly a very minor figure. The importance of the Preface to his
drama lies in the succinctness with which it states an attitude soon
to dominate among Victorian poets and critics. Where Mill and
Hallam insist that the supreme value of poetry lies outside the

* From Henry Taylor, *Philip van Artevelde*, First Edition (London: E.
Moxon, 1834).

sphere of rational thought and moral persuasion, Taylor argues
that poetry is at its best when "sense is at its basis," when it is
reflective rather than emotionally effusive. Although this was by
no means an original idea, it serves to mark for us an important
distinction between the concerns of the majority of Victorian
poets and those of the second-generation romantic poets. The
Victorians, reflecting the spirit of the age, were faced with the
responsibility of reaching an enlarging public, and took upon themselves, even in literature, a heavy moral burden.

. . . The poetical taste to which some of the popular poets of
this century gave birth, appears at present to maintain a more un-
shaken dominion over the writers of poetry, than over its readers.

These poets were characterised by great sensibility and fervour,
by a profusion of imagery, by force and beauty of language, and by a
versification peculiarly easy and adroit, and abounding in that sort of
melody, which, by its very obvious cadences, makes itself most pleasing
to an unpractised ear. They exhibited, therefore, many of the most
attractive graces and charms of poetry—its vital warmth not less than
its external embellishments; and had not the admiration which they
excited, tended to produce an indifference to higher, graver, and more
various endowments, no one would have said that it was, in any evil
sense, excessive. But from this unbounded indulgence in the mere
luxuries of poetry, has there not ensued a want of adequate appreciation for its intellectual and immortal part? I confess, that such seems
to me to have been both the actual and the natural result; and I
can hardly believe the public taste to have been in a healthy state,
whilst the most approved poetry of past times was almost unread. We
may now, perhaps, be turning back to it; but it was not, as far as I
can judge, till more than a quarter of a century had expired, that any
signs of re-action could be discerned. Till then, the elder luminaries of
our poetical literature were obscured, or little regarded; and we sate
with dazzled eyes at a high festival of poetry, where, as at the funeral
of Arvalan, the torchlight put out the star-light.

So keen was the sense of what the new poets possessed, that it
never seemed to be felt that any thing was deficient in them. Yet

their deficiences were not unimportant. They wanted, in the first place, subject matter. A feeling came more easily to them than a reflection, and an image was always at hand when a thought was not forthcoming. Either they did not look upon mankind with observant eyes, or they did not feel it to be any part of their vocation to turn what they saw to account. It did not belong to poetry, in their apprehension, to thread the mazes of life in all its classes and under all its circumstances, common as well as romantic, and, seeing all things, to infer and to instruct: on the contrary, it was to stand aloof from every thing that is plain and true; to have little concern with what is rational or wise; it was to be, like music, a moving and enchanting art, acting upon the fancy, the affections, the passions, but scarcely connected with the exercise of the intellectual faculties. These writers had, indeed, adopted a tone of language which is hardly consistent with the state of mind in which a man makes use of his understanding. The realities of nature, and the truths which they suggest, would have seemed cold and incongruous, if suffered to mix with the strains of impassioned sentiment and glowing imagery in which they poured themselves forth. Spirit was not to be debased by any union with matter, in their effusions; dwelling, as they did, in a region of poetical sentiment which did not permit them to walk upon the common earth, or to breathe the common air.

Writers, however, whose appeal is made so exclusively to the excitabilities of mankind, will not find it possible to work upon them continuously without a diminishing effect. Poetry of which sense is not the basis, though it may be excellent of its kind, will not long be reputed to be poetry of the highest order. It may move the feelings and charm the fancy; but failing to satisfy the understanding, it will not take permanent possession of the strong-holds of fame.

. . . . .

I would by no means wish to be understood as saying that a poet can be too imaginative, provided that his other faculties be exercised in due proportion to his imagination. I would have no man depress his imagination, but I would have him raise his reason to be its equipoise. What I would be understood to oppugn, is the strange opinion which seems to prevail amongst certain of our writers and readers of poetry, that good sense stands in a species of antagonism to poetical genius, instead of being one of its most essential constituents. The maxim that a poet should be "of imagination all compact," is not, I think, to be adopted thus literally. That predominance of the imaginative faculty, or of impassioned temperament, which is incompatible with the attributes of a sound understanding and a just judgment, may make a rhapsodist, a melodist, or a visionary, each of whom may produce what may be admired for the particular talent and beauty belonging to it: but imagination and passion, thus unsupported, will never make a poet, in the largest and highest sense of the appellation.

. . . .

Mr. Shelley and his disciples, however,—the followers (if I may so call them) of the PHANTASTIC SCHOOL, labour to effect a revolution in this order of things. They would transfer the domicile of poetry to regions where reason, far from having any supremacy or rule, is all but unknown, an alien and an outcast; to seats of anarchy and abstraction, where imagination exercises the shadow of an authority, over a people of phantoms, in a land of dreams. . . .

EDWARD BULWER-LYTTON

# England and
# the English*

THE SECTION OF BULWER'S PERCEPTIVE BOOK
presented here emphasizes in a summary way two of the most
important aspects of Victorian literature. Although Victorian vis-
ual arts are frequently marked by a profusion of useless decoration,
there lay behind much of the Victorian aesthetic attitude an
emphasis on utility which Bulwer here remarks. Victorian literature, for its most serious practitioners, was a functional tool. Good
literature should teach, either indirectly or quite explicitly.

Most important, Bulwer's remarks emphasize the extraordinary growth in the popularity of the novel. At the beginning of
the nineteenth century, the novel was not quite respectable. Despite the work of the great novelists of the eighteenth century

* From Edward Bulwer-Lytton, *England and the English* (London:
Richard Bentley, 1833), Book IV, Ch. II "Literature."

(Richardson, Fielding, Sterne, and Smollett), fiction was—certainly among the evangelicals—thought to be not far removed from lying. Macaulay's father tried to discourage him from reading fiction at all. Nevertheless, novels grew in popularity, and with the success of Scott, Dickens, Thackeray, and George Eliot, fiction came of age. Bulwer, it should be noted, was a prolific novelist himself, and he took literary advantage of almost every fad that moved through the first half of the nineteenth century.

. . . The death of a great poet invariably produces an indifference to the art itself. We can neither bear to see him imitated, nor yet contrasted; we preserve the impression, but we break the mould. Hence that strong attachment to the Practical, which became so visible a little time after the death of Byron, and which continues (unabated, or rather increased,) to characterize the temper of the time. Insensibly acted upon by the doctrine of the Utilitarians, we desired to see Utility in every branch of intellectual labour. Byron, in his severe comments upon England, and his satire on our social system, had done much that has not yet been observed, in shaking off from the popular mind certain of its strongest national prejudices; and the long Peace, and the pressure of financial difficulties, naturally inclined us to look narrowly at our real state; to examine the laws we had only boasted of, and dissect the constitution we had hitherto deemed it only our duty to admire. We were in the situation of a man who, having run a certain career of dreams and extravagance, begins to be prudent and saving, to calculate his conduct, and to look to his estate. Politics thus gradually and commonly absorbed our attention, and we grew to identify ourselves, our feelings, and our cause, with statesmen and economists, instead of with poets and refiners. Thus, first Canning, and then Brougham, may be said, for a certain time, to have represented, more than any other individuals, the common Intellectual Spirit; and the interest usually devoted to the imaginative, was transferred to the real.

In the mean while the more than natural distaste for poetry that succeeded the death of Byron had increased the appetite for prose fictions; the excitement of the fancy, pampered by the melo-dramatic tales which had become the rage in verse, required food even when verse grew out of fashion. The new career that Walter Scott had commenced tended also somewhat to elevate with the vulgar a class of composition that, with the educated, required no factitious elevation; for, with the latter, what new dignity could be thrown upon a branch of letters that Cervantes, Fielding, Le Sage, Voltaire, and Fenelon had already made only less than Epic? It was not, however, as in former times, the great novel alone, that was read among the more refined circles, but novels of all sorts. Unlike poetry, the name itself was an attraction. In these works, even to the lightest and most ephemeral, something of the moral spirit of the age betrayed itself. The novels of fashionable life illustrate feelings very deeply rooted, and productive of no common revolution. In proportion as the aristocracy had become social, and fashion allowed the members of the more mediocre classes a hope to outstep the boundaries of fortune, and be quasi-aristocrats themselves, people eagerly sought for representations of the manners which they aspired to imitate, and the circles to which it was not impossible to belong. But as with emulation discontent also was mixed, as many hoped to be called and few found themselves chosen, so a satire on the follies and vices of the great gave additional piquancy to the description of their lives. There was a sort of social fagging established; the fag loathed his master, but not the system by which one day or other he himself might be permitted to fag. What the world would not have dared to gaze upon, had it been gravely exhibited by a philosopher, (so revolting a picture of the aristocracy would it have seemed,) they praised with avidity in the light sketches of a novelist. Hence the three-years' run of the fashionable novels was a shrewd sign of the times; straws they were, but they showed the upgathering of the storm. Those novels were the most successful which bit off one or the other of the popular cravings—the desire to dissect fashion, or the wish to convey utility—those which affected to combine both, as the novels of Mr. Ward,[1] were the most successful of all.

Few writers ever produced so great an effect on the political spirit of their generation as some of these novelists, who, without any other merit, unconsciously exposed the falsehood, the hypocrisy, the

1. Robert Plumer Ward (1765–1846) was a writer on international law and a loyal Pittite, who spent his leisure time writing novels. His first novel, Tremaine; or the Man of Refinement (1825) was extremely popular as was De Vere; or the Man of Independence (1827). His last novel was De Clifford; or the Constant Man (1841). The novels were quite bad and have slipped into obscurity.

arrogant and vulgar insolence of patrician life. Read by all classes, in every town, in every village, these works, as I have before stated, could not but engender a mingled indignation and disgust at the parade of frivolity, the ridiculous disdain of truth, nature, and mankind, the self-consequence and absurdity, which, falsely or truly, these novels exhibited as a picture of aristocratic society. The Utilitarians railed against them, and they were effecting with unspeakable rapidity the very purposes the Utilitarians desired.

While these light works were converting the multitude, graver writers were soberly confirming their effect, society itself knew not the change in feeling which had crept over it; till a sudden flash, as it were, revealed the change electrically to itself. Just at the time when with George the Fourth an old era expired, the excitement of a popular election at home concurred with the three days of July in France, to give a decisive tone to the new. The question of Reform came on, and, to the astonishment of the nation itself, it was hailed at once by the national heart. From that moment, the intellectual spirit hitherto partially directed to, became wholly absorbed in, politics; and whatever lighter works have since obtained a warm and general hearing, have either developed the errors of the social system, or the vices of the legislative. Of the first, I refrain from giving an example; of the last, I instance as a sign of the times, the searching fictions of Miss Martineau,[2] and the wide reputation they have acquired.

A description of the mere frivolities of fashion is no longer coveted; for the public mind, once settled towards an examination of the aristocracy, has pierced from the surface to the depth; it has probed the wound, and it now desires to cure.

It is in this state that the Intellectual Spirit of the age rests, demanding the Useful, but prepared to receive it through familiar shapes: a state at present favourable to ordinary knowledge, to narrow views, or to mediocre genius; but adapted to prepare the way and to found success for the coming triumphs of a bold philosophy, or a profound and subtile imagination. Some cause, indeed, there is of fear, lest the desire for immediate and palpable utility should stint the capacities of genius to the trite and familiar truths. But as Criticism takes a more wide and liberal view of the true and unbounded sphere of the Beneficial, we may trust that this cause of fear will be removed. The passions of men are the most useful field for the metaphysics of the imagination, and yet the grandest and the most inexhaustible. Let

2. Harriet Martineau (1802–76), wrote on social and historical subjects, including a very popular series propagandizing for classical economics called *Illustrations of Political Economy* (1832–34).

us take care that we do not, as in the old Greek fable, cut the wings of our bees and set flowers before them, as the most sensible mode of filling the Hives of Truth!

But the great prevailing characteristic of the present intellectual spirit is one most encouraging to human hopes; it is Benevolence. There has grown up among us a sympathy with the great mass of mankind. For this we are indebted in no small measure to the philosophers (with whom Benevolence is, in all times, the foundation of philosophy); and that more decided and emphatic expression of the sentiment which was common, despite of their errors, to the French moralists of the last century, has been kept alive and applied to immediate legislation by the English moralists of the present. We owe also the popularity of the growing principle to the writings of Miss Edgeworth[3] and of Scott, who sought their characters among the people, and who interested us by a picture of (and not a declamation upon) their life and its humble vicissitudes, their errors and their virtues. We owe it also, though unconsciously, to the gloomy misanthropy of Byron; for proportioned to the intenseness with which we shared that feeling, was the reaction from which we awoke from it; and amongst the more select and poetical of us, we owe it yet more to the dreaming philanthropy of Shelley, and the patriarchal tenderness of Wordsworth. It is this feeling that we should unite to sustain and to develope. It has come to us pure and bright from the ordeal of years—the result of a thousand errors—but born, if we preserve it, as their healer and redemption.

Diodorus Siculus[4] tells us, that the forest of the Pyrenean mountains being set on fire, and the heat penetrating to the soil, a pure stream of silver gushed forth from the earth's bosom, and revealed for the first time the existence of those mines afterwards so celebrated.

It is thus from causes apparently the most remote, and often amidst the fires that convey to us, at their first outbreaking, images only of terror and desolation, that we deduce the most precious effects, and discover the treasures to enrich the generations that are to come!

3. Maria Edgeworth (1767–1849) was an Anglo-Irish novelist who greatly influenced the development of the local color genre. *Castle Rackrent* remains a novel worth reading.

4. Diodorus Siculus was a Greek historian of the first century B.C.

# BIBLIOGRAPHY

Although the following bibliography is extensive, it is nevertheless introductory and makes no pretensions to exhaustiveness. It is designed primarily to provide representative examples of other essays, pamphlets, and books written between roughly 1820 and 1840 and relevant to the concerns of this volume, and secondarily to introduce the reader to some of the most important books and essays about the period and about the writers represented or frequently alluded to in this volume. For primary material I have usually followed the procedure of the volume itself in referring to first editions, although occasionally I refer to important revised editions. Much of the pamphlet and periodical material is difficult of access, although some, by important writers, has been reproduced in collected works or as part of popular editions (as, for example, Carlyle's *Chartism*, or any of Macaulay's essays). Much of the secondary material is modern and still in print (sometimes in paperback), although some technically secondary material (as, for example, Sterling's essay on Carlyle) is not only out of print but, in its way, must be considered primary material as well. Thus, there are three kinds of writing included here: (1) primary material of the kind that might have been included in this volume; (2) secondary material by historians and biographers who write about their subjects from a great distance in time; (3) secondary material written by men who lived through the times they write about or who knew their subjects personally.

Adams, L. P. *Agricultural Depression and Farm Relief in England, 1815–1832*. London: P. S. K. and Co., Ltd., 1932.
Alexander, Edward. *Matthew Arnold and John Stuart Mill*. London: Routledge and Kegan Paul, 1965.

Aldred, Guy A. *Richard Carlile, Agitator: his Life and Times* ("The Word Library"). Glasgow: Strickland Press, 3rd Rev. Ed., 1941.

Altick, R. D. *The English Common Reader: A Social History of the Mass Reading Public, 1800–1900.* Chicago: University of Chicago Press, 1957.

Arbuthnot, Harriet. *Journal of Mrs. Arbuthnot, 1820–1832,* ed. Francis Bamford and the Duke of Wellington. 2 vols. London: Macmillan and Co., 1950.

Arnold, Thomas. "The Oxford Malignants and Dr. Hampden," *Edinburgh Review* (Edinburgh), LXIII (April, 1836), 225–39.

Aspinall, Arthur and E. Anthony Smith (eds.). *English Historical Documents, 1783–1832.* (*English Historical Documents,* ed. David C. Douglas, Vol. II). London: Eyre and Spottiswoode, 1959.

Aspinall, Arthur (ed.). *The Letters of King George IV, 1812–1830.* Cambridge: Cambridge University Press, 1938.

———. *Lord Broughnam and the Whig Party.* Manchester: Manchester University Press, 1927.

———. *Politics and the Press, c. 1780–1850.* London: Home and Van Thal, 1959.

——— (ed.). *Three Early Nineteenth Century Diaries.* London: Williams and Norgate, 1952.

———. "The Circulation of Newspapers in the Nineteenth Century," *Review of English Studies* (London), XXII (January, 1946), 29–43.

Babbage, Charles. *The Ninth Bridgewater Treatise.* London: W. Pickering, 1837.

———. *Reflections on the Decline of Science in England and on Some of its Causes.* London: B. Fellowes, 1830.

Bain, Alexander. *James Mill.* London: Longmans, Green, and Co., 1882.

Baker, Herschell. *William Hazlitt.* Cambridge, Mass.: Harvard University Press, 1962.

Bamford, Samuel. *Passages in the Life of a Radical,* ed. H. Dunckley. London: Unwin, 1893.

Bauer, Josephine. *The London Magazine, 1820–29.* Copenhagen: Rosenkelde and Bagger, 1941.

Bentham, Jeremy. *The Book of Fallacies.* London: J. and H. L. Hunt, 1824.

———. *Deontology; or, The Science of Morality,* ed. John Bowring. London: Longman and Co., 1824.

———. *Lord Brougham Displayed.* London: Robert Heward, 1832.

———. *Rationale of Punishment.* Translated from the French by Richard Smith. London: J. and H. L. Hunt, 1825.

Bentham, Jeremy. *Rationale of Reward*. Translated from the French by Richard Smith. London: Robert Heward, 1832.

Best, Geoffrey. *Shaftesbury*. London: B. T. Batsford, 1964.

Boase, T. S. R. *English Art: 1800–1870*. (*Oxford History of English Art*, Vol. X.) Oxford: Clarendon Press, 1959.

Booth, Charles. *Zachary Macaulay*. London: Longmans, Green and Co., 1934.

Bourne, H. R. Fox. *English Newspapers*. 2 vols. London: Chatto and Windus, 1887.

Briggs, Asa. *Age of Improvement*. London: Longmans, Green and Co., 1959.

Brightfield, Myron F. *John Wilson Croker*. Berkeley: University of California Press, 1940.

Brock, W. R. *Lord Liverpool and Liberal Toryism, 1820–1827*. Cambridge: Cambridge University Press, 1941.

Brougham, Henry Peter. *A Discourse of Natural Theology*. London: Charles Knight, 1835.

———. *The Life and Times of Henry Lord Brougham. Written by Himself*. Edinburgh: W. Blackwood and Sons, 1871.

———. *Speeches of Henry Lord Brougham upon Questions Relating to Public Rights, Duties, and Interests*. 4 vols. Edinburgh: A. and C. Black, 1838.

Brown, Ford K. *Fathers of the Victorians: the Age of Wilberforce*. Cambridge: Cambridge University Press, 1961.

Buckland, William. *On Geology and Chemistry*. ("The Bridgewater Treatises on the Power, Wisdom, and Goodness of God, as Manifested in Creation.") London: W. Pickering, 1836.

Bulwer-Lytton, E. R. *The Life, Letters, and Literary Remains of Edward Bulwer, Lord Lytton*. New York: Harper and Bros., 1883.

Butler, J. R. M. *The Passing of the Great Reform Bill*. London: Longmans and Co., 1914.

Buxton, T. F. *The African Slave Trade and Its Remedy*. London: John Murray, 1840.

Carlyle, Thomas. *Chartism*. London: James Fraser, 1840.

———. *Sartor Resartus*, ed. C. F. Harrold. New York: Odyssey Press, 1937.

Chadwick, Owen. *The Victorian Church*. Part I. London: Adam and Charles Black, 1966.

Checkland, S. G. *The Rise of Industrial Society in England, 1815–1885*. London: Longmans and Co., 1964.

Church, R. W. *The Oxford Movement, 1833–45*. London: Macmillan and Co., Rev. Ed., 1891.

Clark, Kenneth. *The Gothic Revival: An Essay on the History of Taste*. London: Constable and Co., 1928.

Clark, Roy B. *William Gifford, Tory Satirist, Critic, and Editor*. New York: Columbia University Press, 1930.

Cobbett, William. *Cobbett's Legacy to Labourers; or, What is the Right which the Lords, Baronets, and Squires have to the Lands of England. In Six Letters*. London: the Author, 1834.

——. *Cobbett's Legacy to Parsons; or, Have the Clergy of the Established Church an Equitable Right to the Tithes or to any other Thing called Church Property, greater than the Dissenters have to the Same? In Six Letters*. London: the Author, 1835.

——. *Cobbett's Manchester Lectures, in Support of his 14 Reform Propositions*. London: the Author, 1832.

——. *Rural Rides*. London: the Author, 1830.

Cockburn, H. *Life of Lord Jeffrey, with a Selection from his Correspondence*. London: Longmans and Co., 1852.

Cole, G. D. H. *Attempts at General Union. A Study of British Trade Union History, 1818–1834*. London: Macmillan and Co., 1953.

——. *The Life of Robert Owen*. London: Macmillan and Co., 2nd Ed., 1930.

——. *The Life of William Cobbett*. Harmondsworth and Middlesex: Penguin Books, 1925.

——. *A Short History of the British Working Class Movement, 1789–1947*. London: Allen and Unwin, New Ed., 1948.

Cole, G. D. H., and Raymond Postgate. *The Common People, 1746–1946*. London: Methuen and Co., 1949.

*A Concise and Convincing Argument against Socialism; or, the Pernicious Principles of R. Owen Completely Exposed, by a Clerical Gentleman*. London: the Author, 1840.

Croker, J. W. *The Croker Papers*, ed. Lewis J. Jennings. 3 vols. London: John Murray, 1884.

Davies, Horton. *Worship and Theology in England, 1690–1850*. Princeton: Princeton University Press, 1961.

Digby, Kenelm. *The Broadstone of Honor; or, the True Sense and Practice of Chivalry*. 4 vols. London: J. Booker and Co., 1826–9.

Driver, Cecil. *Tory Radical, the Life of Richard Oastler*. New York: New York University Press, 1946.

East, John. *The Patriot, the Philanthropist, and the Christian: A Discourse Occasioned by the Death of the Late William Wilberforce, Esq*. London: J. Chilcot, 1833.

*The Extraordinary Black Book; or, Corruption Unmasked*. Corrected from the latest official returns, and presenting a complete view of the expenditure, patronage, influence and abuses of the government in Church, State, Law and representation. By the original editor. London: Effingham Wilson, 1831.

Fay, C. R. *The Corn Laws and Social England*. Cambridge: Cambridge University Press, 1932.

Faber, G. C. *Oxford Apostles*. London: Faber and Faber, 1933.

Fonblanque, Albany. *England Under Seven Administrations*. London: Bentley and Co., 1837.

———. *The Life and Labours of Albany Fonblanque*, ed. E. B. de Fonblanque. London: Bentley and Co., 1874.

———. "Signs of the Times," *Examiner* (London, October 4, 1829), p. 1.

Fox, Henry E. V., Fourth Lord Holland. *The Journal of the Hon. H. E. Fox, 1818–1830*, ed. Earl of Ilchester. London: T. Butterworth, 1923.

Fox, Henry R. V., Third Lord Holland. *Further Memoirs of the Whig Party*, ed. Lord Staverdale. London: John Murray, 1905.

———. *Memoirs of the Whig Party*, ed. H. E. V. Fox, Fourth Lord Holland. 2 vols. London: Longmans and Co., 1852–4.

Fox, W. J. "Men and Things in 1823," *Westminster Review* (London), I (April, 1824), 1–18.

"Friendly Advice to the Lords," *Quarterly Review* (Edinburgh), XLV (October, 1831), 504–58.

Froude, J. A. *Thomas Carlyle, A History of the First Forty Years of his Life*. 2 vols. New York: Harper and Bros., 1882.

Gash, Norman. *Politics in the Age of Peel*. London: Longmans and Co., 1953.

———. *Mr. Secretary Peel: The Life of Sir Robert Peel to 1830*. London: Longmans and Co., 1961.

Gill, J. C. *The Ten Hours Parson: Christian Social Action in the 1830's*. London: S. P. C. K., 1959.

Graham, Walter. *English Literary Periodicals*. New York: T. Nelson and Co., 1930.

———. *Tory Criticism in the "Quarterly Review," 1809–1853*. New York: Columbia University Press, 1921.

Gray, John. *A Lecture on Human Happiness*. London: Sherwood, Jones and Co., 1825.

Gwynn, D. R. *The Struggle for Catholic Emancipation, 1750–1829*. London: Longmans and Co., 1928.

Halévy, Élie. *The Growth of Philosophical Radicalism*. Translated by Mary Morris. London: Faber and Cowger, 1928.

———. *A History of the English People in the Nineteenth Century*. Translated by E. I. Watkin and D. A. Barker. 6 vols. London: Ernest Benn, 2nd Ed., 1940.

Hamburger, Joseph. *James Mill and the Art of Revolution*. New Haven: Yale University Press, 1963.

Hammond, J. L. and Barbara Hammond. *The Bleak Age*. London: Longmans, Green and Co., 2nd Ed., 1934.

Hammond, J. L. and Barbara Hammond. *Lord Shaftesbury*. London: Constable and Co., 1923.

———. *The Rise of Modern Industry*. London: Methuen and Co., 5th Ed., 1937.

———. *The Skilled Labourer, 1760–1832*. London: Longmans, Green and Co., 1919.

———. *The Town Labourer, 1760–1832*. London: Longmans, Green and Co., 1917.

———. *The Village Labourer, 1760–1832*. London: Longmans, Green and Co., 1911.

Harrison, J. F. C. *Learning and Living, 1790–1960. A Study in the History of the English Adult Education Movement*. London: Routledge and Kegan Paul, 1961.

Hawes, Frances. *Henry Brougham*. London: Jonathan Cape, 1957.

Hazlitt, William. *Spirit of the Age*. London: Colburn, 1825.

Hennell, Michael. *William Wilberforce, 1759–1833. The Liberator of the Slave*. London: Church Book Room Press, 1950.

Hitchcock, Henry Russell. *Early Victorian Architecture in Britain*. 2 vols. New Haven: Yale University Press, 1954.

Hobsbawm, Eric J. *The Age of Revolution, 1789–1848*. London: Weidenfeld and Nicholson, 1962.

Hodgskin, Thomas. *Labour Defended Against the Claims of Capital*. London: Labour Publishing Co., 1922.

Holland, Lady. *A Memoir of the Rev. Sydney Smith*, ed. Mrs. Austin. 2 vols. London: Longmans, Green and Co., 1855.

Holland, Henry E. V. Fox, Fourth Lord of. See Fox, Henry E. V.

Holland, Henry R. V. Fox, Third Lord of. See Fox, Henry R. V.

Holyoake, G. J. *The Life and Character of Richard Carlile*. London: Austin and Co., 1870.

Houghton, W. E. *The Victorian Frame of Mind, 1830–1870*. New Haven: Yale University Press, 1957.

Howitt, William. *The Rural Life of England*. 2 vols. London: Longmans, and Co., 1838.

Hunt, Leigh. *The Autobiography of Leigh Hunt*. 2 vols. London: Archibald Constable, 1903.

Jack, Ian. *English Literature, 1815–1832*. (*Oxford History of English Literature*, ed. F. P. Wilson and Bonamy Dobree, Vol. X.) Oxford: Clarendon Press, 1963.

Jaeger, Muriel. *Before Victoria*. London:Chatto and Windus, 1950.

James, Louis. *Fiction for the Working Man*. London: Oxford University Press, 1963.

Jeffrey, Francis. *Contributions to the Edinburgh Review*. 4 vols. London: Longmans and Co., 1844.

Kelly, Thomas. *George Birkbeck: Pioneer of Adult Education*. Liverpool: Liverpool University Press, 1957.

Kemp, Betty. *King and Commons, 1660–1832.* London: Macmillan and Co., 1957.

Kidd, John. *On the Adaptation of External Nature to the Physical Condition of Man.* ("The Bridgewater Treatises on the Power, Wisdom, and Goodness of God, as Manifested in Creation.") London: W. Pickering, 1833.

Kitson Clark, G. S. R. *The English Inheritance.* London: S. C. M. Press, 1950.

——. *The Making of Victorian England.* Cambridge, Mass.: Harvard University Press, 1962.

Knight, Charles. *Passages of a Working Life During Half a Century with a Prelude of Early Reminiscences.* 3 vols. London: Bradbury and Evans, 1863–5.

Lang, Andrew. *The Life and Letters of John Gibson Lockhart.* 2 vols. London: J. C. Nimmo, 1897.

Lewis, P. A. *Edwin Chadwick and the Public Health Movement, 1832–1854.* London: Longmans, Green and Co., 1952.

Lochhead, Marion C. *John Gibson Lockhart.* London: John Murray, 1954.

Lomax, M. T. *Pugin: A Medieval Victorian.* London: Sheed and Ward, 1932.

Lovett, William. *Life and Struggles of William Lovett,* ed. R. H. Tawney. ("Bohn's Popular Library.") 2 vols. London: G. Bell and Sons, 1920.

Lovett, William and John Collins. *Chartism; a new organization of the people embracing a plan for the education and improvement of the people politically and socially . . . written in Warwick Gaol.* London: H. Hetherington, 1841.

Lyell, Charles. *Principles of Geology, being an attempt to explain the former changes of the earth's surface, by reference to causes now in operation.* 3 vols. London: John Murray, 1830–33.

Lytton, E. R. Bulwer-. See Bulwer-Lytton, E. R.

Macaulay, T. B. "Bentham's Defense of Mill," *Edinburgh Review* (Edinburgh), XLIX (June, 1829), 274–99.

——. "Mill's Essay on Government," *Edinburgh Review* (Edinburgh), XLIX (March, 1829), 159–89.

——. "Sadler's Law of Population," *Edinburgh Review* (Edinburgh), LI (July, 1830), 297–321.

——. "Sadler's Refutation Refuted," *Edinburgh Review* (Edinburgh), LII (January, 1831), 504–529.

——. "Utilitarian Theory of Government and the Greatest Happiness Principle," *Edinburgh Review* (Edinburgh), L (October, 1829), 99–125.

Macconnell, Thomas. *A Lecture on the Signs of the Times.* London: Eamonson, Crisis Office, 1832.

Macculloch, J. R. *Discourse on Political Economy.* London: Longmans and Co., 1825.

———. *A Discourse on the Rise, Progress, Peculiar Objects and Importance of Political Economy.* Edinburgh: Archibald Constable, 1825.

MacDonagh, O. *A Pattern of Government Growth, 1800–1860.* London: MacGibbon and Kee, 1961.

Mack, Mary P. *Jeremy Bentham: An Odyssey of Ideas, 1748–1792.* London: Heinemann and Co., 1962.

Maginn, William. *A Gallery of Illustrious Literary Characters (1830–1838),* ed. W. Bates. London: Chatto and Windus, 1873.

Marchand, L. A. *The Athenaeum: A Mirror of Victorian Culture.* Chapel Hill: University of North Carolina Press, 1941.

Martin, G. Currie. *The Adult School Movement.* London: National Adult School Union, 1924.

Mill, James. *Analysis of the Phenomena of the Human Mind,* ed. J. S. Mill. 2 vols. London: Longmans and Co., 1869.

———. *Elements of Political Economy.* London: Baldwin and Co., 1823.

———. *Essays on Government, Jurisprudence, Liberty of the Press, Prisons and Prison Discipline, Colonies, Laws of Nations, Education.* Reprinted from the Supplement to The Encyclopedia Britannica. London: J. Innes, 1828.

Mill, John Stuart. *Autobiography.* New York: Columbia University Press, 1924.

———. *Mill on Bentham and Coleridge,* ed. F. R. Leavis. London: Chatto and Windus, 1950.

Millman, William. *William Wilberforce and Lord Shaftesbury.* London: Sheldon Press, 1945.

Milner, Gamaliel. *The Threshold of the Victorian Age.* London: Williams Norgate, 1934.

Mineka, Francis E. *The Dissidence of Dissent. The Monthly Repository, 1806–1838.* Chapel Hill: University of North Carolina Press, 1944.

*Modern Papacy Exposed. An Answer to No. I of "Tracts for the Times."* London: Francis Baisler, [1834?].

Monypenny, W. F. and G. E. Buckle. *Life of Benjamin Disraeli.* London: John Murray, 1905.

"The Moral and Political State of the British Empire," *Quarterly Review* (Edinburgh), XLIV (January, 1831), 261–316.

Morley, John. *The Life of W. E. Gladstone.* 3 vols. London: Macmillan and Co., 1903.

Mottram, Ralph H. *Buxton the Liberator.* London: Hutchinson and Co., 1946.

Mudie, Robert. *Babylon the Great: A Dissection and Demonstration of Men and Things in the British Capitol.* London: H. Colburn, 1828.

———. *The Modern Athens: A Dissection and Demonstration of Men and Things in the Scotch Capitol.* London: Knight and Lacey, 1825.

Napier, Jr., Macvey (ed.). *Selections from the Correspondence of Macvey Napier.* London: Macmillan and Co., 1879.

Neff, Emery. *Carlyle and Mill: Mystic and Utilitarian.* New York: Columbia University Press, 1924.

Nesbitt, George L. *Benthamite Reviewing. The First Twelve Years of the "Westminster Review," 1824–1836.* ("Columbia University Studies in English and Comparative Literature," no. 118.) New York: Columbia University Press, 1924.

Newman, John Henry. *Apologia pro vita sua.* London: Longmans, Green and Co., 1864.

New, Chester W. *The Life of Henry Brougham to 1830.* Oxford: Clarendon Press, 1961.

Oastler, Richard. *Damnation! Eternal damnation to the fiend-begotten, "coarser–food," new poor law.* A speech. London: H. Hetherington, 1837.

———. *The Factory Question. The Law or the Needle.* London: H. Hetherington, 1835.

———. *A Speech Delivered at a Meeting Held to Consider the Propriety or Petitioning the Legislature to Pass the Ten Hours Factories' Regulation Bill.* Huddersfield: J. Hobson, 1833.

Oliphant, Margaret O. *Annals of a Publishing House. William Blackwood and his Sons.* New York: Scribners and Sons, 1897–8.

"On the March of Intellect and Universal Education," *Fraser's Magazine* (London), II (September, 1830), 161–9.

Owen, Robert. *The Book of the New Moral World, containing the rational system of society, founded on demonstrable facts, developing the . . . laws of human nature and of society.* London: E. Wilson, 1836.

———. *A New View of Society; or, Essays on the principles of the formation of the human character.* London: Caddell and Davis, 1813.

———. *The Signs of the Times; or, the Approach of the Millennium.* London: Home Colonization Society, 1841.

Packe, Michael St. John. *The Life of John Stuart Mill.* New York: Macmillan and Co., 1954.

"Parliamentary Reform," *Quarterly Review* (Edinburgh), XLIV (April, 1831), 554–98.

Peel, Robert. *The Memoirs of Robert Peel*, ed. Lord Mahon (later Earl Stanhope) and E. Cardwell. 2 vols. London: John Murray, 1856–8.

Pemberton, N. W. B. *William Cobbett*. Harmondsworth and Middlesex: Penguin Books, 1949.

Place, Francis. *Illustrations and Proofs of the Principle of Population*. London: Longmans and Co., 1822.

———. *Improvement of the Working People*. London: Charles Fox, 1834.

"Progress of Misgovernment," *Quarterly Review* (Edinburgh), XLVI (April, 1832), 544–622.

Prout, William. *On Chemistry, Meteorology, and the Function of Digestion*. ("Bridgewater Treatises on the Power, Wisdom, and Goodness of God, as Manifested in Creation.") London: W. Pickering, 1834.

Pugin, A. W. N. *An Apology for a Work Entitled "Contrasts"; being a defence of the assertions advanced in that publication against the various attacks lately made upon it*. Birmingham: the author, 1837.

Quinlan, M. J. *Victorian Prelude*. New York: Columbia University Press, 1941.

"Reform in Parliament," *Quarterly Review* (Edinburgh), XLV (July, 1831), 252–339.

"The Revolutions of 1640 and 1830," *Quarterly Review* (Edinburgh), XLVI (April, 1832), 261–300.

Roberts, William. *Memoirs of the Life and Correspondence of Hannah More*. London: R. B. Seeley, 1834.

Roget, Peter Mark. *On Animal and Vegetable Physiology*. ("Bridgewater Treatises on the Power, Wisdom, and Goodness of God, as Manifested in Creation.") London: W. Pickering, 1834.

Sadler, Michael T. H. *Bulwer and his Wife. A Panorama, 1803–1836*. London: Constable and Co., 1933.

Sadler, Michael Thomas. *The Law of Population; a treatise in the disproof of the superfecundity of human beings, and developing the real principle of their increase*. London: John Murray, 1830.

Singer, Charles, et al. *The Industrial Revolution, c. 1750–c. 1850*. (*The Oxford History of Technology*, Vol. VI.) London: Oxford University Press, 1958.

Southey, Robert. *Essays Moral and Political*. 2 vols. London: John Murray, 1832.

"State of the Government," *Quarterly Review* (Edinburgh), XLVI (January, 1832), 274–312.

*Statement of the Case of the Protestant Dissenters Under the Corporation and Test Acts.* London: Rowland Hunter, 1827.

Stephen, Leslie. *The English Utilitarians.* 3 vols. London: Duckworth and Co., 1900.

Sterling, John. "T. Carlyle's French Revolution," *Fraser's Magazine* (London), XVI (July, 1837), 85–104.

———. "On the Writings of Thomas Carlyle," *Westminster Review* (London), XXXIII (October, 1839), 1–68.

Summerson, John. *Architecture in Britain, 1530–1830.* (*Pelican History of Art.*) London: Pelican Books, 1953.

Tennyson, G. B. *Sartor Called Resartus.* Princeton: Princeton University Press, 1966.

Thackrah, C. Turner. *The Effects of the Principal Arts, Trades, and Professions . . . on Health and Longevity.* London: Longmans and Co., 2nd Ed., 1832.

Thirlwall, Connop. *A Letter . . . to T. Turton on the Admission of Dissenters to Academical Degrees.* Cambridge: J. and J. Deighton, 1834.

Thompson, E. P. *The Making of the English Working Class.* London: Victor Gollancz, 1963.

Thompson, T. P. *A Catechism of the Corn Laws: with a list of fallacies and the answers.* London: James Ridgway, 1827.

———. *An Exposition of the Fallacies on Rent, Tithes, etc. Containing an examination of Mr. Ricardo's Theory of Rent.* London: C. and J. Rivington, 1826.

Thompson, William. *Appeal of One Half the Human Race, Women, Against the Pretensions of the Other Half, Men.* London: Longmans and Co., 1825.

———. *An Inquiry into the Principles of the Distribution of Wealth Most Conducive to Human Happiness.* London: Longmans and Co., 1824.

Thrall, Miriam. *Rebellious Fraser's in the Days of Maginn, Thackeray, and Carlyle.* New York: Columbia University Press, 1934.

*Tracts for the Times.* By Members of The University of Oxford. 6 vols. London: J. G. and F. Rivington, 1833–41.

Tredrey, F. D. *The House of Blackwood, 1804–1954. The History of a Publishing Firm.* Edinburgh: W. Blackwood and Sons, 1954.

Trevelyan, G. O. *The Life and Letters of Lord Macaulay.* London: Longmans and Co., 1878.

Trevelyan, G. M. *British History in the Nineteenth Century and After (1872–1919).* London: Longmans and Co., 1938.

*A True Exposure of the Noted Robert Owen! concerning his late visit to the Queen . . . With an account of the victims of seduction and his new moral marriage system.* London: E. Hancock, 1840.

Vidler, Alexander. *The Church in an Age of Revolution.* London: Hodder and Stoughton, 1962.

Wallas, Graham. *The Life of Francis Place, 1771–1854.* London: Longmans and Co., 1898.

Walpole, Spencer. *A History of England from the Conclusion of the Great War in 1815.* 6 vols. London: Longmans and Co., Rev. Ed., 1890.

Ward, J. T. *The Factory Movement, 1830–1855.* London: St. Martin's Press, 1962.

Wearmouth, R. W. *Methodism and the Working Class Movements of England, 1800–1850.* London: Epworth Press, 1937.

Webb, R. K. *The British Working Class Reader, 1790–1848: Literacy and Social Tension.* London: Allen and Unwin, 1955.

Wellesley, Arthur, Duke of Wellington. *Despatches, Correspondence and Memoranda of the Duke of Wellington,* ed. by his son. 8 vols. London: John Murray, 1867–1880.

Whewell, William. *On the Principles of English University Education.* London: J. W. Parker, 1838.

———. *Remarks on Some Part of Mr. Thirlwall's Letter on the Admission of Dissenters to Academical Degrees.* Cambridge: J. and J. Deighton, 1834.

Whitley, W. T. *Art in England, 1821–1837.* Cambridge: Cambridge University Press, 1930.

Wilberforce, William. *A Practical View of the Prevailing Religious System of Professed Christians in the Higher and Middle Classes in this Country, Contrasted with Real Christianity.* London: Longmans and Co., 1797.

Williams, Raymond. *Culture and Society.* London: Chatto and Windus, 1958.

———. *The Long Revolution.* London: Chatto and Windus, 1961.

Wilson, David. *Thoughts on British Colonial Slavery.* London: Bagster and Thoms, 1828.

Wilson, John, et al. *Noctes ambrosianae.* Revised edition. Edinburgh: W. Blackwood and Sons, 1857.

Woodward, C. L. *Age of Reform, 1815–1870.* (*The Oxford History of England,* Vol. XIII.) Oxford: Clarendon Press, Rev. Ed., 1962.

Young, G. M., *Victorian England: Portrait of an Age.* London: Oxford University Press, 1936.

——— (ed.). *Early Victorian England, 1830–1865.* 2 vols. London: Oxford University Press, 1934.

Young, G. M. and W. D. Hancock (eds.). *English Historical Documents, 1833–1874.* (*English Historical Documents,* ed. David C. Douglas, Vol. III). London: Eyre and Spottiswoode, 1956.

# INDEX